ROBERT STACK
STRAIGHT SHOOTING

WITH MARK EVANS

BERKLEY BOOKS, NEW YORK

This Berkley book contains the complete
text of the original hardcover edition.
It has been completely reset in a type face
designed for easy reading, and was printed
from new film.

STRAIGHT SHOOTING

A Berkley Book / published by arrangement with
Macmillan Publishing Co., Inc.

PRINTING HISTORY
Macmillan edition published 1980
Berkley edition / February 1981

All rights reserved.
Copyright © 1980 by Robert Stack and Mark Evans.
This may not be reproduced in whole or in part,
by mimeograph or any other means, without permission.
For information address: Macmillan Publishing Company, Inc.,
866 Third Avenue, New York, New York 10022.

ISBN: 0-425-04757-1

A BERKLEY BOOK ® TM 757,375
Berkley Books are published by Berkley Publishing Corporation,
200 Madison Avenue, New York, New York 10016.
PRINTED IN THE UNITED STATES OF AMERICA

WITH A STAR AND A STORY ON EVERY PAGE!

After a childhood peopled with Gable and Lombard and Tracy, it was inevitable that Bob Stack would one day be asked the magic question: "Want to be in pictures?"

He did. And after a career of hard work and high times, working and playing with everyone who was anyone in the picture business, it was inevitable that he would one day be asked the magic question: "Want to write a book about it?"

He did. And here it is...

STRAIGHT SHOOTING
ROBERT STACK

"BREEZY AND ENTERTAINING!"
—*Soho Weekly News*

"WARM, REFRESHING...A SENSE OF GOOD, ABSURD FUN MARKED THESE PEOPLE!"
—*Hollywood Reporter*

Acknowledgment

A special Thank You to Mona Bonelli, my sainted aunt, who fortunately kept records of our family history.

For ROSEMARIE,
who makes it all work
—and who makes me think it does,
even when it doesn't

Contents

Prologue, 1

1 Family Album, 6
Or, If You're a Typical American Boy, Why Can't You Speak English?

2 Skeet Is the Name of the Game, 41

3 The Kiss Heard 'Round the World, 66
Or, Osculation for Fun and Profit

4 Three Carloads of Fresh Fish, 91

5 Beloved Son, Bastard #644, 120

6 The Heart Does Not Control the Feet, 164
Or, The Making of The Bullfighter and the Lady

7	The High and the Mighty, 185 *Or, How to Get a Part by Being Low and Sneaky*	
	Intermission, 200 *with* ROSEMARIE STACK	
8	Deirdre, 209	
9	Join the Movies and See the World!, 229	
10	"The Untouchables," 252 *Or, How I Caught Capone, Won the Emmy and Acquired a Lifetime Machine Gun*	
11	Beware the Smiling Lion!, 283	
12	Welcome to Grauman's Chinese—East!, 300	
13	A Tube for All Seasons, 313	
	Epilogue, 346	
	Index, 349	

Prologue

"Who are you?" is a question I hear all the time.

"I mean, who are you really?" the questioner usually adds.

Well, who do you want me to be? A typical American boy so I can give Deanna Durbin her first movie kiss? You've got it! That's me! Forget the fact that my mother had one hell of a time convincing authorities at Ellis Island she wasn't smuggling an alien into the country; this "typical American boy" couldn't speak English until he was six.

When I was seventeen I broke the world's record at the National Skeet Shooting Championships. Again, I heard a familiar refrain.

"Bob, why do you act dumb every time you win a major championship? You say you're lucky. How can you be lucky ten times in a row?"

I thought to myself, *I'm not lucky. I'm good. But unless I act dumb and shuffle my feet, the grown-ups I beat hate my guts*. So if you want me to be dumb, you've got it!

Another I've heard for years is, "You ought to get away from your jet-set society friends and mix with the common people." In fact, I spent all of my bachelor life with racing mechanics, shooters, horse traders, and stunt men. I was a much better athlete than actor or social lion. But if you prefer the playboy image, you've got it!

Jack Warner said, "I could make this kid a star, but he doesn't need me. He's not hungry enough."

Here was a dilemma. What could I say?

"Honest to God, Mr. Warner, I'm not who you think I am. I'm a real schizoid, nutty as a fruitcake, with a hunger that could chew up your whole studio." I knew no matter what I told Jack, he had his own image of me as the athlete playboy who thought of acting as a hobby. Studio heads don't like to change their opinions. They're never supposed to be wrong.

"If you could do something different, change your image," I heard, "you'd be less of a square." My opportunity came along when a director named Doug Sirk said to me, "You're an actor, you should be able to do it all." He gave me my first "real schizoid, nutty as a fruitcake" part. Still I didn't learn. At the preview of *Written on the Wind*, with all the press and studio brass, I forgot the basic credo: "Be what they want you to be." My part in *Written on the Wind* bordered on madness. It was a good role; I won an Academy Award nomination for it. This on-screen character beat up his pregnant wife, caused her miscarriage, and tried to kill his best friend. But did I show up at the preview in a torn T-shirt, a cigarette hanging from my lower lip, walking pigeon-toed, and slurring my words? No sir, old Sam Stupid was there in his all-American-boy outfit, beaming like Pat Boone in a milk commercial. So, of course, everyone was suspicious of the entire proceedings. If they see a maniac on film, they want the same thing in real life, not a phony substitute.

Eliot Ness was a complete stranger to me. This cold-eyed authoritarian was the biggest stretch I was ever asked to perform. Even the cuckoo in *Written on the Wind* was closer to the real me. But after four years, 120 shows, and the international success of "The Untouchables," I was a cop with the unlikely name of Eliot.

"Stack, you've got to be the luckiest guy in the business. How often does an actor get a part he's born for?"

So it goes. But, who am I?

Only twice have I really objected to being described as something I'm not.

One night many years ago, Judy Garland and I were doing

the cha-cha at a small after-hours joint across from NBC on Vine Street in Hollywood. The club was called La Conga, and on the other side of the room, holding up one end of the bar, was "Big Boy" Williams. Guinn Williams was probably the toughest character to inhabit the Hollywoods, a 250-pound ex-rodeo cowboy whose 1930s battle royal with Victor McLaglen had been the talk of the town. Vic had been a professional fighter before becoming an actor, and the two damn near killed each other. They locked the doors from the inside to prevent the weak-hearted from escaping. Neither man would quit, of course, and their bloody battle left both men looking like battle-scarred gladiators on the floor of the barn they had chosen as their arena. The only winner was the doctor.

When "Big" took up polo, he was short on style but long on strength. He didn't just hit the ball as everyone else did. He drilled it for the full length of the field. I tried lifting his polo mallet once, but it took both hands.

When the band stopped playing, there was a pause long enough for me to hear Big Boy Williams in a voice loud enough to be heard in Santa Monica: "That's what I said. Stack is a faggot."

Today I figure that a consenting adult can pretty much play it as it lays, and as the song says, "Different strokes for different folks." But in those dear departed macho days, it was not the thing to say to the world at large. I tried a subtle approach. I walked up to Big and said, "Big, why are you telling people I'm a fag?"

He was plastered to the eyeballs; he looked like a drunken buffalo, eyes glazed, his head wobbling from side to side.

He gave me a lopsided grin.

"Hey, kid, how the hell are you?"

"Why did you call me a fag?" After a pause, and a Charlie Ray foot shuffle, he finally said, "Well, kid, you never take any dames down to the polo games. I just figured you don't like them."

"I don't like them at polo games," I said. "I like them in bed."

"Son of a bitch, kid, that's a good one," said Big. "You know something? You're right. They're a pain in the neck at polo games." Now he began taking off his hand-tooled belt with the gold and silver rodeo buckle.

"Look, kid," he went on, "I don't want to hurt your feelings.

To show you I didn't mean any harm, here, take my belt." And I did. The next morning the phone rang, as I knew it would, with a very hung-over Big Boy on the other end. "Hey, Bob, you were at La Conga last night, weren't you?"

"Yeah," I said. "Why?"

"Well," explained Big Boy, "maybe you can help me. Some son of a bitch stole my belt."

One other time I objected to miscasting was with one of my favorites—in or out of acting—John Wayne.

Wayne had been known to put away his share of firewater, and one night in Mexico in 1950 was no exception. We were a couple of weeks into the filming of *The Bullfighter and the Lady*, and Duke and an assortment of toreros were celebrating something as unique as the sun going down with scotch, tequila, and that deadliest of all Latin potions, Pulque, a drink made from the maguay cactus. It looks like milk, tastes like milk gone sour, and gives you a cactus hangover complete with needles. I noticed Duke watching me with the saddest expression I'd ever seen on his great American face.

He slowly ambled over, put his great paw on my shoulder, and said, "You're really coming off well in the rushes, Bob. The picture looks great. It's a damn shame."

"What's a shame, Duke?" I said.

"That you are a Communist!"

Holy Mother, I thought, *a Communist? That's a new one.*

Next morning, over Duke's shaky cup of coffee, I pursued the subject.

"Why did you call me a Communist last night, Duke?"

"Why'd I call you a what?"

"A Communist."

"Oh, yeah," he said, "it's that girl."

"What girl?"

"The one you go with."

"Who?"

"Hell, I forget her name. You know the one who takes the *Daily Worker*."

"The one who takes what?"

"That red rag, the *Daily Worker*."

"Look, Duke," I said, "I just go out with girls. I don't read their mail. Besides," I said, "my interest is carnal, not political."

"Aw, look, forget it, kid," said Duke. "And if anybody ever

calls you a Communist, I'll set 'em straight." A slow smile illuminated the face of America's favorite cowboy.

I've never had to take Duke up on his offer!

Duke had been highly vocal about his love of country, and had taken his share of teasing as a patriot. But no one could accuse him of being inconsistent.

Once he was approached with a highly lucrative deal to play the lead in a film about General George Armstrong Custer. It is common knowledge that Duke Wayne refuses to make money out of anything that is detrimental to our country's image.

"Custer?" he said. "Custer? That fool, that jerk, that stupid idiot? I wouldn't be caught dead putting Custer's story on the screen!"

Then he paused for a moment.

"Of course," he added, almost as an afterthought, "I'd pay money to see it!"

It is a tribute to Duke's towering reputation that even those in our industry who disagreed violenty with his politics acknowledge him as one of the giants of film history.

So to at least two charges, I took exception. But as far as the rest is concerned, who am I really?

The best place to begin is at the beginning, so if you really want the beginning, here it is.

1

Family Album

Or, If You're a Typical American Boy, Why can't You Speak English?

Sister Susie isn't much of a name for a boy. But my brother James L. Stack, Jr., arrived two years prior to my birth. Anyway, while not exactly a disappointment to my parents, I certainly wasn't an original idea. There was still a bit of confusion after my arrival regarding a name for me, since Susie was no longer appropriate. Forty years later, when a birth certificate was needed to clear me for a Vietnam hospital tour, I was to find that there was still some confusion as to exactly who I was.

My mother named me Charles after my grandfather. My father James Langford Stack, who had his own ideas, changed it to Robert after no one in particular. So I had a choice of what I could call myself. I'm not only the first actor to have kissed Deanna Durbin on the screen, but the only one with two birth certificates, a ploy that may yet serve me in good stead if the progeny of Capone or Nitti ever decide "The Untouchables" was for real and want to even the score with Eliot Ness.

Mother and father divorced when I was only a year old. At the age of three, I went to Europe with mother, while my brother James L., Jr., remained in the States with father. My mother Elizabeth Modini Wood was a great beauty with all the social background Southern California had to offer then. She studied voice in Paris, and I started life as any good French boy should. Nobody thought it important to tell me about the US of A until a few years later.

Before long I began speaking fluent Parisian French. In the summers, we went to Riccione Marina, on the Adriatic in Italy. In those days, Riccione Marina was the watering hole for much of the bankrupt nobility and displaced royalty of Europe. Total recall has never been one of my strong points, but I do retain a series of lap dissolves of those early years: a noon whistle, and the daily ritual of sucking a raw egg washed down with hot cow's blood (an old Italian recipe guaranteed to transform a skinny kid into a lusty he-man). Nevertheless, I remained a skinny kid who learned to hate eggs and can't stand the sight of blood.

I was given a flashlight and allowed to gather snails at night for the larder. There were naps in the afternoon and the opera at night; sailboats bobbing on an azure sea, counterpointed by the sight of sailors cheerfully bashing out the brains of just-caught eels against a flagpole. Being dressed up for seemingly innumerable costume parties—as a Chinese or Russian nobleman or an Apache—was my first taste of show biz.

Not all the residents of that beautiful seaside resort were nobility, fishermen, or fish. Right next door to us was our neighbor Bruno Mussolini. At that time his father Benito was a hero because he made all the trains run on time. His association with Hitler was still years away.

After my afternoon nap, I was used to being put in a basket in the back of the car and taken to concerts or the opera. It was an exciting life, because between the ages of four and six I had already heard some of the best operatic performances in Italy. By now I spoke fluent Italian as well as French, and was working on Spanish. Still no one thought to tell me I was an American.

My mother was a raven-haired, sparkling-eyed beauty who not only knocked all the local swains for a loop, but also set Paris on its ear. She wore the cloche hats and bias-cut chemises of the twenties with a kind of devilish class that made me proud and jealous at the same time. Our apartment was a meeting place for artists, dancers, nobility. How could a four-year-old protect her from the various counts, a prince of Lichtenstein, and the assorted other males that trekked through our small apartment in Paris?

But she was always steadfast and loyal to me. Even when I shot an arrow through the old Spanish Madonna hanging over the fireplace, she only said, "No one told him it wasn't a target." I adored this lady for all her life.

Next door lived the M'Divanis, the general, handsomely mustachioed; the princess, 300 pounds of White Russian charm; and Russa, Nina, David, Serge, and Alexis, their children.

They were from Georgia, not the chitlins and black-eyed peas Georgia, but the little principality adjoining Russia where suspiciously large segments of the population were of royal birth.

Serge spent hours making kites for me which we would fly while the rest of the family plotted to find a way to get into the USA. Finally they decided to pool their resources, and since Alexis was the handsomest, he would be sent ahead to marry an heiress. As soon as he had accomplished his mission, he would send for the others.

Russa was a tall, dark, exotic beauty. She was also a character. She had such panache that she never had to buy any of the haute couture clothes she wore. She'd simply walk into the fanciest couturier and choose what she wanted. When they requested payment, she'd put on her best princess performance.

"Pay *you*?" she said. "I'm going to the gala. I'm Princess Russa M'Divani. I'm graciously offering you the chance to have me wear your clothes."

It never failed.

She wanted mother to pose as her sister and try the same routine. "With your beauty and the M'Divani name, you'll never have to pay for anything." Mother, however, never had the nerve to take her up on it. The M'Divanis lived across the hall from us. I remember the problem of getting the dear old princess, all 300 pounds of her, up and down in the miniature French elevator. She would squeeze in, and then the general and the boys would meet her at the landing and pry her out. Throughout all this she never lost her dignity; her lovely face with the delicate Dresden features always wore a gracious smile.

No matter what America may have thought of them later, to a boy growing up in Paris, the M'Divanis were the most exciting people imaginable, and they treated me as an adopted son.

One day Russa wondered out loud about a topic of strange fascination.

"What would it feel like to be shot?"

Everyone gave an opinion. After a few minutes, we moved on to another subject. Suddenly we heard a tremendous explosion. There was Russa in the doorway, holding the general's 9mm Luger, blood running down her arm, with the most enigmatic smile I'd ever seen on her young face.

"Now I know," she calmly said. (She had shot herself through the fleshy part of the upper arm; the bullet left a mild scar and a legend no Heidelberg saber could match.)

Every president in recent times has been convinced that he could understand the Russians and deal with them from the point of view of an American. I can only say, "Good luck!" Khrushchev undid my old friend JFK with his shoe-pounding diplomacy; others have had even less luck trying to fathom the unfathomable. When you think you've figured them out, ask yourself if you'd shoot yourself through the biceps with a Luger to find out how it feels!

Meanwhile, Alexis had voyaged to America. No sooner did Barbara Hutton set eyes on this irresistible Prince Alexis than she became a titled princess, and the M'Divani clan was on its way to the promised land. (Serge later married Mae Murray, while David latched on to the current femme fatale of cinemaland, Pola Negri, and thus established Georgia's answer to the Gabors.)

When I was about six, mother made plans to return to the United States; I cried. I couldn't speak English, but most important, I knew I couldn't have wine with my meals. In Italy and France at that time, people thought wine killed the germs in the water, and all children drank a little bit of wine with their water. I was convinced I was going to be poisoned when I went to America. In some of the confusion of leaving, no one thought to clarify the passport situation, so our arrival in New York caused a family crisis. Mother had no passport for me, and by now I was too old to travel on hers. I was held at Ellis Island, and dear mama was accused of trying to bring in an illegal emigré. I understood nothing those uniformed barbarians were saying, and promptly confused things further by howling in all the wrong languages. This did little to convince them I was an American citizen. Grandfather eventually came to my rescue, and my life as a displaced person began.

My first words in English were not very dramatic. The traffic signals in those days were metal paddles with "stop" on red and "go" on green. Those were my first utterances in this foreign tongue. We went to California where my grandmother lived. Luckily, mother spoke French, and grandmother, Italian. So while they were around me, all was well. The same cannot be said of my introduction to my brother. He, of course, spoke only English—as well as the language of all older brothers of the world. There was definitely a cultural gap. I was used to asking mother, *"Est-ce qu'elle est mariée?"* in reference to a lady and, after getting the go-ahead to kiss her hand, I went on with, *"Enchanté de vous connaître, madame!"* In Europe a small, well-mannered French boy, kissing a lady's hand, was par for the course. But in California all the ladies thought I was darling. My brother's reaction was equally dramatic. He thought I was a fag.

I early discovered other differences in our cultures. While I had been kissing ladies' hands in Europe and going to the opera, my brother had been living with my father, and was as American as he could be. Jim and his raggedy-looking friends had started a club. Within the club there were many degrees. There were charter members and other categories of varying importance. I naturally started at the lowest degree, and was to be initiated. I almost didn't get past the first ritual of pushing a peanut around the block with my nose.

To really understand what the Stack family was like, it's important to know something about my parents. They were each very special people, unlike any others I've ever met.

Mother grew up in a world of quiet and gracious elegance. There were no televisions, radios, or motion pictures. Mischievous boys could amuse themselves by kicking a tin can around the block. A real adventure might be a ride in the "merry Oldsmobile" parked in the driveway or a chance to visit friends.

Initially, her family lived in downtown Los Angeles, near the center of town. On Sundays, mother and the rest of the family were dressed up and sent to Sunday school. (Her brother Perry inevitably stopped for a detour at Wilson's Pharmacy. Armed with a pocketful of licorice, he always felt there might be a chance to get into a fight and get dirty before going to church with the grown-ups.) Mother, of course, was a well-behaved little girl who avoided such frivolity.

On Sunday afternoons, after a dinner which had been prepared on Saturday, the children went to the cemetery to pay their respects to the departed. Since Sunday was so solemn, the children in the family anticipated the weekend with as much enthusiasm as they reserved for a visit to the dentist.

Eventually the family moved to a beautiful home in St. James Park, one of the nicest sections of Los Angeles. It was in this house that mother really grew up. Today the old house is no longer standing, and in place of the building in which all those children grumbled about attending Sunday school stands another structure: St. Paul's Cathedral.

The house in St. James Park had previously been occupied by a European lady, the Baroness von Zimmerman. The baroness had had a lifelong interest in psychic phenomena. She built a house on her property for the spirits. She would fix elaborate banquets for the various paranormal beings that she knew inhabited the environs. These were consumed with gusto by the local watchman and the neighbors who would wait for the baroness to leave. Then they would indulge in their own form of spirits, with the poor lady never the wiser, convinced that she was communicating with the spirits of the hereafter.

From the beginning of her life, everyone seemed to realize that mother was unusual. She used to swim in Santa Monica at a place called the North Beach House. (In those days, Santa Monica was called North Beach.) One day a man jumped in the water, although he couldn't swim. Mother thought quickly, went to his rescue, and pulled him out of the pool. She was considered a heroine, was written about and praised in the newspaper, and, best of all, given a lifetime free pass to the North Beach House. Swimming was not a pursuit many women enjoyed in those days.

It was only natural for mother to be exposed to music from the time she was old enough to sing simple tunes. My grandmother Mamie Perry had been considered the first musical prodigy of the city.

My grandmother made her operatic debut in Italy at eighteen, singing the lead in a little-known opera, *The Countess of Amalfi*. She stunned the Italians into ten curtain calls as well as an impromptu shower of rose petals from the balcony. At the same time, my grandfather Charley Wood was also in Milan singing under the name Carlo Modini. (They were, as yet, unacquainted.) In retrospect, it may seem odd that perfectly normal Americans couldn't become famous in opera or the concert world without changing their names to sound Italian. But at the time, audiences were highly suspicious of any New World upstarts attempting to sing the classics. So "Charley Wood" was as welcome in Europe as American perfume or champagne.

While in Milan, my grandfather shared the concert stage with the great Nellie Melba. He heard of the new singer knocking them dead in *The Countess of Amalfi* at the opera house, but he was so busy he never had a chance to pursue the matter.

When my grandmother returned to Los Angeles in 1882, she caused the Los Angeles City Council to adjourn for a lack of a quorum. The council members were all at Turnverein Hall to attend her homecoming recital. The reaction increased the demand for local opera houses, and soon the Grand Opera House, the Los Angeles Theater, and the Burbank (named after local dentist David Burbank) were all under construction. The famous impresario Lynden Ellsworth Behymer launched his career selling pictures of actors in the opera houses and running a popcorn and peanut concession. Eventually, Behymer started the Los Angeles Fiesta, the social event of the year. Young Mamie Perry had the honor of being chosen as queen of the fiesta.

Meanwhile, the strain of singing concerts all over the world was taking its toll on young Charley Wood, and he went to Los Angeles to recoup his health. He arrived with glowing letters of introduction to the city's musical folk, and it was natural for him to be invited to William Perry's house for dinner, especially since Perry's eighteen-year-old daughter Mamie was the toast of the far western town of Los Angeles.

After dinner Mamie thought she'd impress her guest with the talents that had thrilled them in Italy. After she finished singing, Mr. Wood applauded vigorously.

"Would you like to sing, Mr. Wood?" she said coquettishly.

"I just happened to bring my music," said Charley Wood, with a straight face. He then proceeded to show Mamie Perry the difference between a gifted amateur and a gifted professional. His months of touring the world with a diva of Melba's stature gave even that old chestnut "Mother Machree" a poignancy never before heard in the City of the Angels. Great-grandfather Perry subtly nudged his daughter with an elbow and whispered, "Don't let this one get away, Mamie." She didn't.

But despite their great singing voices, neither of my grandparents contemplated a permanent life on the stage. Halfway back from Europe on the boat, my great-grandfather had had a talk with his talented daughter.

"Mamie," he said, "I've spent this last year with you in Italy while you were studying voice and preparing for your debut."

"Yes, Father," she said, "and I love you for it."

"I promised you your operatic debut," he went on, "and you've had it."

"Yes, Father."

"So now I never want you to appear again. No daughter of mine is going to make a living singing on the stage."

Charley Wood apparently felt the same way, because he too turned away from an operatic career, and although my grandparents continued to be heard often, it was only at church socials or in the privacy of their home where they harmonized for their own enjoyment. The world of show biz whirled on without them.

When my mother was twenty years old, she was offered a leading part which had been written for her in a Broadway-bound musical comedy. This time it was Charley Wood's turn to say, "No daughter of mine is going to appear on stage in a musical comedy. Opera, yes, but not musical comedy."

When it came to me, much the same thing happened. At about the time I was offered a chance to get into the movies, my cousin Rear Admiral William R. Monroe was aide to President Roosevelt. His wife Katherine Monroe was a social leader in Washington, D.C. When she heard the news about me, a telegram was not long in coming.

"Betzi," she wired my mother, "how can you allow Bobby to be in that crazy business with all those terrible people?" Mother, who had encouraged me in that "crazy business" in the first place, explained that it was my decision, but it was only after Katy learned that my leading lady was to be Deanna Durbin, America's sweetheart, that the okay was finally given.

As for the next generation, my daughter Elizabeth is studying to be an actress. Here's the possible next step in the same old story. I can hear her saying, "Oh, Dad, it's a wonderful part. I'll never get another one like it." I can hear myself saying, "No daughter of mine is going to appear in an X-rated movie!" *Plus ça change, plus c'est la même chose!*

Mother went quietly about her business amid enough accolades to turn any girl's head. Willy Pogani, the celebrated painter, did her portrait. Ina Coolbrith, poet laureate of California, wrote poems about her beauty. The Los Angeles newspapers picked her as one of the six most beautiful girls in the state, and even included her eyes as part of a composite "perfect California beauty." Mother accepted all the public tributes with a combination of modesty and grace that can only be described in one word: style.

Like all young girls, mother dreamed of adventure, and when she went to New York to study voice, the trip whetted her appetite for travel. When it came time for mother and her sister Flissie to make the customary tour of Europe that was considered part of a young lady's education, mother had other ideas.

In 1911 she persuaded my grandmother that the best way to reach Europe was via some exotic adventures in the Orient. Mother was probably dreaming of Omar Khayyam, but the surprises in store during this trip were anything but poetic.

Off Manila Bay, the tour party managed to escape a typhoon. By the time mother had recovered from that shock, they had arrived in China, in the middle of a revolution. The major tourist attraction in China consisted of the public execution of rebels. Mother used to talk about the terror of trying to avoid witnessing the most grisly sight of her life—the pigtailed decapitated heads of rebels being exhibited on stakes by bloodthirsty soldiers—while my great-grandfather was quietly and unknowingly shopping for curios in the basement of the hotel.

"Well," said mother, "we'll really see the sights in Ceylon." The main sight to see there turned out to be a man-eating tiger which was terrorizing the countryside.

Off the coast of Japan, the crew mutinied, and mother found out that piracy on the high seas may be romantic in books, but not if your captain is thinking about tossing *you* overboard. One member of the party died of smallpox during the trip, and my great-grandmother breathed a sigh of relief when they headed through India toward a more civilized destination in Europe.

The trip wasn't all chaos and confusion, though mother got to ride on the back of an elephant in India, saw maharajahs wearing jewel-encrusted turbans, and witnessed something she would never forget: The family was invited to the durbar, the incredible coronation of Queen Mary as empress of India. What girl could forget a chance to meet a real queen just outside the Taj Mahal?

My grandmother was convinced that their troubles were over when mother and Flissie joined their youngest sister Mona in the Mediterranean. The only problem was a delay in booking passage on a ship home. The voyage they barely missed was the *Titanic,* and luckily they returned home safely.

Mother's "love affair with show biz" was a two-way street. It was not so much that show business in general loved her, but one of the most famous stars of the day certainly did.

Wallace Reid has often been called the handsomest actor of silent pictures. He had an Arrow shirt profile with blond hair and a physique that let him do his own dangerous stunts in the action films that were his specialty.

Our lifelong family friend Adela Rogers St. Johns wrote a book recently called *Love, Laughter, and Tears,* recalling that many of the tears shed in Hollywood were inspired by Wallace Reid. A New York heiress once handed a half-million-dollar emerald necklace to his valet as a calling card at Wallace Reid's dressing room. Pretty girls used to hide under his bed and in his closets hoping to catch a glimpse of their idol. The reason for their enthusiasm was understandable. He was a dashing figure, the only amateur ever allowed to drive in the Indianapolis road race, with a stable of his own racing cars that allowed him to drive a different one to the studio each day. He was a good swimmer, boxer, swordsman, and even played the piano, violin, saxophone, and banjo.

Mother had an operatic singing voice, and she met Wallace Reid while studying singing in New York. They were very young, and it was only natural that the beautiful soprano from California would fall in love for the first time with the handsome youth from the East. Full of charm and hopes, he was working for a newspaper at the time, but was not really certain what he planned to do with his life. He came from a theatrical background and was thinking of becoming an actor.

In those days an acting profession seemed even less secure than it does today. My grandparents were understandably less than enthusiastic at the prospect of their daughter marrying a young man with a fine profile but no apparent future.

Mother never told us about him, except when I asked her directly. Then she would look very private and faraway.

"Wally Reid?" she would say. "The dearest man I've ever known." In a tin box—with her lifeguard medal (awarded for saving the man at North Beach) and her autographed photos of Thomas Edison and assorted opera singers—was a picture of Wallace Reid. He was wearing an open-necked shirt and argyle sweater. His blond hair shone like a halo. He was holding a pipe in his right hand and looking directly at the camera with a quizzical, little-boy expression. It said simply, "For Elizabeth, Someday, Billy."

But "someday" never came for mother and "Billy." In those days a young girl wouldn't think of marrying without her parents' approval. During the silent film era, before actors had the Screen Actors Guild to protect them, they were compelled to work terrible hours and some took incredible risks. I was told Wallace Reid was hurt doing a stunt, and that the doctor had given him morphine in the hospital to kill the pain. As a result, he became dependent on the drug, and eventually addicted.

Mother had to find some way to forget Wallace Reid, and for a while she thought of devoting her life to music. The Lombardi Opera Company, a local group of great distinction, offered her a leading operatic role. My grandfather knew the impresario who ran the company, but he felt he couldn't interfere directly. At the same time, my grandparents believed strongly what their parents had told them years before: It would be unthinkable for a girl to become a "professional" singer.

So my grandparents came up with an idea. They simply introduced mother to the most dashing alternative to Wallace Reid that they could find. Their choice couldn't have been more exciting. He was handsome, successful, and full of a wild-eyed Irish charm. James Langford Stack had been master of the hounds in Chicago. In addition to fox hunting, he owned a string of polo ponies, and when mother met this daredevil on horseback, a whirlwind courtship ensued.

When we returned to Los Angeles from Paris, mother took an apartment in a Wilshire district building known as the Bryson Apartments. It is still standing today, only recently being sold by Fred MacMurray who had acquired it some years ago.

Los Angeles was full of nothing but surprises. My old copybook still bears an inscription from those days: *Il mio nome e Robert Stack; abbito al Bryson Apartments."* I couldn't give up my Italian for at least a while.

To soften the shock of finding myself in a country in which no one seemed to speak either French or Italian, mother had brought my French nurse with us to our new home. She was about as much use as teeth on a chicken. One lovely California afternoon, she decided we should have a better look at this foreign city of Los Angeles, and maybe even take in a Punch and Judy show like those presented in the Bois de Boulogne in Paris.

What better place could we start than Main Street in Los Angeles? What my nurse did not know was that Main Street in Los Angeles, even in the twenties, had the highest population of hookers, pimps, and winos west of the Mississippi. After a few blocks, even she caught on and looked for the first available refuge. She noticed the marquee of a movie house announcing an operatic fantasy and quickly led me to safety inside. Neither the nurse nor I could speak a word of English, so it was a case of the blind leading the blind.

I had been brought up on opera in Italy, but this was one I'd never seen before. As far as I could tell, it was about a masked man in love with an opera singer and very jealous of her admirers. He lived under an opera house and killed off the lady's admirers by drowning them, dropping things on them, and so forth. So far, this wasn't too different from Puccini. In the climactic scene, our dweller carried his lady love down to his apartment and began playing to her on a great organ.

As his girl friend reached forward to take off his mask and reveal his identity, my darling mademoiselle said, "Watch now, dear, this is when he is discovered as the fairy prince." There was a slight pause after she pulled off the mask, and then full face into the camera appeared the most ghastly apparition ever put on film. It was Lon Chaney's masterpiece, *The Phantom of the Opera*. I let out a six-year-old shriek of terror and slid under the seat. That night I shared my mother's bed, and I didn't stop shaking for two days. As for mademoiselle, she was suspicious of everything American until the day she died.

The first time I remember meeting my father, he looked at me with a kind of detached amazement.

"Say, he's grown up, hasn't he? He's a fine looking boy."

Then, like a self-made businessman not used to beating around the bush, he asked, "How much do you want for him?"

Mother grabbed me by the arm, yanked me out of the house, and stuffed me in the car. She wouldn't answer dad's calls for two weeks.

But dad was ill now, and really needed mother. He asked her to remarry him, and she did. Mother told me he was once again the man she first married, "The dearest and most thoughtful person in the world." It was only the mandatory booze of the period that destroyed their first time around. So we moved out of our apartment and into dad's big house on Ardmore Avenue. In one complete sweep I acquired a new family, a new nationality, and a whole new perspective on my strange new country. I used to delight in telling people that I got the giggles all during my mother's wedding. I naturally neglected to mention that it was the second time around. It never failed to produce a roomful of raised eyebrows. Today I don't even have to offer an explanation.

Mother and dad were remarried in 1928. The period which so typified my father's life-style was drawing to a close. The wedding was announced in a large headline in the Los Angeles papers. In an ironic footnote, and as precursor of my future television life as Eliot Ness, another article appeared nearby on the same page: "Al Capone wounded by his own gun."

Dad was a character. His rapid rise from newsboy to head of one of the largest advertising agencies in the country was not unlike the exaggerated highs and lows of show business. He was a living symbol of the Horatio Alger legend. He invented such slogans as The Beer That Made Milwaukee Famous. James Langford Stack was a man at home in his era. He roared through the twenties with energy and abandon.

During their "first" marriage, when my mother was in her eighth month of expecting my brother, she and dad went to a movie theater. He asked the manager if he could get mother in without her standing in line, because she was pregnant. The manager said, "You'll have to stand in line just like everybody else." Dad was furious. The next day he called his lawyer, arranged to buy the theater, and fired the manager.

Dad spent a good deal of his time with people like Mack Sennett, Will Rogers, George Bancroft, Leo Carrillo, and many other stars of the silver screen. He had the first motor home on the Hollywood scene. He took a Mack truck and had a house built around it; it had all the luxuries of home, but it never got from point A to B. Although he tried many times to get up the Bishop Grade to his home at Lake Tahoe, he never made it. Like a beached whale, the engine, not designed to move a house, spouted steam and inevitably gave up, holding up traffic for hours. But every summer dad tried again. He had better luck getting there in his Rolls, but the local police in Bridgeport, California, picked him up each time he stormed through their little town. He was too stubborn to slow down, and the local cop began regarding him as a familiar face.

"Nice day, Mr. Stack," the cop would say, as he gave dad his customary speeding ticket.

Dad was convinced that money could buy almost anything. He also felt that he had worked like hell for his, so he deserved it. He paid the servants twice the going rate, but expected his money's worth. If he woke up at 4:30 A.M., he'd ring all their rooms and announce, "I'm awake. Everybody get up!" The turnover was heavy. He had a valet he'd fire once a month, and then forget he'd fired him.

"Where in hell is John?" he would say.

"You fired him yesterday."

"Well, tell him to get back here; he knows I didn't mean it."

After the fifth hire-fire episode, dad had to leave town on business. So did John, for good, with all of dad's wardrobe.

Dad couldn't stand anyone doing a sloppy job. Whenever the chauffeur would blow a shift on the Rolls-Royce (not difficult to do with those old straight-tooth gears), the noise of clashing metal was like a fingernail on a blackboard. Dad would get so mad he'd start pounding the culprit on the back like a bass drum.

He was a close friend of Jack Dempsey and bet $10,000 on him in the second Gene Tunney fight. In 1927, when Tunney won in the controversial "long count" rhubarb, dad never said a word. He also paid up, but in his own unconventional way. It took a few days, but he rounded up 100,000 pennies in 100-pound sacks. Several trucks delivered the sacks to the winner's house. The combined weight of 100,000 pennies was enough to collapse the man's front porch. Dad's only comment was, "Now he's got enough to buy himself a new porch."

In 1927, when Lindbergh made his epic flight across the Atlantic, dad ordered an exact copy of the *Spirit of St. Louis* from Ryan Aircraft, the company that made Lindy's famous plane. The nine-cylinder Wright Whirlwind engine was covered by a cowling that looked like the inside of a safe. This engine could run for 9,000 hours without a breakdown. The beautiful engine cowling shone so brightly you could see it a mile away. The plane itself was a sight to behold. The twenty-eight-foot silver plane was built of spruce wood, piano wire, cotton fabric, and shiny silver steel tubing. Dad was one of the first to have a private plane and a pilot to go with it. Although the plane was a replica of the *Spirit of St. Louis*, the pilot was hardly a replica of Charles Lindbergh. On the way back to Los Angeles from dad's duck lodge near Marysville, California, the pilot pulled up too steeply to clear the mountains, went into a spin, and pulled the plane out just fifty feet from the ground. Dad asked the pilot to take him to the nearest airport. When he got out of the plane, he asked the first person he saw, "What'll you give me for it?" A surprised mechanic said, "I can't afford a plane like that."

Dad said, "Try me."

The mechanic said, "Two hundred dollars?"

Dad said, "It's yours." He took the train home and never flew again.

When he first began his business career, dad became aware of the tremendous possibility for growth in American business. Instead of taking cash payments from some of his clients, he often took stock in their business. As America grew, so did his company. He became a wealthy man, entirely self-made. I used to peek into his private haven at home, the den with the biggest, most forbidding moose head a six-year-old ever saw. I remember the smell of Havana cigars and the clickety-clack of martini shakers. In and out of the shadowy room moved a conglomerate of the greats, dad's polo buddies, and dozens of famous figures of the times.

Also, in the bare cellar stood a bookcase. Even at my age, this seemed a bit peculiar since no chairs or reading lamps were to be found there. In front of the bookcase was a large metal door which, when opened, revealed the largest collection of booze anywhere west of the Mississippi. The prohibition officers would arrive and announce solemnly, "We'd like to check your library, Mr. Stack." He'd say, "Okay, fellas. I've got a few little editions that might interest you." He would take them into the cellar; they would check out the booze and get half smashed. He would send them on their way, staggering down the steps. Little did anyone realize at the time that I would resurface some years later in the role of the incorruptible Eliot Ness.

Dad could be rough and tough. He was an honorary chief of police and an honorary fire marshal in Los Angeles. He had a canary-colored Rolls-Royce with a red light and a siren. The siren and light were very decorative, but the only time I remember his using them was to scatter traffic on the way to the Rose Bowl. One day someone came and removed the siren and light, and eventually the city insisted that he give up his badges. The day of the wheeler-dealer private citizen was coming to an end.

I met my first real movie star at the age of eight. Mother took me to my grandmother's summer cottage in the mountains close to San Bernardino, a town devised for the sale of hitherto valueless land to the Los Angelenos short of enough cash to make it to Europe's watering holes. Venice, adjoining Santa Monica, was another California real estate developer's dream, but this time it was canals, replete with gondolas, mandolins, scenic bridges, and an ahead-of-its-time Italian Disneyland.

Unfortunately, Southern California of the 1920s wasn't ready for this old-world cultural shock, and now Venice's canals all meander forlornly to nowhere, while drug addicts and winos ply the back alleys. But Lake Arrowhead flourished, not only as a haven for Hollywood's greats, but also as a handy location for everything from serials to Jeanette MacDonald—Nelson Eddy love trysts. On one very special day we were awakened by my grandmother's stalwart cook Isaiah.

"There's a movie company just down the road," he said. "Get up, boys, you may never get a chance to see anything like this again."

My cousin Perry and I approached the movie crew stealthily, moving from tree to tree, like Indians, until suddenly we found ourselves face to face with the star. He wore a beautiful beige fur coat and an expression of regal disdain. His face bore not a wrinkle, and his perfect profile was a testament to his stardom. He watched us with no particular interest, turned his back, and sat down. We looked around at these strange intruders. One man with a megaphone was waving his arms and shouting. I knew he was the director, because it said so on his chair. There was a mushy love scene going on, and while the man and woman with "orange guck" on their faces smooched, the director with the megaphone kept telling them what to do. Behind him were two musicians, a violinist and a man pedaling and playing a little portable organ. They were fiddling and pedaling a tune called "The Best Things in Life Are Free." It all looked pretty dumb, because nobody looked as if he were paying attention to anybody else. Then the guy with the megaphone said "cut" and everybody started talking and laughing and smiling. Next, a man with a big scar and black mustache came in and began causing trouble. Now it started getting exciting; I could see the star was just waiting to jump and take care of the dirty rat with the mustache. The director gave the cue, and sure enough, the star ran in, grabbed the scar-faced character, and they wrestled on the ground until the dirty rat gave up. After the scene, the director, who saw us watching, brought the star over and introduced him. I could see now why he was such a famous actor in motion pictures. He had the most intelligent eyes I'd ever seen, warm and sympathetic, but he could also look mean when he had to. We even had our picture taken together. They say that if he could have learned to write, he would have signed more autographs than any actor in the world. But it didn't matter, 'cause I got his paw print, and I didn't care whether Rin Tin Tin could write or not.

Dad was on the boxing commission and Jim and I got to see all the great fights. Dad made sure the older son carrying his name could whip any kid on the block; he did this just as he approached any other project, head-on. He got a world's welterweight boxing champion, Jimmy McLarnin, to teach him. This would have made for a pretty discouraging state of affairs if my brother and I had ever gotten into a fight. Needless to say, any hassle was always resolved short of fisticuffs. Actually, Jim had a straight left that could tear an opponent's head off, but I don't think he ever had a fight outside the ring in his whole life.

Jim also has the ability to endear himself to people in situations that might normally lead to bloodshed. Late one drunken night in a bar, I heard him mutter, "That man's got the biggest nose I ever saw." I looked over, and sure enough the man had a proboscis like an Italian sausage. He said, "I'm going over and tell him."

I said, "Damn it, Jim, don't do that."

But he was insistent. "I think someone should tell him."

"Why for God's sake?"

"Just so he knows I know."

Over he walked, tapped the man on the shoulder, and said, "Excuse me, sir, but you've got the biggest nose I ever saw." By now I was looking around, casing the joint for the handiest exit.

The man turned around, looked at him for a second and said, "You know, you're probably right. How about a drink on it?"

"I'd be proud to," said Jim, and the two went through a bottle of scotch and closed the joint. If I had tried the same thing, I'd have been killed.

One of dad's best chums was Leo Carrillo, an old friend of the family for many years before he became sidekick to the Cisco Kid.

Leo's favorite topic of conversation was his family. His grandfather Carlos Antonio Carrillo was the first provisional governor of California; his father Don Juan Carrillo was mayor of Santa Monica. His favorite tale was of his great aunt Concepcion Arguello, who spent her life waiting at the window of the Garden of Memories in Monterey for a long-lost Russian lover. Leo had so many relatives in California that he would be approached on the streets by small boys he had never seen.

"I'm your cousin," they would tell him. "Lend me two bits."

Leo did everything with flair. One of his pet projects was an enormous Hollywood premiere. A galaxy of Hollywood stars in their Sunday best led a parade downtown on Leo's special night. Klieg lights beamed through the sky. But the grand opening was not for a motion picture; one of Leo's favorite cronies on the vaudeville circuit, a Chinese acrobat and comedian named Sing Ling Fu, was opening a Chinese laundry. Leo just wanted him to open it with style.

Another of dad's best friends was Will Rogers. It was Leo who discovered him. During his vaudeville days, Leo saw Rogers gallop on stage, riding and roping. His hat fell off, and he ad-libbed: "Roosevelt's hat is in the ring; so is mine. I don't know why I said that. All I know is what I read in the papers."

"That's a good line," said Leo. "Keep it in." The rest was history.

My father was a vigorous sportsman, as direct in sports as in business. In the game of polo, if one player crosses in front of the other, a foul is called and a penalty shot given. Dad took the rules literally. If he was on the line of the ball and someone fouled him, instead of pulling up his horse and accepting the free shot, he simply ran over the other horse and rider. Will Rogers was the only polo player as wild as dad. He used to tear down the field twirling the polo mallet around his head like a cowboy about to rope a steer. Maybe that's why they were such great friends.

Dad was also an extravagant gift-giver. As a surprise for mother, he bought a nearly miraculous mechanical bird in Switzerland. It was a songbird, a canary. The canary was life-sized, of solid gold with sapphire eyes and an ivory beak; it was sculpted by hand so that every feather stood out in relief. It was impressive enough in repose, but simply amazing when it was turned on. First came a couple of tentative cheeps, as if the bird were not sure of its audience; next came an appraising cock of the head, a ruffling of the tail feathers, a liquid trill or two; and soon the wings began to flap. Then the canary started swinging on its perch, annihilating its audience with a ninety-second routine that must have taken a Swiss watchmaker years to program.

It was so delicate and complex that it never was run for an audience of fewer than three—or unless Jim or I had done something dandy like not getting in trouble for a week. I loved the little golden bird and, as a child, I thought it was magic.

Mother's bird was the talk of the town. No one had seen its equal, and those lucky enough to view it in action would have given anything to have one like it. But as far as I know, no other bird around could hold a candle to "Betzi's bird" as it came to be called.

Even as worldly a man as Mack Sennett, purveyor of Sennett's famous bathing beauties, was so taken by it that he asked to feature it in a movie. It took a while for dad to give his okay but, finally, he agreed to let it be photographed.

Shortly after my parents remarried, my father became ill. It was 1929, a traumatic year for us; we lost both my father and grandfather. I hardly got to know my father before he was gone. When mother asked the doctor the cause of his passing, he told her that father had died of the period: his Horatio Alger life, his bottle of scotch, twenty cigars a day, his hard work, and harder playing. He was a man for one season, the twenties.

Some time after my father's death, mother wrote to Mack

Sennett to ask for our bird. He may have been the king of comedy to the rest of the world, but he was the blackest of villains to me. "The bird is mine," said he. "Jim [dad] gave it to me, and I'm going to keep it. You can't prove otherwise. Sue me."

Magic is hard to come by, and as Judy Garland sang so wistfully for all of us in *The Wizard of Oz*, "If birds fly over the rainbow, why, then, oh why can't I?" I'll tell you why—because a big burly lout stole my mother's golden bird!

There had been a special magic to those brief years with my father. The zany enthusiasm that dominated the twenties had dominated his life, and in a very unique way some of his energy and vitality had affected all our lives.

Now mother was faced with the prospect of raising two boys alone. She plunged into that responsibility as she did everything else, with good humor and an adventurous spirit.

Mother enrolled me in the Carl Curtis School, a private school on Beverly Boulevard. Carl Curtis had been a fine athlete, and the school which bore his name emphasized having a sound body as well as a sound mind.

Some of the most interesting lessons, however, did not take place in the classroom. Victor McLaglen occasionally refereed the boxing matches. Victor's son Andy was, appropriately, the biggest boy in school. He used his size to great advantage; in the boxing matches he could whale the tar out of all his smaller opponents, and he did this with great seriousness and predictable regularity.

By the time I reached my teens, my brother and I were ready for a year at the Beverly School for Boys. It was one of mother's few uninspired ideas. The school was run by a pair of poor German refugees who had gathered more than their share of roughnecks in the classroom. (In those days they were called juvenile delinquents.) Every type of mayhem broke out during the year, including knife fights, which Jim and I managed to avoid. At the end of the year, we left for Los Angeles High School.

Football, baseball, and the other team sports did not hold any special fascination for me. I had already involved myself in individual off-campus sports and was enthusiastically pursuing competition in shooting. Today, high school is a single, blurred memory for me—a lot of classes and assignments that interrupted the things that really interested me, my off-campus athletics. As an example of the tactics I employed, I turned in the same theme for both junior and senior English. Then, when I enrolled at USC, I dusted off my old high school theme and turned it in again for freshman English. I got an A all three times.

Although my father was gone, there were many reminders of him. Not the least of these was his home at Lake Tahoe. Dad had been one of the first Californians to make Nevada his legal residence. Lake Tahoe sits on the border between California and Nevada. The lake has special appeal because Californians can enjoy the gambling privileges of Nevada by walking across the state line or, in some instances, across an imaginary border in their own living rooms. (It was theoretically possible to have a house built on the border, with gambling legal in the living room, and illegal in the kitchen.)

Dad chose the Nevada site of Lake Tahoe not only because of its beauty, but because there he paid no taxes. After his death, mother continued to spend summers at Lake Tahoe, so some of my happiest memories are linked to that house. Our guest list might include Louella Parsons, Hedda Hopper, a host of opera singers, symphony musicians, and artists of every variety. One of mother's special friends was Carole Lombard, who visited us with her brother Stu Peters in the company of Roscoe Turner, the great airplane racer, who sported a waxed mustache and was accompanied by his pet lion cub Gilmore. I have a photo of Carole Lombard's arrival at the Reno airport. She is standing next to Roscoe Turner's Lockheed Vega, her arms laden with roses presented by her gallant pilot. He has his leather helmet and goggles pushed back on his head, and the devil-may-care grin that suits a heroic aviator. Somehow Faye Dunaway and Warren Beatty and the rest don't make it when they try recreating the period. Trying to copy Carole Lombard is like trying to catch a sunbeam.

One evening Jerry Wills, the local sheriff and bosom buddy of all the Nevada gamblers, took my brother and me to see a new nightclub act. I was assured that the twelve-year-old girl who sang in the show was a prodigy with a voice that no one could forget. She was one of three girls who were billed as The Gumm Sisters.

Judy Garland was already a headliner at age twelve. She was the little one in the middle with the big voice and talent to match. The Gumm sisters all wore bobbie socks and cheerleader skirts, but Judy was the one who jumped off the stage and grabbed the audience even then.

She sang "Zing went the strings of my heart" through her nose, and loud enough to be heard across Lake Tahoe, but the audience adored her. I was sixteen, and not much for twelve-year-old girls. Still, even I picked up her special mix of joy and poignancy. She was always a pro; the audience was something to be manipulated and they gladly played their part. Several years later I remember a benefit at the Biltmore Bowl after she'd made it big at MGM. That night Mickey Rooney and Judy did many of their familiar routines, finishing up with a finale of "God Bless America." Just before the finale, I could see Judy looking up as if asking the Lord for inspiration. What inspiration! On the final "God Bless America," great tears began running down her face. She not only got a standing ovation, but the men picked her up and marched her around the room, and there wasn't a dry eye in the house. After the show, I asked her why she'd looked up before the song.

"Oh, Bobby," she said. "I was looking into the big spot so I could get the tears to work."

Just about that time, Ida May Coverman was second-in-command under Louis B. Mayer at MGM. She was also a friend of mother and thought it would be "darling" if Judy and I had a romance.

"They make such a cute couple," she said. As in every such case, nothing developed. Judy was in love at various times with Artie Shaw, David Rose, and other musical types, while I was researching the list of contract girls. But we were always great chums. She was the first girl I called for a date when I came home on leave from overseas. She made a vulnerable sailor feel like an admiral. Everyone loved Judy, and I was no exception.

My dad's house in Tahoe also eventually became a meeting place for such superstars as Nat King Cole, Sammy Davis, and Frank Sinatra. Nat was my favorite of all the headliners. His gentle, uncomplicated manner was complemented by a purity of talent that touched me like none of the others. Many a night he sat at the piano, silhouetted by the moon path in the lake, and played for the sheer joy of making music until sunrise.

Cal-Neva was a name dreamed up in the twenties for a log-cabin-type nightclub overlooking beautiful Lake Tahoe. The state line ran right through the middle with the gaming tables on the Nevada side and food and dancing in California. Dad's house was only a stone's throw away, and as kids we used to go over and watch the flying-fingered twenty-one dealers and snake-eyed pit bosses plying their trade. We kept watching to see if any extra cards were stuffed up someone's sleeve; we were hoping a Gary Cooper-type character would discover the dice were loaded and take appropriate steps. Our entrance was usually heralded by, "Here come those damn Stack kids again."

I made friends with one dealer, though, who told me he'd come west to retire and raise cattle.

"And since I'm retiring, kid," he said one night, "here's a couple of tips that might prove helpful when you grow up. First, never play cards with a guy with a green eyeshade."

"Why not?"

"Because the eyeshade's polarized. When a player looks through it, he can read the numbers on the back of your cards. Now here's something I don't want you to use, just know about so you won't be a mark." He then proceeded to show me how to mark a deck of cards using only a nail file and some talcum powder.

These two demonstrations have kept me away from the green felt jungle ever since.

It was at Lake Tahoe that I met my first real gangster, a man known by an ominous nickname.

"Bones," the boss of Cal-Neva Lodge, was every casting director's dream of a hoodlum, a 300-pound barrel of a man with no neck, just a smaller barrel for a head, jutting out of his massive shoulders. He had a broken-nosed voice that sounded like a cross between a toilet flushing and the final gasp of a man strangling, a sort of rumbling wheeze. Add to this his little pig-eyes, and the smile of an adder.

He came with high recommendations. He ran all the whorehouses and numbers rackets in the east bay district. Since the feds had clamped down on the hoods in Chicago in the early thirties, many of them had moved west to Reno and then to Vegas. It was only a short step to Lake Tahoe, a slightly more primitive spot, for get-togethers like the later Appalachian meeting of the eastern brothers. The air was crystal clear and the icy waters of the lake prevented a body from ever floating to the top—a definite advantage over the East River or any of the midwestern lakes. Some pretty shady characters had shown up over the years.

But Bones was the first authentic gangster to surface. He scared the hell out of Jim and me, while mother seemed oblivious of these characters. A tall, willowy beauty in a picture hat, mother looked as if she had just stepped out of a painting by Monet. Aside from giving her an old-world touch of class, the hat was protection against the Lake Tahoe sun. She had gotten sunstroke in India many years before.

In those days in Tahoe she would often take the footpath by Crystal Bay to shop for groceries. The same footpath also served the Cal-Neva crowd. One day she came face to face with Bones, our curious neighbor. He took one look at mother's outfit, and after shuffling his feet and doffing his hat, he began to rumble.

"I'd like to take this chance to talk to you, Mrs. Stack," he said. "You've been a hell of a good neighbor."

Mother said, "Thank you," and waited for him to get out of the way.

Bones continued. "Anything I can do for you, let me know."

Mother just looked at him.

"Anybody gives you a bad time, let me know."

Before she could say anything, he went on.

"Anybody gives you a bad time, gets out of line, I take care of them personal, okay?"

Now he began warming to the subject. "If it's something not too important, I'll break his legs."

Mother never changed expression. He went on as if her silence were curiosity.

"Just lay him on his stomach on the sidewalk, stretch his legs over the curb, and snap them right off."

She stood there like a beautiful statue, *Venus de Milo* with arms, wearing a picture hat.

He went on. "And for you, Mrs. Stack, because you're such a good neighbor, if somebody give you a real hard time, we can do even better. You know, there are stories about this lake. The water is so cold, a body never comes up. Well, I can tell you, ma'am, it's not just a story. It's real."

Now mother began coming out of her daze and managed a smothered, "Mr. Bones."

He just held up his hand and said, "My pleasure, ma'am."

Mother never did go shopping that day.

She walked into the kitchen and collapsed in a chair with her hat still on. "What in the world is that man talking about?"

she said to me. "I've never seen him before. What does he mean when he says I'm such a good neighbor?"

"Well," I said, "I guess he appreciates your lack of curiosity. Three people have disappeared this summer without a trace. Rumor has it some pretty strange noises have been coming out of Cal-Neva in the wee hours of the morning."

"My God," she said, "That business about breaking someone's legs and saying that bodies don't rise to the surface of the lake. . . . What did he mean?"

"Well, mother," I explained, "he meant to give you the highest honor a hood can give you—the gift of death. You should feel very flattered."

The following year, Bones was gone. Maybe his other neighbors weren't as good as we were. He was taken away to Sing Sing, and mother lost her biggest fan.

The most unforgettable figure of our Tahoe days was a man called "Weird Frank." Frank joined us at Tahoe during tree transplanting time. This was when mother sent Jim and me and any leftover house guests out to steal willow trees alongside the road to replace the ones the porcupines had eaten. Well, maybe steal is too strong a word. "Thinning them out," is what mother used to call it. "It's really not good for willows to be crowded together like that."

Frank could have been a double for Dillinger. He had straight black hair, bushy eyebrows, steely eyes, and biceps like Jack La Lanne. He told us his father used to beat him with a pipe, and I think we were the first people who were ever kind to him. I only knew him as Frank. If he had a last name it could have been on a post office wall. But mother collected people like some collect stamps, and no questions were asked.

I was about twelve at the time, and he idolized me. That was because I used to take him target shooting. He used to love having his picture taken and posing so you couldn't see that his nose had been broken in three places. The saga of Weird Frank began one evening when he went to a little gambling joint down the road from Cal-Neva and lost his shirt. He came back to the house and got tanked on beer, getting madder and more drunk all the time. He then did something I'd been wanting to do since I was a kid: take a good look at some house dice. He also did it in a very dramatic way. He took dad's .32-caliber Smith & Wesson, went back to the gambling joint, walked in the front door, stuck the barrel in the pit boss's ear, took the dice, and walked out. He took the dice to his room and, with a butcher knife and a hammer, split them each down the center. Sure enough, they were loaded.

Now he'd guaranteed himself a one-way trip to the bottom of beautiful Lake Tahoe, so he figured he had nothing to lose. With a gun in one hand and the dice in the other, he went back once more, pushed the rollers aside, threw down the mangled dice, and demanded his money back.

While all this was going on, mother, my aunt and uncle Mona and Richard Bonelli, and Will Garroway, his accompanist, who was recuperating from a heart attack, were enjoying a leisurely meal. The phone began to ring. It was the local sheriff, a character who protected the local hoods more often than the citizenry. He told mother that because she was such a good neighbor (here we go again!), the boys had agreed not to eradicate Frank as long as he was out of the state by midnight. The only problem was that Frank happened to be nearby and overheard the conversation.

"If anybody sticks his head out," he said, "I'll blow it off."

I found out that under stress, it's usually the most illogical characters that react heroically. Will Garroway, fresh from his heart attack, grabbed a Dunhill cigarette lighter shaped like a pistol. Doing a lousy Bogart imitation, he bellowed, "Put down that gun. I've got you covered."

He found himself looking directly down the barrel of a Smith & Wesson .32. Like an accordian, he slowly collapsed on the floor and stayed there.

"This is ridiculous," proclaimed a voice.

It was mother speaking. She got to her feet, opened the door, and walked out into the night. She stood directly under the porch light and called out to the unseen gunman.

"Frank, stop waving that gun around," she said. "You'll hurt someone. Have I ever lied to you? I promise that no one will hurt you."

Frank stepped out from behind a tree, the gun at his side like a repentent schoolboy.

"You silly man," said mother. "Let go of that gun." Now I jumped up. "Don't let him drop dad's gun," I said. "He'll break the pearl-handled grip on the rocks."

For the first time I saw my mother really angry.

"Bob," she said. "shut up!"

Finally Frank walked toward her hesitantly. They faced each

other for a long moment. Tears began flowing down his face.

"I'd never hurt you or your family, Mrs. Stack," he said. "You're the only ones that ever treated me good. But those crooks cheated me, and I ain't gonna take it no more. I've been cheated all my life." Mother put an arm around his shoulder, and slowly, very slowly, led him to her car. True to her promise, she drove him to the bus station, before the sheriff and his friends made him a permanent part of the Lake Tahoe ecology.

Mother never forced me into show business, but she believed in being prepared just in case. The members of mother's family were all musicians and, in particular, singers. So at an early age I was given a chance to express myself in song. I forgot to mention that dad couldn't carry a tune in a bucket, and I'm afraid his Irish genes overpowered mother's gentler ones. But to mother's dying day, she insisted I had a lovely voice, no matter what weird sounds I made.

Next came exposure to musical instruments. Again mother gave me a choice, hoping I'd choose the piano. But in the music store a shiny, silvery object caught my eye instead, and I took home a clarinet. My older brother Jim chose a saxophone, and together we did imitations of the hounds of the Baskervilles. Our long-suffering teacher was a man named Jack Adair. He was rumpled-looking, wore metal-rimmed glasses, always kept a smile on his face, and believed in "the little people," including spirits and leprechauns.

Jack Adair was also an avid fisherman and used to take us fishing. I think he secretly hated the music lessons as much as we did. He told mother the spirits said she should invest in a New Mexico property that would shower her with oil. The spirits would tell her where to drill a well. Mother used to say she would buy me a chocolate soda when our oil well came in. Jack Adair and mother are both gone, and although I've been left the New Mexico property, I was left no mailing address for the little people who would tell me where to drill. I've long since given up on the chocolate soda.

I was experimenting with music. I played a terrible third sax in my brother's orchestra. He played lead tenor sax, and wasn't much better, but he owned the arrangements and the music stands, which gave him power. Once we played a gig at a decrepit bar in Eagle Rock, a town not known as one of California's music centers. After about an hour, the owner—

a sloppy, unshaven character out of *The Godfather*—approached us with a scowl on his face. He looked like Frank Nitti ready to order a gangland execution.

"My God," he screamed. "That's terrible; you're driving the customers away." His clientele consisted of two winos and a half dozen hookers. Nothing short of a vice raid would move them.

Borrowing a page from an old gangster movie, we agreed to stop playing if he would pay us to keep quiet and leave. We scurried out the back alley, holding our instrument cases like machine guns, convinced that the music business might be strange, but it was profitable.

Once we were mistakenly offered the chance to play at a debutante party at the elegant Town House Hotel in Los Angeles. I think a friend of mother's was trapped into hiring us. (She would have preferred a group of staid string players discreetly hidden behind the potted palms.)

All went well until some joker dancing by switched music on Little Joe, our lead trumpet player. While the rest of us were playing "Night and Day," Little Joe blasted out a rendition of "Stardust" all by himself. The result might be accepted today as avant-garde innovation, a new sound for the "top forty." But back then it turned the debutante party into a cacophonous fiasco.

Our trombone player worked part-time in a nearby mortuary, and between musical sets he delighted in spinning ghastly tales of dissection. We had a clarinet player named Jack Dumont. He had a big talent but a weak stomach. Our trombonist-mortician managed to cap the evening by putting a jar of human brains on Jack's music stand during his Benny Goodman solo of "Sometimes I'm Happy." When Jack spotted the grisly object, he managed to snap our trombone player a look of sheer malice and mutter "son of a bitch" under his breath. Then he threw up.

That spelled the demise of Jimmy Stack's Orchestra. Word had spread from Eagle Rock to Beverly Hills that we were no longer trustworthy. Jack Dumont went on to greater glory, playing lead sax with Lawrence Welk many years later.

Mother was worried that with a house full of women and no man around, I might grow up to be a pantywaist. So she encouraged me to sample the world of sports, and before long I found my life revolving around a variety of macho sports:

polo, hydroplane (speedboat) racing, skeet shooting, sports cars, and motorcycles. Steve McQueen doesn't have to worry though. I ran out of bones to break long before I got very good on the motorcycle!

I adored my mother. She let me race boats, cars, motorcycles, and play polo, so the least I could do was humor her a little when she decided I should take dancing lessons. But tap dancing? My life wouldn't be worth living if any of the delinquents I associated with ever found out. But to please my mother, I sneaked stealthily into the Ernest Belcher School of Dance. As I walked through the front door, I wished that I were anywhere else in the world *except* in a dancing school.

My tap dancing classes were taught by Arthur Prince; Arthur was short and muscular, but with a dancer's walk and graceful hands. He taught Shirley Temple her famous tap number with Bill "Bojangles" Robinson—and he was looking at me curiously.

"Why do you want to be a tap dancer?" he demanded.

"It's mother's idea."

"Yeah, I figured."

He spoke with a kind of strange speech pattern that led my Aunt Mona to say, "My God, Betzi, how can you leave Bobby in the hands of that tap teacher? You know how a young boy can be led astray?"

Aunt Mona was right. Arthur Prince led me astray and was responsible for my first sexual experience. He arranged and stage-managed the whole thing, and I don't feel ashamed regardless of what Aunt Mona said.

But then she had no way of knowing that my questionable tap teacher was the horniest heterosexual I ever met. He was quick to see that I'd be no competition for Shirley Temple as a dancer, and he knew where I really needed instruction.

He led me to that forbidden-to-males sanctum, the girls' tap class, where a lineup of gorgeous Hollywood hopefuls jiggled and bounced in delicious unison, flashing smiles that made this sixteen-year-old forget racing cars, boats, and polo in favor of another international contact sport. One afternoon, Arthur handed me a small blue box with "Rameses" in rococo lettering across the top. He even gave me my final instructions.

"Leave a little extra slack on the end; if this is your first time, you're liable to blow a hole in it. You know the little redhead with the big smile and boobs to match? She thinks you're cute and would love to share your first time."

I wish I could say I was a smash, but I'm afraid my first performance in the arena of love was no better than my tap dancing.

"Practice, Bob, that's all you need is practice," said Arthur. "Don't forget a performer's first obligation is to please his audience, not just himself," my mentor added.

Mother was very happy to see me so enthusiastic about tap class. "Don't give up," she would say hopefully. "You're bound to get better."

"Don't worry, mother, I'm going to practice every chance I get," would always be my reply.

Thanks to my loyal friend Arthur Prince, and to some diligent rehearsal, I received, if not a standing ovation, at least requests for an encore or two.

Eduardo Cansino, a handsome, dignified Latin gentleman, was the head of the Spanish dancing department. His daughter Rita was the talk of the school, a raving beauty with coal-black hair to her waist, and the same ball bearing moves she later used to turn on every male who saw her on the silver screen as Rita Hayworth.

Marge Belcher was the boss's daughter, blond, blue-eyed, and cute as a button. She got her break when Walt Disney singled her out as the proto-type for Snow White. She was photographed in stop action, walking, talking, and dancing, and Walt's animators for the first time gave to cartoons a human with the expression and naturalistic movement he had previously reserved for his animated animal stars. Marge married Gower Champion and brought further honor to the Belcher School of Dance.

I only have a raggedy time step to show for my hours with Arthur Prince. But what the hell? Shirley Temple is a lousy polo player.

Mother worked on the European premise of exposing first to the older son something both sons might eventually want. So Jim enlisted in the Pasadena Playhouse, at that time the Actors Studio of orange blossom land. It was a nest of free-thinking creativity perched in the most conservative WASP community this side of Scarlett O'Hara's Tara.

The Playhouse trained a host of future distinguished alumni for professional careers in the theater. The instruction emphasized classical theater, movement, diction, and performance of plays. It enjoyed an amazing history before going out of existence as both a theater and school. Today the buildings are being renovated and restored as a museum of variety entertainment.

Among the many famous names listed on the Playhouse honor rolls, no one will find that of my brother. He seemed to be getting along fine until one day he bent over to tie his shoelace. At this precise moment, an orange-haired producer-in-residence was passing by. He patted Jim gently on the behind and the chase was on. The producer managed to escape undamaged down one of the phantom-of-the-opera passageways of the old building. My brother's career as an actor thereby came to an abrupt end. I'm afraid, if Jim had caught him, the producer would have come to an abrupt end, too.

When I graduated from Los Angeles High School, I began thinking about college. I would like to say that my career as an actor began in the drama department of the University of Southern California. But there was a twist. My chief drama professor was also sponsor of the polo team, and both of us were interested in the NCAA championship than in Shakespeare. Arizona boasted the top polo team in the west, and regarded polo as a major sport while it was still considered a minor sport at USC. I'm happy to say our team changed all that, and as a member of the team which won the West-Coast Intercollegiate championship in polo, I decided that college was really a lot of fun.

Drama grades were based on the *originality* of one's term paper. I took two sheets of cardboard from newly laundered shirts, unrolled a roll of toilet paper, stuffed the toilet paper in between the cardboard, and wrote some gibberish with an eyebrow pencil. I got an A in drama.

I also took courses in astronomy, which gave me a chance to develop a talent I could use the rest of my life, a talent for finding the darkest lane on Mulholland Drive where I could share my research of the heavens with a feminine companion. I learned how to spot cops in the rearview mirror from almost any position, how to achieve the lotus position in a sports car without one lesson in yoga, and a lot about heavenly bodies in general.

Although my drama course at USC had been generously seasoned with polo, I had become intrigued by the theater as well. Going to the Pasadena Playhouse was out of the question after Jim's experience there. But after college I decided to enroll for some classes at the El Capitan College of the Theater, a school for actors which presented plays under the auspices of Henry Duffy at the Las Palmas Theater in Hollywood.

I remember my initial impression of the theater, a group of young actors practicing speech exercises. It didn't look very interesting until I caught a couple in the corner of the darkened theater obviously running through a love scene. I decided I might get to like the stage after all.

When I was eighteen, I appeared on stage for the first time, as Captain Denny in *Pride and Prejudice*, and had a few lines. The acting bug, with a bite that can have far-reaching consequences, had really bitten me. I was aware, though, that there were strange characters in the theater.

Once, when I told the story of Jim's debacle, a rather strange acquaintance of mine had some advice. "A pat on the ass is only acceptable when the contract with the part you want is in the other hand." We called him Minchie. He was a myopic, dumpy little guy, the best comedian to graduate from the El Capitan College of the Theater. Nature had endowed him with a monk's bald pate encircled by a mousy fringe of brindled fuzz. He had a voice like Tallulah Bankhead's, a unique sense of comic timing, and an unbeatable combination of evil and innocence that fractured an audience.

When I graduated from the El Capitan, we all got plastered, and I proceeded with characteristic tact to ask him if he liked boys. He said yes. I asked why he hadn't made a pass at me. There was a long pause.

"Well, Bob, you have girl friends who don't attract you physically, don't you? That's how I feel about you."

I was relieved to hear this but a small part of me still wanted to know why I wasn't attractive. I wasn't curious enough to research it, however, so I let the matter drop.

Minchie also gave me some advice about Broadway. "Now, Bob," he said, "if you go to Broadway, you'll find many of the producers prefer boys, not just in their plays, but to take home with them. So here's what you should do. When one of them makes a play for you, make sure the theatrical play is a good one with a good part for you. Go along with it until after the opening night. What the hell, you might even get to like it. If not, you can always go back to girls. By then it's too late to replace you and no one will know the difference."

I know two actors who went this route and kicked off good stage careers. The funny part is that both played macho he-man types that bowled over the ladies. I guess that's one way to reach a broader audience.

Mother was truly a Renaissance woman, a member of the best society Los Angeles could muster—a singer, sculptor, writer of children's books, woodcarver, gardener, botanist, metaphysician.... There was almost nothing she couldn't do well.

In the course of growing up, I attended the theater regularly at home. I didn't have to worry about parking or box seats. Mother converted one room in our home to a theater, a sort of playroom with a stage for impromptu recitals where Ezio Pinza, Rosa Ponsell, Lawrence Tibbett, my uncle Richard Bonelli, or any comparably great musical talents could entertain themselves in the company of close friends.

The house was continually filled with opera singers, artists, symphony musicians, actors (both stage and screen), polo players, skeet shooters and teachers (of everything from voice to metaphysics). A typical evening at home might include anything from an opera recital to a seminar conducted by mother's friend Ernest Holmes, who founded the Church of Religious Science. She welcomed them all, and the interaction of these disparate groups made my growing-up years a veritable three-ring circus.

Mother became acquainted with a famous mystic called Astoya. (He had once performed under the name of Nostradamus, the celebrated prognosticator.) Astoya had spent years in the Himalayas learning to control the flight of pigeons. Astoya's gifts were amazing, and he only used them occasionally. Once he came by mother's house for dinner. When we'd finished, he turned the lights down low. We touched hands in a circle, and things began to happen. First papers on a desk across the room began to rustle and then, as if in a whirlwind, they spun off the table and up in the air. Cocktail glasses on the bar began to clink against each other. The finale was unbelievable: The big dining room table must have weighed 500 pounds but slowly, and very gently, it rose into the air and sailed majestically over our heads into the next room. I could hear the silverware rattling in the drawers as it sailed overhead, and I remember hoping they wouldn't open and spill all over us. They didn't, and the table settled gently into the next room. The next day, it took five men to get the table back where it belonged.

Astoya also had the gruesome ability to pierce his flesh without drawing blood. He got a kick out of sticking hatpins through his cheek and tongue like a living shishkabob. He could also control his heartbeat, but the stunt almost cost him his life. He had himself buried alive in the middle of a baseball diamond, and remained there for twenty-four hours. He told my grandfather to make sure they got him out at an exactly specified time. Some of the assistants were a few minutes slow getting him out of the ground. Astoya was bleeding from the nose, almost dead. Grandfather convinced him to abandon that part of his routine.

It was with some sense of pride that I realized that some of mother's most memorable musical evenings were provided by a member of our own family.

Richard Bonelli, who married my Aunt Mona (herself a fine violinist), was first baritone with the Metropolitan Opera. He was also a mechanical engineer whose name was originally Richard Bonn. But baritones were expected to be Italian; hence, Richard Bonn became Ricardo Bonelli. To this day, in his eighties, he can make shivers go up my spine when he opens his throat and that dark, golden sound pours out. At his thirtieth wedding anniversary, he accompanied one of his pupils in a duet. (He's also a great teacher.)

I remember once being called aside by the concertmaster at a Hollywood Bowl rehearsal.

"Go up to the last row," he said. "You'll never hear a baritone like this again. Listen to the pianissimo." Sure enough, up in peanut heaven, one could hear the crystal clear Bonelli tone without artificial amplification. He is one of the few baritones who was equally comfortable with the tenor repertoire. Whenever he sang, I could hardly wait for him to smack those high ones. He always had another half-octave in his pocket.

When my darling Aunt Mona announced that she was going to marry an opera singer, Jim and I indulged in a good deal of grousing.

"Gee, an old, bearded, grouchy opera singer, that's all we need in the family. Now we won't have any fun."

Dick Bonelli made his entrance in our lives driving a twelve-cylinder Pierce Arrow roadster, battleship gray and three miles long, and sporting a cap straight out of *Autocar* magazine. To back up my first impression, he later took me to the salt flats in Utah, the site of most of the attempts at land speed records. Here, he introduced me to his old friend Ab Jenkins, the holder of more world's auto speed records than anyone. He let me sit in his "Mormon Motor II" while the two discussed valve timing and volumetric efficiency.

The first Mormon Meteor engine was built for him by Augie Duesenberg. I was later allowed to drive this beauty on a road paralleling the salt flats. I shot up to 120 mph in no time and felt that particular exhilaration and freedom only a racing car or speedboat can bring.

Sitting in the cockpit, closed in from the distractions of the outside world, the hood stretching almost to the horizon, the giant vertical fin in back, the chrome exhaust stacks making the most visceral sound there is... Heaven could wait!

Richard Bonelli is regarded by many as the successor to the world's greatest baritone Tito Ruffo. Ruffo's voice was darker and stronger, but the similarity was striking. When Uncle Dick was starting out, one of his first appearances was in Havana in *Il Trovatore*. On the same day, Tito Ruffo had agreed to perform a few songs for charity before the opera began. As Dick tells it, "All I had to do was follow the world's greatest baritone singing Spanish songs before a Cuban audience."

Ruffo naturally brought the house down. Now it was up to the young American with the manufactured Italian name. The first baritone aria in *Trovatore* is hardly a show-stopper, but when Uncle Dick finished in Havana, there was an ovation led by Tito Ruffo himself. From way back in the peanut gallery came a voice: "Now we have two Ruffo's!"

Richard Bonelli had the same misfortune in coming after Tito Ruffo that every tenor had in following Enrico Caruso. Although Dick had a brilliant career—first baritone at the Metropolitan Opera, world-renowned concert and recording artist—he was always in the shadow of the man who led the applause for him in Havana when he was beginning his career.

But even with Richard Bonelli in the family, I wasn't thinking of a career in opera. From the time I first handled a shotgun, I had been captivated by an exciting new sport: skeet!

2

Skeet Is the Name of the Game

My Grandfather Charley Wood had been a trapshooting champion. He won the Los Angeles Bluerock (clay target) Championship in 1910, breaking fifty-eight targets without a miss. When I was thirteen years old, my uncle Perry presented me with my grandfather's 20-gauge L.C. Smith, took me out to a skeet range, and I was hooked for life.

Skeet is a Scandinavian word for "shoot." It's also the name of a game in which clay saucers are thrown by slingshot arrangements while people with shotguns try to break them as they fly by. It's not a blood sport, unless you count the occasional damage to a beginner's shoulder or nose caused by too short a stock. Skeet is a lot of fun; it gives the same feeling of satisfaction as does throwing a rock through a greenhouse window—minus the thrill of having to dodge the cops.

If you go west on Pico Boulevard, past the San Diego Freeway, on your left is a small, private airport called Cloverfield. Back in the thirties, in the middle of what is now a gaggle of tract houses, stood a nondescript shack surrounded by a couple of skeet fields. Even the skeet fields were in a peculiar form of juxtaposition, since an arroyo ran down one part of the property. Anyone shooting skeet had to either bend over like Quasimodo or rock back on his heels to maintain his balance as he went from station to station. This was the Los Angeles-Santa Monica Gun Club, the site of my happiest memories as a teenager, and the supreme domain of Harry Fleischmann.

I couldn't have found a better teacher than Harry Fleischmann. Harry was captain of the All-American Skeet Team, and a great character. He was the black sheep of the Fleischmann family. The family had many millionaires, but only one Harry. Only slightly immoral, at heart Harry was a hustler and inveterate gambler. He would rather have hustled a buck than earned $1,000 legitimately. He was a big man with massive arms and neck, a swarthy complexion, and a driving will to win, revealed only by his chain smoking and fingernails chewed to the elbows.

An ex-tugboat captain and sometime movie villain, Harry was also a violent man who bit off the ear of a Long Beach gambler when he caught him with three dice instead of the customary two. But to me, he was a proxy father, a little unconventional perhaps, but a real pal. His photograph—showing Harry holding his old model 31 Remington Pump Gun and wearing an expression swiped from his other student, Clark Gable—says simply, "To my pal Bob, Sincerely, Harry."

I soon found that, as a happy accident of nature, I was gifted with terrific eye-hand coordination. This is a big advantage in fast-action sports such as tennis, car racing, and skeet. It has nothing to do with talent, just a lucky combination of genes. The result of being able to cut that extra hundredth of a second in reaction time is that fast-moving objects look as if they're moving more slowly. That's why I used to look forward to darkness or heavy winds. Bad weather would always bring my lucky inheritance into play.

The quickest way to improve at any sport is to get a good swift kick every time you make a mistake. If the computer in your head is quickly trained to send out the right message, instead of wasting time experimenting with the millions of wrong ones, you're on your way to being a champion.

The next requirement, as expounded today in cybernetics, is to observe only the best athletes so the subconscious picks up a visual picture of the procedures that separate the champion from the pack. Bobby Jones learned his classic swing by caddying for great golfers; he learned to be good without first being bad. Under Harry's guidance, I became an expert shot in a hurry.

If you have never tried skeet shooting, imagine what it would be like to hit a moving object with a stream of water from a garden hose. It's not enough to aim directly for the object, because there's a split-second delay between your shot and the moment you hit the moving target. So you have to shoot where your instincts tell you the target will be.

The best shots not only hit the target, but they develop their own special styles of shooting. I copied Harry's slapdash, rough-and-ready style of mounting the gun aggressively and shooting as fast as possible. My friend Alex Kerr was one of the best shots in the country, and unlike Harry, he handled a shotgun like a precision instrument. (Today he is the owner of Kerr's, the fanciest sporting goods store in Beverly Hills.) Skeet shooters, like golfers, talk about an outstanding swing in mounting their guns. Alex possesses the most beautiful swing in skeet, and I consider him one of the two best shotgun shots in the world.

I made other friends at the skeet field. Like Harry and Alex, they were grown men and, to a teenager, being accepted as their equal meant everything.

"Lefty" Bill Davis, a skinny, carefree, lovable, free soul, shot his best with a hangover. Grant Ilseng, many times all-American, ambidextrous in skeet as well as trap, was—along with Alex and me—a hall of famer.

It is customary to shoot skeet in five-man squads. Although Harry's teaching had turned me into a teenage crack shot, you can imagine my reaction when he asked me to join him, Alex, Bill, and Grant as a full-fledged competitor. I could hold my own with the others in shooting. But being accepted on the California Five-Man Skeet Team while still just a boy had an influence on me that's affected my whole life. I began to learn what it was like to be part of a team. Each of us was more interested in beating the hotshot eastern teams than winning individual championships. I found later on, for example, that the success of "The Untouchables" as a team effort meant more to me than winning the Emmy for best actor. What angered California shooters was that we were treated like poor relatives. Skeet was invented on the East Coast, and the easterners said we were all fair-weather shooters who couldn't hit our hats unless the sun was shining. (I had a chance to answer that argument when I won the Western Open at the Pacific Rod and Gun Club near San Francisco. It was foggy, and some skeptics even accused me of shooting by sound.)

The time was 1935 and every young skeet shooter in the country was dreaming of the same thing: the first National Skeet Shooting Championship, to be held at Cleveland, Ohio.

This was the event we'd been waiting for, a chance to meet the eastern competition head-on. For me, the prospect was a special thrill. I had been proving myself as a skeet shooter in Southern California. But if I went to Cleveland, I would have to face a host of teenagers who had won enough trophies to fill a house from top to bottom.

Instead of merely giving me whatever I might want, mother, in her effort not to spoil me, always gave me a choice of two things. When it came time to go to Cleveland, I was given just such a choice: the trip to Cleveland or the cocker spaniel I'd wanted so badly. I gave up man's best friend for the moment and chose the trip to Cleveland. Harry promised mother he would look after me. No one asked who would look after Harry.

When we arrived in Cleveland, I realized what I was up against. The first shock to my system came when I showed up for practice. Lead-off man was a short, thin, sixteen-year-old Oklahoman in cowboy boots. I couldn't tell what he was wearing for a jacket, because every inch—front, back, and even the sleeves—was plastered with emblems and medals from major championships won: Great Eastern, Lordship, State Champion, Long Run, World's Record, etc. This was my first exposure to a scare jacket, a shooting coat so loaded with honors that many times the opposition was intimidated before the first target was thrown.

If that didn't do it, the next thing did. He held out his hand and drawled, "My name's Billy Clayton." Now I *knew* I should have stayed at home and taken the cocker spaniel. I was going to have to shoot against the legendary Billy Clayton, the most honored junior shooter in America. I'll say this for him—he had class. He snapped a quick look at my old beige shooting sweater with leather patches on the elbows to cover the holes (and a patch for shooting one lousy twenty-five straight on the chest) and he never changed expression.

The next day, however, practice went out the window. Our

squad was scheduled to shoot in the morning, and I looked forward to my first national competition with a mixture of excitement and terror. Harry promised to awaken us on time. But he played seven card stud all night and forgot to leave a call. By the time I put my gun together, the rest of the squad had already started shooting. In fact, the four hotshots had already shot fifty of the required hundred targets.

I joined the squad and smashed my first fifty targets without a miss. Shooting in the normal way, with my rapid-fire friends, I was ready for anything. Then the shock came. The rest of the squad had finished the second fifty targets while I had been polishing off the first fifty. So I had fifty more targets to go, and no one to shoot with.

For the first time, I realized I had a chance to win the United States Junior Championship. The mighty Billy Clayton had a ninety-six on the board. His chief rival was the Kentucky state champion Max Marcum, who had a ninety-eight. If I shot forty-eight out of fifty, I would tie Marcum, and forty-nine would make me the national champion.

Shooting alone was unheard of in skeet; it's a tradition to shoot as part of a squad. One of the officials came up with a brilliant idea.

"We can't let him shoot alone," he said. "Find another junior so he can finish shooting as part of a pair."

It turned out that the only available junior was his daughter. She was twelve years old and had shot only once before. I didn't know what she was doing at the National Skeet Shooting Championship, and I didn't care.

Imagine playing mixed doubles at Wimbledon with a partner who has never seen a tennis racket, or catching a pass in the Super Bowl when the quarterback has never seen a football.

The squad of red-hots was huddled around the field, waiting to see how the dummy from California and his twelve-year-old partner would do. I had to help my companion load her gun, a practice not recommended in a national championship. She broke seven clay targets out of fifty.

I was lucky, too. I had faced competition before, but nothing like this! I smashed forty-six targets, which gave me a ninety-six, in a tie for second with Billy Clayton.

People have asked me occasionally how anyone can take the pressure of sitting in the audience at Academy Award time waiting for that hellish, "And the winner is..." I can tell you that, facing those final fifty targets, I felt more pressure at age sixteen than I have ever felt in show business.

By now I was in shock, and nothing mattered much anyway.

I had to face a tie-breaking shoot-off with Billy Clayton. We both went straight to station seven, the easiest target on the field. Billy stepped up and missed the target. I broke nine and turned to him.

"Look, Billy," I said, "I don't want you to give me second place just 'cause you feel sorry for me." I couldn't figure out how the world's best junior could miss a straightaway.

He looked at me as if I were nuts.

"What the hell are you talkin' about?" he said. "I was tryin' to hit it. I just plain missed it."

So began a friendship that lasted until he died of cancer several years ago. Billy was from Oklahoma, only about 5'5", and shot in cowboy boots. He only moved the gun a couple of feet or so, while the rest of us manhandled ours. He shot so fast it seemed as if the gun went off by accident; he had more style than anyone else I've ever seen. He turned skeet shooting into an art form.

Another time, at the Western Open at the Pacific Rod and Gun Club, I was shooting miserably, hitting targets on the top, bottom, front, and back, but I was lucky and shot 100 straight. Billy pulverized ninety-nine and "just plain missed one." I walked up to him and said, "I don't deserve this thing [a big grandfather clock for the champion]. I didn't hit one damn target in the middle. You ought to have it."

He said, "Are you gonna start that malarkey again? On paper, every target that's hit looks the same whether you crush it or chip it. Take your silly grandfather clock and run."

The following year, I had another chance at national competition, this time in St. Louis. I thought that history was going to repeat itself but, at the last minute, I had some unexpected bad luck. I got hold of some bad shells, a load slower than usual, and shot the worst score of my life, a humiliating seventy-nine. After watching me slouch around with my eyes on the ground for two rounds, Harry Fleischmann said, "Now listen! I don't care if you miss every damn target. Get your head up and act like a man or you can't shoot on another team."

I should explain (for non-shooting readers) that a lead ball is found to fit the barrel of a gun. The number of lead balls that make a pound determines the gauge. For example, twelve balls to the pound means the gun will be a 12-gauge gun. The bigger the number, the smaller the barrel, and the more difficult the shot.

Each event was listed according to gauge. Harry's advice was well taken. The next day I shot a ninety-nine and won the 20-gauge championship. (Billy Clayton was there, too, and he won the 410.) A teenager named Dick Shaugnessy won the 12-gauge, and the three of us were named First Team All-American. Our scores stood up against the old pros, and none of us was over seventeen.

But more important, our five-man team had a day to remember. Harry, Alex, Bill, Grant, and I not only broke the five-man team record, we also destroyed the eastern team's credo of shooting deliberately in absolute silence with every man for himself.

Our California five-man team broke precedent with all that Roseland, New Jersey—the classiest eastern team—stood for. They shot as individuals, with the captain of the all-American team, Frank Kelly, as lead man. There was absolute silence, and each went about his job as if the other four didn't exist. Only at the end of the round did anybody speak.

With Harry Fleischmann as our lead-off man, it was a three-ring circus.

"Work on 'em," we said. "Keep your head down; grind 'em up."

If anybody missed, he was told how and why by the shooter behind him. The national championships had never seen anything like this. We helped each other, and the result was that our individual scores improved. We became the hottest team in the country, setting the styles for all five-man teams to come.

Instead of stalling or using the old, deliberate eastern style, the man behind would step up and shoot the very second the station was clear. We not only beat them, we set a record for the "fastest competition round ever shot."

Not long ago I was going to Houston for a golf pro-am, and I dropped Billy Clayton a note. I wondered if we'd recognize each other after so many years. His reply was simple.

"I've been taking cobalt treatments for cancer, so if you come in after dark, I'll just stand out in the parking lot and glow."

Billy Clayton, my old chum with the scare jacket, cowboy

hat, and classy shooting style, always stood out from the rest.

One day, we decided to try our hand at turkey shoots. In the farm country outside Los Angeles County, local farmers would offer a live turkey as a prize to anyone who could successfully break five consecutive clay targets. A twenty-five cent entrance fee was all that was required, and since the average farmer was not usually a champion shot, few turkeys were given away.

Harry, Alex Kerr, and the rest of the group dressed up in overalls and denims. We made sure we were in old clothes and looked appropriately weather-beaten. Then we assumed our best corn-pone accents and arrived for the turkey shoots dragging the guns on the ground. (For good measure, we managed to pick up some old beat-up guns which looked as if they had last been used during the Civil War.)

Once in sight of the clay targets, however, we went to work as if we were shooting in the nationals.

By the time we had won four or five turkeys, the judges realized we were suspicious characters from the big city. We knew that tar and feathers were no longer fashionable, but we decided to beat a hasty retreat just in case. We took off in our truck filled with turkeys, and escaped to another town a few miles away... where we started all over again.

By the end of the day, we had managed to win thirty or forty turkeys. Suddenly we realized that we had to do something with the birds, who were already gobbling away in a chorus of protest. I knew we couldn't simply stick them away in the attic—"or anywhere in the house," said my mother, who normally made allowances for my misadventures but wasn't about to have turkeys wandering around the house.

We decided to give the turkeys away to anyone who would take them. A lot of people had free turkey banquets that year and, hopefully, at least one or two of the birds got a reprieve as pets, at least until the next Thanksgiving.

Shooting was full of surprises. My first problem arose when I went to shoot away from home. I stood behind a middle-aged gent who wore pigskin gloves and a pheasant feather in his hat, and shot so slow I thought he'd caught his glove in the trigger.

On my first target, he jumped and said, "Watch it, son. The gun went off on you, didn't it? Funny thing is you broke the target."

He offered some advice. "No, no, son, you're doing it wrong. This is a game of science. You just can't shoot blind and trust to luck like you're doing."

Then he told me what was wrong with my gun. I was shooting granddad's old 20-gauge with the barrels cut off. It wasn't a skeet gun, but it seemed to be working well.

I kept saying "yes, sir," trying to be polite everytime he'd give me instructions and tell me how lucky I was. By the time I had broken my first fifteen targets without a miss, I could see his expression change.

"My God, you're doing that on purpose, aren't you? You're really trying to shoot that fast. Well, let's see if you can break the rest of them."

I did.

He then took off his pigskin glove, shook my hand, and said, "Son, I think maybe you made a fool of me out here. Congratulations on a fine round. Maybe next time you'll give me a few pointers, speed me up a little. Okay?"

"Yes, sir," I said.

"I'll be proud to shoot with you any time, son."

"Thank you, sir." That's how I met Ralph Cook Scott, one of the finest gentlemen ever to grace a skeet or trap field. He taught me more than I could ever hope to teach him: Gun manners, or how to handle a gun like a gentleman; how to win without being a pain in the neck; how to lose without envy or self-pity; how to appreciate beautiful workmanship in a shotgun and to respect the talent and dedication of the artisan.

He owned some of the most beautiful shotguns I'd ever seen. One in particular, an L.C. Smith Premier Grade double barrel with magnificent engraving and gold inlays, took my breath away. I used to just stare at it with my mouth open.

One day I passed Ralph as he was shooting this jewel and summoned up enough nerve to ask him if I could put it to my shoulder.

"Letting someone shoot a fine gun is like letting someone take out your best girl. You've got to be sure she's handled gently and with respect."

Even though I had just won the National Skeet Championships in St. Louis, he still gave me a lesson on how to open and close the fine double barrel before he let me shoot it. As far as I know, I'm the only other person he ever did let shoot it. I've played polo. I've raced cars, outboards, and hydroplanes. I've taken part in competitive archery, golf, and tennis. But I've never met a greater bunch of people than in skeet and trap shooting. I never went through the classic generation gap, because the men on the skeet field treated me as a colleague, taught me, encouraged me, gave me hell when I did something stupid, and kidded the socks off me every chance they had. It is hard to describe the thrill of a sixteen-year-old boy accepted as a man and a member of the world's best five-man team.

In those days, skeet shooting was one of the most popular sports in Hollywood, and since Harry was the best shot in town, it was only natural for him to teach the stars to shoot. He knew more Hollywood stars personally than Louella Parsons. Some of his clients were Robert Taylor, Fred MacMurray, Fredric March, Andy Devine, Gary Cooper, Mike Curtiz, Jack Conway, Frank Morgan, Gene Raymond, Eugene Palette, Fred Stone, Carole Lombard, and Ginger Rogers, to mention a few. Many of the male stars' wives participated as well. Henry Hathaway's wife Skip and Gary Cooper's wife Rocky were among the best of the women skeet shooters. Rocky held a world's record for a while. Harry's clients weren't all actors, however. He also gave lessons to Howard Hughes, Barron Hilton, and Ernest Hemingway.

In this odd way I got to know some of the world's most famous people. They weren't really celebrities to me—just grown men I could easily outshoot because I had been blessed with some natural physical skills.

As a result of skeet shooting, I met one of Harry's favorite pupils, an actor who could really shoot. His name was Clark Gable. Harry taught Clark Gable to be a pretty fair shot. Harry also ran a duck club near Bakersfield, California, where he, Clark, Frank Morgan, Jack Conway, and others went on weekends to play cards all night and get plastered. They would stagger out at 4:30 A.M. to suffer hangovers compounded by the blast and recoil of heavy 12-gauge duck loads.

Harry was a master at making a client think he'd hit a duck when he'd missed it by a country mile. He could time his shot exactly with his client's. A slap on the back was enough to convince his somnambulant guests they were jim-dandy hunters. He only pulled this on "sportsmen" he considered hopeless, never on an experienced shot like Gable. Harry himself was the best duck shot I've ever seen.

Much has been written about Clark Gable. But not many

people have been privileged to see the private Gable, a man who thought it more important to protect a chum in trouble than to preserve the thing he treasured most, his reputation.

One Saturday afternoon, the tribe had been shooting and had a few birds over the limit. Frank Morgan had been dipping his beak since the day before. He was in no condition to greet the game warden who suddenly materialized from behind a bush. Frank was a gentle and charming man when sober. But he had been known to change from the "Wizard of Oz" into a Warner Brothers heavy when bombed. He blasted the game warden, who had only asked for his license.

Then Gable arrived from Beverly Hills. Being the gent he was, he immediately tried to clear things up. By this time, the furious game warden was going out of his way to find some reason to put Frank Morgan away. He finally found the extra birds, and was about to take Morgan in when Clark said, "Those birds aren't Frank's. They're mine."

"Are you sure, Mr. Gable?" demanded the warden. "You know there are too many there."

"Yep," said Gable. "They're mine."

Clark got himself what has been estimated as a million dollars' worth of bad publicity. The game warden notified the press, and Clark Gable, the sportsman, the man's man, became an overnight "game-hog" and law-breaker. I knew how much this hurt Clark. But he stuck to his story, and only a very few of us knew he'd taken the blame for someone else.

One of our fellow sportsmen was Spangler Arlington Brough, a boy from Pomona who made it big in the flicks. The old Los Angeles-Santa Monica Gun Club was one of the few places where no one gave a damn about his profile; we considered him just another turkey.

He was the least likely, but the handsomest, movie star I ever saw, actually shy and even apologetic about his fame and good looks. He was the prototype of the matinee idol. As Ronald Reagan said in his eulogy, he was a gentleman in every sense of the word, more at home outdoors than on a movie set.

Calling him "Spangler" is a genuine dirty trick. His stage name was the only thing phony about Bob Taylor.

An eighty-year-old former cattle rustler summed it up when he met Bob Taylor during the filming of a western. "That Taylor fellow ain't never growed himself an ego."

Bob never thought of himself as a star; he wanted to be one of the boys.

He could always take a joke. One of the stories flying around the club dealt with a hunting trip he once took with Andy Devine. After much beer and a long haul over back roads, they could not refuse nature's call. As they were irrigating the desert in unison, Andy looked over and said, "That doesn't look like it belongs on the world's greatest lover." Without missing a beat, his friend said, "I know, but don't tell my wife. She thinks they're all the same size."

Many fabulous characters came into the fields to shoot. Late in the afternoon one weekday when the club was about to close, in about 1936, a tall, lanky figure with a fedora hat and a beautiful blond in tow came to a screeching halt in a black convertible. He got out of the car, took the girl's arm, and hurried off to the back of the skeet field. I had never seen Harry Fleischmann, the club's proprietor, carry anyone's gun before. But for this clown he not only carried the guns but the shooting coats and shells, and almost saluted. I was shooting late that day, practicing for the national championship, so I decided to sneak over and find out who the beautiful dolly in the formfitting pink slacks was. It didn't take long to find out that her name was Ginger Rogers. But it took a month and a bottle of rye before one of our guys got Harry to give them the name of the mystery man. I thought Ginger Rogers was something else, but the mystery man with the big car and the private manner didn't mean a damn thing to me. His name was Howard Hughes.

Eventually I got to know Howard through shooting. Although he liked his privacy, he visited the gun club to enjoy the sport. He was highly intelligent, and not the least bit eccentric—then. I'm convinced that the many serious plane crashes he survived made him the strange and reclusive hermit the world now remembers.

Hughes's worst accident happened when he was testing an experimental plane with counter-rotating propellers. He slammed into the ground a block away from my mother's house in Beverly Hills. He was only saved by the quick action of a passerby who pulled him from the plane before it burned. Mother told me it was a miracle that anyone survived that crash without being affected in some way. I think he was. Anyone who has seen the film of Howard Hughes defending himself at the Senate hearings on the "Spruce Goose" knows that earlier in his life he was hardly an incompetent eccentric.

Harry died while still a young man, before the outbreak of World War II. He had enjoyed his life of mischievous mayhem, and it would be hard to underestimate the influence that shooting and Harry had on my life. By the time I was eighteen, I started turning to other sports. But to this day I can't drive by the old site of the gun club without thinking of Harry and the marvelous friends I made there.

I grew up surrounded by men who loved fast cars and faster boats. It was only natural for me to be wild about speed.

I suppose I can blame most of the crazy things I've done in speedboats and racing cars on a wild, bald-headed Dane named Al Jepson. One night when I was about fifteen, I dropped by a garage run by Joe Mozzetti to listen to the racket of the hopped-up roadsters and smell the burning castor oil. In those days, racing mechanics used castor oil in their engines, as much for its pungent aroma as for what it did. A teenage boy would react to burning castor oil the way a fashion model would to a gallon of Chanel No. 5. The irregular heartbeat of an idling racing camshaft did for my generation of postpuberty males what Raquel Welch does for this one. In the midst of the candy-apple paint jobs, with racing stripes, burnished chrome, and flaring exhausts, stood an old black Ford Model A roadster. The cloth top looked like a tent from war surplus; it seemed as out of place as a little old lady in tennis shoes might among city slickers. Sitting in the front seat like a sinner in church was the driver. He wore a felt hat to match his nondescript coat, an open shirt over his muscular frame, and a look of peaceful innocence on his Scandinavian kisser.

I was later to learn that this look usually led to some kind of contest of courage, or fistfight. That particular night I had seen the last of the gleaming engines and was about to leave when this chap asked if I wanted to see his engine.

"It's like a loyal friend. It never lets me down," he said.

Why not? I thought to myself. *If it makes the guy happy.* He opened the hood to reveal a motor as ratty-looking as the rest of the car... mud and dirt all over it. The intake manifold and the carburetor were different, but I figured they were replacements from the junk yard.

"Want to take a ride?" he said, still maintaining his look

of innocence. "This is a real good stock Model A."

For those of long memory, a "real good Model A" was hardput to go sixty miles an hour with a tailwind. As the hotrods began fanning out into Santa Monica Boulevard, I hopped in and he fired it up. A telltale *tha-bump, bump, tha-bump-bump-bump* should have warned me that this was not the way Henry Ford meant his creation to sound. We cruised to the first stoplight. When the light turned green, everyone turned on. Suddenly the ridiculous old crock surged out with the rest of the speedsters. I looked over at my companion, who kept looking straight ahead, innocence itself, while he slammed through the gears in two spectacular speed shifts.

We were now tailgating a beautiful crimson overhead-valve, underslung job. When the owner looked back and saw the old black Model A chewing on his exhaust, he stamped on the throttle, and soon I found myself flying down the street at ninety miles an hour. I knew it was ninety because I now realized that under the coating of grime was a very professional speed- and tachometer. When the crimson job had run out of horsepower, my driver gave me a wink; we swung out and blasted past him at over 100 miles an hour. This ploy of fitting an old car with a souped-up engine has since been picked up by Paul Newman, whose Volkswagen with its Porsche engine has humbled many a Mercedes or Datsun 280Z.

After ducking down side roads to evade the cops, we managed to sneak back to Mozzetti's garage, lights out and engine off. So began an association that lasted over thirty years and gave me the most loyal friend I've ever had.

Al Jepson was a race driver and master mechanic. He picked up his trade the hard way, building up his own jalopies and racing the bullrings at county fairs. The bullring must be the toughest of all races—a flat half-mile of dirty ruts and no banked turns. The car moves sideways, continually out of control. If you don't grab the lead and hold it, the rest of the race is spent driving blind with a mouthful of mud!

Al soon became "King of the Bullrings" until his car spun 360 degrees and drove his right leg through the hip joint a foot or so. He insisted that the cast be set with a bent knee so he could drive his car. (He went on to win the AAA championship that year.) He then became ride mechanic at the Indianapolis 500 when the cars were two-seaters, and now he was wheeling a ridiculous Model A with yours truly.

It was no time at all before *our* Dry Lakes roadster, a glamorous relative of the black Model A was under construction. Except during a World War II stint overseas, Al and I always had a project cooking. We took that Model A roadster to the races at Lake Miroc and won the class we entered at 115.68 miles an hour. He sucked the goggles off the competition with an engine designed by Al and his friend Ed Winfield, an automative genius and inventor of the Winfield carburetor and Novi engine.

Racing buffs would invariably ask Al how he managed to stuff so many "horses" in a four-cylinder Ford; he would pick up his old sledge hammer and waggle it, saying, "I did it with Old Betsy here." Everyone who's driven a sports car has wished for a magic fifty horsepower more to glide by those $30,000 Ferraris. While our little four-cylinder beauty was hammered out in my garage with much more enthusiasm than money, it did house one nifty surprise. There are very few secrets among the highspeed car buffs. The souped-up Model A's were all three-speed transmissions. All the Ferraris had to do was wait until the Model A's had run out of "horse" in third gear, quickly slip into fourth or even fifth, and watch the nuts and bolts come flying out the exhaust pipe of the Model A.

One sunny day on the way to Bakersfield, Al and I were testing our secret weapon when what should loom on the horizon but a small black Ferrari Ameriga, all twelve cylinders spewing venom; the smell of burning castor oil and the scream of double overhead cams presented a challenge hard to ignore. The Ferrari driver recognized us as a souped-up Model A and decided to play the old second-gear trick.

As we got up to fifty mph in second, I looked over at the driver of the Ferrari, since he could see when we decided to shift gears. He, with an arrogance only a Ferrari owner can afford, put both hands on the wheel to show he'd just leave his car in second, too. But instead of shutting off at sixty-five mph as he expected, our little beauty kept seventy-five... eighty.... By now the Ferrari was pushing past the red line on the tachometer and still we accelerated; in a final burst of speed we reached ninety-five mph. We looked over and saw a black puff of smoke and suddenly the Ferrari dropped back with a blown piston.

The Ferrari distributor called the next day. "What the hell did you do to my customer?" he demanded. "He's telling everybody in town that Stack has a Model A that goes ninety-five mph in second, and he's selling his Ferrari and suing me for publicly humiliating him."

Good old sneaky Al had done it again. He had installed a Columbia two-speed axle—a supposedly impossible job on a Model A—and had hooked up a shifting arrangement to the clutch. This gave us six speeds forward and two in reverse, the latter in case we ever had a race going backward. While the Ferrari driver was watching my hands, I had simply pumped my left leg which threw us into a gear never before encountered—a case of the foot being quicker than the eye. For the Ferrari to have kept up with us in second gear, the engine would have had to turn 13,000 rpm's, a feat even the great Enzo Ferrari couldn't manage. But Model A's, souped-up or not, were not my only interest. Motorcycles entered my life along with Al and stock cars.

A motorcycle is a two-wheeled vehicle which uses the rider's legs as fenders and his head as the radiator. In case of a crack-up, replacement fenders and a new radiator are not available at your friendly neighborhood body shop.

As opposed to Steve McQueen, who was a tiger the first day he got on a motorcycle, my own first exposure to the vehicle was slightly less heroic.

"Want to take a ride?" said Al, in his usual innocent fashion.

"On what?" I said.

"A motorcycle," came the reply. He wheeled out a vintage two-wheeler left by somebody as payment years before.

"Do you know how to drive that thing?" I demanded, remembering the souped-up Model A.

"I know how to drive anything," he said. With the matter settled, I jumped on the back, and we lurched off toward Hollywood Boulevard. I soon found that he had never driven the damn thing before, but I was at the age when I knew I would never die, so it didn't matter. We zoomed off toward Hollywood, and roared down Las Palmas, a narrow street with no palms, toward Mozzetti's garage. But Jepson kept right on going past the garage toward Santa Monica Boulevard, a stop sign, and the five-o'clock traffic.

"I think you'd better hit the brakes about now, chum!" I screamed.

"I did a block back," said Al, breezing along, "but they didn't work and it's stuck in third gear." He threw the motorcycle on its side, screamed through the stop sign, somehow wedged us between a bus and a truck, and slid down the trolley tracks for 100 yards. I left my maniac driver when he dumped the cycle. While he had the motorcycle between him and the pavement, I had only my pants. So when I finally got up, friction had chewed up the bottom out of my pants and Hollywood got its first taste of "mooning." This momentous event occurred thirty years before Marlon Brando, James Caan, and Bob Duvall decided to show their behinds to the world—and mine was in living color!

Jepson made me get on that miserable contraption again, and ride back to Mozzetti's garage, so no one would think we were "chicken."

"Any other way, we'd lose face," he explained.

I was unconvinced.

"I'm not worried about my face; it's my ass I almost lost."

Many others in the picture business took to motorcycles with varying degrees of success.

Andy Devine had a Harley Davidson with saddlebags that his ample bottom lapped over and seemed to engulf. Dick Powell had a shiny Triumph, all spit and polish. Clark Gable, Victor Fleming, and Keenan Wynn could be seen at the local hill climbs. Some had near tragic accidents. Van Johnson slammed into a car and was seriously hurt. After Carole was killed in a plane crash, Clark could be seen tearing down Sunset Boulevard at speeds way over his ability. (Not an actual suicide attempt, but it sure as hell seemed second cousin to a death wish.)

I never liked motorcycles much, and I guess the feeling was mutual. I ran out of flesh to bruise and bones to break on one wild ride to Lake Tahoe. Actually, I never got to Tahoe, but I'm getting ahead of myself. Al Jepson had just put together a super-cycle, a four-cylinder English Ariel designed for dignified, casual riding. The addition of high-compression pistons, Winfield cams, and different drive gears once again turned an innocent-looking package into a guided missile. Carey Loftin, the dean of Hollywood stunt men, and an old chum, came up with the idea: We'd cross the desert at night to keep from being charbroiled, and hit the mountains at sunup. I didn't intend to take the last part literally. It was one in the morning and colder than taking a cross-country ride during the Ice Age. We both had on two pairs of pants and three sweaters, and Carey felt the addition of a little brandy might help. It did, at first. After taking a swig at high speed, Carey absentmindedly threw the top away. We now had a portable spray gun showering Henessy all over everything.

Carey said, "We'd better drink it before it blows away."

"No sense wasting it," I agreed. So my trusty companion and I had our fun. By 2 A.M., I am told I rode standing on the seat like Buffalo Bill at a rodeo. This was a trick I had never before attempted, and it was only when I tried getting off the motorcycle in Mojave, a small town in the middle of the desert of the same name, that I encountered my first problem: I was still moving at a healthy clip and no one, not even Carey Loftin, looks good getting off a two-wheeler at twenty mph. I jackknifed the motorcycle, turned a series of somersaults, and slid on my stomach right up to the entrance of an all-night cafe. It took a while to get served. The old geezer behind the counter kept mumbling about the damn drunks giving his place a bad name.

So we left Mojave, jewel of the desert, and pointed ourselves north, coffee mixing nicely with the brandy. The coffee and the next 150 miles managed to sober us up.

The sun was coming up as we reached Bishop, gateway to the Sierras. Mojave was soon forgotten. The Bishop grade is famous as a continuing grind of endless turns heading from the desert floor to the mountains—a stretch many vehicles are lucky to make without breaking down or boiling over. This seemed as good a place as any to see if Carey's hand-built Crocker could take Jepson's creation. We screamed up the canyon, riding the racing pegs, sparks flying off the exhausts, and I steadily pulled away from the black Crocker.

The end of the grade is a long radius turn to the left, nicely banked, which I took at eighty mph. With crystal clarity, I remember each moment. I was singing the "Cow-Cow Boogie" one instant; the next, I was talking to a seven-foot pheasant that kept flapping its wings and kicking gravel in my face. This last scene, which was in color, slowly dissolved into an out-of-focus close-up of Carey Loftin saying, "Stick your tongue out. Come on, Bob, it's important."

I stared at him in disbelief, wondering why I should stick my tongue out at my good friend. His answer came all too quickly.

"To see if your back is broken."

I tried sticking my tongue out, but it wouldn't work. My mouth was jammed full of gravel, like a latter-day Demosthenes. I looked around and saw myself on a soft shoulder of the highway, my cycle ten feet away. I tried getting up and fell into Carey's arms. Now I spat out the gravel, and finally, with a look of triumph, slowly stuck out my tongue.

I had managed to hit a patch of gravel kicked out by a car, hidden from my field of vision, doing a U-turn. Luckily, I was going so fast I missed the asphalt and flew into the soft shoulder. I broke both ankles and peeled off most of the right side of my face, including my eyelid. This gave me a strangely grotesque look, that scared off even the usual friendly truck drivers we tried to flag down.

Finally, some kind soul dumped us off at a gas station called Happy Jack's, where I spent hours lying on an old army cot listening to two locals laying bets on my survival while Carey tried to get me a room in the Bishop hospital.

When he finally succeeded, I was subjected to the Bishop hospital treatment, which consisted of putting on an ointment to heal the tattered skin. Next, my brother flew down from Tahoe and took me to the Reno hospital. There they scraped off the ointment with a brush designed by the Marquis de Sade and put on an evil-smelling powder.

I felt the results when the navy called me for my physical. I managed to get in the back row to do the required knee bends and jumps by clutching a corner of the wall. I never rode a motorcycle again.

I had no time to waste regretting the loss of motorcycles. I had discovered a new source of interest, and the object of my affections had to be seen to be believed!

She was a beauty! Man, was she ever! With a figure that was out of this world! In fact, the figure was about twenty grand—so that was the last I thought about getting that most beautiful of sailboats, an Olympic six-meter. Instead I joined the powerboat racers, more commonly known as "stinkboats," and learned that in this style of water sport the devil takes the hindmost, the object is to win. In those days, refugees from a gas pump and road mechanics would look for excitement in the water. There were also a few straights, including Guy Lombardo, but they raced Gold Cup Unlimiteds, with Rolls-Royce Merlin engines, and provided matching racing outfits for everybody in the crew. Our gang looked more like a crew of Marlon Brandos, straight out of *A Streetcar Named Desire*.

I quickly learned the etiquette of closed-course speedboat racing. As in the world of autos, my mentor was again that Danish maniac mechanic, my best friend Al Jepson. We had just built a racing runabout and were testing it before our first race.

I soon found out that the only thing I could expect in racing boats was the unexpected. We swapped ends on the first turn.

"A little slippery, isn't it?" I said.

"Well, yeah," came the reply. "I guess I forgot to put on the stabilizing fin."

The race started, and we somehow got around the first turn without hitting anybody or running on the rocks. A boat without a fin tends to keep sliding sideways.

We were at Long Beach Marina Stadium—a narrow band of water with big boulders lining the shore—which had been used for the 1932 Olympics' rowing, or scull, races. If you lost control and wound up on the shore, you became what the locals call a rock sandwich.

On the second turn, the boat in front of us spun out and we slammed into it. Surprisingly enough, we almost cut the rival boat in half with no damage to us. I slowed down and Jepson reached over my shoulder and jammed the throttles back open.

"Come on, let's move it!"

I couldn't believe my ears.

"What about the other boat?" I said. "What is he going to do?"

"Swim," said Al.

It was nice that the owner of that boat could swim, because his boat had already sunk. I felt rather guilty winning the race while the other driver was out in a rowboat with a long stick trying to locate his sunken property.

Much later that night, I told Al how I felt.

"You know," I said, "I've just never seen one boat cut another in half like that before."

"Well, kid," he said, "I'll tell you a trade secret. They have races so somebody can win. There's no point in firing up the engine if you're just going to drag your butt 'round a course. I knew this course was kind of slippery, so I took out insurance. I went to a blacksmith and had him make a bow plate out of boiler plate steel and sharpen it just in case. It worked, didn't it?"

Many years later, I found myself feeling a strange kind of *déjà vu*. In an early "Untouchables" episode, I had to blast into Al Capone's brewery in a truck with a piece of sharpened boiler plate steel mounted on the front. I wondered if Ness ever knew Al Jepson.

At about this same time, in Ventnor City, New Jersey, an inventor named Appel had designed the first three-point hydroplane. Once, on a trip East, I couldn't wait to go to Ventnor and see this new development. So Al and I arranged to stop off and take a look. Unlike many of the classic V-bottom boats of the past, the three-point hydroplane didn't push through the water. It rode on a tunnel of air, providing a cyclonic breakthrough in speed. It was based on the principle of using three points, the two stabilizing areas and the propeller.

We brought back a three-point hydroplane to California, the first one on the West Coast. When I took the boat into the water for the first time, at Lake Elsinore, California, I ran it up to seventy miles an hour. It felt as slippery as a bear on ice skates.

"There's something wrong with this thing," I said. "It feels as if it wants to fly."

"You idiot," laughed Al, with his usual subtle charm. "It's *supposed* to fly."

It was only natural for me to enter competitive racing. My brother raced in the International Motorboat Regatta in Venice, Italy, and I went along as a kind of caboose. I had been fooling with outboards since I was thirteen, and I couldn't wait to put the new three-point hydroplane in a race.

But boating wasn't my only interest. I was dating a lovely girl named Cobina Wright, Jr., at the time.

Cobina Wright, Jr., also known as "Little Cobina," was a beautiful, willowy blond with blue eyes. She had an indomitable mother who had brought her up during the depression with wits and a lot of intestinal fortitude taking the place of money. "Big Cobina" made her daughter a celebrity by being on speaking terms with everyone in the blue book and cafe society; they took her in like an orphan in a storm. Even when Big Cobina forced her to sing at chic boîtes, which Little Cobina hated, she was still accepted by the 400 as a society chanteuse and no points were lost. Philip of Greece, now married to Queen Elizabeth II of England, was smitten by her; Big Cobina sneaked me a letter or two to prove it. Little Cobina sailed through all this as unspoiled and charming a young lady as you'll ever see.

Cobina's counterpart was Brenda Frazier, another beauty, but with opposite coloring. With dark hair and brown eyes, she looked a little like Gene Tierney. These were New York cafe society's darlings during the period of Woolworth (Wooly) Donohue and Shipwreck Kelly. They were so well known that Jack Benny introduced two Brooklyn comedy telephone operators named "Brendah" and "Cobinah" on his radio show.

Cobina and I drove down to San Diego for the most important race of the season. I couldn't wait to show everyone how Appel's invention worked. But I was the one in for a surprise. For some reason, buoys, or markers, were placed all along the straightaway as well as at the end. I took off in my three-point beauty, flying over the water.

Then, as I drove straight toward the sun I turned the boat around, one buoy before the last marker. I found out later that I hadn't run the full course; though I had won by a mile, I was disqualified for missing the last buoy.

I sent Cobina back to Los Angeles with a friend. I was so damn mad that I disappeared for three days. (I spent the three days in Santa Monica at a bar called The Bucket of Blood, drowning my sorrows.)

My next and almost final adventure with buoys came at Lake Yosemite. For months Al and I had been aiming to break the world's five-mile speed record. But on a short course, the sharp one-buoy turns slowed the boat down too much. Lake Yosemite had the perfect course: five buoy turns we could barrel into at over 100 mph, skittering sideways at full throttle like a spaced-out crab, with only the rudder as a brake.

Hydroplanes race over the water at 2½ miles a minute. Saul Pett, correspondent for the Associated Press, described hydroplane racing as a wet earthquake, riding a berserk firecracker in a big cocktail shaker. They throw up a spray sixty feet high. A small can floating in the water can put a hole in the boat, and a submerged log can convert one into assorted canapes.

The unlucky ones end up like Orth Mathiot and Thompson Whitaker, who felt their boat, Quicksilver, go out of control in front of 150,000 spectators. It nosed down and plunged to the bottom of the lake, with the drivers, strapped in by their seatbelts, going to their deaths. Bill O'Mara, the TV sports announcer, was visibly shaken as he turned to the camera and led his audience in the Lord's Prayer, a grim reminder that in a hydroplane, triumph can turn to tragedy in a single second.

A three-point hydroplane is its most vulnerable in a high-speed turn. It doesn't bank like the conventional V-bottom hull. Instead, it leaps, shudders, and makes the damnedest noise imaginable—like a hailstorm on a tin roof. You're convinced that it's coming apart in small pieces. A rounded sponson, or pontoonlike object called a slip chime, allows it to slide sideways without turning over. But it's easy to get in trouble when the trough the boat hits is deeper than the slip chime. This was a lesson I would soon learn the hard way.

Jepson kicked off our world record attempt by getting plastered the night before the race and punching the commodore of the yacht club in the nose before passing out under our boat trailer. The next morning, he was as useless as tits on a bull.

The race had a clock start, not the conventional lineup with a starting flag. A clock start has always been a tricky affair. In theory, you should time it exactly so that as the giant hand reaches zero, you are a second or less from the starting line and, ideally, under a full head of steam. Some of the more heroic types synchronize a watch to the judge's clock, go back about a half mile, and try to hit the line wide open. This makes for an interesting situation when two or three of the less hardy types are milling around, cluttering the narrow starting chute. A classic photo of Lou Fageol's Gold Cup boat shows the craft upside-down, twenty feet off the water, going 160 mph across the starting line—a shortcut to becoming a bionic man. Of course, if you guess the wrong way and cross the line before the gun, you have to go back and do it again.

In the first heat the delicate Winfield carburetors that ordinarily responded to the master's touch were so out of adjustment I was lucky to get the boat across the starting line and chug around the five miles like an asthmatic paddlewheeler.

When I staggered in, Jepson was soaking his head in Lake Yosemite, knowing I would have done it for him otherwise. In a final frenzy of scraped knuckles and flying screwdrivers, he got the carburetors adjusted. I didn't even have a chance to buckle my crash helmet before the gun.

This time, my mad Danish friend had done his job! The Thunderbird was lifted into her tunnel of air and we flew around the course. We had arranged a signal. If I broke the record on the first lap, he was to wave a rag as I came by. Sure enough, as I stormed past the judge's stand, there was Jepson, waving a greasy rag over his head. We had made it, almost!

I saw a flash of a patrol boat doing the unforgivable, leaving a high-speed wake. I hit the first part of the wake and took off for about twenty feet. I knew the second half was somewhere between number one and number three buoys, but the water was too choppy for me to see it. I could either stay wide open around the turn and hope I didn't catch a sponson in that damn wake—in other words, I could continue trying to break the record—or slow down between buoys one and three, and play it safe. If I made the latter choice, I knew the record would fly right back into Lake Yosemite.

I stayed on the throttle and as I came around the second buoy, I hit a trough that was three feet deep, with a two-foot slip chime. It was like catching my heel on a rug. I was suddenly airborne, doing a perfect barrel roll. Unfortunately, however, I was in a boat, not a plane. I was thrown out on my head. The crash helmet I had had no time to buckle came off, whacking me in the eye. I never found out what happened next. As I came to, I was surprised to see two patrol boats converging on me. There was actually only one, but I had split vision for a week, and a headache as bad as Al Jepson's.

My mother got used to calling to check on how my racing career was doing. When a voice on the phone said, "Bob isn't here," she automatically said, "All right then, give me the hospital." But this wonderful lady understood. She never fenced me in.

In my middle years, I feel twinges, occasional muscle spasms, and assorted aches and pains left over from my glamorous, brainless youth. But each one has a memory. The permanent bump on my wrist reminds me of Bran Muffin, my beautiful chestnut thoroughbred lady, the granddaughter of Man O' War, who lost her right front shoe at full gallop in a twelve-goal polo championship at Riviera Country Club. The muscles that pulled away from my rib cage on the left side tell of my motorcycle fiasco with Carey Loftin. A blue mark on my left eye is the result of my being hit by my goggles as the crash helmet flew off at Lake Yosemite. The hairline cracks in my front teeth came from a polo ball hit by the University of Arizona's number-two man in the NCAA play-offs. Even

"The Untouchables" left its mark: an occasional migraine caused by George Kennedy's two-handed thump on my neck when he played a giant deaf-mute.

The flesh is weak, but the memories linger on!

3

The Kiss Heard 'Round the World

Or, Osculation for Fun and Profit

Whenever I am asked about the beginning of my movie career in Hollywood, I have to say that I began not in Hollywood but in Universal City.

Universal City is unique in many respects. Perhaps the only city in the world founded specifically to produce motion pictures, it is located near Studio City, a Los Angeles suburb.

Today Universal City is also a major tourist attraction, with a large hotel and guided tours for the public. A ticket entitles the bearer to a tram ride around the lot, a chance to watch an exhibition of movie stunts and special effects, and even an opportunity to catch a glimpse of Universal's current reigning superstar, the shark from *Jaws*.

Universal City is not geographically part of Hollywood. It was founded in 1915 by Carl Laemmle, the president of Universal Pictures, whose private name for the studio's large tract of land in the San Fernando Valley was "the bottomless pit." The treaty which ceded California to the United States was signed on this location in 1847. On this historic piece of real estate, Laemmle proceeded to build a unique empire.

In the early days, tourists were invited to sit in grandstands and watch the filming. They could buy peanuts and watch the flocks of white chickens which were Laemmle's pride and joy. (Employees could buy eggs from the studio at a discount.)

As the head of the studio, Carl Laemmle was a feisty and colorful man who began his career in pictures by winning a legal battle with the monopolistic "trust," a group of pioneer film companies which controlled the fledgling movie industry.

Throughout the studio, everyone knew who was boss. Only five feet tall, Laemmle had provided Universal with its name after spotting a truck advertising "Universal Pipe Fittings." Even the signs which said Keep Off The Grass displayed his personal signature. Producers and directors had to mind their manners when talking to their office boys. Anyone on the lot might be a relative of the man known affectionately as "Uncle Carl."

One of Laemmle's unknown relatives was William Wyler, who went on to become one of Hollywood's most celebrated directors, and my boss at Liberty Productions.

Like most heads of studios, Uncle Carl enjoyed the limelight. On one occasion he was involved in negotiating the most unusual contract ever suggested in Hollywood—an on-camera appearance by Pope Pius XI. Uncle Carl was enthusiastic about the idea of photographing His Holiness making a Papal statement to the world. When the Vatican requested that the studio make a sizable donation to charity in lieu of compensation, Laemmle, in characteristic fashion, sent a telegram to his European representative: "Forget Pope!"

After running the studio for a number of years, in 1929 he announced his chosen successor, who was, not surprisingly, Carl Laemmle, Jr. He gave the studio to his son as a birthday present. The younger Laemmle, called "Junior" by everyone, was only twenty-one, but he was determined to leave his mark on the studio. It was during his regime that the studio produced such classic horror films as *Dracula* with Bela Lugosi and *Frankenstein* with Boris Karloff.

Eventually, the studio ran into a dire financial crisis and was sold in 1936 to a group of financiers. When I arrived at Universal in 1939 the studio was no longer in the Laemmle family. The new owners had discovered over seventy friends and relatives of Uncle Carl on the payroll—including more than one who would have had to come back from the great beyond to collect a paycheck. To replace the Laemmle regime, the new owners decided that the studio needed a major new asset, a superstar who could save Universal. They found one in a pretty twelve-year-old girl with an incredible singing voice. Her name was Deanna Durbin. Born Edna Mae Durbin, Deanna began her astonishing career in Winnipeg, Canada. In late 1935, MGM was searching for a girl who could play Ernestine Schumann-Heink, the celebrated opera singer, as a child. Deanna's voice had captivated everyone at Metro, including Maestro Andrés de Segurola, the Spanish opera singer and vocal coach consulted by the studio. A mustachioed bass who had toured Europe and directed Havana's national theater, de Segurola said that young Deanna had the voice of a fully mature adult. He became her teacher, and the studio was enthusiastic. Louis B. Mayer decided to dispense with the name Edna Mae, and since she was called D.D. by her friends, Deanna quickly acquired a new name.

Unfortunately, Ernestine Schumann-Heink died, the project was abandoned, and Deanna left MGM. She continued studying with Maestro de Segurola, however. She was given the lead in *Three Smart Girls,* and eventually turned up in a Universal feature *100 Men and a Girl*. This film, about a girl who organized an orchestra and persuaded Leopold Stokowski to conduct it, became a smash hit. At fourteen, Deanna Durbin became what is today called a superstar. Stores sold merchandise bearing her name. Toys and school supplies using her name or face were found everywhere. A national fan club which called its members "Deanna Durbin Devotees" began following her every move. A journal (naturally called *Deanna's Diary*) reported the tiniest details of her activities. Everything from what Deanna ate for breakfast to her handwriting (which was analyzed by a graphologist) was eagerly awaited by thousands of people. The school board assigned a private tutor to work with her because it was impossible for her to go to school without creating a major traffic hazard.

Away from the set, Deanna was quiet and reserved. It was understandable that she try to preserve whatever aspects of her private life she could, since the public was never far behind. To her fans, she was always the girl next door. But her home life could hardly be called that of the typical American girl. She lived in an Italian villa near the estates of W.C. Fields and Cecil B. DeMille. Her home was a maze of terraced gardens and lily ponds. There was a large swimming pool, and even an economic waterfall which turned on and off, courtesy of a handy push button.

For those of little memory or too young to recall, Deanna Durbin was a motion picture phenomenon. Barbara Streisand, Faye Dunaway, and Raquel Welch together wouldn't have had the impact she had as America's sweetheart, that darling girl with the golden voice. Perhaps the innocence of the late thirties in America had something to do with it.

Every parent wanted her for a daughter, and every young man felt sure he was the one to break through that curtain of sweetness and carry her off in his Hudson Terraplane. More to the point, she was "big box office." Universal Studios kept its gates open just because the bank held Deanna's contract as collateral. All America was up in arms over Deanna's growing up and having her first screen kiss.

Deanna had been maturing despite the studio's desperate measures. Nature was endowing her with a blouseful of goodies, as my racy older brother would say. The studio wardrobe department was doing everything possible to keep her thirteen years old forever. Suffice it to say, nature won! This presented a problem of monumental proportions. She was going to have to be allowed to grow up. Ninety percent of all child stars did not successfully make the transition into adult stardom, but every effort was to be made to carry Deanna through this dangerous time.

Someone came up with the idea of creating a Cinderella story around her. It wasn't exactly original, but it was suitable. Prince Charming had to be an unknown, prefabricated by the studio, a prince consort beyond reproach, or at least beyond any escapade reported by Louella or Hedda. Coincidentally, I was taking voice lessons from Deanna's singing teacher Maestro Andrés de Segurola. I managed to improve my sound from a bullfrog's croak to the mating call of an Irish wolfhound. In despair, the good maestro suggested that I visit Deanna on the set to hear how the human voice was capable of sounding. My eyes had hardly grown accustomed to the sound stage, when a short, sandy-haired gentleman sidled over to me and said, "Wunderbar, would you like to be in the movies?" I looked around, wondering who might be the subject of this query. When I realized he was looking at me, I said "of course," never giving it a second thought.

The man was Joe Pasternak, one of Hollywood's most powerful producers. No one could have been more surprised than I. Universal had been looking for months for Prince Charming, and Pasternak thought I was it. I didn't feel very charming when I overcame my initial delight and found out what was in store for me.

First came a photographic test. I sat on a piano stool, while someone lying on his back on the floor spun me around. Academy Award winner Joe Valentine was the cinematographer. He kept things moving with comments like: "My God, look at that profile. Okay, spin him around. Full face is no better. Okay, spin him.... The other profile is worse.... Spin him!" He went on and on and on! "At least the back of his head is okay," he concluded.

I felt a natural enough temptation to jump off the piano stool and give Joe Valentine a knuckle sandwich. But before I knew what was happening, I found myself being pulled onto a sound stage for an acting test. The girl assigned to test with me was Helen Parrish, one of Deanna Durbin's regulars, a gorgeous face with body to match. One look at Helen convinced me that I had been rewarded for not giving Joe Valentine a black eye. This was more like it!

When the verdict was handed down from the front office, the news was good. Universal had found a thoroughly unsuspecting Prince Charming, profile and all. Deanna Durbin had her first screen lover, and I had a new career. The year was 1939. The major stars who had known me as a champion skeet shooter were quick to recognize that Clark Gable and the other sex symbols had nothing to fear. ("We've lost a good shot and probably gained a lousy actor," said Spencer Tracy, expressing their basic point of view!)

On the set of *First Love,* Deanna was completely self-contained, courteous, private, almost aloof, off camera. On camera, she had the luster very few in our profession possess, particularly in musical numbers. The plots of her films were adjusted to give her a chance to sing a variety of arias. I remember her singing "One Fine Day," from *Madame Butterfly.* In this scene, Cinderella thought she had lost her prince. At the end of the scene, she saw me, the tears running down her face.

She rushed toward me, we embraced, and the film ended. It was a good thing the cameras were over my shoulder. The crew and I were welling up, right along with her. She could

THE KISS HEARD 'ROUND THE WORLD

be very convincing. But all was not beer and skittles. Although a star is always present when his or her scenes are being shot, they sometimes leave the set if someone else is being photographed in close-up, and let the script girl read their lines. Deanna's penchant for leaving the set after her close-ups led to my first love scene with a blackboard.

Henry Koster was the director, a gifted man, and he did his best. He said, "All right, Bobby, do you see this chalk mark?"

I nodded.

"That's Deanna," he continued. "Now you see her. You notice she's pretty. Now she's beautiful. Now she looks at you."

The chalk mark didn't smile or say anything.

Koster continued to rhapsodize while he expected me to gaze at the chalk mark in rapt attention.

"You love her. You adore her."

No matter how many times I looked at that lousy cross, it never looked like Deanna to me. After a couple of hours, my right eye began turning in like a part-time Chester Conklin. This was my introduction to the world of illusion.

One of the reviewers of the movie later singled me out in this scene as the most promising new romantic lead to emerge in a long time. Happily, she attributed my myopic, slightly cross-eyed look, to passion, not confusion and boredom with a blackboard.

Movie makeup was full of surprises for a young man unaccustomed to worrying much about his looks. One day, before shooting began on *First Love,* I was ambling down the main street of Universal. I saw a white-smocked gentleman beckoning to me from a doorway. I walked over to see what he wanted and, instead of the customary "hello," he said, "Step in here and let me look at you." Curious, I obeyed him.

He led me by the arm to a sterile white operating room filled with what looked like hundreds of decapitated heads. On closer examination, the decapitated heads were wigs stands on which makeup men stick the hair, beards, mustaches, and such, when actors go home.

"You know," he said, pushing me into a makeup chair, "no blond has ever made it as a leading man."

By now I began to get the queasy feeling I should have kept on walking.

"Wavy hair looks feminine," he added, pulling the mysterious tools of his trade from the many drawers that surrounded him. Finally, with eyes squinted, looking like a hawk who has spotted the hen-house door open, he said, "Did anyone ever tell you you have an inverted hair line?"

I was nearly convinced I was in the hands of a nut who had escaped from a nearby sanitorium, white smock and all. As I looked desperately around the room for means of escape, my eye stopped on a familiar golden statuette: FOR OUTSTANDING ACHIEVEMENT IN MAKEUP TO JACK PIERCE (the Oscar!).

I sighed a nervous breath of relief and settled back into the chair.

What other actors had the honor of having an Academy Award winner as makeup man? Jack Pierce was one of Hollywood's greatest makeup men, but his most famous creations were the title characterizations in *Dracula* (for Bela Lugosi), the *Invisible Man* (for Claude Rains), and those stalwart matinee idols in *The Mummy and Wolfman*. Jack Pierce's most famous creation was, however, the Frankenstein monster played by Boris Karloff.

At this time all the major studios tried to duplicate the trademarks of success. If Gable was king at the moment, every new actor tried desperately to furrow his brow and do Clark's famous "Gable gargle." No matter what a young actor (or young actress) might look like, every effort was made to bend nature in the direction of a sure thing.

When Jack Pierce got his hands on me, Robert Taylor was the reigning star of the moment. With me in his clutches now, Pierce began casually enough with, "Let me show you how you'd look with darker hair. Don't worry," he added, "it's only a rinse; it'll wash right out."

After a short procedure, there I was, a Latin with black, wavy hair and blue eyes.

"So far so good," said Mr. Pierce. "But that wavy hair ruins the effect. Let's take out some of that wave to give you more strength. Don't worry, it'll only last a few hours."

Now out came a device familiar to many a lady of an earlier period: a curling iron, or in my case, an uncurling iron. This seemed hardly the image for a character who spent his life playing polo, lifting weights, or shooting skeet, so I made him draw the curtains so no one would witness this last experiment. When he was finished the result was far from spectacular. My hair now had the texture of a wire brush, and my expression of muted horror did little to enhance the picture. Jack seemed to think it looked great, and maybe it did, compared to the lead in *The Phantom of the Opera*.

Rather desperately, I convinced him I thought it looked fine, but I argued that since the studio had signed me the way he had found me an hour before, I didn't want to give them a surprise, even such a nifty one, my first week at Universal.

With a smile worthy of Father Christmas, he instantly made preparations for the reparation. He washed my hair for a few minutes and then I heard a muted chuckle.

"Isn't that funny," he said. "I haven't done that since I was an apprentice."

My face was under water, so I let him go on.

"Most of the actors want the effect to last through a movie. I guess I forgot this was only a temporary job."

I finally surfaced and sputtered, "What?"

"You see," he explained, "I should have straightened the hair first. When you use a hot iron on the rinse it sets it like a dye."

"You mean..." I stammered.

"Yes, you now have straight black hair," he smiled encouragingly. "I think it's an improvement."

Over what? I thought.

"Well, anyway, now that we've fixed most of what's wrong," he said, "let's finish the job. Let's fix that inverted hairline."

My hairline had never been such an object of scorn before, but by now I figured, what the hell, why not?

He took a small triangular piece of black hair backed by hairlace, and after a few moments of adjusting and judicious trimming, he glued it to my forehead covering the offending inversion.

He stepped back, then crept toward me like a 35mm Mitchell movie camera coming in for a close-up, and then moved back again. Finally he spoke.

"*Now* you look like a movie actor!"

I opened my eyes, which I had held closed during this last experiment, and saw myself in the three-sided mirror. A complete stranger, someone I had never met but who looked vaguely familiar, looked back at me with an expression of wonder.

He looked—wait a minute—he looked just a *little*, a *very*

little like Robert Taylor, seen through a funhouse mirror.

When I arrived for the first day's shooting of *First Love*, the assistant director called, "Places!" Henry Koster walked right past me yelling, "Where's Stack?" Then he turned to me and said, "Who are you?"

There was a long pause, worthy of Macready, the famous stage star whose trademark was a dramatic silence between phrases. "My God," he exclaimed, looking at the widow's peak. "What happened to you?"

On this note of confidence, I began my first motion picture. Other surprises were just around the corner. I quickly learned that *close-up* was the most magic of all show biz words, and also the most elusive. Established stars not only fought for them, but carefully considered which side of the face would be on camera, how much light shed on it, etc.

I seemed to be getting my share of close-ups in this first attempt. The studio, however, had forgotten to tell me about a time-honored Hollywood practice. All the film shot does not necessarily end up in the picture. Between the cup and the lip, slips occur in a clouded chamber called the editing room. The film cutter, or editor, as he likes to be called, does his best to see that the star of the flick is protected. Everyone else appears no more than is necessary. This is called "staying with the money."

The *First Love* premiere was unqualified madness. I prepared myself, went into shock, and the aftereffects still remain.

The studio did not allow any of us to see the rushes of *First Love*. The first time I appeared on screen that night, I had no idea who that black-haired idiot was. Whoever he was, I couldn't help wondering where he learned to speak in that weird, hollow voice.

Oh, my God, it's me! I thought to myself. *I don't look and sound like that, do I?* I contemplated sliding under my seat. But since nobody seemed to notice, I began waiting for those crucial close-ups. The camera cut in to pick up Deanna, and I leaned forward to see the shot of me that followed. I was nowhere to be seen. Suddenly, in a blinding flash, I realized that an entire scene can be played spotlighting the star, with just an astral voice and one ear representing the other actor.

The famous kiss turned out to be a bit of a letdown, too. Like a girl in a see-through blouse who keeps her arms crossed all evening, much was promised, but damn little was actually seen. The studio backed out at the last minute, cutting the kiss from a satisfying smooch of three seconds to a millisecond peck.

When *Life* magazine offered us its cover to feature the kiss, the studio turned it down as too controversial! This was the final straw. In *today's* Hollywood, Julie Christie and Warren Beatty could reprise their famous *in flagrante* love scene in *Shampoo* on the city hall steps without attracting attention from a national magazine.

As for public reaction to my debut, it followed a Hollywood tradition. The makeup department's attitude seemed appropriate for Mad Hatters and March Hares to me, but there was very definite method in their madness. The big studios felt that an actor, in order to reach the public, had to be presented in a specific mold. The mold might change from week to week, but if a specific image seemed to be working in the box office, every actor was expected to fit. If his ears, nose, or other features failed to conform, the makeup boys took over. When columnists described me as "looking like a young Robert Taylor," the studio purred with approval. Jack Pierce had succeeded.

Much of the motion picture business made no sense at all. I was accustomed to sports in which the best shot took home the trophy, and to be the best shot required a lot of practicing. But in the movie business, it's very possible for an actor to achieve the height of success before ever really learning his craft. Shortly after the premiere of *First Love,* I happened to be in a theater in New York, when a group of girls learned that Deanna's Prince Charming was in the audience. They tore down the aisles in pursuit. As I left the theater, they chased me out to the cab and, when I leapt inside, they lifted the wheels off the ground. Not entirely sure whether they found me irresistible or wanted to tear me limb from limb, I finally got away, wondering what I might have missed if I had let them catch me.

I had no idea what I had done to merit all this feminine attention, but I decided to enjoy it. In later years, I realized the incredible illogic of films. Stardom can be instant, but the phenomenon can disappear just as quickly. It depends on fate, luck, and all kinds of intangibles.

Another new element introduced in my life at that time was the fan magazine. Especially in the forties, these publications delighted in parading before the public the indiscretions and eccentricities of anyone whose face happened to appear on a movie screen. If an actor refused to be obligingly indiscreet, the magazines made up something. Any casual date could be turned into a heart-wringing passion. I'm glad that my mother saved many of these old articles about me. I enjoy them today. They're the funniest things this side of Mark Twain's Mississippi River, and their tales are twice as tall as any he ever wove.

One magazine dubbed me, "the Adonis on Wheels." Another introduced me as "the young man who committed an act of osculation with Deanna Durbin."

Sometimes, the studio publicity department planned "parties" to be attended by actors under contract and photographers. The actors were provided with noisemakers, hats, and everything else they needed to make it appear they were having a good time. The photographers would snap their pictures, and then everyone would pack up and go home. A really "wild" party might last ten minutes longer than the two hours normally required to take all the photos.

It's never a good idea to read things into photographs. At one point I had my picture taken with Lana Turner. We were supposed to be discussing Lana's interest in crocheting. (What else would a man be discussing with Lana Turner?) Lana was regarded as one of the most beautiful actresses in Hollywood. Since the premiere of *First Love*, the fan magazines had been madly speculating about the girls I dated. I asked Lana out and took her to see my racing hydroplane. The mechanics on the pier nearly fell off when they saw Lana (probably wearing one of the sweaters she crocheted) walking over to inspect my boat. Since I was involved in hydroplane racing up to my ears, I naturally assumed that Lana would be just as fascinated. I spent a marvelous evening getting the boat in racing condition. Unfortunately, I was so engrossed in what I was doing that I failed to notice that Lana—unaccustomed to being ignored, and not sharing my enthusiasm for camshafts, manifolds, and such—had simply picked up and left. (Lana and I should have stuck to crocheting.)

The "most ridiculous fan magazine" award would have to go to the writer who dreamed up a feature depicting me sharing an interest in bowling with Diana Barrymore. But the magazine snapped a picture, decided we had to have a mutual interest, and settled on bowling. (If Diana and I had ever gone near a bowling ball, one of us would probably have been tempted to throw it at the other.)

While the fan magazines were solemnly describing my on-screen osculation with Deanna Durbin, I was thinking about my future. There was a special magic in making movies and, now that I had had a taste of films, I couldn't wait for a whole banquet. Although I had next appeared in *The Mortal Storm*, a serious drama for MGM, Universal wanted to repeat the formula of *First Love* in a new film called *Nice Girl*. Deanna and I were paired again. I began to think the movie industry, despite the madcap confusion and innocent nonsense, must have a sense of continuity after all. I saw myself emerging as a serious actor, building up to roles in films like *Citizen Kane* and *Gone with the Wind*, always opposite a long line of gorgeous girls who couldn't wait to see me cast as their leading man. Instead, after *Nice Girl*, I found myself working in one of the most forgettable westerns ever made, a nonmasterpiece called *Badlands of Dakota*. Instead of another beautiful girl, I had to work with Broderick Crawford.

Like any young actor, I was more than a little enthusiastic when I signed a contract with Universal. But I soon had the opportunity of discovering the lot of contract players. The Universal contract called for seven years of universal servitude (no pun intended). In those days they paid $150 a week, with a yearly option. The actors could be dropped at any time. There was also a suspension clause. The studio could determine when not to pay us for twelve weeks, and they had the right to lend us to other studios. (Naturally when the studio lent an actor to another studio, it charged its opposite number a substantial fee. But the actor went right on earning $150 a week.)

Like all major studios, Universal had gathered under its protective and, in many cases, suffocating wing, a potpourri of talents, big and small. The syndrome of the major studios no longer exists; at that time, however, the studio served as a combination benign father, protecting you from the insecurities of the outside world, and corrupt jailer, arbitrarily controlling your destiny to satisfy his own selfish ends.

The arguments between studio and contract player were endless. (The studio was quick to remind any actor that the system could make you a star. "The casting director giveth and the casting director taketh away" was a familiar motto, all to familiar to a number of pretty starlets who found out in a hurry what the casting director wanted to "taketh away" from them, preferably on a comfortable couch.) The studio insisted that the actor owed it blind allegiance, which included an acknowledgment that the front office had the right to put the actor in as many bad pictures as it saw fit.

The actor, in turn, had to admit that the studio had given him an opportunity. Nevertheless, my response was still, "This gives you no right to destroy me by sticking me in every piece of garbage on your schedule or keeping seventy percent of my salary when you decide to loan me out to another studio (or, worse yet, arbitrarily refusing to loan me out for the part of my life)."

There were some interesting faces appearing in Universal pictures then. Marlene Dietrich, Fred Astaire, and John Wayne were on the lot, and my fellow contract players included a broad spectrum of talent: Allan Jones, Bob Cummings, Richard Arlen, Abbot and Costello, and the Andrews Sisters.

Sometimes the Universal family had overtones of a Charles Addams cartoon. For example, Lon Chaney, Jr., and Brod Crawford—partially out of boredom and perhaps from having played too many Wolfmen and Count Draculas—used to play a game between camera setups. The classic paper, rock, and knife game of grade school took on eerie proportions. The loser's slap on the wrist became a roundhouse smash that led to bloody blisters, in turn giving way to a stream of crimson which hardly endeared them to the wardrobe man.

Their other favorite pastime was kicking each other in the shins with high-heeled boots until the blood ran. The dialogue went something like this:

"Oh, that hurt. That's a good one... son of a bitch! That's the best one yet! I think you broke my leg."

When the game was over they would walk away slapping each other on the back and laughing. We called them, "the monsters."

Andy Devine was the only real chum around from my skeet shooting days. He was a damn good shot, and one of my best friends. Andy had always been convinced I should have been a professional skeet shooter, particularly after seeing me in such sterling Universal movies as *Badlands of Dakota* and *Men of Texas*. In the former, I played a teenage sheriff with dyed black hair and a scowl to match, galloping all over the Universal back lot protecting Ann Rutherford from the likes of Brod Crawford. On second thought, maybe she needed protecting. In *Men of Texas* I played a reporter in the Old West and managed to do for the press what I had done for law enforcement in *Badlands of Dakota*.

A bit later on, a beautiful, dark-haired, voluptuous dancer named Yvonne DeCarlo appeared in a Universal effort called *Salome Where She Danced*. Romantic desert pictures, more commonly known as "tits and sand," became the rage. Every actor's career fluctuated according to the current fads and fashions. Contract actors, including an enthusiastic, handsome young man with a Bronx accent, were thrown into every uncast role. To audiences used to the bizarre casting of Universal Studios, "Yondah lies de castle of me fahdda de Caliph" delivered by Tony Curtis to his lady love gave even the stoutest fan of "t and s" pause. Tony never stopped. He used every facility the studio offered. He studied fencing, riding, stunt training, acting, diction—and graduated from Universal with an Academy Award nomination for one hell of a performance with Sidney Poitier in *The Defiant Ones*.

I quickly found out that much of the Hollywood legend was not fantasy. Life on and off camera at Universal was, to say the least, zany.

At about this time, Universal had a casting director straight out of the famous stag film, *The Casting Couch*. An actor's problems were nothing compared to those of the poor stock contract girls. Their extracurricular services were not laid out (I mean "not spelled out") in the contract, but they were nevertheless expected to perform. I confirmed this firsthand one day when I passed the casting office and saw one of our starlets burst out the back door screaming bloody murder, bra in one hand, blouse in the other, and only her in between. I'll say one thing for the casting fellow, though: He never chased them once they escaped the casting office.

Happily for the contract girls, this casting director imported for his very own a very well-endowed lady from south of the border, and proceeded to try to make her a star. She became quite well known not only as an actress of the "t and s" variety, but for several other quirks. She had one habit which in no way endeared her to the poor guy assigned to clean her dressing room.

On the back lot location, the studio provided the actors with a group of fungus-green, canvas, tentlike structures; they were hotter than Hades, and had no facilities for answering nature's call. The assistant director would scream for an actor's presence on the set, only to find that he had taken a long walk to find the nearest men's room. The lady in question found a simple solution to the problem. Perhaps partially in protest against the shabby dressing room and partially because she was too lazy to walk half a mile to tinkle, she answered nature's call in the natural way. After about a week of this and several unanswered complaints (after all, she was the boss's girl friend), the gent in charge of her dressing room came up with an ingenious answer: he decided to sprinkle the floor with quicklime. The following day, everything proceeded on schedule, until the quiet was shattered by a scream of which Medea could have been proud. This time when the lady let fly, a cloud of sulphurous smoke engulfed her and flames began licking at her feet.

Those of us who were in on the plot tried to convince her that it was a supernatural manifestation, the god of Universal's back lot striking back. The topper was that the casting director couldn't find a legitimate excuse to fire the maintenance man. From then on, she could be seen along with the rest of us peasants walking the long half mile to the comfort station.

As I continued working at Universal, I began between scenes to explore the lot. Universal was a small village unto itself. The gray and white cottages each contained their own families: producers or directors working on their separate projects, ranging from the sublime to the ridiculous. Easily identifiable on the ridiculous side were such unbelievably zany characters as the Ritz Brothers, Abbott and Costello, and a host of child actors who attended a special school right on the studio lot. It was only natural for the movies to turn to children as natural scene stealers. This did absolutely nothing to improve the disposition of Universal's favorite exponent of cantankerous intoxication, W.C. Fields.

Fields's problems with child actors had started at Paramount, when the studio gave him a pint-sized co-star with the unlikely name of "Baby Leroy." Ronald Leroy Winnebrenner was discovered by Paramount after an extensive search of several Los Angeles orphanages. It seemed the studio needed an infant who resembled Maurice Chevalier, the star of their projected feature *Bedtime Story*. The director spotted Leroy, said "*oo-la-la,*" and Chevalier acquired a supporting player. Then, to the consternation of Fields, Paramount decided he was next on the list of Leroy's adult companions. In a series of films ranging from *Tillie and Gus* to *Alice in Wonderland* (in which Baby Leroy played the joker in a deck of cards), Fields encountered his youthful nemesis. Fields allegedly decided to cope with the tiny scene stealer once and for all by spiking Leroy's orange juice with vodka.

When the normally docile Baby Leroy responded as if he'd had one too many, Fields ambled onto the set instructing the crew to walk the infant around and sober him up. "If he can't stay sober, why does he come to work?" said Fields with a look sly enough to set Mae West's heart aflutter. Fields's most cherished possession was a cocktail shaker, which he kept in his dressing room or affixed to his chair on the set in a holder he made himself from some old wire. He would invariably arrive late to work and, with one of his servants, make an enormous scene of moving the assorted articles in his wardrobe and other possessions into his dressing room.

"What's in the cocktail shaker?" a studio guard asked him one day.

"Pineapple juice," said Fields, with a straight face.

Fields consumed enough "pineapple juice" to earn him a place as the state symbol of Hawaii. He disliked people who appeared drunk in public, and somehow, no matter how much Fields drank, the alcohol seemed to have little effect. He was as irascible as ever.

One day a member of the crew, perhaps remembering the fate of Baby Leroy at Paramount, decided that no such nonsense would take place at Universal. So he secretly poured some real pineapple juice into Fields's cocktail shaker. When the comedian discovered the mischief afoot, he came storming out of his dressing room loudly demanding, "Who put pineapple juice in my pineapple juice?"

Fields, like Robert Benchley, spent his time at the Garden of Allah, the legendary apartment hotel frequented by stars, where on several occasions he tried unsuccessfully to walk on water. Everyone assumed his confidence was the result of too much liquid refreshment, but he managed to keep his bulbous nose above water until someone could jump in the swimming pool and rescue him whenever he fell in.

Fields's most dramatic performance was never used in his

films. When the great earthquake struck Southern California in 1933, Fields was in the process of making a motion picture. The chandeliers began swaying, the walls began rattling, and the floors shook. Starlets screamed and rushed off the stage. A stampede of extras, crew members, actors, gossip columnists, and even fearless producers hurried off the set as soon as everyone realized that an earthquake was taking place. Fields, however, presumably gaining courage from his daily intake of pineapple juice, couldn't understand what all the commotion was about. He walked past the camera, muttering and mumbling to himself, trying to figure out why everyone was running around. True, the walls were shaking, but for Fields, it didn't seem a bit unusual.

With Fields's passing, Hollywood lost an original character. There was never one like him before, and will likely never be one again. I met his son in the navy. He was a teetotaler with very little sense of humor, which is probably understandable.

A sense of dignity at Universal was maintained through the efforts of the Ritz brothers. Harry, Al, and Jim Ritz felt that their every action should project an image of aristocratic refinement. They shook hands while holding eggs, sprinkled flour on the chairs of the stars, and passed around shoe leather sandwiches. They fed vinegar pop to the crew, presented studio executives with gifts which exploded, and passed out to the cameramen cigars which blew up. Occasionally, they dropped lighted matches on the toes of actors, and harassed the watchmen by walking in and out of rooms. Since they all looked alike, the poor watchmen couldn't decide who was on stage and who wasn't—to the delight of the Ritz brothers.

One of the favorite Harry-Al-and-Jim operations was to pay the electricians to wire the director's chair. When he shouted "action," the startled director would get some unexpected action of his own. Most of the Ritz antics came straight out of vaudeville. Once, in Syracuse, the three brothers fell through the boards of a stage, and literally stopped the show while a carpenter hurriedly replaced the floor. Al Ritz once slipped and fell through a bass drum. He wanted to make the fall a regular part of the act, but the theater would not go along with the idea.

In those days at Universal, an actor might accidentally get a big laugh on screen with a surprise gag or facial expression. If the audiences were rolling in the aisles, the lucky performer could expect to repeat the performance for years to come.

Billy Gilbert, a plump ex-prizefighter, sneezed his way into the hearts of audiences everywhere. To Gilbert, a sneeze was no small matter. He would give the audience a glimpse of the tickle creeping up on him, use his finger to try to stop the sneeze, lose control, and explode in a hysterically funny *"ah-choo."* His career featured such zany performances as Sneezy in Walt Disney's unforgettable *Snow White and the Seven Dwarfs* and Hermann Göring in Charlie Chaplin's *The Great Dictator*.

In later years, a Hollywood trade paper created a problem for Gilbert. A Universal property man with the same name had recently died, and the trade paper announced his death. The Gilbert household was bombarded with telephone calls. When Gilbert called the newspapers to announce he was still alive, a startled columnist demanded to know if Gilbert could prove he wasn't a prankster, but the real McCoy. He inhaled, paused for a moment, and then let the mightiest of sneezes explode out over the telephone wires.

Hugh Herbert, another of Universal's regulars, discovered his trademark while working on a Wheeler-Woolsey film, *The Diplomaniacs*. After a night on the town, Herbert unexpectedly found that he had to shoot on location. While standing under a tree with Louis Calhern, he heard the wind howling and he began crying *"woo, woo, woo-woo."* For years to come, he was known as the "woo-*woo*" actor. In the zany world of Universal, an actor could be typecast in the strangest ways.

As a young actor, I had the very pleasant shock of breaking into pictures with some of Hollywood's finest actors and directors. Since the contract system was the only aspect of the picture business with which I was familiar, I assumed that a contract actor was popped into pictures of quality. It was an equal shock to find out that a contract actor could go from a masterpiece to a piece of cheese as quick as the studio could say, "Here's your next assignment!" But I learned that any film could produce its share of amazing characters, and there might be a story behind the enigmatic smile on the face of almost anyone on the set.

While standing on the set of *A Little Bit of Heaven*, I saw a vaguely familiar face among the extras. There was something about the smile, the way this man looked at the cameras, that seemed to ring a bell. I knew that a whole supporting cast of silent film actors were making cameo appearances in our film, and then I realized that this man, working as an extra for seven and a half dollars a day, had once been the biggest star in Hollywood. Ironically, no one else seemed to notice Charles Ray, an actor who had seen his flame blaze through the Hollywood skies only to slip away like an elusive comet.

Charlie Ray was born in Illinois. He had come to Hollywood during the silent film era, beginning as one of the Ince players. He played small parts at first and emerged as the equal of Wallace Reid, Harold Lloyd, and Fatty Arbuckle. He gained a reputation for wholesome pictures in the days of Theda Bara and the solid-marble bathtub. At his peak, Charlie Ray was earning $11,000 a week, one of the highest-salaried actors on the Coast.

Like many actors, Charlie dreamed of producing his own pictures. He tried to establish his own studio, raising (and subsequently spending) two million dollars to produce his own motion picture, *The Courtship of Miles Standish*. His friends' reactions were unprintable; most of them thought the film so bad that they stopped calling him on the phone. The critics were not so silent and, within a short time, the onetime idol of the silent era faced financial disaster. The phone stopped ringing. Charlie tried opening a flower shop. It failed. Then he tried a bookshop with similar results. Finally, he attempted to launch a magazine. Nothing seemed right.

Charlie ended his career in a sad, ironic comeback attempt. He got a job at Universal as a silent extra. The onetime star of the 1920s became an anonymous prop on the set, standing quietly with the other extras who once would have auditioned to do a walk-on in his films.

Sadly, *A Little Bit of Heaven* did not relaunch Charlie's career. He fell victim to an impacted tooth shortly after the film was completed. The infection spread to his jaw, and he died at the age of fifty-two, still a relatively young man with only memories of the grand and glorious days of the silents.

Charlie was not forgotten. In recent years, in a final ironic twist of fate, silent film historians have rediscovered Charlie Ray. His photograph has even been displayed in the library of the Academy of Motion Picture Arts and Sciences. I regret not having been old enough to work with him when he was one of Hollywood's biggest matinee idols.

THE KISS HEARD 'ROUND THE WORLD

• • •

Surrounded by stars, starlets, and lovely ladies, it's no wonder a young, impressionable actor might have fallen frequently in love, usually but not always unrequited.

Today we have TV commercials in which Pete Rose, Joe Namath, and Walt Frazier end up fondling a luscious dolly. This is the time of the macho athlete-lover; they, not the movie types, are the sex symbols.

In those earlier, more innocent days, most of us in sports got recognition only from the other poor bums who shared our workouts. The ladies couldn't have cared less and, even though I was in the movie business, I was still mostly an athlete and fan at heart. One of my favorites was a real star.

Betty was my first bout with unrequited love; it was a doozie. I fell, or thought I fell, for Betty Grable. She had already been married to Jackie Coogan and had hit the high spots with swingers like Harry James, so I must have been as exciting to her as a bowl of Jell-O. Of all the glamor girls in cinemaland, she had the most gorgeous figure; that world-famous shot of her looking over her shoulder in a white bathing suit warmed the libidos of millions of America's fighting men in World War II. The pinup was born. She made sex look like an all-American hobby everyone should enjoy, and about as illicit as apple pie.

I was so awed by having a date with my first real movie star, I took her out and treated her like the girl next door—a way in which even the girl next door doesn't want to be treated. I also gave her a love bauble, a gold heart with the notes and lyrics of "I've Got a Crush on You" engraved all over it. (I had already given away the first skeet trophy I ever won. Over my mother's strenuous objections, I had presented that token to Lana Turner.) But my gift to Betty was the first one I bought in a jewelry store. When Betty left me for Harry James (after only a week), I had a wonderful time feeling sorry for myself and nursing a dandy hangover. But after a few days, my recovery complete, I had a much more meaningful relationship with my loyal Thunderbird than with America's pinup with the dimples on her knees.

While working on the film, *Nice Girl*, I met the hoot of Hollywood's zaniest parties, Robert Benchley. I thought, if anything would help me forget my week's romance with Betty Grable, a good party might do the trick. So I accepted one of his invitations to drop by the Garden of Allah, his newly discovered stomping ground.

The Garden of Allah was a complex of pink Mediterranean-style stucco buildings built around a large swimming pool. Benchley, the celebrated writer, humorist, and wit, was most comfortable in New York, holding forth at the famed Round Table at the Algonquin Hotel, where Marc Connelly, Dorothy Parker, George S. Kaufman, and Alexander Woollcott flashed the wits they were famous for. But Benchley had discovered the Garden on one of his Hollywood sojourns, and while he was in California the Garden became his favorite place.

Coincidentally, my brother Jim found the pleasures of the Garden equally appealing, and he had moved into one of the bungalows. The Garden was started as a country home in the 1920s. Sunset Boulevard was still a rural road in those days, and the villa was converted to a hotel by actress Alla Nazimova, the first woman to be publicly billed as a "movie star." Nazimova added an *h* to her first name, and the Garden of Allah was born.

There was almost always a party at the Garden and half the time no one knew who was giving it. One evening I decided to drown my sorrows over Betty Grable in double martinis. In no time, I had passed out in Bob Benchley's hallway. Although I was in my new Italian suit, the arriving guests began using me as an ashtray. Before I took the final dive to oblivion, Bob Benchley came up with a suitable tag line: "Enjoy yourself, Bob, you deserve it. If I'd known how tough acting was, I wouldn't have written all those lousy reviews of you actors when I was a critic."

The Garden of Allah could be compared to today's swinging-single condos. Of course, a lot of those acting like singles were doubles, but nobody kept score, and Hollywood was always ahead of its time. Shortly after my unrequited love affair with Betty Grable, I met my first older woman. She must have been all of thirty and was a well-known European actress with a husband conveniently left at home in the old country. She took it upon herself, like a dedicated Berlitz professor, to better equip me for life in Hollywood. To this dear lady I will be eternally indebted. Her enthusiasm and imagination brought an excitement to learning I never knew existed.

Benchley, with his irreverent attitude toward everything and everybody, quickly emerged as one of the prime movers of the mischief and mayhem that became the trademark of the Garden. One day I saw Benchley and his friend Charles Butterworth pushing each other around the grounds in a wheelbarrow. ("A new game—subway," explained Benchley, with a rakish grin.) Once, he discovered the switchboard at the Garden was unattended. He left a note reading, "How do you know I might not be having a baby?" and signed it.

While Scott Fitzgerald was writing *A Diamond as Big as the Ritz* in one of the villas at the Garden, Dick Stagg, the swimming instructor, was busily pulling assorted writers and actors out of the 40' x 60' swimming pool. (Somehow antics at the Garden always ended up with someone in the pool fully clothed.)

Too much clothing was seldom the problem at the Garden. One celebrated actress was fond of wandering about her villa in the nude. She also had a pet monkey who enjoyed riding on her shoulder. One day a telegram arrived, delivered by the Western Union boy, who was horrified to be greeted at the door by the naked actress. He stammered and stuttered for a moment and then, with great aplomb, handed the telegram to the monkey and fled from the den of iniquity as fast as his legs could carry him.

Benchley, like everyone else at the Garden, enjoyed shattering the illusions of anyone he considered a stuffed shirt. One day he called the former German kaiser, Wilhelm, in exile, and when the once mighty ruler picked up the telephone, Benchley explained that he just had a desire to speak German. He was an inveterate note-leaver. Once he left a note for the milkman at Grant's Tomb. Another time, he stuck feathers to his legs and then went to a physician with complaints of a rare disease which the startled doctor could not diagnose. Benchley also once ran an advertisement in the trade papers describing his acting specialty as "society drunk roles."

After Nazimova's death, the Garden survived a variety of scandals, a sheriff's auction, and a star-studded wake in the form of a gala costume party. The buildings were then torn down, and a Savings and Loan Association was built. Progress claimed a host of Hollywood memories and an ironic brand of zany humor which could only have been the product of a man like Benchley and his age. The demolition of the Garden, a repository of many of the mad, irreverent doings of the gifted free spirits of a happier time, marked the disappearance of an important part of my life.

Another vivid part of my life at that time was the Flag Room. It was on Whitley Terrace, a small curving street wandering into the Hollywood Hills, midway between Highland and Cahuenga. It came to rest in a cul-de-sac of jumbled apartments irregularly stacked on top of each other like building blocks put together by a drunk. Each apartment was perched dangerously on its neighbor. Over each apartment grew a luxurious, tangled web of vines creating a veritable Garden of Eden effect. It was here that I learned about the birds, the bees, the barracudas, and other forms of Hollywood wildlife. A friend of mine, Alfredo de la Vega, had come up with the idea that we should each convince our mothers we needed a hideaway for meditation and study. When our mothers surprisingly agreed to this arrangement, we promised ourselves to study our favorite subjects even harder than before.

One room in particular was the highpoint of our hideaway; it was guaranteed to stimulate a damsel's interest beyond anything as trite as etchings. The room itself was no bigger than a full-size bed; the ceiling was too low to allow an adult to stand fully upright. The walls and, in particular, the ceiling were plastered with flags from every nation. So no matter where you looked there was always something to hold your interest. I devised a game that required the lady of the evening to memorize the flags on the ceiling in a given time or pay the penalty. Since she was already in a horizontal position, paying the penalty was usually no problem.

Just to keep the game interesting, we kept switching the flags around so no ringers could ever memorize their order. Our landlord lived directly above us. He was a one-legged boozer of prodigious capacity who never seemed to mind the racket downstairs as long as the door was open. Around the shank of the morning, say two or three o'clock, we would hear the *clump, clump, clump* of his wooden leg as he came to collect his toll, a beer glass of straight scotch.

The Flag Room became as well known locally as the Pump Room in Chicago. De la Vega brought a nice-looking fellow to the studio one day, and introduced him as "Ambassador Kennedy's son John." I am happy to say that Jack Kennedy found occasion to further his geopolitical studies and gain future constituents at our little pad on Whitley Terrace. (When campaigning for the presidency and talking about his experience in international relations, he never publicly discussed the Flag Room. Yet Alfredo and I always believed ourselves responsible in some small way for Jack Kennedy's early interest in remembering which flag represented which country.)

In passing, I think it's worth mentioning that I've known many of the great Hollywood stars, and only a very few of them seemed to hold the attraction for women that JFK did, even before he entered the political arena. He'd just look at them and they'd tumble. I often felt like asking him why he wasted his time on politics when he could have made it big in an important business like motion pictures.

I'm not about to list the cast, since I still live in California, but suffice it to say that through those humble portals passed a guest list that ran the gamut from the chorus line to Academy Award winners to the great Oval Office.

Those were good times for me, but for all the charm and innocence of Hollywood's golden era, those times also produced unspeakable horrors and harsh realities. While I was kissing Deanna Durbin, Adolf Hitler was starting a war.

The invasion of one country after another by the Nazi armies was a stark contrast to the fresh optimism of Deanna Durbin's films. If Deanna was America's sweetheart, this reality of war was best illustrated by the fate of another young girl. In Holland, Anne Frank joined her family in a makeshift attic, to live in fear and cold terror as they hid from the Nazi barbarians.

Anne Frank is known throughout the world today for her diary, a document full of the kind of courage and strength that manages to discover love in a world riddled with hate. *The Diary of Anne Frank* was published in twenty-one languages and subsequently made into a motion picture. Anne Frank never had the opportunity to be a real-life Cinderella. She died in a concentration camp. But despite the horrors of war, she could write in her diary that people were really good at heart. Few of us remember that one of her fondest dreams was expressed in the caption for a small photograph of herself in her diary: "This is a photo as I should wish myself to look all of the time. Then maybe I would have a chance to come to Hollywood." When the world discovered the possessions that this beautiful and optimistic child treasured during her family's hiding, they found my photograph. Anne Frank, like millions of other young girls, dreamed of finding her own "first love."

For all of Hollywood's departure from reality during those years, that very departure made it special. If, in some small way, the film industry brings a touch of magic to the Anne Franks of the world, our reward can only be measured in the intangible terms of human feeling.

4

Three Carloads of Fresh Fish

In the summer of 1940, England was being bombarded by the Nazi onslaught. Nearly everyone was convinced that Germany would win the war, and word came from London that the British Red Cross was in desperate need of funds. One morning, in a burst of patriotism, my mother announced that the best way of raising money for the British Red Cross would be a benefit play.

"Why don't we put one on?" she said.

We chose R. C. Sheriff's *Journey's End*, an heroic story of the courageous English soldiers of World War I. Since Hollywood's contingent of English actors seemed to be rather more successful than the locals, we thought we'd be assured of a star-studded night. The set was simple enough: a dugout with the thunder of battle created offstage by sound effects and while someone in the wings threw dirt onto the stage to simulate the near miss of a shell.

I was to play Raleigh, the very young, callow, second lieutenant whose innocence and experience as a soldier matched mine as an actor. Tom Skinner, a good actor who deserved better, played Stanhope, the idealistic, sensitive captain. Jon

Easton, the only professional working actor of the lot, was Osborne, with the crusty heart of gold. The only part left was that of the colonel of the brigade. Gil Stuart was the only English acting chum I had, so he was elected, with walrus mustache and much graying of hair, to play a fifty-year-old martinet whose pomposity was supposed to show what swell guys the rest of us were in contrast.

A diminutive lady with enormous eyes and a strange Oxfordian accent was enlisted as our gallant director. Her name was Helena Sorrell.

The program also proudly announced the services of Director of Special Effects, James Stack, Jr. Mother planned the evening with her usual flair. During the intermissions, refreshments were served on the terrace. She also planned to clear the studio for dancing after the performance. As opening night drew near, we began getting ticket requests from some of Hollywood's biggest stars. What was mild confusion during rehearsals began to build to raw panic.

Nothing was working out right. The collapsible set always let go at the wrong time, burying the actors in mid-sentence, doing little to bolster anyone's confidence. The sound effects record did not arrive. An album did turn up, but what was supposed to be DB 213A "Machine-Gun Sounds, Scattered and Intermittent Rifle Fire, Varying Explosions, and 75mm Cannon" turned out to be DB 213B "Bird Calls and Assorted Pastoral Sounds including Cow Moos."

Our opening night audience was a veritable who's who in Hollywood, a guest list suitable for any premiere. The front row was occupied by: C. Aubrey Smith, the dean of the English colony; Jean Hersholt, president of the Academy of Motion Picture Arts and Sciences; Basil Rathbone and Nigel Bruce, the Sherlock Holmes and Dr. Watson of the screen, who were equally close friends off camera; Edward Arnold and his charming wife Olive; Edward G. Robinson, that dear, gentle, talented friend, and his wife Gladys, herself a very gifted painter; the consul general of Great Britain; Boris Karloff; Walt Disney; Walter Wanger; Louis B. Mayer; Judy Garland; and Mickey Rooney. The rest of the audience was almost as impressive. None of us had any delusions about the reason for the stellar turnout. During the Battle of Britain they would have turned out for a sheep shearing or a taffy pull if it would help the British Red Cross.

The first act went pretty well. Midway through the second

act, I heard a great confusion backstage and much muted swearing.

"Damn it, it's not my fault. The damn thing fell off! Go beat on a tin can while I try to find it." Jim had lost the phonograph needle for the sound effects. To create the illusion of an explosion, a stagehand was supposed to toss dirt on the stage, but no sound cues to help him, the stagehand goofed. On my first exit, he caught me full in the face with dirt, driving me right back into the dugout.

"Those big German shells don't make much noise, do they?" I stammered, trying to cover the ghastly stage silence. I cleared the mud from my eyes and once again attempted my exit. This time I managed to elude the maniac with the shovel.

The *pièce de résistance* was next on the agenda. Our director had decided that an offstage cry for stretcher bearers was not enough. She demanded a feeling of reality, and devised a solution: what she called "sound in perspective," a forerunner of stereophonic sound. Six members of the cast were lined up fifty feet apart from backstage to across the street. We had only rehearsed this during the day, so we were all surprised at its amazing effect at night. It began with a loud holler nearby, "Stretcher bearers—stretcher bearers—stretcher bearers—stretcher bearers..." fadding to a faint "stretcher bearers."

The audience had little time to assimilate fully the effect of our sound in perspective before there was a scream of outrage from down the block.

"If you don't shut up, you're gonna *need* stretcher bearers."

Happily the show staggered on and later I heard murmurs from Helena of "probably an Axis sympathizer" in response to our neighbor's complaint.

Gil Stuart, all done up in colonel's pipe, mustache, and riding crop at port arms, looked like a frozen halibut. His entrance was fine until he opened his mouth. Out came a strangled Esperanto. His line was, "Oh, Stanhope old boy, good news. They're sending a carload of fresh fish up from Railhead."

What came out the first time was: "Good news. They're sending a carload of fresh fish heads up by railway."

When he saw Stanhope's horror-stricken expression, he pressed on with even more enthusiasm.

"Yes, it's good news. They're sending a carload of French rails up from Fish head."

Apparently Gil was determined to outdo Harry von Zell's

famous introduction of Herbert Hoover on radio. (No one could forget the announcement, "Here he is, folks, Hoobert Heever. Heebert Heever... Hervert Hoober... Hoobert Heever.... Yes, sir. It's the president of the United States.")

Gil finished with, "Yes, it's really good news. They're sending a carload of railheads, and some fresh fried footch . . . I mean fesh frish French fetch, fresh fatch, frish frash, frash frish. . . . *FFMMMMMMMMM.* . . ." He a took a long pause, then slowly pulling himself up and with a look into space, as if listening to a distant drummer, he gave a jaunty waggle of his crop, spun on his heel, and swaggered off to thunderous applause, proving once again why Britain won the war.

In *Journey's End* the "letters from home" sequence is supposed to pull a tear from the most hardened of audiences. This night, when I reached for the now familiar missive from my true and ever-loving fiancée, some joker had replaced it with a large French postcard graphically illustrating the arts of fellatio, sodomy, and several improvisations I never knew existed.

As I read my letter from home, my barely covered hysteria was interpreted by some as a delicate and sensitive reaction, "a stifled sob that so eloquently showed Raleigh's loneliness and need of love." Throughout my spotted theatrical career, my reviews have usually been about as valid as that one.

To the surprise of all, the dugout roof collapsed on cue and the show was over. It wasn't long before the audience and cast, too, were all in varying stages of collapse, having toasted the British with a feeling of camaraderie the survivors of Dunkirk must have felt.

It is difficult today, in light of the traumatic events which have torn nations and civilizations apart, to remember our national mood in the early 1940s. A day did not go by when gloomy reports were not broadcast over the radio, always reiterating: Germany, or, more literally, Hitler's Nazi war machine, appeared to be goose-stepping its way toward victory after victory, each one bloodier than the last. Today terms like "Maginot Line" seem isolated in textbooks. In those days they were dangerously real. It appeared entirely likely that our European allies would collapse in the face of the Nazi onslaught.

When the United States entered the war, Hollywood plunged headlong into the fury. A host of movies depicting the Nazi threat were made. Everyone from Sherlock Holmes to Donald Duck (who said, "We Heil, We Heil, Right in Der Fuhrer's

Face") was placed in a prowar, pro-America, anti-Nazi stance. But before Pearl Harbor, before we abandoned our official stance of neutrality, it was a very different situation.

Congress had a strongly isolationist element which opposed America's entry into the war. Officially, we were subject to the Neutrality Act which implied, at least in public, that our government took no official position.

It was under these conditions that I made the startling transition from Deanna's Prince Charming to active participant in the grim reality depicted in *The Mortal Storm*.

The Mortal Storm was Hollywood's first involvement with powers outside the realm of show business. Phyllis Bottome's best-seller, along with *Confessions of a Nazi Spy*, did not go unnoticed by the Third Reich. About two weeks into filming, an official-looking gent arrived on the set and was seen talking to the producer Victor Saville. By the expression on Victor's face, I knew the news wasn't good. Then I saw Robert Young pacing back and forth, his hands behind his back, mumbling, "My children, what about my children?"

It took a while for the news to filter down to me. The Swiss consulate had received word from Germany that everyone connected with *Confessions of a Nazi Spy* and *The Mortal Storm* would be "taken care of" when Hitler won the war. Since Hitler's war machine had pierced the "impregnable" Maginot Line in a few days, and now stood on the edge of the English Channel, the threat seemed more than mere hyperbole.

The German-American Bund, a pro-Nazi organization whose members waved American flags and wore swastika armbands at rallies, began making ugly noises. The atmosphere on the set was tense. Fights broke out, and the book-burning sequence almost got out of hand. The most demonic scene in the film was played by a New York actor doing his first movie. His last Broadway credit had been as a dancer. His name was Dan Dailey, and he brought such ferocity and sadism to his part as head storm trooper that during his harangue to the soldiers, a woman visitor from Austria who happened to be visiting the set fainted and had to be taken to the hospital.

As Otto von Rohn, I played the part of a young Nazi who failed to recognize the destruction of his own family. The key figure in the story was Viktor Roth, a beloved scientist played by Frank Morgan. Other members of the cast included Robert Young (as a dedicated storm trooper), Margaret Sullavan,

James Stewart, and the distinguished Russian stage star Maria Ouspenskaya. Rounding out the cast were William T. Orr, Bonita Granville, Dan Dailey, and Ward Bond.

The film was as far removed as imaginable from the fantasy world of Deanna's films. Freya, the character portrayed by Margaret Sullavan, died in the arms of the man she loved after being shot while trying to flee across the border. The professor himself died in a concentration camp. One by one, the members of the family succumbed, either as victims of the growing terror or as its unfeeling instigators.

At this same time, in 1941, I looked forward to my most exciting part to date, the young Polish flyer in *To Be or Not to Be*. The film called for a good, light comedian who would make love to a beautiful woman in her dressing room while her husband was delivering a Shakespearean soliloquy on stage! I knew I could handle the comedy. But I was startled to find out that my love scene would be played opposite one of Hollywood's most glamorous stars, Carole Lombard.

In the forties all America was in love with Carole Lombard. If Clark Gable had become Hollywood's king, Carole was most definitely his queen. On screen or off, she had a style all her own. She was a combination of many qualities. She was a cool and sophisticated lady who felt comfortable at an elegant dinner pouring tea and using a silver service. But she was equally at home with wild and woolly sportsmen who usually wouldn't welcome any woman, even one as beautiful as Carole, to their hunting lodges.

Any young actor would have given anything to work with her. In my case, however, there was a problem. Most young men found Carole irresistible, and I was certainly no exception. Carole was not a new acquaintance for me; I had first decided she was irresistible when I was thirteen years old. Carole knew my mother, and came to stay at our house at Lake Tahoe while getting her divorce from her then-husband William Powell. Of course, I instantly fell in love with this beautiful blond movie star. Love naturally isn't the same at thirteen as it is ten years later. But I found myself comparing all other women to Carole, sometimes an enthusiastic little girl and sometimes a painfully grown-up, sensuous star. I began giving Carole shooting lessons. Perhaps the reason I loved her so much was that she was always aware that the boy is a "man to be." She never condescended; we were two equals.

When she gave me an autographed picture, it was for me alone, just between us. In the photo she was standing as only she could—languidly, with one arm leaning against a wall, in a delicate, diaphanous negligee, partially back-lit. In today's Hollywood there are actresses who need to depend on explicit shots and dialogue to match, in order to establish an image. But there was more romance, mystery, and sex appeal in that photo of Carole than in any twenty combined Playboy centerfolds.

At Lake Tahoe, Carole became an outstanding shot with the shotgun. After hitting a particularly hard target, she'd let out a whoop and throw her arms around me. On the other hand, if she missed an easy one, she could swear like a trooper. Today, Hollywood is rediscovering the Lombard memory. There are those who exaggerate Carole's freewheeling language. I prefer to remember the other side of Carole Lombard. She could be "just one of the boys" on the skeet shooting field. But then she could be fragile and feminine, the tears streaming down her face, as she talked about Bill Powell. She said that the marriage hadn't worked but that Bill Powell was a great guy! One minute she could be wisecracking, clowning, and using a four-letter-word vocabulary she wouldn't dream of employing in front of my mother. The next minute, she was all glamor and feminine charm.

Of course, Clark Gable was the only man for Carole; even I couldn't fault that. Clark and I used to shoot at the old Los Angeles-Santa Monica Gun Club. Gable was a good shot. One of my biggest satisfactions, however, came when Carole proved she was a better shot than Gable on a pheasant hunt. When Carole wiped Gable's eye (When someone shoots a bird that another person has missed, this is called "wiping your eye"), she couldn't resist sending me a telegram, which I still have: "Bobby, I love you because you're the best, Carole." But Clark was a gent. He used to brag about her beating him in shooting, as long as it didn't happen too often.

When it came time for me to play opposite Carole, I found that positions were reversed. Clark and Carole both knew that I had been an all-American world record-holder in skeet shooting at seventeen. The stars at the gun club knew I could whip them easily. But when I walked onto a sound stage, I was no longer an object of admiration; I was a beginner stumbling into a world where my former shooting pupils reigned as gods.

Six years had passed since our shooting lessons at Lake Tahoe. Now Carole was married to Clark, reigning as the king's queen. Nothing had changed; she was still Carole. But now I saw her as one of the most brilliant comediennes in the business, not just as a marvelous shot and glamorous friend. During the shooting, I was so nervous in close-ups, I often moved out of range of my key light, the last thing an actor wants to do. She'd gently maneuver me right back into focus. This was a courtesy never repeated in my long and spotted career. She was given to such kindness. Still pictures are always an arduous, self-conscious experience. Today the studio sometimes uses individual frames from the film itself for publicity shots. But in those earlier days, the stars were expected to strike poses while a still photographer went to work. The photographer might yell at us to strike some mood ("passion" or "mayhem" was typical). I was terribly inexperienced. In fact, whenever Carole saw me begin to freeze, she hissed at me, "Come on, you're as lousy at this as Pop [her pet name for Gable]. You're supposed to have ants in your pants for me." The reminder of Gable was not really helpful. With Gable's image now in front of me, the ants didn't materialize. But all was not lost. She winked at Bob Coburn, that master photographer. The 8 × 10 glamor camera was whisked away, and in its place a wind machine and a small rapid-sequence Rolleiflex appeared. Suddenly, with the wind machine roaring and her blond mane flowing behind her, she started our still session by throwing her arms around my neck and almost strangling me.

"Loosen up, professor," she said, shaking me for good measure. "We're supposed to be having fun." We did.

The shots were fabulous, and this incident remained for me one of the many examples why Carole Lombard was a very special person.

Clark, of course, was also special, though in other ways. The public Gable is too well known to require further analysis. (Clark wouldn't have approved of analysis anyway. He was too busy living life to the fullest and having a good time.) There was a perpetual twinkle in his eye. He took tremendous pride in being a man's man.

But while the public Gable was having fun, the private Gable was a professional from the top of his grin to the tips of his toes. He felt a great responsibility to his job as an actor, and had no time for fits of temper or other nonsense.

Once the cameras stopped rolling, Clark's sense of humor took over. He couldn't be serious regarding his status as a matinee idol. It was as if he had his own private joke. He couldn't really understand why so many women thought he had been put on earth to fulfill the dreams of the opposite sex. But as long as enough of them felt that way, it was perfectly all right with him; he decided to enjoy himself. Considering the circumstances, who could blame him?

But sometimes, even the king was hoist by his own petard. Once, on location in Japan, Clark visited a geisha house. Many of the girls were very pretty, and Clark naturally noticed the most beautiful one of all and decided that they should be better acquainted. The lady in charge, however, took a dim view of the American movie star. She didn't mind a handsome celebrity having a night of fun. But the geisha Gable was given was very special. She was sponsored by a powerful Japanese banker, who regarded her as his personal property. She was expected to cultivate all the feminine arts and charms she could, but save them only for him.

Gable was used to having his way with the ladies. (When he walked into a shop near the duck lodge at Lake Tahoe to buy a pair of boots, the girls literally would fall over.) The *mama-san* at the geisha house was in a dilemma. She couldn't say no to Gable; nor could she let the banker find out about the actor after Gable went back to Hollywood. So she devised a unique solution. The beautiful young geisha was permitted to spend an evening with Gable, serving him dinner, making him comfortable, everything arranged to persuade Gable that it would be a night to remember. Then, when the scene was about to reach its natural denouement, the girl said quietly, "I am very shy. Can we turn out the light?" Obligingly Gable said yes in the dark.

The banker's special geisha was whisked away, and a second girl substituted. When Gable woke up in the morning, the first girl was back again, in time to give him breakfast. He assumed he had made a conquest, and went back to Hollywood congratulating himself on the fact that even in Japan, he was hard to resist. Clark never found out what happened, but word was passed to the crew.

No one ever learned what the banker thought about all this, but I thought the lady who ran that geisha house missed her calling. She should have come back to Hollywood with Gable. As an agent in the film industry, she could have made a mint.

Gable loved a challenge, even if it came from a swaggering boy (me) who should have known better. One day, at the Racquet Club, I decided I was old enough to take on the king and stared manfully at him, challenging him to match drinks.

Unfortunately, he looked me right in the eye, which should have warned me to stick to skeet shooting. He was seated at a table with a beautiful girl, as always, who looked as if she had stepped straight out of a novel by F. Scott Fitzgerald. Her wide picture hat and flowing white dress complemented Clark's casual attire perfectly. Clark was in his element, relaxed, confident, having a good time. If I wanted to drink, he'd be glad to oblige. After a preliminary drink or two, we had a five-wine dinner. By the time the fifth round came, my nerve began to fail. I was also deathly ill.

I often stayed at the Racquet Club, and I managed to excuse myself and go to my room. I have no recollection of what happened after I collapsed on the bed. But I woke up in the morning with a grade-A hangover, and when I came downstairs, the scene that greeted me did nothing to improve my constitution. I walked out from the awning into a white-hot glare of sunshine and reflected light. It was like the Sands of Kalahari. As I staggered toward the swimming pool, I managed to focus on a happy-looking group at poolside.

There was Gable, elegant, at ease, sitting at his table by the pool, wearing a white shirt open at the neck, looking as if the good life were just getting better all the time. Next to him was the beautiful girl in her picture hat. I wobbled out, and Clark saw me. "Hey, Bob," he called, "come on over. I've ordered you breakfast." I walked over to the table and sat down. I didn't have much to say. Chagrin and nausea mixed in equal parts. The waiter came around the pool, carrying a tray with my "breakfast." Gable had ordered me two double martinis.

The king picked up a glass and toasted me with a grand gesture, winking at the same time. I wouldn't drink. But Gable, enjoying himself and the situation, looked me right in the eye again. He was telling me, very gently, not to play a man's game until I had really become a man.

Several years later, after seeing my performance in *Written on the Wind*, he looked at me in a serious moment and said, "Kid, I think you're going to be all right." Like many rugged men, Clark didn't always show his emotions or feelings off camera. But the message was there just the same. Clark Gable and his good friend Ray Hommes were always welcome guests at the duck lodge. I'd known them both since I was a kid, and Ray and I even won the California State Two-Man Team Championship. This was as big a surprise to us as it was to the competition. By then I'd given up competing for skeet trophies in favor of more nocturnal sports. I showed up two minutes before the entries closed and bumped into a slightly hung-over Ray Hommes. "Want to shoot in the two-man team?" he asked me. "It looks like one of the hotshots wants us."

So we shot in the last squad and won the damn thing.

At that time, my brother Jim and I frowned on anything which took away from the tradition of duck shooting. No outboards were allowed, and the sole means of transportation to the birds a mile away in the tules were "tule splitters." (These narrow, unpredictable boats take a bit of experience to handle; otherwise the result might be an unplanned exploration of underwater flora and fauna. They are pushed along by the use of ten-foot poles which also serve to balance the whole shaky project.) Ray stands about 6'6"—a great stork of a man. He chose this particular windy day to wear a waterproof cape worthy of *Phantom of the Opera*. He and Clark got into the boat with guns, shells, and two bottles of White & McKay twenty-one-year-old scotch.

As Ray raised his arms to pole the boat, the wind caught the cape, and away they went. He was smart enough to use the pole as a rudder, but they were going too fast to stop without turning over. I saw them sail out of sight past our property toward the West Butte Duck Club, two miles away. They finally got into the West Butte territory and had a dandy shoot. When the president of the club came over to arrest them as poachers, he took one look at Gable and invited them both to dinner; they spent the night there. The next day, Clark tried poling and dumped the boat, Ray, and the guns into the water only twenty feet from the boat landing. The next year, Jim and I decided to get outboards for our guests.

The night after his total immersion, Clark dragged out the twenty-one-year-old White & McKay scotch and, after Ray had gone to bed, we proceeded to make sure it wouldn't be twenty-two years old.

Clark finally put down his drink and looked me in the eye without his customary ironic twinkle.

"You know, in all the time we've known each other, we've never talked about the business. I get enough of that crap on the set. I also was never sure if you were serious or, more important, if you were any good. I saw a couple of the last things you did, and I think maybe you've got a chance. But I'll tell you one thing. It's not like winning the nationals or busting the record in a speedboat. It's not a sport; it's a kind of craziness. But even so, there are rules. The first and most important is to be a professional. Know your lines, show up on the set on time, don't foul up the author's intent, and when the makeup comes off, the performance stops.

"Remember, if you like what you see up there on the screen, ninety percent of the credit goes to the writers, directors, crew, and the cutter. When it doesn't work, it's like hell on earth; when it does, it's like getting paid for having a good time.

"Now let's cut the bull and get back to something serious like duck shooting."

Clark, along with Ray Hommes and Barron Hilton, later joined a fancy duck club called Venice Island, on the Stockton River. I didn't get to shoot much with him after that. But one time, many years later, Barron invited me up for a shoot. Clark was gone by then, but not forgotten.

On a shelf in the main room stood a bottle of White & McKay twenty-one-year-old scotch, with Gable's glass alongside; underneath lay his old Parker 12-gauge. The King is dead, but long live the king wherever he is, and wherever he is, I hope there are beautiful women, plenty of good scotch, and a duck pond loaded with mallards.

There have, of course, been other kings and queens in Hollywood. (The public relations boys are creating new ones every day.) But there is a reason, a special reason, why the memory of Gable and Lombard stays with us. They possessed a special brand of dash, style—an ability to live the good life to its fullest. In *That's Entertainment*, Gable dominates the screen as no one else could. Gable could keep the public's attention with his personal magnetism, his charisma, in a way that no other major stars could equal.

We lost Carole right after *To Be or Not to Be*. News of the tragic plane crash that took her life was all too soon in coming. My autographed photo of Carole disappeared—along with my picture of Fredric March as Mr. Hyde, autographed in purple ink—with a host of boyhood memories. Clark went on, of course, to marry my good friend Kay Williams, and continue his career as a Hollywood legend.

Even as he grew older, Clark Gable insisted on competing, on proving that he could still keep up with younger men. Shortly before he made his last film *The Misfits*, our mutual friend Ray Hommes said, "I'm worried about Clark."

I said, "Is he sick?"

He said, "No, but if Marilyn Monroe doesn't behave herself, God knows what might happen when they work together."

I only knew Marilyn Monroe at the beginning and just before the end of her career. I first met Norma Jean Daugherty before she changed her name, when a good-looking Hungarian actor named Eric Feldari took her to one of our swimming parties. She wore a white bathing suit, which she filled beautifully, but then so did most of the other pretty girls. I remember only that she appeared to be shy and somehow on the outside of everything taking place at the party. I tried being a good host, and every time I'd ask if she wanted anything, she'd say, "No, everything is fine."

Feldari found a more communicative companion, and when the party broke up, she was the only one left. Finally Bill Burnside, a man many years her senior, took her home. He became a close friend to her and, as it turned out, shot many of her last still pictures.

Now, as Marilyn Monroe, the shy girl I met had become an international star with a reputation for being very difficult to handle on the set. She was quite insecure and went through an agony of doubts and frustrations before walking onto a sound stage.

So much has been written of Marilyn, so many best-selling books and quotes from the famous, that we all forget she was a classic throwback to Hollywood's golden years, when everyone was out of time, when success and self-destruction became synonymous.

The most beautiful woman ever to grace the silver screen died in a sanitarium in her twenties. Barbara LaMarr was so breathtaking she was called the too-beautiful-to-be-real girl. Several threatened suicide, and they say one even carried out the threat, all for love of beauteous Barbara.

Jean Harlow was my choice of the sexiest lady in motion pictures. The irony is that she hated the sex symbol trap that brought her nothing but envy, misery, and death. There was another suicide, but this time more tragic than the others. Her husband Paul Bern killed himself, left a note saying that he did it for her. Bill Powell, the only man she ever loved, and who loved her, was afraid to marry her. The sex goddess image was too much even for him. Jean Harlow died at age twenty-six.

Poor Marilyn escaped none of the tortures of being a sex symbol but at least she lived long enough to worry about her first wrinkle.

I never saw Clark Gable happier than just before he left to do *The Misfits* opposite Marilyn. I don't think he liked the Arthur Miller script that much but, pro that he was, he went on a crash diet and was ready to give it his best shot. It's hard to believe this man they called the king was as excited as a kid to be working with Montgomery Clift, but therein lay his charm. He never stopped being a fan of his profession and the best people in it.

Of course, his competitive drive made him do his own stunts at an altitude of 6,000 feet, and the problems of working with Marilyn Monroe must have torn him apart inside. But on the outside, he did his best to understand and even help this poor, sad, displaced young woman.

After the heart attack no one really thought was serious, Clark had Chasen's cater his dinners in the hospital. We all thought he'd be out in a week. I wrote him a note, "Hurry up and get off your butt. We've got some duck shooting to do." An hour after I mailed it, I heard on the news that he was dead.

I was privileged to know both these great stars in the days when they were young, happy, and full of life. The pictures of Carole and the awkward young man I once was are now hanging in my den. They serve as a constant reminder that neither Gable nor Lombard took their own lives too seriously. A touch of humor, a dash of spice, and the ability to act unconsciously larger than life. Somehow, they made the rest of us feel the same way.

Working on *To Be or Not to Be* also provided one of the great thrills of my incipient movie career: a chance to be directed by the legendary Ernst Lubitsch. Of all the directors in Hollywood, none was considered to have a greater flair for comedy than Lubitsch. Jack Benny thought Ernst Lubitsch the greatest director of all. A small man with dark hair and surprisingly sad eyes, Lubitsch had enormous enthusiasm for dancing, good cigars, and *himbeeresaft*, a cold raspberry juice drink which reminded him of his European boyhood.

Lubitsch's trademark was a unique attention to little things, small details which told an entire story in a single close-up. A book on a desk, a piece of jewelry, any pose or shot that could indulge in ironic commentary on the human failings of his characters, would be ideal for his satiric imagination. Wit, irony, charm, satire, and a lighthearted acceptance of man's vulnerability had distinguished the Lubitsch comedies from dozens of others filmed in Hollywood.

Lubitsch had once been a comedian in Berlin. He had discovered Pola Negri, the star of silent films, and reached the peak of his career directing such comedies as *Ninotchka* starring Greta Garbo. So it was perhaps the most ironic twist of fate that so much controversy eventually surrounded *To Be or Not to Be*, Lubitsch's satire on the Nazis who invaded Poland.

From the beginning, it was clear that Lubitsch had boundless energy. (Ben Hecht once described him as resembling a kangaroo on a pogo stick, because of the zest with which he bounded from one idea to another.) In the cutting room, he didn't just edit film, he attacked it. Yet he was sensitive to the feelings of writers. He once called Samson Raphaelson, one of his favorite writers, and asked him to make a special trip to the studio. When Raphaelson arrived, Lubitsch asked his permission to change *one line* of dialogue in a script. Few directors would show a writer this courtesy, especially if they were as creative as Lubitsch.

Lubitsch was enthusiastic about the United States. He once expressed his joy over the prospect of working in America. "Ziegfeld Follies," he exclaimed, "pretty girls. . . . I will like America." He loved chewing gum, which he called "California fruit," and American music. (He told a reporter his hobbies were "d'piano, d'cello, and d'shimmy.") On the set of *To Be or Not to Be* he had no time for a megaphone or the artificial trappings of directorial authority. He would hop about the sound stage, ready to give instructions and encouragement, or to demonstrate the way he wanted a scene played with his own unique sense of comedic timing.

He could laugh, cry, and grimace on cue; his hands would move in wild gesticulations as he made his points. Usually, actors would be quick to follow instructions. If not, Lubitsch was ready to give them another demonstration.

With his sense of irony, he understood that *To Be or Not to Be* was ahead of its time. Today it is regarded as a classic, a film worthy of its great director and clearly marked by the "Lubitsch touch."

Today it is difficult to explain the very real fears which existed during the prewar era. But many Americans were convinced in the forties that a German air attack on the United States was a possibility. Blackouts were required. Residents of Bel-Air, where Lubitsch lived, agreed to serve as block wardens, to insure that all the lights on the block were turned out, thus providing no targets for passing enemy planes. Lubitsch, doing his patriotic duty for his adopted country, discovered a house with all the lights on. He raced up and down the block, shouting instructions to the offending neighbors, all in his thick German accent. Laurence Olivier, living nearby, heard Lubitsch screaming German oaths at the owner of the house with its lights on.

The script for *To Be or Not to Be* was written by Edwin Justus Mayer, and based on a story developed by Lubitsch and Melchoir Lengyel. Controversy developed immediately over a scene in which Sig Ruman, playing a Nazi general, reacted to Jack Benny's rendition of a Shakespearean soliloquy with the line, "What he did to Shakespeare we are now doing to Poland."

The audience at the sneak preview of the film roared with laughter at the scenes between Jack Benny and Carole Lombard. But the Sig Ruman line brought dead silence from the audience. Following the preview, Lubitsch and some of his friends stopped for a drink and to exchange reactions. His friends were unanimous: The line in question must go!

Lubitsch insisted the line was necessary. He would willingly cut a poor joke from a film, but when his friends insisted that the line was in bad taste, Lubitsch disagreed. Samuel Hoffenstein, the famed writer of light verse, happened to be in the nightclub, and when he passed the director's table, he, too, stopped to protest the use of the destruction of Poland as the subject of a joke.

A chorus of critics were quick to agree. *Time* magazine supported Lubitsch, but virtually every other major critic insisted the line was offensive.

Nor did the public understand. Jack Benny's father, furious when he saw the comedian dressed in a Nazi uniform, walked out of the theater. It took Jack an hour to persuade his father that the picture was really a comedy.

Eventually, Lubitsch felt it necessary to write to the newspapers, explaining his point of view. Lubitsch was angry that critics emphasized his German origins in their criticism. He said, "What I have satirized in this picture is the Nazis and their ridiculous ideology. I have also satirized the attitude of actors who always remain actors regardless of how dangerous the situation might be, which I believe is a true observation." He went on to praise the gallant people of Poland, and to demand that critics confine themselves to a legitimate discussion of whether or not satire was an appropriate genre for the subject matter. He was deeply hurt by implications that he personally found anything about the invasion of Poland amusing.

Had Lubitsch lived longer, he would have seen *To Be or Not to Be* regarded as one of the great classics of Hollywood. It was a privilege to be associated with this film, which has helped to make the name and legend of Lubitsch among the most respected by filmmakers today.

If participating in films such as *The Mortal Storm* and *To Be or Not to Be* was one of my greatest thrills, the same could not be said for my publicity tour with Louella Parsons. One of the fringe benefits of being a contract player was being told that you had volunteered for a publicity tour. These tours helped promote the studio's pictures and made Louella a lot of money.

On my particular tour, in 1940, I was scheduled for a seven-show-a-day personal appearance gig with Louella, Mike Frankovich, Binnie Barnes, Sabu the elephant boy, and a few other assorted poor souls. It was not our overwhelming love of these junkets that sent us around the country. But no one turned Louella down in those days, unless he was planning to leave the picture business prematurely. Actually Louella wasn't a bad old gal. She had been a friend of the family since the Lake

Tahoe and Carole Lombard days. But she did have her peculiarities. Her sneakiest and most valuable asset was looking either stupid or drunk, and getting exclusives in the process. When she seemed her most plastered at parties, she would have pencil and paper in her lap, taking down every juicy word. She could never remember where we were on tour, and our final number would be thrown into a state of confusion by "Lolly's" poor grasp of geography.

As a finale, someone had come up with the brilliant idea of having Louella say a fond farewell to the audience while the rest of us were wiggling and twisting around the stage in the background, singing and doing the cha-cha to the accompaniment of maracas. Louella would tell a packed house in Chicago how delighted we were to be in Minneapolis. (In Minneapolis she had already said we were happy to be somewhere else.) I sometimes drew the lucky assignment of trying to make sure Louella knew where we were, without losing a beat of the cha-cha.

Minor matters of geography did not distract Sabu, however, this fifteen-year-old East Indian had become a star after he appeared in a movie called *Elephant Boy*. He had large, liquid brown eyes filled with a sad innocence that belied the string of knowing blond "fans" who visited his dressing room, every hour on the hour, sometimes in pairs. The rest of us consoled ourselves by assuming it had something to do with his diet of curry and straight scotch. Brenda Joyce, a beauteous blond who was later to become another Jane to Lex Barker's Tarzan was a welcome addition. She and I did a boring number on a park bench about young love. Boring to the audience, perhaps, but I am happy to say that it beat the hell out of doing the cha-cha with Louella.

Mike Frankovich was an ex-football player turned radio announcer. When the master of ceremonies got sick, Mike stepped in and told some terrible jokes he'd been telling us for weeks. After the first hesitant laugh, he was bitten by the comedian's bug. Suddenly we had a new permanent MC. Mike went on to become the head of Columbia Studios and producer of such hits as *Butterflies Are Free*. But his joke-telling really hasn't improved.

In Steubenville, Ohio, he played a trick I'll never forget.

Just before the show, he told me that my romance with a certain dolly might lose me fans, because fans like their idols unattached. When I was in my dressing room, he instructed the audience not to applaud when I walked out on the stage. The audience went along with the gag but, in the meantime, a couple came late and missed Mike's request. After the usual speech, in which Mike praised me as the all-American boy, Deanna's Prince Charming, I ran out to the acclaim of the few and the silence of the many. There was a deafening silence that reached the rafters, broken only by three claps from the latecomers which faded after two seconds. Even a performing seal gets a little applause and, just as I had become accustomed to being unnoticed by the public in my premovie days, I had finally adjusted to being somewhat in the spotlight. The walk out to center stage felt like the last mile. I have never felt so absolutely lost in my life. Finally, when I reached the microphone, he said under his breath, "I told you romance might kill you off." I stood there like a refugee from a wax museum. Then, finally, the dirty rat said, "Let's show Bob how we really feel about him," and the place fell apart!

Seldom does Hollywood shake off its self-satisfied superiority and remember its beginning as a non-descript village of nickleodeon salesmen. But it took only one word to do it: *Garbo!*

In 1941, Camille was coming out of retirement; Queen Christina was deigning once again to share her nobility with the peasants; and Metro-Goldwyn-Mayer had somehow convinced the mysterious Swede to do a comedy called *Two-Faced Woman*, to be directed by that diplomat and master of female foibles George Cukor. Cukor was recognized as the town's finest woman's director, who had tamed the worst shrews Hollywood had to offer.

The Gold Rush had nothing on the mass of young male hopefuls who attacked MGM when word got out that there was a romantic juvenile lead to be cast. Like lemmings, they descended on Culver City with swollen biceps, deltoids at the ready, and biographies filled with extravagant lies. The chance to play opposite Garbo had Walter-Mittied every young man in town into seeing himself as another John Gilbert. After a massive screening process it boiled down to that most nerve-wracking of Hollywood tortures: the screen test. Here you become part of a fleshy production line with rejection and humiliation the norm while the word "Star," like a vision of sugar plums, spells itself out in flashing lights on the marquee of each participant's overwrought imagination.

I was fidgeting in the makeup room wishing I could locate Jack Pierce to glue on the hated widow's peak, just so I could look a little like Robert Taylor in *Ninotchka*. Then I heard "Cut, print, okay, next!"

George Cukor, always the gentleman, met me and explained the test. It was a happy, "tennis anyone?" young-people scene and looked easy. He said, "Bobby, I want you to be light, charming, and gay." (In the forties, "gay" meant happy.) I made my entrance, got through the first line only to be stopped by Cukor with "No, Bobby, much lighter."

So I tried it again, "much lighter," but was interrupted with, "No, Bobby, no, happy, be happy, I want a big smile."

With the idiotic grin of a Cheshire cat, I once more attacked the poor defenseless scene.

"That's it, Bobby, only more like this."

Many good directors tend to exaggerate a scene to give the actor the key. However, in George's case the exaggeration, plus endless hours guiding Hollywood's leading femmes, produced a surprising result. I saw my image of John Gilbert suddenly become Joan Crawford.

I began to form a horror-stricken vision of myself in ballet slippers and tutu, making my entrance on tippy-toes. My final effort was the ultimate fiasco. My subconscious wouldn't let me copy Cukor's bizarre speech pattern, until I lost my voice completely. My entrance was joyous, the grin was devil may care, but what came out of my mouth was pure Peter Lorre. This hoarse croak lasted through the entire test. The next day, George Cukor called.

"Bobby, I just saw the test."

Oh Lord, I thought. *I'll never work again.*

"It was really very good, light and full of fun."

I could imagine.

"There's just one thing though, your voice came out a little hoarse, and we could hardly hear you."

That's a blessing, I thought.

Then this kind, gentle man said, "I suggest you see a dear friend of mine, Mrs. Fogler. She's world famous and I know she'll help you."

The next day, I went to see Mrs. Fogler, a charming, gray-haired lady, who handed me a *Hamlet* soliloquy and asked me to read.

"Why you have a perfectly splendid voice," she said. "Why

are you here? By any chance did Mr. Cukor send you to see me?"

I nodded.

She paused and gave me a quizzical look.

"You know, you'd be surprised how many pupils he's sent me."

My good chum Bob Sterling got the part. The movie was not a success, and Greta Garbo never again graced the silver screen. Much later, after four years on "The Untouchables," I was called "the great stone face," and asked why I never had a light moment or gave out with a grin.

I was tempted to say, "I'm afraid to, 'cause when I do, I lose my voice."

In 1942, I acted in my first real war picture. It was called *Eagle Squadron*, and it would be hard to forget.

Eagle Squadron was produced by Walter Wanger. This film was responsible for a whole series of memories, some poignant, some touching, and some funny. I don't know what category to assign to my off-screen working relationship with one of my co-stars.

Walter Wanger had been responsible for bringing such stars as Jeanne Eagles, Claudette Colbert, Ginger Rogers, and the Marx Brothers to the screen. So when word came that the love interest in *Eagle Squadron* would be portrayed by a renowned stage actress, I expected someone really extraordinary. The someone turned out to be a sad and thoroughly mixed-up lady with a famous name: Diana Barrymore.

I didn't really dislike Diana. I felt rather sorry for her. She had grown up in the shadow of the most famous theatrical family in the world. Her father John Barrymore was a legend, and while his self-destructive drinking habits made life impossible for his friends, relatives, and colleagues, no one could deny Barrymore's consummate acting skill.

Diana had managed to acquire many of the outer trappings of being a Barrymore: the inclination to drink away her problems, a fiery temper, and an erratic emotional perspective. But she had had neither the time nor the training to acquire the enormous technical foundation in acting that other members of her famous family had had. The result, of course, simply compounded her own frustrations. She wanted to be a Barrymore in every sense, and unfortunately this included the least appealing qualities of John Barrymore.

Diana had a special way of playing a love scene. She would

lean forward and, out of the upstage corner of her mouth, the side invisible to the stage audience before which she was used to performing, she editorialized. "As an actor, you really stink," she might coo.

Once, we went to see the rushes. Diana was endearing. "I don't understand it," she said. "How can anybody who is as lousy as you are look so much better on film?"

I just smiled and said, "Maybe I'm not as lousy as you think I am, and maybe you're not as good as you think you are." Also starring in the film were Eddie Albert, Nigel Bruce, Leif Erikson, Jon Hall, Isobel Elsom, and the great English star Gladys Cooper. But one of the most memorable performances in the film came from a man who wasn't an actor at all: the famed journalist Quentin Reynolds.

Reynolds had experienced a long personal association with members of the real Eagle Squadron, American fighting men who had volunteered for service in the RAF and who at that very moment were being killed in the deadly air war taking place over Britain. He had written a book, *Only the Stars Are Neutral*, devoted to the story of Eugene "Red" Tobin, a onetime MGM office boy, who became top man in the Eagle Squadron and was killed on the same day Reynolds had planned to give him a birthday party. Wanger acquired some film footage of Tobin climbing into his spitfire. One of the film's many tragic ironies, it was the last time he was ever photographed. The audiences for *Eagle Squadron*, of course, had no way of knowing that the man they saw getting into his plane was on an actual mission from which he would never return.

We also met John M. Hill, a pilot officer in the RAF, who came to Hollywood for an eight week sabbatical from the war. He had been leading a squadron of night fighters taking off from a British airport when a fuel truck ran across his path in the dark. The result was a broken leg, a temporary leave from the RAF, and a job as our technical advisor.

The screenplay was written by Norman Reilly Paine and was based on a story by C.S. Forester. But it was Reynolds's voice which gave the film's introduction its special quality.

Reynolds had recently returned from the Russian front, and he brought us news of the war: sad, terrifying details of the struggle which was enveloping the world. Today the battles and memories have receded into the volumes of history books and statistics but, then, they were as real as the ordeal of our MIAs in Vietnam.

Reynolds began narrating the introduction to the film in his compelling voice: "*Eagle Squadron* is the story of some of our countrymen who did not wait to be stabbed in the back. They quit their college classrooms... their jobs... went to England ... saw ghastly death come from the skies. They asked no favors... became respected in the RAF as one of the finest fighter squadrons. I knew these boys.... I saw them fight.... I saw them die. These boys who did not wait... these few to whom so many of us owe so much...."

Then he mentioned the men by name. It is doubtful that many Americans would remember the names of these flyers today. But every one of these men had been killed in action, a grim reminder that *Eagle Squadron* was more than a motion picture. It was the record of real men fighting and dying in a real war which was actually taking place over England.

I portrayed an American test pilot who came to England and saw his best friend killed in his first battle across the English Channel. Wanger sent Merion Cooper, his friend and a prominent producer, to London where, working in cooperation with the British Air Ministry, he acquired actual film footage of several squadron raids. We have a view of the cliffs of Dover, pilots bailing out over the channel, and actual German antiaircraft guns in France. The British government was sensitive about releasing the films but, after six months of cables, letters, and transatlantic phone calls, the Air Ministry finally said yes. Two prints were sent to the United States, one by clipper, one by boat. *Eagle Squadron* was the first commercial film to show actual Spitfires in combat.

When the squadron went into action, their planes bore a Disneyesque eagle wearing boxing gloves, posed in a belligerent fighting stance. *Eagle Squadron*, as a film and as a symbol of some courageous men, was an experience I like to think will not be forgotten.

While filming *Eagle Squadron*, I was in constant touch with my old and dear friend Gilchrist Stuart, of "Fresh Fish from Railhead" fame. He started in our business at the same time I did, and had the scars to show it. By now mother had unofficially adopted him, and he was a frequent and always welcome house guest. At dinner he would regale us with his newest adventures or, in most cases, misadventures.

Gilly had arrived in Hollywood at the request of Arthur Rank, one of England's most important film producers. He went to the El Capitan College of the Theater, intending to lose his heavy British accent. It took him only a few days to realize the dollies found the accent irresistible, and his renditions of "Once More into the Breach, Dear Friend" were jealously referred to by his fellow students as "Once More into Your Britches, Dear Friend."

When Rank asked for a recording of his voice to check the improvement, he sounded worse than when he had arrived. Exit Arthur Rank.

Another reason Gilly didn't lose his English accent was that he was very proud to be a member of the English colony in Hollywood. Having left foggy London for sunny California, the British could be seen rushing around the UCLA campus, protecting a wicket, nose-diving into a scrim in rugby, or spending the afternoon with croquet mallets in hand at Howard Hawks's or Sam Goldwyn's. Where else could one find a cricket team including Ronald Colman, Basil Rathbone, Nigel Bruce, David Niven, George Sanders, and Roland Young?

The undisputed dean of the English colony was an urbane character actor named Sir C. Aubrey Smith. When I worked with Sir Aubrey in *Little Bit of Heaven*, he said he hadn't missed a Hollywood cricket match in sixty-four years. The unflappable Sir Aubrey always had the last word. When a local drunk became abusive in a restaurant and demanded, "What do you have to do to get a glass of water in this joint?" Sir Aubrey turned around and quietly suggested, "Why don't you try setting yourself on fire?"

He had even once managed to get the best of George Bernard Shaw. As a young actor, he had played a small part, a policeman, in one of Shaw's plays. He asked Shaw for permission to play the part as an Irishman. The unsuspecting Shaw, not imagining what was in store, said yes. When Shaw went to see the play, he was astonished to find the young Aubrey Smith made up to look exactly like Shaw himself.

Right after the war, Gil got a part in *Forever Amber*, the film version of a best-selling novel about the mistress of Charles II of England. It starred Linda Darnell, Cornell Wilde, and John Russell, and was directed by Otto Preminger. Gil was in it, too—heroically, as it turned out.

Working with Otto was an experience similar to total immersion and shock treatment combined. He's one of that old school of tyrannical directors; he believes that real blood on the actors is better than makeup. The first night of location shooting, Gil came home with a great gash on his leg. He was dressed in a floppy seventeenth-century hat, silken bloomers, and pointy-toed boots. In a chase scene across the ninth hole of the Riviera Country Club (doubling for the sake of the movie as an English country-side), his bloomers had caught on a tree limb. He gallantly finished his ride in his shorts, with the silken pants streaming behind him like a battle flag.

The following night he showed up with two black eyes. He'd forgotten that horses in the days of the movie had no martingales, the piece of leather that keeps the horse's head from coming back in the rider's face. When the chase went into a ditch, the horse's head naturally came back as it went downhill, bashing him in between the eyes. Presto! Two black eyes and overtime for the makeup man.

Filming went on for a month. When Gilly came home one night, mumbling something about not being hungry, and went upstairs to his room, I went up to check. This time he'd broken his nose in a sword fight and didn't want to ruin dinner with his unsightly appearance. His big moment came when he found himself postured on his horse directly behind Linda Darnell and Cornel Wilde for their farewell scene. In rehearsal, he gave the horse a little kick to see if it would move, and was pleased to see it make a nervous sidestep. When Preminger screamed "action" Gilly, thinking it was now or never to get some notice, gave the horse a stab of the spurs. What happened next exceeded his wildest expectations. The horse reared, pawing the air with its front hooves, and leaped forward until its hooves were directly over the heads of the two stars. For a moment everyone froze in place like figures in a French tapestry: two lovers in the foreground with the great warhorse towering over them. Gil desperately hauled in the reins and the horse came back over on top of him, scattering extras all over the Riviera Country Club.

There was a long pause.

"Mr. Gilbert, are you trying to kill my two stars?" said Preminger. "I've been watching you try to kill yourself but, my God, this is going too far. Mr. Gilbert. Watch what you're doing!" Preminger continued, screaming in his best storm trooper dialect, which panicked the already edgy horse.

Behind Preminger's eyes was the hint of a twinkle.

"If you are ready, Mr. Gilbert, we'll try again, this time without so much talent, please."

In the next take, Gilly was happy to remain quietly in the background. Otto Preminger had noticed him and "Mr. Gilbert" was better than "hey you."

When times are rough in the flicks, many of us take to the boards to pay the bills. Gilly was certainly no exception. At a lean moment, he got a role in *White Cargo*, a racy play in its time about an Englishman gone to seed for love of a native girl, Tondolayo. It seemed harmless enough but, as it turned out, there were certain risks in the play, depending on how raunchy a performance the girl delivered. Gil's performance in *White Cargo* was one none of us could forget, least of all Gil.

He told me he felt a sense of foreboding when he saw that the actress playing Tondolayo was wearing a stripper's G-string and energetically masaging her nipples with an ice cube prior to her entrance. "This ought to give those horny bastards their jollies," she murmured while slinking seductively onto stage.

Her first line, after an impressive pause, was, "I am Tondolayo." On opening night, she had no sooner said "I am Tondolayo" when from the balcony, as if on cue, came a voice announcing, "And I am going to lay you."

From there, things got worse. She began doing bumps and grinds. Fights broke out. The cops arrived with the paddy wagon and carted the whole cast off to Lincoln Heights Jail, the Devil's Island of Tinseltown.

I didn't go to the opening night performance, and I was the most surprised person in the world when Gil called me to arrange his bail. After I posted bail, we closed a couple of bars. He finally came out with his only comment on the fiasco.

"My God," he said, "I'm a jailbird because of a frozen-nippled nitwit."

Because he had a distant Canadian relative, Gilly decided to join the Canadian Scottish Highlander. He apparently yearned to go into battle in kilts with his knobby legs for all to see.

He would come down on leave from Canada and, every time, he was a different rank. First he was a sergeant, then a corporal, then a private. We never knew how to address his mail.

One balmy summer day, he arrived on a week's leave. Everyone was around the pool in bathing suits. He was in kilt and jacket, and even the most pneumatic of the many pretty starlets there couldn't get him to doff his uniform. I happened to be passing his room after he'd taken a shower, and I quickly realized why.

Perfect geometric squares of raw sores and scar tissue marched across his back like some angry disease.

With great embarrassment, he explained that the only way he was able to get leave was to volunteer for an experiment. Mustard gas was the problem. The British were still worried that Hitler might use the kaiser's favorite weapon. When they decided to test two dozen salves as possible antidotes, Gil offered his services as a guinea pig. Before the antidotes were tested, they applied mustard gas to his back. Some of the salves worked, and some didn't, so Gilly ended up looking like a patchwork quilt.

"Anyway," he mumbled, "there was something about me and an officer's wife, and I'd never get leave through normal channels but I promised Betzi I'd come down in June, so here I am." Gil hadn't changed.

Before we took off for different part of the world, we managed to flabbergast most of the populace of Beverly Hills by our antics. I drove around with Gil on my motorcycle, Gil on the pillion seat in his kilts, me in my navy uniform, just a navy man and friend. Heads turned and Gil got the "God knows what uniform this is, Harry, but it must be an ally" look.

After World War II, when times were tight, Gil wore a ratty-looking sport coat with as many holes as Swiss cheese. When I left a check for fifty dollars on the dresser, I hoped he'd take the hint. The next day, mother received fifty dollars' worth of roses. Still in his crummy coat, he thanked me profusely and said he'd pay me back later, which he did.

Gil Stuart's sorties into the arena of love were not without drama either. One particular incident (which has since become a classic) took place on a balmy summer night in the fifties. Gil had gone to his favorite watering hole, Hollywood's version of an English pub on the Sunset Strip called Ella Campbell's. Here he mingled with the other expatriots, throwing darts and looking for quiff, the empire's equivalent of a cooperative female companion. His dart scores were never high, since his eye was mostly on the bar, looking for a more important score. Finally, he saw the girl of his dreams, a luscious, heavy-lidded blond in her twenties, who was throwing admiring glances his way. The two hit it off instantly, and she found Gil's accent, the one that cost J. Arthur Rank ten thousand dollars to try to eradicate, "too sexy for words." They both drank it up until closing time, and weaved out to Gil's vintage Jaguar SS100 roadster in search of the nearest motel. There were three conventions in town, and the first vacancy was way out on Ventura Boulevard in the San Fernando Valley.

As Gil opened the motel door for his lady, she stumbled and almost fell on her face.

"Darling, I have to tell you a secret," she said. "I'm a little drunky-poo. Why don't you get us some coffee? I want to be at my best for you." She gave him a lingering kiss. "Hurry back, lover."

Gil hurdled into the Jaguar roadster and soared down Van Nuys Boulevard in search of an all-night coffeeshop. There was only one problem. It was 3 A.M. and, in those days, the San Fernando Valley used to roll up the sidewalks by eleven. So he had to drive half way to Santa Barbara before he found a joint open. He rushed back in the direction of his lady love, coffee carton in hand, when he suddenly realized he'd forgotten the name of the motel. He reached into his pocket and began to breathe more easily when his finger wrapped around the motel key. He stopped under a street light and looked for the name. There was the room number: 227! But that was all, no name or address on the key.

The identifying tag had dropped off, probably when he threw himself into his car. Between the coffeeshop and Universal Studios, there were at least fifty motels of varying shapes and sizes. He was too bombed to remember any details beyond his panting partner who was waiting expectantly to fulfill his wildest desires. So he did the only logical thing. He began knocking on every motel door number 227. By the time he got to his tenth motel, the local constables were there to escort him to the Valley jail.

When he told them the sad tale of his search for a love lost in an unknown motel room, the station house fell apart, and all charges were dropped.

But somewhere in a motel on Ventura Boulevard in room 227, a fifty-year-old, heavy-lidded blond may still be anxiously waiting for a cup of coffee and her long lost British lover.

Gil coutinued to be one of Hollywood's busiest character actors. He spent months in Tahiti with Marlon Brando, Trevor Howard, and Richard Harris making *Mutiny on the Bounty*.

He also played the sneaky butler in *The Sound of Music*. In between, he found time to tackle the Cresta run at St. Moritz. He could do it all!

Not very long ago, I called Gil to see how he was.

"What's new?" I said.

"I've got cancer," came the forthright reply.

"Oh, my God!"

"Not at all, old man. I'm taking chemotherapy. As a matter of fact, I've got my own little pump that pushes the stuff through my throat. It's supposed to take away all the nasties. Can you hear it?"

From the other end of the phone came a muffled *tick-tock, tick-tock*.

"Damnedest thing happened the other day. I was doing a part in a TV show, and drove the sound man crackers. He kept saying, "I hear an alarm clock ticking somewhere." The director thought he'd flipped.

"What do you mean an alarm clock?" the director asked.

"Well," said the sound man, "It sort of moves from place to place."

"You mean like the crocodile in *Peter Pan*?" he demanded.

"Something like that," said the sound man.

Gil then told me he went to the wardrobe man and together they wrapped insulation around the little pump so the sound man wouldn't be fired. The little pump didn't get the job done though. Not long after, Gil was hospitalized at the Motion Picture Country Home, a home created by the film industry for those who have contributed years of service. I never even knew he was there. His wife Sasha said he told her, "It's a messy business; let's keep it to ourselves. No sense in making our friends unhappy." He never did, which is a fine enough legacy for any man.

5

Beloved Son, Bastard #644

In World War II the macho types who won all their battles on the silver screen were expected to do the same with their makeup off. Gable, who was too old in the first place, put himself in the embarrassing position of publicly working his way up from the rank of private. He tried to be just plain GI Joe, but the press drove him crazy. He finally escaped by volunteering as a tail-gunner on a B–17 in bombing missions over Germany. Lee Marvin was a marine in the South Pacific, Louis Hayward a combat photographer, Wayne Morris a navy fighter pilot, while Ty Power took his perfect profile through Marine boot camp where life was one continual fistfight.

I had played so many flyers in movies that I decided the Navy Air Corps was for me. The uniforms were the jazziest. So down I went to take the all-important eye test. This worried me a bit, since years of shooting had given me a dominant right eye, and I wasn't sure I could pass the depth perception test necessary for tricky carrier landings. We were supposed to line up two markers, ten feet away, by pulling a couple of strings.

Before taking the test, I had some advice from a self-styled expert standing in line behind me.

"Don't worry about the markers," he said, "just line up the strings where all the other guys lined 'em up, where they're dirty."

"Thanks," I said and I did.

While I was lining up the dirty strings, I was imagining my wings being pinned on, and brave carrier landings under fire. My dreams were rudely interrupted by the doctor.

"Sorry, fellow, you'd better see an optometrist. You're practically blind."

While I had turned my back to talk to my friend, the dirty doctor had moved the markers, proving once again that cheaters never prosper—or, more to the point, never turn your back on a doctor.

But I was lucky! Happily, only a few years before, I had been an all-American with a shotgun, and this allowed me to enlist in the navy as a gunnery officer. I got my share of "what's an actor doing in a man's job?" but this had its advantages, often leading to side bets and a trip to the shotgun range. I could win enough to keep me in bourbon for the rest of the month. I broke the machine-gun range record at Pensacola, so I was assigned to teach gunnery using these noisy monsters. Little did I know that I'd still be fooling with the damn things twenty years later on "The Untouchables." My job was to teach air-to-air gunnery, an absolute *must* for the aerial gunner who would try to protect his plane from enemy fighter attack. This was an uphill battle; our gunners, in the rear of our dive bombers, had to face Japanese Zeros with 20mm automatic cannons. The pilot had armor plate to protect his back, but it took a very tough customer to sit in the rear alone, facing backward, looking down the throat of that Japanese flying artillery with only a .30-caliber pop gun. Our gunners were volunteers. On any given day, our volunteers could see front-page photos of pilots walking away from their shot-up planes and the rear gunners being hauled off in the meat wagon. The mortality ratio was something like three to one, gunners to pilots. As a result, torpedo and dive bomber squadrons in the Pacific were being held up for lack of gunners.

One day I got orders to report to the chief of naval operations, who told me I had the dandy job of taking five decorated combat gunners, just back from the Pacific, and making a tour of naval stations trying to find volunteers. The tour with my five, delinquent heroes would make a book in itself. How we all kept from being court-martialed, I'll never know. My stalwart crew traveled ahead in buses, and I flew in later to meet them at our destination. This left them unescorted, and they made the most of it. The buses were filled with delicate electronic training devices to entice the unwary sailor. This equipment was dumped in the back, so mattresses and a bar could be rigged, transforming the buses into portable cat houses. When I arrived at each destination, there would be complaints from outraged mothers whose innocent daughters had been misused or had run away with sailors in official navy vehicles. They also left a trail of demolished bars and unpaid bills. At age twenty-one, I was "the old man," in charge of a bunch of swingers that put Hollywood's best to shame. Great Lakes Naval Training Base was our crowning disaster. It was the dead of winter, and the crew called, saying they'd be delayed because of snow. To make things worse, a crusty old admiral was in the audience. Five minutes before show time, the buses arrived.

This was the wrong evening to be searching for volunteer gunners. The morning paper had featured another photo of a navy pilot walking away from his fragmented plane, as the rear gunner was carried off on a stretcher. When I walked out, a swabby hit me with, "What about the picture in tonight's paper?" I quickly responded with my introduction of the five aerial gunners just back from combat in the South Pacific.

"You can judge for yourself how these men came out of combat!" I said. The first to step out proudly, wearing all his battle ribbons, was Jack, our chubby, machinist-mate, also known as "Jack the Joker." From the front, his uniform looked impeccable. His hair was slicked down, and his shoes glistened. But from where I stood, I could see he'd torn the seat of his pants and sewn it up with green thread. The result looked like the rear end of a Raggedy-Ann doll.

He also had the worst black eye I'd ever seen; it was only partially covered by pancake makeup, obviously borrowed from one of the crew's groupies.

He backed up to his chair, sat down, and gave me a big

wink. Number two, a pocket-size, red-haired Romeo from Scolly Square, had his right arm in a sling. The other three were successively worse. Lined up, they looked like the trio in the painting *The Spirit of '76*. (All they needed was a flag, a fife, and a drum.) There was a burst of nervous laughter from the audience. I looked over at the admiral, who never changed expression. He looked like a heavy-eyed hawk.

During one of the technical displays, I asked Chubby Jack what the hell happened.

"Just doin' what you said to do, Lieutenant," he said.

"What did I ever say to get you in a battle the day we had an admiral in the audience? The shape you guys are in, the only volunteers we'll get are Japs."

"You always said us navy gunners should be treated with respect."

"Yeah, so?"

"So we carried out your orders, Lieutenant. Those army bastards in that bar down the road got a lot of respect for us now."

When we finished, I saw the admiral coming our way. We all snapped to attention. He threw me a quizzical glance, then slowly panned over my ragged troop, his eyes chest-height, taking in only the battle ribbons.

"You should be very proud of your men, Lieutenant," he said.

"Oh, yes, Admiral," I said fervently. "I'll never find another crew like this."

If I found it hard to take the rules and regulations of the service seriously, I had good reason. A devil-may-care attitude ran in the family.

My uncle Perry Wood, or "Uncle Poo" as I called him when I was a small boy, has always been a smash with the ladies, and still is. He's also always had a wild streak that I like to think I inherited. But I never would have done the things he did in the service. He and Tay Garnett, the famed director, were old chums, and joined the Navy Air Corps in World War I. They did the same thing to protocol that the kaiser's troops were doing to Belgium.

There must be as many bastards in the world as there are sons of bitches, and both are generally preceded by descriptions as dirty, rotten, or miserable. They are seldom described as beloved. If I hadn't been part of the air corps, and bumped into a remarkable Chinese lady, I would have been like all the other dime-a-dozen bastards in the world. Instead, Ma Chung adopted me, and I became one of her beloved sons, Bastard #644.

Ma Chung was an attractive and seemingly ageless Chinese woman. She could speak perfect English and Chinese. She wore mandarin coats and, though small in stature, she was tall in qualities that made her friends remember her for years.

To be one of Ma Chung's "bastards" was not to be taken lightly. Others included admirals, generals, and the heavyweights who ran the show in World War II. But her favorites were the combat pilots, in need of TLC (Tender Loving Care), and for them, Ma made her house in San Francisco a haven filled with joy and camaraderie. There was no rank or title in Ma's house, the bastard number was all that counted. I can think of no other place on earth where an admiral couldn't throw his weight around and a lieutenant with a lower number could outrank him.

Ma Chung's story began in the China-Burma-India theater, where she befriended General Clair Chennault. A partially deaf, retired US Army Air Corps captain, Chennault had taken over the job of building the Nationalist Chinese air force. His flyers included a wild group of men who flew the China skies in battered P-40s with noses painted to look like the mouths of grinning sharks. These "Flying Tigers" were the special favorites of Ma Chung, who had watched them fighting the undeclared war before Pearl Harbor. Most of America had never heard of General Clair Chennault and his little band, and couldn't have cared less about a few crazy American flyers on the other side of the world. But Ma Chung did. If the war was illegitimate, and if the Tigers were bastards, she would adopt them as her beloved sons. So began the Bastards Club.

When she came to San Francisco, she opened the doors of her house to flyers in the other services and some special nonflyers she called "kiwis." (The kiwi is a flightless bird.)

No social pedigree was necessary; she just had to like you. Ma particularly liked a sexy-looking blond in mink and diamonds who was always the life of the party and carried a roll of bills that would choke a horse. I only saw her a couple of times. She arrived and left in a limousine a block long with a driver who looked like Frank Nitti's brother. Much, much later, I learned that the girl was Virginia Hill, a girl friend of hoodlum Bugsy Siegel and the reputed bag lady of the mob. But at Ma Chung's in 1943, she laughed, looked pretty, and no one gave a damn, least of all a bunch of flyers who had their hands full with Hitler and General Tojo.

At various times, I had duty on a couple of aircraft carriers. I was rocket-training officer for a dive bomber squadron, and taught "quad fifties." The muzzle blast of four .50-caliber machine guns untied your shoelaces and left you shaking like Don Knotts.

But my worst job was giving refresher courses to B–24 bomber crews who were rusty. At times, this could be the dumbest, most dangerous job in the navy. To save time, I was supposed to check out the waist gunners on the B–24 (they're the ones you see in all the World War II movies, standing up and firing out the sides of the bomber). At the same time the pilot was giving a brand-new fly-boy a lesson in how to handle the "flying coffin." B–24s were called flying coffins because there was no way for crews to get out of the damn things except through the bomb bay.

Naturally, every sloppy landing made those of us riding steerage very nervous. A bomber is supposed to fly level and drop bombs. The gunners are supposed to protect the bomber from enemy fighters. This is pretty basic and the way it's always been. For this type of gunnery training, a smaller, faster plane pulls a towed sleeve, which looks like a wind sock on a long line, and the gunners shoot at it as it comes by.

Simple, right? My first experience was my worst. It took no time to learn that these characters had their own set of rules. A little knowledge is a dangerous thing, especially if that knowledge is the false security of a couple of useless flights over enemy territory. This doughty crew had flown over a Japanese island or two at 30,000 feet. They'd never seen a Zero but they had all the answers.

"Hey, what the hell are you doing?"

I'd just noticed the gunners were taking out their gun stops, which were designed to keep them from shooting their own planes.

"No sweat, Lieutenant," they said condescendingly. "That's how we do it out there."

I checked with the pilot and he gave them the go-ahead. I thought *what the hell, it's his plane*, forgetting it was mine, too.

The towed sleeve came by and they shot holes all over the sky, nowhere close to the target. Next time, the pilot tried to bring his gunners closer. He slammed the big bomber over on its side, in what a fighter pilot would call a high-side run, and attacked the towed sleeve. This left him with the right wing in line with the towed sleeve. The starboard gunner who had cleverly taken his stops out, just as cleverly followed the target and put three .50-caliber slugs right through the wing. I grabbed the gun and got on the horn to the pilot.

"Are you going to keep doing aerobatics?"

"Why, you scared back there?"

"Yeah," I said, "but I guess we're both in the same plane, right?"

"Yeah, right."

"In that case, you may not want to make anymore fancy moves. Your gunner just shot three holes in your starboard wing, one through the main spar."

"You better watch it back there."

"Get this turkey on the ground and let me out. I'm not getting combat pay. And I'll tell you guys something: If that's the way you do it out there, I'll put money on the Japs."

The landings were always slow, suffocating suspense. I began to appreciate the lot of a bomber instructor. The B–24 has four engines with four throttles which are controlled by the four fingers of the right hand—which takes some adjusting. Eventually I could handle anything the gunners did, but I never got used to the landings. After I finished my job for that particular flight, I was still a prisoner of another unrelated insanity.

I suggested letting myself out by parachute after gunnery practice, but no one went along with my idea. So I squeezed into the back of the cockpit and joined the party. Each young pilot had the gray, ashen look of a death row regular. On final approach, sweat started forming on the upper lip, and the right hand that controlled our destiny turned into an arthritic claw. I can still hear the senior pilot saying, "Relax, relax. Don't freeze on the throttles. Don't worry, I'm here if you need me."

The grim-faced pilots, however, knew perfectly well that once the landing was committed, the big beast had a mind of its own. After three months of slamming into concrete runways like a giant yo-yo, two things happened. I began losing my hair, and I got my orders to go to the Pacific. There I did little to win the war, but at least my hair grew back.

Tom DeMott, one of my old drinking chums, had the lowliest, least appreciated, and potentially most dangerous job on the ugliest boat in the navy—a sixty-foot tub made of wood, one .50-caliber machine gun forward. It had a crew of five. Tom's job was to wander around the Pacific alone, checking on enemy ship movements. This led him to such garden spots as Guadalcanal, Iwo Jima, and the big Japanese naval base at Truk. He would skulk on the horizon, hoping the boat's low profile would keep him invisible to enemy ships, but there was no protection against the occasional Japanese planes that used him for target practice. He got so tired of having the boat poked full of holes, he carried strips of doweling the same size as the Japanese machine-gun bullets to plug the holes. He became so frustrated fighting his private, anonymous war that when he returned to Pearl Harbor, he stayed gassed for a week.

One day, he not only got his revenge, but notified the navy of the existence of Tom DeMott. He was sailing back into Pearl Harbor after two weeks of stumbling around places no US ship had a right to be. He had his shirt off and was lying on a deck chair he had appropriated from the officers' club pool. He looked over his shoulder and saw the Third Fleet steaming in. Carriers, cruisers, and destroyers were strung out for a mile.

He looked over at his equally crazy executive officer Clarence Klopsick.

"We've got the right of way, don't we, Klop?"

"That's what it says in the navy's rules of the road, skipper."

"Okay, hold course."

Admiral Nimitz's flagship let loose a blast that shook the harbor.

"Stay clear!"

Tom held course, which put the picket boat and the flagship on collision course. Again the flagship boomed: "Stay clear!" Tom never budged from his deck chair, beeping his message across the water loud and clear.

"Check US Navy rules of the road. I have right of way."

The huge aircraft carrier loomed over the tiny wooden picket boat. Then suddenly with a flurry of flags and signal bells, the mighty Third Fleet began turning. From that day on, he was known as the crazy bastard who turned the Third Fleet around.

When Tom's new orders came through, he figured it was back to the States. Not at all; the navy finally recognized Tom's existence. He was told his small boat experience made him invaluable! I was in the Pacific when Lt. Thomas DeMott, Jr., was assigned to Operation "Olympic," the planned invasion of the Japanese mainland. The Japanese had built their defenses in concentric rings from the coast to the center of the island so that they could fall back gradually in case of invasion.

To understand what the invasion of Japan meant, you'd have to understand a kamikaze attack. The paralyzing shock of seeing another human aim himself at your ship with the intention of using himself as a living bomb took some adjusting. Everyone in a war figures to play the odds and, until the appearance of the "sons of the divine wind," it was always somebody next to you who figured to cop it. Now the whole gang found themselves sitting in the middle of a bull's-eye, and all the rules of warfare went out the window. The breaking of the Japanese code gave the US an insight into what an invasion of the Japanese mainland would be like.

In short, all of Japan was preparing to defend the mainland with its most effective weapon: the kamikaze attack. Orders went out to all remaining units to prepare for suicide missions to defend the homeland. One-man submarines, frogmen, and even ancient biplanes were to be rigged for the one-way trip. Precious gasoline stored underground and fast burning alcohol were used to fuel planes for the short hop. The emperor's picture, final orders, and all codes (still thought to be unbroken) were to be burned. Operation Olympic would not go unnoticed; a reception committee was waiting for Tom DeMott and his friends. It was estimated that over a half million Americans would die in the operation. Tom was to be in the first wave. Tom had no regrets about the atomic bomb.

I was in the navy for three and a half years, and the memories form a collage. There was Naval Air Station, Jacksonville, where the Free French cadets came to learn to fly, also teaching us how to live, with naked ladies running up and down the halls and coed showers. A French CO had assigned them to learn to fly that widow-maker, the Gull Wing F4U. Only half of them survived training. My CO at Alameda Machine-Gun Range was a dead-ringer for Captain Queeg; we all hated him so much that we kept notes on his nefarious deeds so if one of us was court-martialed, we could all testify against him.

Then there was my roomie Joe Shelt who mistakenly pulled the air raid alarm instead of the fire alarm and blacked out most of Oahu and almost his navy career at the same time. At one point, I myself was headed for a court-martial, but found after a long dressing-down that the brass was really after Lieutenant Stark, not Lieutenant Stack.

Suddenly, it was over. There was a deadly moment of silence when the bombing of Hiroshima was announced, and then we filled a twenty-gallon drum with everything alcoholic we could find, and chugalugged on V-J Day. (A mixture of bourbon, brandy, red wine, and rum topped off with that staple of all navy alcoholics, torpedo juice, 160-proof alcohol drained from torpedoes and strained through a loaf of bread.)

Then there were all the flyers, sailors, and soldiers I swore I'd look up when I got out and never did. The memories are still very much with me.

Mononucleosis is called the young people's infection, intern's complaint, and kissing disease. In 1945, I was young all right, but far from being an intern. I was teaching machine gun out in the boonies. The kissing part might have proven an interesting way to contract something or other, but the only familiar face belonged to my commanding officer. He looked like Porky Pig and displayed the disposition of a tarantula. Still, I couldn't escape the bug.

One morning, I looked in the mirror, and a large frog looked back. The glands on my neck had swollen. I did my best not to look into the mirror, which is difficult enough while shaving. I was convinced after a few days of no change that my only chance was to hide out.

It was in this glorious condition that I learned of an offer that would have been any actor's dream, a fantastic contract from Liberty Productions. Liberty represented a revolutionary new concept for motion pictures. Three of the best directors in the business—William Wyler, George Stevens, and Frank Capra—had joined forces in an independent production company. Jimmy Stewart and I were to be the only actors under contract to these directors. In those days an independent company, not affiliated with any of the big studios, was totally unique, and I considered the chance to work with these giants a once-in-a-lifetime opportunity.

I only had a few weeks before my return to civilian life and, fortunately, no representative from Liberty came around to see what a strange-looking leading man they had signed.

William Wyler had just completed *The Best Years of Our Lives* and word was out that it was a heavy Oscar contender. Frank Capra was finishing shooting *It's a Wonderful Life* with Jimmy Stewart, with equally good reports. Sadly for me, the success of these films put George Stevens, who was scheduled to direct my film, under tremendous pressure. Judy Holliday was signed to appear as my leading lady. But Stevens was faced with the prospect of producing a motion picture that could stand beside those of his partners, both of which had already been acclaimed as classics. After months of delay, Stevens was unable to satisfy himself that he was really ready with the right script and the right approach. Liberty Productions folded and I found myself adrift.

The adjustment from gunnery instructor to civilian actor wasn't a small one. After several years away from Tinseltown, I wasn't entirely sure how I would react to the picture business or, perhaps more important, how it would react to me.

On my first night home, I went to the Mocambo, a club in Hollywood where I had enjoyed many good times before the war. I was seated alone at a table, wondering how things had changed while I had been away. Suddenly I saw two familiar faces. Across the room, I had been spotted by a pair of movie legends. But to me they were old friends, the first reminder that the war was over and I was really home. They knew I was lonely and not sure what was going to happen next. They got right up and deliberately crossed the room planting themselves directly in front of my table.

Bob Hope and Bing Crosby greeted me with big smiles.

"Hello, Bob," they said. "Welcome back!"

It was good to be home!

Home, of course, was about to change, because mother had suggested that once I left the service, we should look for a new house.

A brand-new house is a known quantity and can become, like your own child, an extension of your ego. An old house has nothing to do with you; like an adopted child, it was created by others whose life and tastes you are invading. If you are lucky, it may adopt to you.

Colleen Moore's house on 345 St. Pierre Road in Bel-Air gave us just such a feeling—as if we were moving into a private part of someone else's life. Mother believed that so-called inanimate objects had life, that they merely had different rates of vibrations. In that case, the house's past history was enough to give it a constant case of the shakes. Mother's only comment when we took our first tour through it as owners was "such a lovely house with terrible memories." Among the memories had been an attempted murder, rape, and just about every sexual deviation in the book.

It was a large Mediterranean house, vintage 1928, with a rolling lawn down to a tournament tennis court, a large tile pool, and a cabana with dressing rooms and barbecue in between. In the mid 1920s, Colleen Moore was number one at the box office. She was a young actress who decided not to copy the glamorous queens, but to break the molds. So she invented the flapper. A free soul with Dutch-boy haircut, shapeless dresses, and a jaunty kind of sexiness that became the trademark of the jazz age, she was immortalized by the world-famous cartoonist John Held, Jr., as "his girl." Her boyish bob became every girl's symbol of the free woman, the roar in the Roaring Twenties.

She married John McCormick, a producer who helped build her career and eventually almost destroyed her. When their marriage broke up, she sold the house pretty much as it was furnished and with much of her memorabilia still in various closets. There were labyrinthian passageways and other curiosities. Chief among these was a monkey house of exotic tile, a wishing well, a powder room covered with silk caricatures of Hollywood's greatest from Chaplin to Colleen herself, a wonderful 1928 projection room, and a theater.

We lived there for five years before I noticed a door next to a room where the gardner kept his tools. The lock was tight and rusty, and hadn't been opened in years. I called a locksmith, who finally broke it free. The door was heavy and opened slowly. Then I could see why. It was lined with metal. I fumbled for the light switch and suddenly, like Ali Baba at the cave of jewels, I saw the treasure of 345 St. Pierre. There it was! I was looking at a lead-lined room filled from floor to ceiling with shiny cans of 35mm film. It was as if the films were waiting to be shown to Colleen's guests that night. Old film is touchy stuff and often self-destructs after a period of time. It can also be dangerous. It used to be called nitro cellulose before the government forced the studios to abandon a substance with many of the properties of dynamite in favor of safety film. Luckily, it was perfectly preserved.

As I stepped farther into the room, I found I'd stumbled into more than just an old cache of film. Neatly placed next to some of the reels were acetate phonograph records. Colleen was one of the few actresses to handle the successful transition from silent to sound movies. This then was the industry's first effort to make movies talk. The poor projectionist must have felt like a one-man band, trying to start the projection machine and spin the record at exactly the proper time. I rushed out and rented a 35mm silent projector. (The old films ran at sixteen frames per second. Modern sound films run at twenty-four. This is why silent movies appear to jerk, stop, and start, on modern projectors.)

Now the golden years of our business began unveiling themselves to me, an audience of one, in a way no retrospective could ever do. There were westerns, musicals, love stories, and home movies with Hollywood's biggest stars mugging like children—even Chaplin doing Doug Fairbanks imitations. There were newsreels of premieres with Valentino looking like a teenager, Mae West looking like someone you'd like to come up and see sometime, and Colleen, accompanied by a very young social secretary named Mervyn LeRoy who would later be a top director. There were motion pictures that began in black and white and went to sepia for the romantic scenes. There were musicals that began in sepia, abruptly went to color for the big production numbers, and back to sepia. No one was quite sure in what direction to go. Of course, there were samples of sound, a quality that many of the Hollywood famous fervently hoped would never succeed. There were reels of Colleen's tests for movies she never made. She's the only actress, to my knowledge, who rented a studio and made tests of herself at her own expense for parts she wanted. The final curiosity was a screen test of New York's ubiquitous Mayor Jimmy Walker, strutting his stuff in top hat, white tie, and tails, which seems to answer the question of why he spent so much of his time 3,000 miles away from his home base.

I'll tell you something. Whatever they paid Colleen, she was worth it. The lady was a star. It was as if I'd stepped back in time thirty years, watching a girl in her early twenties who might be appearing next on the "Tonight Show." She was cute as a button, topical as a zipper, and probably one of the few actresses in the world with one brown eye and one blue one. I became an instant fan. I told Louella Parsons about our discovery, and she printed it. In a few days, I received a letter from Mrs. Colleen Moore Hargrave in Chicago. She had forgotten all about the films, which, considering the John McCormick problem, was understandable. She asked if I would give them to her, which, of course, I did. But for a small moment, I had a taste of what had put the hick town of Hollywood on the map. I had lived briefly in the company of Barrymore, Garbo, and Chaplin, and I hated to leave so soon.

Events that later became part of the house's terrible legacy began to occur not long after the house was completed. John McCormick became more of an alcoholic as Colleen's career zoomed. Finally, one day, Colleen asked for a divorce. McCormick, in a drunken rage, seized her by the throat and almost killed her. He probably would have, if the chauffeur hadn't heard the commotion and come to her rescue.

At one point John McCormick was in danger of being fired by the studio, but Colleen, the top box office star of the year, telephoned the head of the studio and announced herself as Mrs. John McCormick. If the scene sounds familiar it should. Our close friend Adela Rogers St. Johns adapted it for the original version of *A Star Is Born*. Colleen's story had a happy ending, best told by Adela as a master chronicler of that era. After McCormick's death, she met and married Homer Hargrave, a widower with two children. She moved to Chicago, where she became a civic leader and her fabulous dollhouse became a legend. She discovered a life every bit as exhilarating outside pictures as the life she had led as one of Hollywood's brightest stars.

Adela, incidentally, remembers our home before it became ours. She had gone to school with my mother, and when she wrote recently about the house, she brought back a host of memories. Bebe Daniels and Ben Lyon had played bridge in the card room with Tommy and Frances Meighan, while John Gilbert resolved his relationship with Greta Garbo in the library. Jean Harlow had often descended the staircase.

But while packaging Colleen Moore's films, I noticed an extra reel, apart from her collection and sealed in a very different container. I wondered what this film might be. When

I ran it through the projector, I realized that it was an ironic legacy, not from Colleen, but from the free spirits who rented the house after Colleen sold it.

The film was an original print of *The Casting Couch*, a stag film in which a pretty starlet completes her "audition" by disposing of everything but her high-button shoes. It was an odd reminder that 345 St. Pierre Road had been the scene of a most bizarre story after the property changed hands.

One of those who rented Colleen's house after her departure was Freddie McEvoy, world-renowned playboy and bon vivant. Freddie's best friend was Errol Flynn, who was a constant house guest. Errol's old buddy Bruce Cabot completed the unholy threesome.

By coincidence, when I returned to civilian life after my time in the navy, I began squiring a beautiful dark-haired young lady named Irene Wrightsman. She was oil millionaire Charles Wrightsman's daughter, and Freddie McEvoy's ex-wife.

Freddie McEvoy was an international playboy, a devil-may-care character who tried to make his living marrying heiresses—in Irene's case, an eighteen-year-old one. The first Mrs. McEvoy was in her seventies when he married her, and very sharp. Although she owned more oil wells than she could count, all Freddie wound up with after the divorce was his monogrammed blazer with matching slippers. As for Irene, Papa Charles disinherited her, allowing Freddie to win the title of "world's worst fortune hunter" a second time. Nevertheless, he was a fearless, fascinating man, member of Britain's Olympic bobsled teams, and one of the originators of the Cresta run at St. Moritz (instead of a bobsled, a flimsy wooden platform is used with the luckless passenger's chin a few inches off the narrow run of sheer ice).

I realized that events had come full circle. Freddie McEvoy had once rented this house and had invited Errol Flynn and Bruce Cabot as house guests. The gardener soon told me about how the lawn down to the pool had often been used for more than landscape; curious races were held there, starting at the house and finishing in the pool. The vehicles were cocktail trays mounted on wheels; the passengers were naked ladies; and I guess everybody was a winner except the neighbors.

Mother heard that the blue room had once been locked tight—after Errol Flynn was accused of rape—with official-looking lead seals put there by the police to make sure no one disturbed the evidence.

I moved into the room where Errol Flynn had taken advantage of poor Betty Hansen, or vice versa. I remembered the case well. Who could forget it?

In November of 1942, Errol had faced his worst crisis, a charge of statutory rape. And so, only a few weeks after becoming an American citizen, Errol faced an American judge and jury to answer the charges. Although the details are forgotten today, at the time of the trial, every detail (and as much as the press could discover about Errol's assorted escapades) was reported nightly in the newspapers.

Errol was defended by the celebrated criminal lawyer Jerry Geisler, who surprised everyone with an eleventh-hour cross-examination of a key witness. Errol was implicated in two separate incidents involving girls who were under age; he was accused of statutory rape by Peggy Satterle (on the boat *Sirocco*) and by Betty Hansen. Geisler proved that Flynn could not have been in the bunk on the boat with one of the underage charmers: The girl had claimed to see the moon rising, but a rising moon was only visible from the porthole *opposite* Errol's bunk. (I have a feeling the jury thought the story was bunk, too.)

The girls turned up in court dressed like characters out of *Rebecca of Sunnybrook Farm*. But a certain worldliness in the eye and a telltale wiggle of their behinds somehow tipped the jury.

Errol was judged, if not exactly innocent, at least no guiltier than his accusers. But for the rest of his life Errol was saddled by a reputation he detested. He was the target of all the jokes and uncensored stories one could imagine. "It's better with your socks on" and "in Like Flynn" became household phrases. He had a strange sort of pride, and he found the sudden contempt of the public an enormous shock.

Errol's shady background, however, never betrayed him in his films. When he donned the costumes of Don Juan or Lord Essex, he was class and style personified. The ruffled shirts and lace cuffs made a fascinating contrast to his pantherlike walk and his athletic dexterity in the action scenes. He also possessed a mischievous, little-boy look—with the left eyebrow at half mast—that contrasted strangely with the pencil-thin mustache and the hint of cruelty about his mouth.

Errol was not only a man of action, he was also an observer of life. One day Irene and I were invited to his house for a cocktail. The wait was interminable; the butler kept insisting that Mr. Flynn was in the steam bath. Trousers, shorts, and socks littered the living room, while a trail of dress, hose, and shoes led around the corner straight to the new steam room. This was Errol's not so subtle way of making sure his friends knew how he was occupied. Finally, he made his entrance, beaming, hair neatly brushed, in a terrycloth robe. I never did see his female companion.

On his way through the many rooms, he said, "Why don't you kids have a drink on the couch, and I'll be down in a half hour. I have some calls to make." As we sank into the inviting couch, I naturally put my arm around my date and gave her a kiss.

With a sly grin she said, "I hope you don't mind an audience."

"An audience?" I said.

"Errol," she answered. "He's probably upstairs watching."

For the first time, I noticed the mirror on the ceiling. Knowing Flynn's taste, I might have passed if off as something to amuse his guests. But, actually, it was a two-way mirror, which Errol used to amuse himself. He also had a camera mounted to document the more imaginative performances conducted on the couch. Later, he would show his home movies at the most inopportune moment. Like it or not, I'd had my first encounter with the incredible world of Errol Flynn.

If there ever were an actor whose off-screen exploits made his on-screen escapades seem tame, it was Errol Flynn. Errol's involvements with a variety of beautiful girls gained him predictable notoriety in Hollywood, but few people realized that for Flynn, his movie-colony adventures represented a comparative settling-down.

Errol once described himself, as a young man, as a Tasmanian devil, a carnivorous marsupial known for its extreme ferocity. When young Errol was ferocious about anything or anyone, she was usually very pretty. His first adventure came when he ran away from home after getting caught playing "doctor" with the girl next door. That was the beginning and from that moment on, Errol stormed through a series of escapades which took him from his native Tasmania, through

New Zealand, to the most and least civilized parts of Australia and the South Seas. Errol had two loves: the sea and members of the opposite sex. After short stays on land, he was invariably forced to retreat on yet another journey. The leading ladies might change, but one element was repeated without fail: Errol, like Don Juan, would be pursued by furious husbands, fathers, and older brothers, all prepared to dump him in the Pacific Ocean if they ever got close enough to strike the first blow.

Errol's travels, by land and sea, took him through Ceylon, North Africa, and Macao, where he sampled opium, gambling, and tours of the local bordellos. ("I didn't always participate," he said afterward. "If I'm in La Scala, and I go to see *Carmen*, I don't necessarily get up on stage.")

He launched his career as an actor by displaying an impressive resume which stated that he had brilliantly executed starring roles in a series of nonexistent plays.

In any situation, he never lost his sense of humor or his capacity to acknowledge his own vulnerability. He was notorious as a practical joker, and the targets of his pranks were often his leading ladies. The first time he worked with the very dignified Greer Garson, he greeted her with a hearty slap on the behind. She thought it hysterically funny. Errol had a grand time by sneaking into the leading lady's dressing room, and depositing a dead snake in her underclothes. Olivia de Havilland was not amused.

Once, in a particularly emotional scene with Bette Davis, Flynn discovered his co-star's enthusiasm for realism. She struck him with a blow severe enough to be judged a technical knockout. He protested. She insisted. He protested again. She continued to use a real blow. Finally, the chivalrous Flynn made it clear that if she struck him, he would hit her back. Bette Davis played the scene, missing Flynn's face by inches.

Sometimes the ladies provoked actual retaliation. He threatened to give his friend, columnist Hedda Hopper, a "kick in the pants" if she didn't cease and desist from calling attention to his latest *amour*. Hedda persisted, and Flynn, true to his word, hauled off and kicked her in a Hollywood nightclub. ("She's an especially good pal," he later said. "She just needed a kick in the pants.")

But Errol was talented in many ways, including athletics. Flynn's trainer on *The Great John L* was sure that his pupil could have been a professional fighter. The same was said about his skill with foil and saber. He was so sure of himself, he seldom bothered to learn the routines; instead, he counted largely on his reflexes. One day, however, he was filming a sequence with Al Cavens, the Belgian fencing master, and used the wrong parry. Flynn was nearly blinded.

All actors desperately try to find security in an insecure business, and the obvious play is to borrow someone else's. Thus, the cockney lilt and stylized "takes" of Cary Grant have served hundreds of beginning performers, as well as such established ones as Craig Stevens in "Peter Gunn" and Tony Curtis in *Some Like It Hot*. Clark Gable loaned George Montgomery, Dale Robertson, David Janssen, Burt Reynolds, Lee Majors, Clint Walker, and Jim Brolin a bit of his built-in machismo while they were developing their own. And Brando was the security blanket for the talents of Paul Newman, Jimmy Dean, and many other graduates of the Actors Studio. His Stanley Kowalski is still the source from which the rebels of the moment (Dennis Hopper, Al Pacino, Jimmy Caan, among others) draw sustenance.

Flynn's role model was John Barrymore. Flynn was so obsessed by him, he would have given anything to do his life on film. I'm convinced that he even followed Barrymore's tragic pattern of self-destruction in the final years of his life when he became an alcoholic as well as a registered narcotics addict.

Barrymore was Flynn's house guest during his last days, when no one else was enthusiastic about putting him up. But Errol so admired this shadow of the world's greatest actor, he accepted his eccentricities and unsanitary habits. Ironically, at the nadir of Flynn's own career, he was asked by Jack Warner if he would make a comeback effort in *Too Much, Too Soon*. Flynn played Barrymore on the screen and, finally, won the acting reviews he had pursued all his life. (Too much, too late?)

To see this magnificent physical specimen, with a body and face every male in the world envied, slowly and methodically destroying himself was hardest of all for his friends. No one accused him of being a good actor. But put him in costume, in a period that gave him the chance to use the inherent qualities of an adventurer, and he was a smash. In the few movies he made in everyday, modern clothes, he seemed somehow smaller and insecure. None of these films was successful.

Mother, Jim, and I gave a party during World War II for some navy flyers who had survived several battles floating around the Pacific in rubber rafts. Lots of pretty girls were to be in attendance, of course, to greet our heroes.

Errol had his own private radar for sighting lovely girls. The conversation went something like this.

"Bob, this is Errol."

"Yeah, Errol?"

"I hear you're giving a party for some swabbies."

"Yeah, Errol."

"Also that there'll be lots of young, beautiful girls."

"Yeah, Errol."

"And in particular, Gloria DeHaven."

At this point, I blew up.

"No, damn it, Errol, she's not even eighteen yet, and you're not invited."

When the party began, we somehow convinced the beautifully illegal Gloria to leave early. Two minutes after her departure, Flynn breezed in, quickly sized up the situation, gave me a knowing smile, and headed for the bar. From then until 4:30 A.M., when I threw everybody out, he took over the party. He started spinning sea stories with the navy flyers and soon, drinking, laughing, and relaxing, they surrounded him. The starlets departed pretty much unnoticed, and Errol Flynn, the lady-killer, the destroyer of America's morals, stayed on and on, making a group of lonely guys feel as important as they probably ever felt in their lives.

There was, of course, the other Errol. I spent one miserable dinner at his house refereeing a nonstop battle between him and his pretty new wife Norma. After a couple of hours, the dialogue rose to this:

"What can you do with a bastard like that?" Norma would demand.

"It takes a bitch to know a bastard," Flynn would respond.

Finally, the battle came to an end, with Norma shouting, "We don't have one damn thing in common!" As if on cue, Errol jumped out of the chair, ran upstairs, ran back down, and threw a monstrous rubber dildo onto the middle of the table.

"We have *one*!"

I went home.

Errol hated decorum and would do anything in his power

to make sure a conventional evening turned into a disaster. One party he gave was a classic. It was black tie. His butler put on his fanciest Buckingham Palace manner to greet just about everyone I'd ever seen in Hollywood. The champagne was Cordon Bleu, the caviar Beluga, and the guest list ranged from Hollywood's elite to pimps, hookers, and touts.

Errol seemed to take a certain glee in mixing the snobs with the slobs, then sitting back to watch the outcome. If it turned out like the Mad Tea Party, so much the better. This night, he took no chances, and orchestrated what is still the maddest party I have ever attended. Louella Parsons had written something to incur his wrath, so he planned to work her into the evening's festivities. First, he sent word to Finocchio's, a famous San Francisco cabaret featuring female impersonators. He asked if they could provide a performer who resembled "Lolly." Then he arranged for the makeup department at Warner's to transform a middle-aged transvestite into the most influential gossip columnist in the country. All the while, the real Louella—uninvited—remained blissfully ignorant of Errol's plan.

About two hours into the party, when everyone's attention had been softened by hard liquor, Louella (the fake) made her entrance. Whispers went through the crowd: "It's Louella "

"She's finally arrived," one of the starlets said, hoping for an eventual mention in her column.

Errol said nothing. Resplendent in chinchilla, looking like an over-sized koala bear, "she" began circulating. The face was an endorsement of the genius of Hollywood's makeup men. Even her voice, as she apologized to darling Errol for being late, passed the test. It was a little foggy perhaps, but nothing her "bad cold" couldn't explain away. By now, the guests were pretty foggy, too. Errol cleverly kept "Lolly" in movement on the chance there might accidentally be one sober guest in the house. After ten glasses of champagne, in as many minutes, Errol's store-bought Louella began coming apart.

She confronted a dignified old character actor with a leer and a wig slightly askew, and inquired, "I'd like to know how you English keep your peckers up."

Next came references to the private sexual habits, preferences, or eccentricities of the more dignified guests. Before the wig fell off and the crying jag began, this refugee from

Finocchio's managed to kiss or insult more of Hollywood than the real Louella did in a year.

Errol stayed just sober enough to provide the coup de grace. To keep things moving and make sure the décolletéed ladies stayed on their toes, he released from various parts of the house his special surprise: two hundred white mice. The scene changed from Hollywood's most glamorous party to a disaster film with Errol doubling as C.B. DeMille. Women raced around screaming, skirts over their heads, bumping into trays, breaking glasses. Some took refuge in the pool.

Errol stood in the middle of the holocaust, his satyr's grin as evidence of a most successful evening! Nevertheless, my sharpest memory of Errol is still the time he spent six hours entertaining the navy flyers. As we were walking out to his car, after many drunken good-byes, he suddenly said, "You son of a bitch, you play it cool and never hit the papers. But I'll bet you get more quiff than I do, and I'm supposed to be the world's greatest lover."

"If I do, it's only because I'm not impatient," I said. "I try to wait until they're legal. I can't afford Jerry Geisler."

With a wave, Errol was in his car and screaming off into the dawn. In the gray light, I could just make out the battered Hollywoodland sign, tilted and running downhill so the final letters petered out into the manzanita bushes. Once arrogant and proud, but now a symbol of poignant decay, the sign was like my friend.

In the last scene of *The Adventures of Don Juan*, Errol said, "There is a little of Don Juan in every man and, since I am the real Don Juan, there must be more of it in me." The same could be said of Errol himself.

Whenever I think of Errol and the Hollywoodland sign, I am reminded how much Hollywood has changed physically over the years. Today the Sunset Strip looks like a patchwork quilt of neon billboards. Every character who leads a rock group (and a few from under a rock) seems to have paid to project his own image—glowing, flashing electrically and otherwise—or giant, overpowering display structures that overlap each other like a deck of cards.

In the old days, a personal billboard on the Strip was really big news. I remember one which for a month announced "Lank Rivers Is Coming." Then it changed to "Lank Rivers Is On His

Way." Finally it read just "Lank Rivers." Lank Rivers never appeared, and the sign was allowed to deteriorate until after a couple of years, it just collapsed. One wiseacre said, "No wonder Lank Rivers didn't make it. He was too pooped. He's been coming for two years."

To this day, none of us has ever found out who Lank Rivers was. But that was the old Hollywood, positive, youthful, optimistic in every sense, ready for an era of pictures whose only justification was that those who made them (or watched them) had fun.

The war had changed my outlook, just as it changed all the boys who went into the service. I had emerged from the service as a man, and it seemed logical that I would begin playing a man's roles in motion pictures. But I soon discovered that the industry still thought of me as a boy, and I found myself cast as a boy who had a crush on the girl next door. (Coincidentally, the girl next door was played by a new star, an incredibly beautiful teenaged Elizabeth Taylor.)

A Date with Judy was typical of the musicals which MGM turned out in the forties. The plot was light, frothy, and full of fun. No one took himself too seriously. The script gave everybody a chance to sing. And some extra glitter was added to the solid financial reputation of the MGM lion.

Philip K. Scheuer summed the film up in the *Los Angeles Times*:

> Romances all the time. The Foster household consists of Judy (Jane Powell), her father (Wallace Beery), her mother (Selena Royle), a kid brother, and a maid. The Pringles are Carol (Elizabeth Taylor), Oogie (Scotty Beckett), father (Leon Ames), and a butler (Clinton Sundberg). [Also included were Xavier Cugat and Carmen Miranda.] Judy and Oogie had been childhood sweethearts, but Judy now has a crush on Stack who is attracted to Carol and vice versa. Judy suspects her dad of falling in love with Miss Miranda, but Carmen is really engaged to Cugey who is devoted to himself and his chihuahua. Mr. Pringle, a widower, is in love with the stock market. This leaves Foster's maid and Pringle's butler unaccounted for, but they don't seem to be in love with anything, not even their jobs. I can't say I blame them.

One of the more unusual aspects of *A Date with Judy* for me was the opportunity to work with Carmen Miranda, "the Brazilian Bombshell."

Although Carmen had already appeared in a number of films in the United States, English was still a mystery to her.

"Why does the studio think I have an accent?" she protested to me one day. "What do they expect from a Souse American?"

Carmen loved fast cars (and once drove hers straight through her own garage door) and eleven-course meals. But her famed appetite couldn't top an escapade by another legendary gourmand—Harpo Marx. Harpo, in full view of his astonished friends, once capped an enjoyable meal by proceeding to salt and pepper the check which had been deposited before him by a haughty waiter. He ate the check while the waiter tried to figure out how to deal with the situation.

It would be hard to imagine a greater contrast than that between *A Date with Judy* and my next picture, which put me in a very familiar role: right in the middle of World War II. I wasn't attached to any particular studio and the film at Warner's, a picture called *Fighter Squadron*, gave me a chance to work with one of Hollywood's most colorful directors, Raoul Walsh.

Raoul had lost an eye to a jack rabbit that crashed through the windshield of his car while he was speeding one night to Palm Springs. Instead of a glass eye, he sported a black patch which gave him the look of a benign pirate. He was a man's man, not given to small talk, and at his best with the macho stars of the period. He was respected as an action director, but the more tender scenes embarrassed him. He also rolled his own cigarettes. This gave him a bit of business to escape uncomfortable situations, such as love scenes.

When I asked him how he wanted us to play the first romantic scene, he began to mumble uncomfortably.

"Well, you see, you're a guy and she's a girl," he began. This didn't sound very encouraging. He went on for a few moments, as if unable to make up his mind how to explain the birds and the bees. Finally, he resolved the whole problem.

"What the hell," he said. "Just do what you'd do with a girl." With that, he ambled off, rolling his cigarette. He turned his back to the camera, and I took it from there, doing what came naturally.

Jack Warner summed up the studio's attitude regarding our director, when he said, "To Raoul Walsh a tender love scene is burning down a whorehouse."

Raoul was happiest as a man of action. In his youth, he had

been a horse wrangler who roamed the wildest mining towns of the West. His favorite story involved an adventure in Mexico when he made a film about Pancho Villa. He did his work under the constant eye of Villa's armed guards. When it came time to film a mock battle between Villa's men and the government soldiers, Villa's followers simply dressed up in the uniforms they had taken off the bodies of enemy soldiers who had been killed in battle a few days earlier. (Happily, when I worked with Raoul, the costume department supplied all the uniforms.)

His protégés included some of the most legendary names in Hollywood. He launched a Hollywood trend for westerns because he wanted to help his friend Tom Mix make a comeback when Mix's career reached a low ebb. Would westerns ever have been the same if Raoul hadn't discovered a muscular ex-football star from USC with the unlikely name of Marion Morrison? The young gridiron hero very nearly was given the stage name of "Mad" Anthony Wayne. Instead, he settled for John Wayne and started his long ride to glory. Another one of Raoul's finds was discovered when George Raft refused to play a character who had to die on screen. Walsh came up with a replacement: a gravel-voiced bit player named Humphrey Bogart.

Clark Gable had warned me that Raoul was a practical joker. The king had been the victim of a special Walsh prank. Raoul once turned a deodorized skunk loose in Gable's tent on a camping trip. He had told Gable that skunks were afraid of whistling, and let Gable whistle enough tunes to fill a concert program before walking in and calmly disposing of the skunk. George Raft was the target of a similar prank. Raoul told Raft he would have to jump off a bridge while the cameras were rolling, because George's double was unavailable. Just as Raft finally summoned up the courage to do the jump, convinced by Raoul that the studio would pay for his funeral if he missed, a dummy was brought in front of the camera to take the dive.

Raoul was a grand and royal friend, however. Once, he posed as an insurance agent in order to smuggle a prize bottle of cognac past a dour nurse to the dying John Barrymore.

Raoul stopped playing games whenever he thought people were being unfair. Well past the age of brawling, he took on a group of bullies with his fists because one had uttered a racial slur about Sammy Davis, Jr., a man he'd never even met.

When the German government, at the height of Hitler's power, invited him to make a film in Berlin, he suspected their motives. He was wined and dined by Ribbentrop, whom he remembered as a heel-clicking champagne salesman, and by Goebbels, Himmler, and even Hitler himself (who Raoul thought was insane). He discovered that they wanted him to persuade his friend William Randolph Hearst to trade a rare painting to Hitler. Raoul suggested that the Nazis offer, in exchange, some Grecian columns which had belonged to Hearst before they were sunk by a German U-boat in World War I. They don't make directors like Raoul Walsh anymore!

Raoul used a technique I'd never seen before. He would *listen* to a scene (not watch it), and have his assistant Russ Sanders, the former USC football great, tell him if there were any visual mistakes. As an actor, having a director turn his back on you before you open your mouth is hardly a vote of confidence. But his method, listening to the dialogue like a radio broadcast, must have worked, for his list of credits is phenomenal. He was also famous for helping actors get a start. At one time Raoul had under personal contract a black-haired, handsome ex-truck driver who also doubled as his chauffeur. With Raoul's encouragement, his protégé turned actor. In a manner that typified the old-time directors, Walsh rode the young actor unmercifully.

"You big dumb bastard," he yelled. "Don't just get in the center of the camera and stay there like a tree, *move!*" With this auspicious beginning, a young ex-truck driver who had recently changed his name from Roy Fitzgerald to Rock Hudson made his screen debut.

Rock and I later worked together in two movies, and he proved to be a gentle giant, a gentleman, and when given the chance, as in *Giant*, a big talent.

The postwar years were exciting in many ways, and I quickly learned that, for an actor, the excitement often started when the cameras *stopped* rolling. One of my strangest adventures began innocently enough when several of my friends were invited to dinner at the home of Henry Willson.

Henry Willson (with two *l*'s) was a young man who decided to invade Hollywood and make his mark. Willson became an agent and discovered (and named) Guy Madison, Tab Hunter, Rory Calhoun, and his biggest triumph, Rock Hudson.

However, it was my old chum William T. Orr who came

up with the greatest put-on of the lot. When he was head of Warner Brothers Television, a meeting was held to decide the name of a lusty young western actor. "It's got to sound macho, create a word picture, grab the women. It's got to be as sexy as an erection."

Bill didn't miss a beat. "How about Ty Hardin?" Which, if you substitute an *o* for the *i*, is about as sexy as you can get. This is another example of the taste and care that go into the planning of a Hollywood career.

One evening, Henry invited Bob Sterling, Craig Stevens, and me to dinner. In the middle of the soup course, the phone rang, and it was for me.

"Hello, Bobby. It's Dolly. How are you, darling? Why don't you drop by for a drink? I'd love to see you." The voice was a sultry cross between Ava Gardner and Lana Turner, breathy and inviting. I've survived, more or less, in Hollywood because of a little man who resides in the back of my head and who, like J. Arthur Rank's trademark, swings a large hammer against a gong when all seems not according to Hoyle. This may have lost me many nights of mad, sensuous pleasure, but at least it's kept me out of jail. The little man was swatting the gong, so I decided to investigate further.

"Dolly?" I said. "Dolly who?"

"Dolly Johnson, silly. I'm a great friend of Jim."

"My brother?"

"Who else?"

"How is he? I haven't seen him for a couple of months."

"He's just great."

"How are Jim, Jr., and Billy?"

"Couldn't be better."

The little man went into overdrive like Jack La Lanne on KH_3. Jim doesn't have any children.

"I'll be right over," I said.

Hollywood has long been the land of the hustle, and I don't mean the dance. When you remember that show business had its antecedents in such rowdy enterprises as the medicine show and the shell game, more sophisticated ploys can only be considered variations on a theme. Like a bird dog on point, I smelled the epitome of the hustler's craft, a combination of a good performance and perfect timing called "the Badger Game."

The idea is to lure a patsy to a deserted apartment or house for a drink and the promise of something more visceral. The lady, after a couple of drinks, announces she'll put on something more comfortable and returns shortly in a creation that leaves little to the imagination. A couple more belts, and she is draped all over the poor patsy. Then, wonder of wonders, the door is flung open, and a muscle-bound, irate "husband" bursts into the room. Here's where the performers are allowed to improvise, depending on how the mark reacts. Anything from slapping the "wife" and threatening to work over the poor patsy, to hauling out a .45 automatic and announcing he's "going to shoot you both, and no judge will ever convict me" is permitted.

The negotiations can go like this: "I've got shots of you and my wife that will cost you $10,000 or they'll be in the hands of the newspapers by morning, and you'll be selling cars."

I never would have gone alone, but I figured with all three of us, there wouldn't be much anyone could do. So Craig and Bob joined me, and we were off.

The house was found at a good and vaguely familiar address on Benedict Canyon. It was decided that I should go in alone. I rang the bell, and a bountifully endowed blond, with purple eye shadow and fingernails to match, greeted me. She had bypassed the "I'll get into something more comfortable" routine, and was *already* in something more comfortable—that is, next to nothing. She greeted me with, "Darling, I'm so happy you dropped by," delicately slid her tongue halfway down my throat. As she led me into the living room, I was not surprised to see her close the door but not latch it. The entrance of the irate husband can be spoiled if he has to fool around with keys.

She languidly made a double martini, while the law of gravity gently, and oh so slowly, began disrobing her. The negligee would slip a bit, and then she would move her arms so it would hang on her generous contours, all the while maintaining an expression of childlike concentration. The robe would be allowed to drop further until, innocently reaching for the ice, she halted its journey on a cooperative nipple. Altogether, it was one hell of a performance. All at once, she indelicately ripped off the negligee and plastered herself against me. I saw the door open. There was a beat or two of silence, and finally one of the rover boys spoke.

"We hear there's a party going on," said Craig.

"How about a drink?" Bob chimed in.

Dolly spun, not bothering to cover her femaleness, and growled at Craig and Bob, "Who the hell are you?"

"You asked me by for a drink," I said jauntily. "I knew you wouldn't mind my bringing my chums."

Just at that moment, the door burst open and the "irate husband" charged in. He looked like an unemployed lifeguard, tanned and muscular.

"Get your hands off my—." He stopped in mid-sentence. Bob was making a martini, as Craig handed him the vermouth. I was helping with the ice. His undraped "wife" was standing in the middle of the room trying to figure out what had gone wrong.

In a way, I felt sorry for him. The actor had learned his lines, but somebody had switched the material. He stood there looking as if he'd rather be at Zuma Beach. The same can't be said of Dolly whose tongue was as active in her mouth as somebody else's. We finished our drinks and left, followed by a string of four-letter words that would do credit to a stevedore.

When we returned to our house, I called the Beverly Hills police and told them the story. Beverly Hills has the most specialized, most sophisticated police force in the world, and will investigate the most bizarre problems of its citizenry. I asked them to call me and fill me in later. In twenty minutes, I got the call. Dolly and friend had skipped, leaving only three empty martini glasses, and a still-smoking cigarette. The house belonged to a screenplay writer on vacation in Europe. Thanks to a set of skeleton keys, he had been their inadvertent host. Who knows, you might catch Dolly's act yourself someday. If so, share it with a couple of friends. It may not be as exciting, but it's one hell of a lot cheaper.

Shortly after the war I began thinking about the theater. I had planned, when I first decided to try being an actor, to go back to New York and really learn my craft. When the chance to kiss Deanna Durbin changed my plans, I heeded Spencer Tracy's advice not to turn down a sure thing.

So I became a movie actor but, like Walter Mitty, I occasionally fantasize a gala opening night as Hamlet or as the agile lead in a musical, with my Arthur Prince time step becoming a Bob Fosse tour de force, and the audience embracing me with their enthusiastic applause and maybe a bravo or two.

Then comes the gnawing feeling that if I hadn't listened to Tracy and *had* gone to New York to work on stage, I could have been—who knows?—perhaps an Olivier or a Burton.

I guess I can hand Walter Mitty the blame for my adventures or misadventures on the stage. Although my great-grandfather owned a Los Angeles Theater back in the 1890s, my association with the living theater has been no love match. It's been more like mutual suspicion.

Broadway is a magic word to all actors, no matter how gifted, untalented, rich, poor, famous, or unknown. That tapestry of masochism and humiliation coupled with the Napoleonic dream of performing before fans who respond every night, as if on command, is an irresistible temptation.

In 1949 I received my first opportunity to involve myself in a legitimate stage effort. Armina Marshall (wife of Theater Guild's boss Lawrence Langner) asked me to play in a revival of Belasco's *Girl of the Golden West* at the Westport Country Playhouse in Westport, Connecticut. If the play were a success, it might go to that magic place, Broadway. Without thinking twice, I said yes.

Westport is the classiest of summer theaters. The New York critics come up from the Big Apple to review the shows. The casts are usually all Broadway types, so it's almost like doing a show in New York. The cast for this play included June Havoc (Gypsy Rose Lee's baby sister), yours truly as "Mr. Johnson of Sacramento," and Murvyn Vye as Jack Rance, the sheriff. (The play had been performed before it was made into an opera by Puccini.) Unlike film actors, stage performers used to be given only their own lines, not a full script. The cue sheets, known as "sides," would contain a word or two of the previous dialogue to cue the actor's entrance. As a tip of the hat to Belasco, we were to use the original sides, which were kept in a vault, and try within reason to play it straight. This was no mean feat, since this antique play had the actors doing "asides" (talking directly to the audience). June Havoc was the darling of the Theater Guild, highly experienced, and an absolute love.

Murvyn had just finished a smashing run on Broadway as Jud, the lecherous heavy in *Oklahoma!*, and was the strangest character I could have encountered this side of Times Square. He stood about 6'2" and had a bald head, black beetle brows, and a brasso voice that came out of his shoes. I soon learned why he was such a lecherous heavy on stage: He practiced full-time offstage. In summer theater, young, dewy-eyed hopefuls do much of the work building sets, making costumes, etc., in exchange for the chance to watch the professionals at work and to play an occasional small part. Many of the girls are from sixteen to nineteen years old, and very anxious to learn. Murvyn did his best to accomodate them with private lessons in his room.

"What you need is experience," he would rumble. "Little girl, let's go run over some lines." For someone who spent so much time "running lines at night," Murvyn still had the sides for the first act in his hand two days before opening night. It got so that June and I would rehearse alone and try to figure a way of covering the gaps when Murvyn's turn came.

The story of the *Girl of the Golden West* is simple. A girl who lives in a western gold mining town falls for a stranger called Mr. Johnson, who, it turns out, is a thief. The sheriff, who has eyes for the girl, is jealous, but gets his revenge when he finds the wounded Mr. Johnson hiding in the girl's room. In the climax, she bets her virtue for his unconscious body in a game of cards with the sheriff—winner take all.

To complicate matters, there were position marks we had to hit on stage. They were critical spots where we *had* to stand so that special effects would be on target. When the sheriff searches the girl's room, and finally gives up, he puts his hand out to the girl. On cue, one of the apprentices, peeking through a small hole in the loft, squeezes a rubber bulb, and a drop of "red blood" makeup is supposed to fall onto the sheriff's hand. He then looks up and says, "Aha, he's up there."

Murvyn was so worn out from his nightly adventures that, when he wasn't wandering around the wrong part of the stage like a zombie, he'd be flaked out and forget his entrance.

Girl of the Golden West was to be the opening show of the Westport season. Following us was *Private Lives* with Tallulah Bankhead. I was always one of her big fans, and I wish I could say Tallulah Bankhead and I hit it off. I hate to admit it, but I had to slip that most gifted of American actresses a Mickey Finn to try to save our show. It began with Lawrence Langner's garden party, at which one show's actors were supposed to meet the other actors and famous locals. Miss Bankhead had been on a bender and her eyes looked like two fried eggs. She still managed, however, to sway regally over to me like Regina in *The Little Foxes*.

"Young man," she said in her rich baritone, "I hear you're going to resurrect Belasco's *Girl of the Golden West*."

"That's right, Miss Bankhead," I said.

"I hear you're also going to play it straight."

"That's right, Miss Bankhead."

She threw back her head with that wonderful, lascivious Tallulah laugh.

"You're going to have your hands full, young man, because I'm going to be there tonight with noisemakers to make sure you *don't* play it straight."

She was still laughing as she turned and wobbled off toward the bar. I didn't actually slip her a Mickey. I just made a deal with the bartender to make her drinks triples. Miss Bankhead did not grace us with her presence opening night.

But we had enough problems without Tallulah and her noisemakers. As soon as the curtain went up, we found nothing had changed since rehearsals. June and I still had to work around Murvyn, who not only forgot his lines, but kept jumping to the wrong act.

After one desperate flurry of improvisation, with June on one side of the stage, me on the other, and Murvyn in the middle, we knew we were in deep trouble.

"I think what the sheriff means is..." I would say.

"It seems to me the sheriff is saying," June would continue.

So it went. June and I finally ran out of things to say, and we all stood there like posed figures in a tintype photo. Then Murvyn, who naturally had the next line, did something I'll never forget. During that deadly pause, he very slowly walked downstage, pulled a chair toward him, put his foot on it, and, with great authority, looked straight out into the audience, leaving June and me stuck like dummies on opposite sides of the stage—making it seem to the audience that the sheriff was the only one in the show who knew what he was doing.

John Lund, who played Yank in *The Hasty Heart* on Broadway, later gave me an explanation for Murvyn Vye's surprise move.

"Oh yes," he said, "that's an old trick. Next time someone tries that, just follow him downstage, tap him on the shoulder, and say loudly, 'It's your turn.'"

In the second act I noticed that Murvyn had dropped his voice an octave lower than in rehearsals. I've often been told what a nice deep voice I have, but next to Murvyn, I sounded like Tiny Tim. I got my first laugh in the play when, in my dramatic confrontation with the sheriff, I tried to drop down to Murvyn's level and my voice broke. I sounded as if I was yodeling my lines.

Somehow we got through the first two acts, and came to the third, with all its complications. In spite of our problems, the audience seemed to be going along with our efforts to do right by Mr. Belasco, and hung in there, even during the asides and old-fashioned dialogue. We were now in the middle of the last act, and I figured the worst was over. I figured wrong.

In rehearsal, Murvyn had never hit his mark for the blood dripping on his hand, so the stage manager had painted a big line with a bloody hand on it only a blind man could miss. I made my "wounded" entrance and staggered up to the loft to hide. A few moments later, the sheriff stormed in, in a flurry of phony snowflakes, and played his scene with June. It was time for the dripping blood.

I was lying down alongside the apprentice who had his eye glued to the peephole, waiting for the cue. I heard the cue, "Can't you even say good-bye, girl?" I looked down and wonder of wonders, Murvyn was on his mark. Then I looked over and saw abject horror on the apprentice's face. "The damn bulb is stuck," he said. "The stuff must have dried out. I can't squeeze it."

By now Murvyn realized something was haywire, so he did what every experienced performer would do. He repeated the line and moved to make it appear he was pleading with the girl, not just filling a gap. As Murvyn moved forward, the apprentice finally got the bulb to work but, in his excitement, he squeezed so hard, not just a couple of drops but the whole bulp emptied.

Just as Murvyn said, "Can't you even say good-bye, girl?" with hand eagerly outstretched, one quarter pint of "blood" landed on his bald head in a great flood, running copiously down his face. He looked as if he'd been scalped. He stood there for a moment, then slowly wiped his face with his hand, like Guy Kibbee. His next line—"Aha, he's up there"—got the biggest laugh ever heard in the Westport Country playhouse.

We still had the card-playing scene to do before the night was over. The scene had never worked in rehearsal, and there was no reason to believe tonight's performance would be any different. But now I breathed a sigh of relief; my dialogue was over and all I had to do was be unconscious and slump over the poker table while the sheriff and the girl played for my body—at least according to Mr. Belasco. June was really stuck: there was no way she could cue Murvyn during the poker game. All she could do was hope one of the apprentices had actually used the lines while "gaining experience." At Murvyn's second line, the rat race began. He took a great pause which he filled beautifully by scratching his head, shuffling his cards, clearing his throat, and finally leaning back in his chair.

Luckily I'd turned my face away from the audience and had learned the sheriff's lines just in case. We now began a three-way poker game. June would deliver her line; I'd whisper Murvyn his cue, and he'd play it as if I were a teleprompter. This was how we finished the play.

The local papers were kind to everybody, but the *New York Times* was something else. First, the reviewer noted that it took a "lot of guts to do Belasco's old play." He further wrote, "June Havoc was bright and spunky as the girl, but seemed to have lapses in concentration."

"Robert Stack," the critic went on, "a Hollywood refugee, wasn't bad as Johnson, but we're not sure whether his innocent, dazed look was a performance or the real thing." Next came the clincher. "Murvyn Vye as the sheriff was just right. He brought us a character that had the courage and timing only achieved by a well-prepared professional, a performance the others can learn from."

Well, I learned this much. The next time around, I'm going to prepare my part as Murvyn Vye did, and if I don't wind up in jail on statutory rape charges, or in the alcoholics' ward, I hope to find the courage and timing of a "well-prepared professional."

Ten years later, I again bumped into Murvyn. This time I was doing "The Untouchables," and instead of playing Jack Rance, the sheriff, he played a sleazy dope pusher. He gave a good performance, didn't blow any entrances, and knew all his lines. But there was something missing. He didn't have that special *joie de vivre* he had had at the Westport Country

Playhouse. Maybe he was getting too old to "run lines" all night.

When Murvyn eventually moved out West to latch on to some of that TV gold, he got himself a business manager. He had a habit of giving parties at Chasen's, the favorite restaurant of the Hollywood biggies, for twenty or so casual acquaintances, so he was always in hock. Finally, his poor advisor set down an ultimatum: no more fancy parties, no expenditures without his okay, or Murvyn could find himself a new manager. One night Murvyn was having a beer at the local bar and noticed a sign on the wall: $100 REWARD FOR ANY BOBCAT CAUGHT IN THE LAUREL CANYON AREA.

He hurried home and rigged a trap from a packing box he'd found in his garage, and baited it with a piece of ancient fried chicken. Then he ran a clothesline from the trap door to his bedroom, tied it around his foot, and went to sleep. He caught three bobcats in as many weeks. The three hundred dollars gave him enough for another splurge at Chasen's, for which he paid in cash. When his business manager read about the party in *Variety* he hit the roof.

"Where'd you get the money?" he said. "Did you sell the car? Hock your watch?"

"No," Murvyn said, "I earned it."

"Not at any studio you didn't. I checked," said the manager. "How'd you earn it? Don't lie to me. Tell me the truth or you can get yourself another manager."

Murvyn looked him straight in the eye and rumbled, "I earned it trapping bobcats!"

If I thought Murvyn Vye would be the most difficult co-star of my career, I was badly mistaken. I was destined to work in a motion picture with a co-star who never forgot his lines, and was perfectly capable of annihilating anyone who upstaged him. Working with a live lion in two dimensions is bizarre; in the first commercially produced three-dimension film, it was an experience that had to be seen to be believed. Like so many of these adventures, it began in the usual innocent way.

The phone rang. It was my agent.

"How'd you like to be the first actor in Three-D?"

"Three-D what?"

"Three-D! Third dimension. It's a brand new process that's so real everything seems to jump off the screen."

"Sounds great for Tarzan pictures."

"Damn it, Bob, be serious. How many firsts have you had in your life? Sure, you were the first to kiss Deanna, but that's ancient history."

"How does this process work?"

"Well, you know, it takes two eyes to see anything in depth—it's like the old stereopticon. An eye doctor named Gunzberg has invented this system that synchronizes two cameras."

"How does that give you Three-D?"

"This is where it gets tricky. He puts a different Polaroid filter on each camera and on each sychronized projector."

"Then what?"

"Then you wear matching Polaroid glasses to separate the left camera from the left eye and the right camera from the right."

"Glasses?"

"Yeah, they hand out cardboard glasses with your ticket."

"What's this turkey called?"

"Bwana Devil."

And so I plunged into *Bwana Devil*, an experience I'll never forget in three glorious dimensions. In particular it would be hard to forget Arch Oboler, a leprechaun with thick magnifying glasses and an ever-present cap to cover his crop of pink skin that took the place of hair. However unimpressive he looked, he was dubbed the "master of the eerie." Even in radio, he managed to scare the socks off an audience, and his anthologies (including the famous "Lights out!") gave many an avid mystery fan sleepless nights. With him as our director, we set sail off into the great unknown.

Bwana Devil was, if not a steal, a heavily borrowed version of *The Man-eaters of Kumaon*, and several other grisly tales of terror set on the dark continent. But for reasons of thrift, the Paramount Ranch, a hundred or so acres of nothing located thirty miles north of Los Angeles, became our Africa.

Here, Arch set out to build a railroad, vintage 1900, with matching engine and cars to puff their way to disaster. After the technicians had laid the tracks and a giant crane gently lowered the vintage train on them, it sure enough began to look as if we were going to make a movie. The synchronized cameras were locked together side by side, set a predetermined distance apart. It soon was clear that these Siamese twins were the stars of the picture. Never has an actor been accorded so much attention by director and crew as Gunzberg's two-eyed monster was. We soon learned about no-man's land.

There was a line about six feet from the camera that we were never to cross or we would find ourselves "in the audience." It was perfectly fine, even recommended, to throw rocks, spears, fireballs, or anything handy at the camera to scare hell out of the audience, but we were told if part of us crossed the forbidden line, the offending part would hang out over the first six rows as if disembodied.

Oboler had a bunch of spears and shields, and he said they were authentic Masai weapons. Then he announced that he was ready to film a Masai lion hunt, the coming-of-age ritual in which young men are given the honor of going on a lion hunt with only a spear and shield. If they survive, they are warriors. Since there were no Masai available in Los Angeles County, Arch did his recruiting for the lion hunt in Watts. He told his recruits they were to dress in native garb and play brave Masai warriors. No mention was made of their co-star, Leo the Lion.

But I'll say one thing for Arch: His casting was first class. His warriors went into the wardrobe tent a bunch of zoot-suited, gum-chewing pool sharks, and came out looking like Masai—superficially anyway. He told them all to form a circle and get used to waving the spear and shield. While the fellows were getting in the mood, the animal trainer took his young, tame lion and led him to the middle of the ring. I don't know who was more shocked, the Masai warriors or the young lion. Oboler picked up the bullhorn and told his now petrified performers to close the circle and, as though hypnotized, they did. As the circle kept getting smaller, the lion began running around the diminishing circle faster and faster. The warriors began acting as if the hunt were real. Finally, the lion spun on his haunches and tried to leap over the circle of spears. He didn't quite make it, knocked a couple of the warriors flat, and disappeared in the distance. It took two days to find the lion, who by now was a nervous wreck. Our Masai from Watts got the biggest hand I ever heard a cast and crew give a group of actors. The bus was ready to take them back, but they stuck around in costume all day. As they finally left, I heard one say, "We've been on a lion hunt, an honest-to-God lion hunt, with a damn spear. No other son of a bitch in Watts ever did that."

In the film, I played a young engineer in charge of building a small railroad through Africa. Our family's dear friend Nigel Bruce was a Dr. Watson-type doctor, and lucious Barbara Britton was my doughty wife who came out to the bush to surprise her engineer husband and furnish some 3-D cheesecake for the viewers who by now, no doubt, were getting edgy dodging spears and charging lions.

It wasn't the easiest acting job I'd ever had; I can't be held entirely to blame with lines like: "Those infernal devils. I'm going to sit in the middle of that field tonight, and if those devils want me, they can come and get me!"

Strangely enough, the basis for the story was true. Two lions working together with almost human intelligence had wiped out several villages and actually stopped the construction of such a railroad. The bloodiest scene of all was quite factual. The two lions, working from opposite ends of a railroad car, had methodically masticated all the passengers. When reproduced in 3-D, this incident had an effect on the audience beyond even Arch Oboler's expectations.

Finally the picture was finished, and it was time for the unveiling. None of us had been allowed to see the rushes. None of us had any idea if the process was going to work or if the audience would even wear the cardboard glasses.

There was much fooling around with the glasses and joking about 3-D before the lights dimmed, but when the titles appeared, you could feel a sense of anticipation. Something different was going to happen in that theater. We were all in on a *first*, the first commercial 3-D film ever made. Now the picture began. First an African landscape, the Serengeti Plain, appeared. Then the audience realized that the nearest tree was stretching its branches over their heads. The train puffing toward the first row was sure as hell going right through the theater.

My God, we thought, *it really works*.

The damn glasses didn't fit, and if anyone tipped his head, he saw two of everything, but the idea worked. I knew we had them when the first spear came flying out of the screen and everybody ducked and screamed. All was not perfect, however. In Barbara's love scene with me, she wore a flimsy negligee. She did the unforgivable: She crossed over the line and stood too near the camera. Her right bosom, magnified like a pink Goodyear blimp encased in lace, proudly thrust itself over the first ten rows. When I kissed her romantically on the neck, my nose poked through the invisible barrier like a torpedo and I became Pinocchio.

Just when everyone was getting used to 3-D, along came the scene with the two lions in the railroad cars. People in the audience jumped out of their seats; some even fainted. Oboler had finally achieved every horror-movie director's dream: He literally scared the crap out of the audience.

Jack Warner sat through the first half, but left before the mayhem broke loose. A few days later he picked up the trade papers and read that *Bwana Devil* was breaking box office records. He immediately called Bryney Foy, a producer best known for his speed as a filmmaker.

"How soon can we come up with a Three-D picture?" he demanded. "This *Bwana Devil* thing is making a mint."

"I just happened to have the perfect story," Foy replied confidently. *"Murder in the Wax Museum."*

"We already made that."

"Yeah, but we'll change it a little and give it a new name. How about *House of Wax*?"

"Great."

"Who'll direct it?"

"André de Toth isn't doing anything."

"Stick him on it!"

André "Bondi" de Toth is a Hungarian who looks like a cross between a man in the Van Heusen shirt ad and a pirate. His black eye-patch gave him a rakish, romantic appearance better suited to being in front of the camera than behind it. But for some reason, when he appeared on the set of *House of Wax*, the familiar patch was missing.

House of Wax, a nickel-and-dime forerunner of such spectacles as *Towering Inferno*, tried to do for arsonists what *Bwana Devil* did for masochists. Here, instead of being eaten by lions, you could be burned to a crisp in delicious 3-D, all for the price of a measly ticket.

Vincent Price played the mad operator of a wax museum who couldn't be bothered sculpting the various historical characters for his exhibition. Instead, he collected live ones and dipped them in wax as if they were human candles. When everything eventually caught on fire, the effects were ghastly enough for one reviewer to suggest that the audience bring vomit cups.

Jack Warner was pleased as punch and happy to take credit for choosing a "director who knew how to handle the complexities of Three-D." One day Jack Warner noticed de Toth on the lot wearing the familiar eye-patch again.

"Why is he wearing the patch?" demanded Warner. "He didn't have it when he was shooting *House of Wax*!"

"Since this was Warner Brothers' first Three-D movie, he didn't want you to worry," came the reply.

"Worry about what?" said Warner. "He's done one hell of a job."

"I know, but it took a lot of guts, Jack, for you to give him this picture, considering."

"Considering what?"

"That he's only got one eye."

"I know he's only got one eye. Herbert Marshall had a wooden leg and most of our female stars have plastic tits. So what?"

"So you know it takes two eyes to see Three-D. With one eye, he can only see two overlapping, blurred images. De Toth never knew what he had on film."

There was a long pause.

"Well, I was right," snapped Warner. "He's one hell of a director; he's got imagination."

After the successful premier of *House of Wax*, Jack Warner issued a statement to the press, proclaiming 3-D the wave of the future.

"Soon everyone will be carrying Three-D glasses the way they do fountain pens today," he said. Nevertheless, in spite of his optimism, Warner's first and unfortunately last 3-D picture was *House of Wax*. *Hondo*, a western with John Wayne and Geraldine Page, began in 3-D, but was released as a normal motion picture when the craze for movies "in depth" faded away. But Mr. Gunzberg's flash in the pan shook up the entire industry, and soon Cinemascope, VistaVision, and stereophonic sound came along to woo waning audiences away from that "boob tube" in their living rooms and back to the theaters. Today, Universal has "Senseround," which literally shakes hell out of audiences during the inevitable explosions, earthquakes, and roller-coaster rides. Mike Todd, Jr., tried to sell "Smellavision," with various scents wafting through the audience.

Three hundred and sixty degree wraparound screens, with multiple cameras, include the audience as part of the show without those silly glasses. These screens are now under development. This, coupled with the special-effects wizardry of *2001*, and *Star Wars* should bring to motion pictures what Arch Oboler dreamed of doing more than twenty years ago. Just remember, when you are hurtled to a distant galaxy in the company of R2D2 and C3PO and friends, it all began with Arch Oboler and a turkey called *Bwana Devil*.

Whenever an actor reaches a low ebb in his career, he contemplates retiring to become a used-car salesman. There is an alternative to become a pitchman for used Datsuns, however. You can go to work for a producer who turns out forgettable, low-budget films with actors who hope that these indiscretions will be forgotten as their stars rise to greater glory. In the early 1950s, my own career reached one of its less inspiring moments, and I found myself accepting an offer to play the lead in just such a film: Sam Katzman's production of *The Iron Glove*.

The Iron Glove co-starred Ursula Thiess and Alan Hale, Jr. It was a costume drama. I wore tights and sang a song, and if that wasn't enough to kill off an already ill-fated film, I don't know what else would. The film told the story of Charles Wogan of Rathcoffay and Sergeant Gaydon O'Toole, bodyguards of James Stuart, pretender to the throne of England in the early eighteenth century. I was told to use a dubious Irish accent throughout the film.

Katzman was very watchful of his budget.

"Lights go out in twenty minutes," he would say at a rehearsal. We had to do the job quickly; otherwise we would find ourselves locked out of the studio. Dick Crockett, a stunt man, worked with me on the swashbuckling swordplay. We hadn't had time to really choreograph our moves.

"Ad-lib it," said Katzman. "Lights go out in twenty minutes." I had memories of a drunken Errol Flynn once nearly losing an eye when he adlibbed a fencing match. But I pressed forward.

Crockett insisted that we go on with the show.

"I don't know the routine," I protested.

"We've got to wing it," said Dick. "If we don't, the old bastard will shut the lights off."

We began fencing, and I threw myself into the scene with enthusiasm. I nearly cut Dick Crockett's ear off. Blood was streaming down his face, but he insisted on keeping the fight scene going. When the lights went off, Katzman came down on the set. I threw the sword in his direction.

"You son of a bitch," I said. "Look what you made me do to my good friend Dick Crockett." Sam still shut the lights off.

A story, which may be apocryphal, attributes one of Hollywood's most bizarre episodes to Katzman. One of his relatives was working in scaffolding, or, as the crew says, "up high." The man had a heart attack and died on the spot. As the body was being carried down from the scaffold, Katzman scurried around the set. His grief was apparent.

"Come on, come on," he said. "Let's not sit around wasting time. Lights go out in twenty minutes."

Sam Katzman was not really unusual for a producer. He was simply concerned with saving a lot of money, getting the job done in a hurry, and making a profit. If there were some minor casualties along the way, it was all part of the business.

If ever there were a plum part in a film, it was Curly in *Oklahoma!* On Broadway, *Oklahoma!* was, for years, the most successful musical in history. (Its box office records have since been surpassed, but only by a handful of musicals.) The show represented a milestone in the history of musical theater: one of the first shows to feature a book (and therefore a plot) which could stand on its own. *Oklahoma!* also represented the debut of a new songwriting team Richard Rodgers and Oscar Hammerstein II, joining forces after Richard Rodgers and Lorenz Hart had dissolved their partnership of many years.

To many things even more exciting, the movie of *Oklahoma!* was to be photographed in Todd-A-O, the new widescreen process which seemed to forecast a whole new era in cinematography. In short, the lead in *Oklahoma!* was a part any self-respecting actor would give his eyeteeth to get.

No one could have been more interested than yours truly, when word was announced in 1954 that the film version of *Oklahoma!* was planned as a significant departure from the Broadway musical approach. Instead of casting singers in the leads, and treating the acting as an incidental matter, a unique decision had been made. The film version of the Rodgers and Hammerstein classic would emphasize the plot of the story, with strong stress laid on the actors' interpretations. The script was to follow closely the play, *Green Grow the Lilacs*, Lyn Riggs's classic work on which *Oklahoma!* had been based.

Every young actor in town participated in an assembly line

of screen tests. (One of the first to be rejected was an unknown actor from New York named James Dean.) The procedure for the tests was simple. Each actor was given a scene to prepare and then perform in front of the camera.

I decided to prepare my scene with the assistance of my friend George Zhdanov, an eminent director who once had his own theater in association with Michael Chekhov.

George's wife Elsa Schreiber is an equally celebrated director and acting coach. Together, they have personally provided the approaches to specific characterizations used by many international film stars. One of the peculiarities of our profession is that stars seldom acknowledge the advice or assistance of a coach or director. This is in direct contrast to ballet or opera, in which established stars of the Met or the Royal Ballet regularly go to classes. George and Elsa have a list of clients which reads like a who's who of Academy Award winners, and I know of several major stars who will not make a move without consulting them.

One of the ironies attached to my experience in trying to get the part of Curly was that while George and I were downstairs at their house preparing *my* interpretation for the *Oklahoma!* test, Elsa was upstairs coaching Gordon MacRae for *his* test for the same film.

An actor often needs a sounding board, someone in whom he has confidence, to build a personal and assured approach to characterization. The script contained some directions. Most were very basic and simply called for Curly to stand up or walk around. George and I decided to develop our own approach to blocking the scene. Instead of simply taking the script's direction, I decided to move around according to impulse. Instead of just talking to the girl in the scene, I decided to pick her up.

Virtually everyone else was following the directions in the script to the letter, so George and I decided that at least I could do something different.

When I arrived for the test, I saw actors walking in and out the door as if everyone in town was after the role. The filming began, and I was photographed doing the test my way. The temporary director started giving me directions but, since it was only a test, I had the option of doing it my way, and I did.

The initial reactions to the test were very positive. I was told that Fred Zinnemann liked it, and when the music director told me that Oscar Hammerstein II was enthusiastic about me, everything seemed to be very promising. I really wanted the part and knew I could do it well. After some delay, I finally received word that the odds were strongly in my favor. But fate had one last surprise in store. After hearing that both Zinnemann and Hammerstein had indicated their preference for my test out of hundreds of others, sudden word came from New York. Capitol Records had acquired the rights to release a record album in conjunction with the filming of *Oklahoma!*. All the leads in the movie would have to be played by actors who could record an album for Capitol. Gordon MacRae, who had a strong voice and had been testing all along, was signed for Curly.

Several people at the studio decided to cheer me up.

"You should be very proud of yourself," they said. "The studio loved MacRae's voice, but they didn't approve of his test. So they're going to use your test as a model for him to follow."

Even today, when I hear, "Oh, what a beautiful morning," I still can't help singing one line: "The corn is as high as a lyricist's aye."

6

The Heart Does Not Control the Feet

Or, The Making of The Bullfighter and the Lady

Ernest Hemingway once said that all true stories end in death. Nowhere is this more true than in Mexico where just about every hot, sunny Sunday afternoon, in the center of the bullring of the Plaza de Toros, a man can, by his own choosing, come to grips with all the essentials of life and death in a single instant. He may emerge triumphant in an indescribable moment of glory or be cut down in sudden violence and the chilling reality of his own fear.

In 1950 the furthest thing from my mind was an intense personal involvement in bullfighting, not to mention an appearance in the ring. Although an actor may be called upon to do many exciting things on the screen, the essence of acting is illusion. When the camera stops, the role ends. When I began preparing to play the part of a young American matador, I had no suspicion that this role would affect my life so deeply. Until then I had had no experience with bulls or fighting them, and even less interest in the subject. Nevertheless, when my very old friend Andy McLaglen invited me to go to Mexico for a couple of days, with Budd Boetticher and John Wayne, it seemed to be a perfectly simple jaunt.

THE HEART DOES NOT CONTROL THE FEET

Little did I know that this innocent-sounding junket would lead to the death of one man, the goring of two others, the rebirth of one of Mexico's greatest toreros, and the debut of one crazy actor in a Zacatepec bullring.

Few Americans have achieved success in the bullring. A whole chapter in Hemingway's *Death in the Afternoon* was devoted to Sydney Franklin's exploits. Barnaby Conrad jumped into a Mexican bullring to prove his courage, and eventually became a torero and the leading American writer on the subject. One of the few Americans to achieve success in Latin bullrings was Budd Boetticher, and the film called *The Bullfighter and the Lady* was to be based on his life.

Budd Boetticher has been described by many as a great romantic; just as many think he's nutty as a fruitcake. But everyone agrees he has what a matador would call a "surplus of *cojones*" (nerves of steel that defy translation).

Budd has been everything from a good amateur boxer, horseman, and football player, to successful Casanova and bullfighter. Anyone who is not an aficionado of bullfighting may not realize that bullfighters prepare by degrees to become matadors. The final test before becoming a full-fledged torero is called the *alternativa*. The new matador has a sponsor, or *padrino*, who is always an experienced torero. In Budd's case, his mentor was Armillita, one of Mexico's most revered toreros, fondly known as "the Pope" ("El Papa").

While I regarded the trip to Mexico as a jaunt, it was really a rather unique audition. John Wayne was to be the producer of Budd's film *The Bullfighter and the Lady,* and the Duke's idea of a test was to see if I flinched under pressure when faced with the real thing. He felt that if I was going to be believable as an on-screen matador, I had to be tough enough to have some similar qualities off camera.

Our destination in Mexico was Xayai, a small village built around a bullring. We rode for seemingly endless hours, bouncing along the narrow dirt roads better suited for the mule-drawn *carretas* than a gas-burner. By the time we arrived, we had collected Armillita, his twelve-year-old son, and various members of "the Pope's" *caudrilla,* or bullfighting team.

"Say, Bob, we're in luck," Budd said with a gleam in his eye—which I later learned usually meant trouble. "The local *ganadero* (bullrancher) happens to be testing some brave young cows today, and he's invited us to make a few passes."

When breeding fighting bulls and race horses, blood line is all important: hence, the *tienta*, or test, of the prospective bull-breeders, the young cows. Here the young cow (*vaca*) is tested for bravery. If she passes the test, she's saved for breeding. If not, she winds up on someone's barbecue. Only one in ten is found brave enough to mother a fighting bull. Male calves are not used, because the male calf might grow up one day to be a fighting bull. The bulls have good memories, and would remember fighting a man with a cape, even as an exercise, so they can't be tested for courage and bravery.

Although many people think of a bullfight as a ritual in which the matador tries to avoid the bull by adroit footwork, what actually takes place in the ring is just the opposite. The matador allows the bull to charge directly at him, and then works the bull around his body by using the cape to guide the bull past him. The basic ritual depends on the fact that the bull is seeing a torero for the first time when he enters the ring and may be fooled by skilled manipulation of the cape.

The term "cow" as applied to the young animals we were to test is deceiving; these creatures bear no resemblance whatsoever to gentle, smiling Elsie. They are lean, tricky, and, though lighter than young bulls, make up in speed and in the size of their horns what they lack in weight.

When the *vaca* is charging at everything in sight, toreros can practice passes, or guests are given the chance to make idiots of themselves. The *tienta* took place in the Xayai bullring. Friends and family of the *ganadero* gathered around. The atmosphere was one of festive enthusiasm, not unlike that at a local football game.

Budd explained the Armillita would begin by demonstrating the proper procedure at a *tienta*. He selected a particularly feisty little cow, displaying pass after pass.

Then it was my turn. I had participated in some pretty wild sporting activities in my life, and Armillita made this matter of caped passes seem so easy that I figured I wouldn't have too much difficulty. It looked as if all Armillita did was stand still and wave the red cloth, while the little cow obediently followed every move of the cape, behaving as docilely as a performing seal.

When I got the cape in my hand, I stood in what I thought was a copy of Armillita's stance, confidently waved the cape, and was immediately knocked flat on my back. Everytime I tried to get up, that miserable little female knocked me down, trying to stick her miniature horns in all my vital parts. Duke Wayne, Boetticher, and McLaglen were no help; they must have thought my performance was the funniest thing since Laurel and Hardy. Finally I threw dignity and old-world tradition out the window, and bulldogged the little monster like a rodeo cowboy. I threw my entire weight against the *vaca*, tying her up in the cape and trying to wrestle her to the ground. I decided that I had something to learn about the art of *torear*.

Andy McLaglen's turn was next. Andy is quiet, self-effacing, with a puckish smile and tousled brown hair. At 6'7" he was the only pal of John Wayne who could see Duke's bald spot. His mild manner belies the fact that he has one of the best punches in Hollywoood. Since he was taller and heavier than I, he was harder to knock over. But he looked like a giraffe trying to tie his neck in a knot when he tackled the *vaca*. He finally draped the cape over his adversary's head and got the hell out.

By now I realized that however easy bullfighting might look to the casual observer, it was a ritual for men of experience. If my debut as a matador hadn't been a picture of grace or style, I felt I could be forgiven. Even the toughest character could lose his cool when first facing a fighting cow.

Just about this time, Armillita's twelve-year-old son Manolo jumped in the ring. He challenged the same animal that had deposited me on the ground. As the cow charged, he began executing a complicated series of passes with the muleta.

"Those are *naturales*," Armillita proudly explained. "Now watch those. Those are *derechazos*." He began explaining to us the different types of passes used by an experienced matador. If the fighting cow had been damaging enough to my ego, little Manolo delivered the coup de grace. I returned home convinced this was one "audition" best forgotten.

A few days later Budd called to tell me that I had the lead in the movie. He also told me that I could look forward to the most interesting co-stars ever, the fighting *toros* of Mexico. "You've just seen the cows," said Budd enthusiastically. "Wait till you see the bulls."

I couldn't wait!

For a month, I worked regularly with Budd. He explained that as soon as we went back to Mexico, I would be taking lessons from some of Mexico's finest toreros. I read the script of the film, and learned something about my character. My role was that of a young American, not unlike Budd Boetticher on his first trip to Mexico years before. This young man would be captivated by bullfighting and, in exchange for skeet shooting lessons (a special touch for me), he would persuade a great Mexican torero to train him for the ring.

As I began going more deeply into the subject, I started to understand Budd's enthusiasm. The script was a good one. The complex subject of bullfighting would be shown to the audience through my character's eyes. As I learned, they would learn with me. Gilbert Roland, Katy Jurado, Joy Page, and Virginia Grey rounded out the cast. John Wayne remained in the States, but planned to join us as we progressed in our filming.

Budd and I flew directly to Mexico City and went almost immediately to the Plaza Mexico. Outside, we saw the imposing statues erected in tribute to the great Mexican matadors. The Plaza is the biggest bullring in the world, an amphitheater of overpowering size. Even when empty, there is a mood, a special feeling about the Plaza that surrounds you as you climb the steps near the entrance. On Sunday afternoons the place is teeming with cheering crowds; the rest of the time the deserted bullring is quiet, eerily still, and lonely. As I walked around the Plaza Mexico for the first time, I thought the bronze statues of dead toreros surrounding the ring looked like headstones in a cemetery.

Shortly after arriving at the Plaza, I was introduced to the man who had been hired to double for me in the film. His name was Luis Briones, and he was a torero of legendary skill. In his last fight, he had been gored in the head, the horn slipping in past his left eye. Miraculously, he was neither blinded nor killed. No one talked about it, but after the terrible goring even the experts didn't know how he would react when facing the horns again.

Bullfighting is completely unionized in Mexico. Every matador belongs to the union, and the head of the *syndicato* is always very powerful. Briones had quarreled with Señor Gaona, who ran the Plaza Mexico, and had almost been forced into retirement. Now, hired by an American film company, Briones would be making his comeback appearance in a Mexican bullring.

To us, the bullfighting sequences were simply part of a

motion picture, but to Luis Briones they represented a second chance at a career about which he felt passionately. Intense, emotional, and possessed by a fierce sense of determination, Luis Briones was facing his own private challenge. He would prove himself to all Mexico.

I also met Felix Briones, Luis's brother. He had been hired on as insurance in case anything happened to Luis during the filming. The toreros at the Plaza Mexico were among the most famous in the world: Carlos Arruza had been the rival of Manolete, perhaps the most legendary of all matadors. Critics seriously suggested that Arruza could hypnotize a bull with his skill.

Our initial business experience south of the border was something of a jolt. For several weeks we waited for a crew and a sound stage. Nothing was available. While the studio continued keeping actors on the payroll, the delays seemed impossible. Our production manager Nate Edwards couldn't figure out what was wrong, or why everything moved more slowly than a group of turtles.

Finally, Ruben Padilla, our Mexican liaison, provided the answer. "Who has taken care of the *soborno*?" he said.

"*Soborno?*" we all said at once, wondering if this was some mysterious form of paperwork which had been neglected.

"The bribe," he said. "All the crews in Mexico are controlled by the union, the *syndicato*. Haven't you arranged to bribe someone there to provide you with a crew?"

Nate, who regarded such chicanery as unspeakably dishonest, was horrified. "I've never bribed anybody," he said.

"In most Latin countries, it is the custom," said Ruben Padilla.

The next day, he arranged for us to visit the beautiful, streamlined glass building which housed the offices of Mexico's *syndicato*, the equivalent of the Screen Actors Guild.

"How do I bribe someone?" demanded Nate.

"Give the man the money," said Ruben.

We all went in with Nate to the main office, where we were greeted by a local official. We exchanged pleasantries, talked about the weather, and about local bullfighting. After a few minutes of this, Ruben gave Nate his best cloak-and-dagger look. "Now," he whispered. Nate was obviously feeling more uncomfortable than he would have had he awakened from a sound sleep and found himself in the middle of Mexico's largest bullring. He took out of his pocket an envelope filled with $10,000 and dropped it on the table.

The gentleman behind the desk was not subtle. He picked up the envelope, examined its contents, and then said matter-of-factly. "By the way, señores, tormorrow you have a crew and one of the best sound stages in all Mexico. Would you care for some tequila? Salud!"

Our next encounters with trouble were with the fighting bulls of Mexico. Unlike human protagonists, there's no amount of money to dissuade a charging bull from doing what he loves to do best: thrusting his horns into any target unfortunate enough to get in his way.

For the next twelve weeks, I was allowed into the private world of some great toreros. Because I approached them humbly, asking for their help, every bullfighter I met made me welcome, and spent hours showing this particular gringo their expertise. My first exercise was "running the horns." Usually an aspiring bullfighter will depend upon the boys who hang around the ring to run the horns for him. But in this case, Briones did the job himself. The novice matador learns to use the cape, while someone pretends to be the bull, charging at him and carrying a special set of horns. This protects the beginner, allowing him to practice his passes without using a real animal—which could be fatal.

I learned quickly that the beginner is sometimes fooled by the deceptive ease with which great toreros handle the cape. Every pass with the cape requires constant practice, just as a virtuoso musician or star athlete perfects the most difficult moves and makes them look easy. A pass can look flashy in front of a mirror, and yet not work with a bull.

The basic pass is called *la veronica*, named after the woman said to have held out a cloth to Christ on the road to Calvary. Then there is the *chicuelina*, invented by Chicuelo: the matador pulls his right arm toward his body as the bull's horn is going by his legs, then he spins toward the bull and revolves completely around. I was shown the spectacular *manoletina*, a pass created by Manolete: the torero faces the bull and stands between the muleta and the bull. As the bull charges, the matador turns and the bull passes under his right arm, hopefully, a very flashy pass. Then there are the *naturales*, the basic left-handed passes, and a drop to the knees with one's back to the bull, a *desplante*.

To my surprise, I learned that there are as many approaches to the passes as there are matadors. Some toreros augment their passes with *adornos*, feats of great skill, designed to elaborate their performance. (An example would be the matador who drops to his knees or turns his back and virtually invites the animal to kill him, confident that the animal will not charge.)

I realized that it takes years of practice (not to mention talent) to execute the passes well. But I had to learn to handle the cape and muleta well enough to fool the camera at a distance. For close-ups, I would be doubled by the finest toreros in all Mexico.

During hours of instruction in the techniques of the cape and muleta, I gradually discovered the mystique of the bullring. Like most Americans, I had never explored the world of bullfighting in detail. I learned that nothing takes place in a bullfight which is not related in some way to classical tradition. There are many types of fighting bulls; their coats, markings, and physical appearances are described by the term *estampa*. There are more than sixty *estampas*, covering every possible physical detail. The fact that a bull is a *nevado* ("snowed upon," with small white spots) or a *carivacado* (with an elongated snout) may be irrelevent to its fighting ability. But a genuine aficionado wants to know everything, including blood lines, about the fighting bulls he sees in the ring.

When I took my first lesson, the only thing I knew about a bull's horns was that they were long, sharp, and deadly. I also knew I felt comfortable staying as far away from them as possible. I soon learned that a list of the varieties of horns could fill a small dictionary. A bull's horns may be described as *astiagudo* (sharp-pointed) or *astifino* (thin, polished). Horns can be white, black, or even green; they may curve very close together, out to the side, or not at all.

Fighting bulls have been bred for centuries to be brave, to charge everything that moves, and to kill that moving target. They are not domestic cattle, and are raised on ranches exclusively devoted to providing bulls for the arena. The aficionados love the bulls which charge directly at the cape.

I had an opportunity to see both the public and private sides of the men who must deal with the unpredictable public adulation as well as unpredictable bulls. They live with a combination of exultation and fear on a daily basis. And they must always demonstrate courage and honor. A bullfighter normally begins as a *novillero,* or apprentice. Eventually, he may graduate to become a full-fledged torero. (The term toreador appears only in *Carmen,* not in the Mexican bullrings.) Each matador has a *cuadrilla,* a group of five ring assistants. There are three *banderilleros* who place darts or *banderillas* in the bull's neck and cape the bull into position. There are also two *picadors,* men on horseback who use lances, or *varas,* to pick the bull before the torero takes over.

I was allowed to mingle freely with the *cuadrilla,* and to attend the *sorteo,* or drawing of the bulls. At noon on the day of the fight, the senior *banderilleros* gather as representatives of the various matadors. They draw lots from a hat; the clips of cigarette paper contain numbers which determine which bulls will face which matadors.

Even the process of dressing for a fight follows a ritual pattern. A matador wears the *traje de luces* (suit of lights), a lamé-trimmed costume that may weigh as much as twenty-five pounds. I still treasure my own suit of lights, which I wore during sequences of the film. The suit includes the traditional shirt (*camisa*), pants (*taloquilla*), jacket (*chaquetilla*), vest (*chaleco*), Cape de Paseo (dress cape), slippers (*zapatillas*), and pigtail (*coleta*). While the matador is dressing, friends and colleagues may wander in and out, wishing him good fortune or asking for his autograph. In private, he will pray to the Virgen de la Macarena, and attempt to make peace with himself before stepping into the ring.

While I concentrated on learning to handle a cape, and on the basic techniques of footwork and control, I could not escape the mystique of bullfighting. I began to understand why it was so important for Luis Briones to return to his days of glory. A famous matador occupies a position in Spain or Mexico for which there is no parallel. Phenomenally successful athletes in this country may become famous and wealthy—matinee idols. But the matador is even more. He becomes a national hero, a symbol of courage and tenacity to everyone in his country. It is this intangible emotional element that defies description. It must be sensed and experienced to be understood. It can also disappear if the matador disappoints his fans. Manolete was an international idol, a hero to the Spanish people.

Yet, near the end of his career, the bullring crowds sang songs ridiculing him; they sang parodies of the lyrics which had been written in his homage only a few years before. Still, when he died, the nation mourned, just as Americans mourned the deaths of the Kennedys and Martin Luther King.

Bullfighters lead an exaggerated, fast-paced life. Many of them seem larger than life; they live for the excitement and thrill. I took one wild, unholy car ride with Silverio Perez from his ranch in Tescoco to Mexico City. The trip proved two things to me: first, that bullfighters are crazy, and, second, that they command the respect, love, and sometimes hatred or contempt of people. This particular night, Silverio had argued with both his wife and his mistress. He was so out-of-his-skull drunk as he drove the car that I was lying on the floor in back waiting for a crash. I wasn't disappointed. Racing around one of the traffic circles on Reforma, he slammed into a brand-new Cadillac. The driver of the Cadillac was a big bruiser with a mustache. He slowly got out, looked at his mashed car, then stormed over to Silverio's car, yanked the door open, and reached in as if bent on destroying the culprit. Suddenly, he froze in wonder.

He slowly hauled out the plastered matador, and then, wonder of wonders, a big grin spread over his face as he wrapped his arms around Silverio in an embrace.

"Matador," he said, "it is an honor for me to meet you."

He even took us back to the hotel and waved a jolly goodbye as he drove away in his damaged, but honored Cadillac.

After the fights, I was welcomed as a friend to celebrate or mourn what had happened in the ring. To be accepted by the matadors meant more to me than any acceptance I have ever known.

The first part of the film took us to the most remote haciendas in Mexico. On the way, I happened to notice a discarded bathtub full of slabs of meat sitting in the sun, layered with flies.

"A bull killed by lightning," the interpreter told me. "Good for *carnitas*."

I assumed *carnitas* was a pet dog. I was wrong. *Carnitas* proved to be our dinner: barbecued anything that was killed or had died that day.

These ranches out in the middle of nowhere had no electricity, but communication between them was a simple arrangement. Built into each hacienda was a tower. By Morse or some other code, and by using a mirror in the day and a lantern at night, messages were sent to neighboring ranches. Since there were no screens, all the great outdoors joined us indoors. What I first thought were raisins in our food proved to be whatever could fly or crawl in at lunchtime. When we arrived at the Ganaderia (bull ranch) Zacatepec, I saw a herd of fighting bulls for the first time. They were black specks in an unbroken panorama of wildflowers.

Señor Muñoz, the *ganadero*, invited us to dinner. By now I thought I was prepared for almost anything. But when I arrived at the main house, I nearly went into shock. The parade of servants was an instant reminder of how deadly fighting bulls could be. The man who served soup had a twisted back, which made him look like Quasimodo; a one-armed waiter poured wine.

No one offered an explanation until midway through dinner, then I was told that these men had been gored working outside. Those who survived became household help.

On this note of cheer, Budd announced that we would choose the fighting bulls tomorrow. Boetticher is a man with an insane kind of charm, a sort of Pied Piper of Pamplona. I had played polo, so at least I could ride a horse, although I tried to forget about what could happen if the horse accidentally stepped in a gopher hole. Somehow, gopher holes kept appearing in my imagination all during dinner.

The next morning, we went out to look the bulls over. For a number of years, some matadors had been encouraging breeders to breed smaller, less dangerous bulls. But every role in our film, even that of the bulls, was to be cast by Budd, and he wanted the biggest, bravest bulls he could find.

"Look at number twenty-three, isn't that a beauty?" he would yell. "What a rack of horns on sixty-three!" Budd would ride up within twenty yards of a group of bulls. All the time, he slyly watched me out of the corner of his eye. I was damned if I was going to be bluffed out by my crazy director; I felt we were playing an old-fashioned game of chicken. If a bull started to charge, we'd spin away, the bull returning to the herd, and we'd start all over again.

The purpose of our exhibition was simple. By testing which of the bulls charged aggressively while we were on horseback, we had an idea which bulls might prove the bravest in the ring.

ROBERT STACK
"MY LIFE IN HOLLYWOOD"
Including photos from his personal collection

Me and my best girl

My first movie star Rin-Tin-Tin, Mother, and me

Every skeet shooter's dream—a world's record

Jimmy Stack's band (I'm the guy in the white socks)

Carole Lombard, a thirteen-year-old's first love

Doing a Robert Taylor imitation with Deanna Durbin in <u>First Love</u>

With Maggie Sullavan, Bill Orr, and Jimmy Stewart in <u>The Mortal Storm</u> or How We Got on the Nazi Death List

Playing the boy next door in <u>Nice Girl</u>, with (left to right) Franchot Tone, Bob Benchley, Deanna, Ann Gwynn, and Nan Grey

The only time I was Spencer Tracy's equal—
on the polo field

The King and I

Taking over the controls in <u>The High and the Mighty</u> with John Wayne

My favorite photo session: with Carole Lombard in
To Be or Not to Be

Ambassador Kennedy's son visits the set

Recruiting aerial gunners for the United States Navy, me and my delinquent war heroes

A date with the real Judy

Watching Gilbert Roland's death scene in <u>The Bullfighter and the Lady</u>

My first tienta

An actor's dream—the role of Kyle Hadley in <u>Written on the Wind</u>

Finding out I'm a daddy: Jack Carson, Rock Hudson, Dorothy Malone, me, and Bob Middleton

As Eliot Ness

With the Untouchables: (left to right) Abel Fernandez, Paul Picerni, and Nick Georgiade

Eliot Ness makes the cover of <u>Look</u>

My family: Rosemarie, Elizabeth, and Charlie

A dancing lesson

The good life, courtesy of Capone, Nitti, and friends

Señor Muñoz watched our carryings on through binoculars.

"Macho," he said, shaking his head as he observed our hijinks, *"Pero, unpoco loco!"*

By now, Duke Wayne and his long-time chum Jimmy Grant had flown down to Mexico and planned to join us at our next stop.

Our filming moved along smoothly until the company moved to Querétaro. "This is an historic site," exclaimed Budd with his usual enthusiasm. "Maximilian was assassinated here!"

I should have guessed instantly that trouble was just around the corner. The first surprise in Querétaro was considerably more than a minor mishap. In the script, the character portrayed by Gilbert Roland was supposed to hurt his hand and fight an unpicked bull with left-handed passes only.

Three toreros were dressed identically to do Gilbert's fighting; the job was too difficult for a single matador. We hoped to get enough usable footage from all three toreros to make it appear that Roland had accomplished this feat. One of the three was Felix Briones. On his fifth pass, the bull came in head high, hooked, and caught him over the eye, laying his scalp wide open.

When I finally found Felix, after the doctors finished working on him, he was sitting in a darkened room of the hacienda. He turned toward me and I saw great tears running slowly down his face.

"I have ruined the movie and disgraced Mexico," he said.

He spoke not one word about damn near having had his head torn off. The Briones brothers seemed to be treating the movie as a test of bravery and honor instead of an entertaining motion picture.

While in Querétaro, Duke hosted a party that lasted all night. All hell broke loose. Many local characters had been recruited as extras. They were casually invited to join our company, but we later discovered that the guns they wore on and off camera were full of live ammunition.

By the time they had joined the crew for a combination of wine, women, and tequila, they were ready for some excitement. Mariachi bands had been providing music all evening, but by 4 A.M., when I was trying to sleep, the boys outside were just beginning to loosen up. I heard the familiar and unpleasant crack of a bullet as one whizzed by, tearing through the adobe walls, and passing two feet over my head. Duke, Budd, and I received the same treatment. The Mexican cure for party poopers worked. The party went on till sunrise.

The next day, I asked Budd why the ranch hands, would-be toreros and just plain adventurers, played their games with live ammunition.

"Machismo," said Budd.

Because the world of bullfighting is filled with danger, matadors accept life and death as an everyday occurrence. It is sometimes easy to forget how dangerous the bulls really are.

When we first arrived in Mexico, we heard stories about an incredible display of courage by Diego Fortuna, a retired bullfighter who had been living in Spain. In 1929 a bull accidentally escaped and charged down the streets of Madrid, goring anyone who got in his way. He terrified a large crowd of people until Fortuna stepped forward, used his overcoat in place of a cape, and distracted the bull until his wife arrived with his sword. He killed the bull and won the Cruz de la Beneficencia from the Spanish government. I never suspected that we would witness a similar feat of courage right there in Querétaro. The bullring itself, although quite small, was typical; adjoining it was a smaller ring where bulls were drawn by lot for the Sunday bullfight. Local animals were never used for our filming. The studio trucks would deliver our own bulls in advance, and they would be waiting when the company arrived. On Sunday, Budd and I went sightseeing.

Suddenly, we heard screams coming from the bulls' quarters. One of the *caporals* or bullhandlers had spent the night drinking tequila. In a moment of drunken abandon he forgot the long pole used to move the bulls into the stalls and tried to make a bull move into the ring by slapping him on the rump. The bull had spun and hooked him with his deadly horns and was goring him. Suddenly, from nowhere, Luis Briones appeared, decked out in his Sunday suit. We were not filming and no one was prepared for action. I remember wondering, what in hell Luis thought he could do without his cape.

Even in street clothes and with no advance warning, Luis Briones was the master matador. He hurdled the stone fence which stood between him and the nearby ring, took off his hat, and threw it toward the bull like a Frisbee. The bull charged toward the hat, then turned and started toward him. By now, Felix had heard the noise and had joined his brother. Between them, they worked the bull away from the poor *caporal*, using their bodies, hats, and even a handkerchief. The bull charged one, then the other, in a ring one-tenth the size of a normal bullring. For sheer courage, I've never seen anything to top it.

They gradually worked the bull so that another torero could extricate the injured man. The poor *caporal* was severely hurt and was taken directly to the hospital. As it happened, the bull which wounded the man belonged to the studio, not to the local ranch.

The local citizenry were up in arms. As they saw it, an "American bull" had almost killed a Mexican. The chief of police told us to get out of town fast. He had learned that some hotheads were getting a posse together and, if the *caporal* should die, the chief couldn't be responsible for our safety.

Under armed guard, we got out of there in a hurry. The next day we received word that the *caporal* had died during the night.

Our next destination was Mexico City. We returned to the capital city of Mexico to photograph the climactic fight in the Plaza Mexico. I thought everything that could possibly happen during the filming of a motion picture had already happened in Querétaro. How wrong I was!

For *Bullfighter*, my hair had to be bleached blond. Since we were shooting in black and white, it was felt the contrast was needed to differentiate between the Latin toreros and me, the gringo bullfighter.

Poor Luis Briones, my double, also had to undergo the bleaching treatment. Unfortunately, they never managed to get his hair to turn blond, even after blistering the top of his head repeatedly. He was so ashamed of his newly acquired orange hair that he only went out at night, and then only with a beret.

In my case, no one had told the hairdresser that in Mexico City the water is turned off in the afternoon. She had me all soaped up in the bleach, only to discover, when the time came to rinse off the junk, that nothing would come out of the water faucets but a loud, dry belch. In a panic, our hairdresser Hazel finally met the emergency by rinsing me in 7-Up and root beer. But, by the time she made her move, I was bleached as blond as Betty Grable and very sticky to the touch. The flies loved it!

The language also proved a problem for me. Even the simplest question could turn into a major communications crisis. One of my conversations might run something like this:

"Hey, Roberto, you from America? What you call yourself?"

"Me? American!"

"Hey, Roberto, you a *maricon*?"

"That's right, American. Roberto is *maricon*." (*Maricon* is Spanish for homosexual.)

"Hey, Roberto, what you do in the war?"

"I taught machine gun."

"Chinga?"

"That's right, machine gun."

"Roberto teaches *chingas*." (*A chinga* is a whore, naturally.)

Fortunately, we confined ourselves to discussions about such scintillating topics as the weather and the price of tortillas. I had the feeling that a serious discussion of Mexican politics might start World War III before the translator arrived!

A few days before our arrival in Mexico City from Querétaro, ads had been taken in the papers, announcing free admission to a *corrida* with Luis Briones, Luis Castro, Andrés Blando, Chicuelin, etc. This announcement assured not only a full house, but the rowdiest crowd ever assembled in the Plaza. Briones was famous throughout all Mexico. In addition, word had been spread that this *corrida* would feature the biggest bulls seen in the Plaza Mexico in twenty years. The chance to see an ostracized bullfighter trying for a comeback against giant bulls proved an irresistible lure. People poured into Mexico City from a hundred miles away. The fights were bonafide fights, but we were going to film them for use in the movie.

Five cameras were to be used. The action would necessarily be improvisational. We had learned from Felix's goring that bullfighters cannot follow a script. So Luis was told to forget the script and run his own show.

But Luis Briones was marching to a different drummer. In our talks, I kept telling him that *The Bullfighter and the Lady* was only a motion picture. Luis only shook his head. There he sat, a tiny brown man in a big leather chair, with delicate hands and the most somber expression I ever saw.

Finally he said to me, "Maybe a motion picture for you, Roberto, but not for me." He seemed to be speaking almost to himself. "Tomorrow, I am either the greatest torero in Mexico, or the deadest."

I realized that Luis saw this *corrida* as a real bullfight, a chance to redeem himself before all Mexico City. The cameras might be rolling, but this would be Luis's personal confrontation with death in the afternoon. I was enormously impressed with the man's dignity, but I was also frightened for him.

The climax of the motion picture was to be the Plaza Mexico bullfight. The plot was simple: The veteran matador who had taught my character how to fight had been killed, and now, as an American facing a hostile crowd which blamed him for the death of a Mexican hero, my character was supposed to enter the ring and prove his courage. Of course, although I would enter the ring with the others, Luis Briones would do the actual fighting.

To describe the emotion I felt in the *paseo,* the parade leading into the bullring, would take a book. I stood near the main gate to the bullring, surrounded by six of the finest toreros in Mexico. The Plaza Mexico was a great amphitheater teeming with people. The crowd was noisy, ready and eager to cheer wildly or shout its angry displeasure, depending upon what happened. The Plaza Mexico seemed set for a combination of events: Christians versus lions, and an auto-da-fé.

Normally, a motion picture is nothing more than a re-creation of reality. But here, any semblance of fantasy had vanished; it was all too real.

The crowd went into a frenzy as soon as I stepped into view. The sight of a blond gringo was hardly welcome.

"Hey, blondie," someone shouted in Spanish. "Throw us a kiss."

That was the nicest thing anyone had to say to me all afternoon. The rest was unprintable, in English or Spanish. The bullfight had not even started and already a half dozen fights had broken out in the stands. It was a very angry crowd for some reason, a crowd spoiling for trouble. I could see the sun reflecting off knife blades. I prayed that Luis would triumph, or our unhappy experience in Querétaro would seem like a skirmish in the face of what this crazy mob might inflict on us.

The band played "La Virgen de la Macarena," the traditional bullfight melody. When the trumpet sounded, the "Door of Scares" was flung open, and out burst an enormous animal. It looked like a piece of monumental statuary.

The huge bull made a rush at the *banderillero's* cape. When it found nothing solid to sink its horns into, it furiously pounded its horns against the *burladero,* a small wooden barrier a torero can duck behind for safety if he is in trouble. The *burladero* was knocked flat against the wall. A large gasp went up from the crowd. We suddenly realized, along with the throngs of onlookers, how huge the bull really was. Luis stepped out onto the sunlit sand.

An eerie hush settled over the Plaza. Luis made a few passes. The *picadors* thrust their lances into the bull, and now the show began.

The muleta is a small cloth with a stick running through the top so that it can be held with one hand. When passes are made with the right hand (*derechazos*), the sword is also used. It extends the end of the muleta, making it a larger target.

The left-handed passes (*naturales*) have a target only half the size. These are the classic or "money" passes. If the bullfighter has only the *naturales* in his repertoire, and can execute them well, he can always find work.

With a combination of fear recalled (his terrible goring in the very same Plaza a few months before), fear present (the biggest bull he'd ever fought), and a raging anger against Gaona, Impresario of the Plaza Mexico, who had kept him out of his bullring for so long, Luis Briones was magnificent. The highlight of any bullfight is the *faena,* the combination of passes leading up to the kill. The aficionado often says that passes, by themselves, do not constitute a bullfight. It is the careful combination of passes, the step-by-step design and pattern of the work with the muleta, which makes a bullfight exceptional. To the aficionado, a bullfight has the same intense drama as a play or an opera. A masterful *faena* must be orchestrated with a foundation of basic, functional passes, followed by a series of daring *adornos*. These stunts demonstrate the courage of the matador.

Luis put together a *faena* which no one in the Plaza Mexico would ever forget. He included all the classic and showboat passes. He had even read the script on the sly, and did a series with his toes planted in his hat, the ultimate arrogance.

After tying together two *arrucinas* (the most dangerous pass in bullfighting, with a handkerchief-sized target), he turned his back to the bull. He dropped to his knees and looked over at me with a crooked grin.

The crowd went wild when Luis executed a perfect kill.

Even Gaona, Luis's old nemesis, was jumping up and down, yelling, waving his scarf. The prodigal son had returned. Or so I thought.

Not quite. With that incredibly haughty torero's swagger, Luis sauntered about the ring, as flowers, hats, and mantillas rained around him. Then, he took his sword and strode briskly toward Gaona's box.

Good, I said to myself. *Now they'll make up and Luis's problems will be over.*

Luis walked across the ring to Gaona's box, all right. But instead of making up, Luis looked directly at Gaona, and made an unmistakable international gesture suggesting what Gaona could do with his bullring. Gaona paid no attention to the insult. Luis was taken back into the family in spite of his audacity.

The following morning, headlines in the newspaper *Ovaciones* confirmed Luis's success. "Briones Colossal," exclaimed the papers. "Bullfighting returns to Mexico!" Luis, himself, was pleased and moved. We didn't know how much until Luis saw himself on screen.

As the film began running, and he made his first pass, I heard a quiet "olé" from the back of the projection room. It was Luis. As the tempo of the passes increased, so did Briones's enthusiasm. By the final, climactic *faena,* he was on his feet, yelling and cheering. "Look at that, an *arrucina,* by God!" he exclaimed excitedly. "What a bullfighter! There's nobody like you! You're the greatest! Olé, Luis!"

People often joke about actors having schizoid personalities, seeing themselves on the screen but reacting as if they were seeing someone else. The matador seemed no different. Luis left the projection room convinced he was Mexico's greatest torero. Fortunately, all Mexico agreed, and so did his friends among the movie's crew.

The last part of *The Bullfighter and the Lady* did not take place in Mexico City, but in a *tienta* in Zacatepec. Although an audience always sees the scenes of a motion picture in order, people often don't realize that the ending of a film may be shot before the beginning. It all depends on the schedule, which is influenced as much by travel conditions or budget as by the chronological order of scenes ina script.

So, although we had completed the most important scene of the film—the big bullfight—we had some unfinished business. From the very beginning of the film, I felt it important that the audience be convinced that my character was actually fighting in the final bullfight in the Plaza Mexico. Budd shared my view that the best way to convince the audience would be to include, earlier in the picture, some scenes of me in close-up, participating in a *tienta*. Up to now I'd never fought any big animals, but what had begun as a fanciful idea, began to seem very important to me. I wanted to find out what would happen if I faced a decent-sized animal in the ring.

Budd knew me so well that when I mentioned doing a possible *tienta*, he told me it was set for the following day. I signed on the dotted line, and faster than you could say "waiver," the studio was cleared of any responsibility. To experienced toreros, the *tienta* is not dangerous or thrilling; it's just a routine day's work.

But at least one participant in this particular *tienta* was standing outside the bullring wondering how he'd ever gotten into this situation. As I waited outside the ring in Zacatepec, I thought about the toreros I had met during my stay in Mexico. I thought of their courage and wondered what it would be like to experience, even in the relatively subdued atomosphere of a *tienta*, a moment which could only be understood by those who stand directly in the path of a pair of sharp horns attached to a large black animal that wants to do away with you.

A couple of novice bullfighters who came to watch noticed that I was obviously an American, even though I was doing my best not to look nervous. What ensued was a scene out of a comedy.

One of the *novilleros* approached in a friendly way. "Are you going into the ring?" he said.

I nodded.

"Are you a *novillero*?" he asked, his face brightening.

"No," I said. "I'm an actor. My name is Robert Stack." He looked confused.

"Suerte," he said, and walked off shaking his head.

As I waited for my turn, I recalled the events of the last few days. With impeccable timing, I chose to come down with dysentery for the seventh time since my arrival in Mexico.

The toreros all helped to build my morale in their own special way. The night before, I had been invited to view a short film called *Muerta en las Cuernas*, or *Death on the Horns*. It was short only because it consisted entirely of matadors being gored. All the major gorings of the last twenty years were included. There was no story, no plot, no characters, just people flying through the air, being torn to shreds or impaled like shish kabobs. All the toreros thought it was great fun.

Of course, I would not be facing a bull, but a fighting cow, a *vaca*. "Don't be afraid," said one torero. "Even the great Juan Belmonte was once nearly killed by a fighting cow. It was only an accident. If Belmonte himself respected the *vaca*, why should you expect perfection after only a few weeks' training?"

Señor Muñoz had also helped make my day by providing *vacas* which were more than twice the size I had anticipated. "Roberto, they are big, yes," he said, as if reading my mind. "But I personally made sure you are fighting only those with horns that turn in. There's less chance of being hooked, unless, of course, you are hit head-on, in which case you will be hit by both horns. Try not to be hit head-on."

I'll try to remember that, I thought.

Budd gave me the signal. It was my turn. I walked forward and prepared to fight in my first *tienta*. The crowd seemed receptive to the idea of watching *"un poco loco gringo"* in the *tienta* ring for the first time. The bleacher seats were loaded with spectators; most of the spectators were loaded, too. The blood-red wine being squeezed out of a hundred *botas* was ominously reminiscent of the previous night's film.

One of the girls in the crowd had a long silver streak in her hair. She was a *procunista* (a fan of the great Luis Procuna) confided one of the *novilleros*. He explained that the girls who followed the career of the celebrated matador dyed their hair with a silver streak to match the natural streak in his own.

Luis Briones rejected the first two *vacas*, made only one pass on the third, and then nodded his head.

"Go out now and do *manoletinas*," he said, grinning at me.

Why in hell he chose that miserable pass for me to do, I'll never know. It's the pass in which the matador stands between the bull and the muleta, exposing all that is mortal and unsure to all that fortune, death, and danger dare, as Shakespeare would say.

But Luis was the director of this scene. I trusted Luis Briones, and he knew how I felt. The night before the *tienta*, we had received word that the famous American matador Sydney Franklin would be attending. The picture was officially over, and after the *tienta*, a fiesta complete with mariachi music was planned to celebrate what the gringo did (or didn't do) in the ring. Before I went to bed, Luis invited me for a nightcap. As the bar was closing, he toasted me.

"Roberto, we love you," he said. "You are a good man, and you have a brave heart. Unfortunately, as you may know, the heart does not control the feet. If you run, do not be ashamed." I knew I wouldn't run.

What I *would* do, however, was entirely open to speculation. Few words can describe the feeling of being in a ring with animals bred to annihilate whatever moves. As I felt my manhood trying to creep up into my stomach, I fatalistically placed the muleta behind me. My heart stopped and everything went into slow motion.

The *vaca*'s tail flew up, and she was on her way. The charge was as pure as Luis had predicted. A photographer was on hand to capture my reaction. The *vaca* charged, hit the muleta, and went flying past me, under my arm, brushing my back. In the second shot of the before-and-after sequence, I was looking over my shoulder with an expression that meant "son of a bitch, it worked."

From then on, it was ecstasy, pass after pass. I thought I was Manolete. Of course, I wasn't, and the first one to realize this was the *vaca*.

A telescopic lens caught what happened next. I was feeling right at home in the ring. I looked relaxed and confident. I actually loved my deadly black partner. She was following every nuance of the red cloth. So I decided to try some *naturales*.

In the telephoto lens of one camera, I could be seen starting one pass, then getting hit, and disappearing up out of the frame before dropping back into the next frame like a yo-yo. I scrambled to my feet.

I jumped over the *barera*. The matadors all crowded around, slapping me on the back.

Luis Briones was all smiles. "Roberto, you son of a bitch," he said, "you are a bullfighter now!"

7

The High and the Mighty

Or, How to Get a Part by Being Low and Sneaky

The High and the Mighty, by Ernest K. Gann, was a best-seller published in 1953. It took the country by storm. It must be one of the original disaster stories. In the book, a plane loses the use of two engines, but the crew manages to get it home. Gann caught the public's love for the vicarious experience of potential disaster, much as *Jaws* or *The Towering Inferno* have more recently.

After heavy negotiating, John Wayne bought the motion picture rights, and the battle to get a part in the movie was on. Every actor in Hollywood with a guild card, and some who had retired to the security of real estate and insurance work, came out of the woodwork to take a crack at it. The part of Sullivan, the plane's captain who goes berserk under pressure, was a good enough role to tempt anyone to try desperate measures.

Like everyone else, I read Ernie Gann's novel and was fascinated by the psychology of Captain Sullivan. He was superficially a clear-eyed, normal human being. But under his normal exterior was hidden a basket of snakes, a touch of madness that would have to be revealed in the actor's eyes.

The actor portraying Sullivan would have to play the role from the inside out.

I believed I could play Sullivan, but I thought carefully about the people I would have to convince. High on the list was the film's director "Wild Bill" Wellman, member of the legendary Lafayette Escadrille in World War I, deflator of producers and stuffed shirts, and the terror of every actor in town.

One acting stud whose only previous dealings with the Almighty had been taking his name in vain, decided to join the Catholic church. He just happened to end up in the same parish as Wellman, although it was thirty miles away from where the actor lived. Another potential Captain Sullivan tried dating one of Wellman's pretty daughters. (The actor in question had a hard time explaining to his fiancée that his extracurricular activities were only part of the casting game.)

In my case, I depended on my secret weapon, my agent Bill Shiffrin. Underneath his elegant Italian silk suit lived the spirit of P. T. Barnum, a spirit an actor needs in his agent. The casting of the movie became a national concern, not as intense as the one for *Gone with the Wind,* but ferocious just the same. In the midst of this intense competition, Duke Wayne put his arm around Bob Cummings at a movie premiere on coast-to-coast TV and announced with a grin, "Here's Captain Sullivan, folks."

It looked bleak for me, even though Bill Shiffrin assured me that he had a plan.

No one had invited me to read for Wellman and, given Duke's public endorsement of Bob Cummings, I was tempted to give up.

The co-producer of the film was Duke's partner Bob Fellows. I couldn't have felt gloomier when Wayne's secretary told me that my chances to get the part were poor. "I don't really see you in the part," she declared. As an afterthought, she added, "Neither does Mr. Fellows."

On this note of impending disaster, Bill Shiffrin began his maneuvers.

"Trust me," he said, as he set to work. He attacked the problem as if he were a general plunging into battle. Every hour on the hour he sent a telegram to Wellman.

"Stack is perfect for Sullivan!" screamed the messages. "Stack *is* Sullivan!"

It wasn't too long before Wellman, furious at being badgered so, was ready to toss the next messenger from Western Union out the window. It was the only time in my life that I ever let anyone go to those extremes to land a part I really wanted. Finally, with customary warmth, Wellman said he would see me. "Any silly son of a bitch who wants a part this badly can come into my office."

The first thing I noticed about "Wild Bill" Wellman was a special look in his eyes. Vance Breeze, the famous test pilot of the P-38, had it. (Breeze was the man who tested the first twin-engine fighter plane, a dangerous job he did with supreme flair.) My roommate during World War II, Buck Mazza, had it, and he proved himself a war hero. Wellman's eyes were clear, blue, cool, and piercing. It was as if he could see straight through me.

He sat back in an enormous chair, his feet up on the desk, his hair windblown, as though he'd just been flying in an open cockpit. His blue eyes were like radar, seeming to react to the slightest movement anywhere around him. He would not be frightened of a swarm of enemy planes or impressed by a Hollywood snow job. He was not a man to be conned or intimidated. When I sat down across the desk from him, he immediately began to talk. He did not waste time on the amenities. "All right, Stack, what makes you think you can play Sullivan?" he demanded.

I took a deep breath.

"This part can't be acted, Mr. Wellman, it must be felt," I said. "It has to come from the inside out. There's no room for tricks or gestures inside the cockpit. This story has to be played in the eyes. I'm the only actor in town who can do that. The only actor who understands Sullivan." All this was said in a single breath. I'd never spoken about myself this way before; nor have I done so since. But I really believed what I said, and I knew those lie-detector eyes would pick up on any flattery or false humility, so I was as honest and straightforward as I could be.

"Do you know that crazy bastard Duke has already promised Sullivan to another actor?"

I said nothing. We stared at each other, me fighting to keep my eyes pinned to his. Finally, he broke the tension.

"Well, hold on to your hat. I'll have an answer for you tomorrow. You can get the hell out of here now, Stack. One more thing; tell that SOB Shiffrin to stop sending me those damn telegrams!"

At nine o'clock the next morning, Shiffrin called. It was good news.

"Wellman said to tell you if you can sell the audience the way you sold him yesterday, you'll be a smash as Sullivan." Then, ever the optimist, he added, "If you don't, Duke Wayne will strangle both of us." But he was chuckling.

I had known men like Sullivan in the service, and here at last was a part I could play that related closely to a personality type that had always fascinated me. Here was a man who wasn't what he seemed to be. Everyone thought they could pigeonhole him on the basis of his calm, superficial exterior. The challenge to an actor would be to maintain the veneer, yet reveal the intensity of the potential sickness underneath.

I wasn't exactly looking forward to my first meeting with Duke on the set. No star of his magnitude likes making a public statement only to be undercut by one of his employees, even as gifted an employee as Bill Wellman. But Duke was that rare jewel in our profession, a pro whose respect for a great director, a John Ford or a William Wellman, was boundless. As I walked on the set the first day, resplendent in my captain's uniform, Duke wrinkled his forehead, shook my hand, and said, "Mr. Cummings, I believe."

The real test would be our first scene in the cockpit together. Wellman, who had been so charming in the office, turned into a raging tiger on the set. It took me a while to learn that his temper was a secret weapon he used to keep actors on their toes. (In other words, scare the hell out of them.) Nor did he confine himself to scaring actors. Once, during the filming of a picture, he decided to use bizarre means to encourage a stunt man to put some extra zest into a scene. He dashed out from behind the camera, charged at the bewildered stunt man, tore off every stitch of the man's clothing, and left him standing there in his birthday suit, trying to figure out whether to give the director a punch in the mouth or run for cover.

Doe Avedon, a lovely New York actress, came to the coast to portray the head stewardess. In one scene, Doe simply had to walk up the aisle, serve coffee, and adjust a pillow here and there while the special-effects man vibrated the plane—the first sign of impending disaster. After about twenty takes, during which nothing went right, Doe finally stumbled over a nonexisting object in her walk up the aisle.

From behind the camera came a roar. "Good God, Avedon, can't you even walk straight? It's not a tough scene; all you have to do is walk up the aisle without falling down."

Our courageous stewardess looked at Wellman and spoke for all of us when she said: "Mr. Wellman, you've got me so frightened, my knees don't work."

Away from the set, however, Wellman was a pussycat and couldn't stand hurting anyone. But, once behind the camera, he was so unpredictable that actors were constantly thrown off guard. He could tongue-lash an actor into a bowl of jelly. Then suddenly he would mutter, "My God, now what's wrong? Don't tell me I've hurt your feelings? I didn't know actors had feelings."

Everyone knew that Wellman had been an actor himself and, when he stopped yelling and spoke softly, it made us want to please him all the more. Because he demanded the very best of everyone, actors would strive to better their performances. This made Wellman a great director.

Since he personally had cast me as Captain Sullivan, Wellman went out of his way to make sure I didn't expect special treatment or his automatic approval. My wonderfully mad roommate Robert Newton and I often hid out in our dressing room to keep out of sight of our mighty leader.

One day, by accident, I happened to cross Wellman's field of vision. I could see the wheels spinning as he focused on this unfamiliar object. Most of my scenes were still to come, at the end of the picture.

"Where the hell have you been, Stack?" he thundered.

Looking him straight in the eye, I said, "Hiding, Mr. Wellman."

"Hiding?" he said, as a slow, ironic smile formed on his face. "I'll get to you later." Unfortunately, he was true to his word.

From the start, Wellman let the cast know he was going to be unpredictable. "I had a book full of notes before we started shooting," he said, "but after I saw your screen tests, I threw the book away and started over." The press interpreted this comment as a sign that Wellman was hopeful the cast would exceed his expectations. The rest of us weren't sure that he didn't mean it another way.

Ninety percent of my scenes took place in the cockpit, with only a few in the cabin with the passengers. As is true of most motion picture productions, the guest stars are photographed first, so I soon found myself saying fond farewells to my fellow players, as if the movie were finished, even though I hadn't played my first scene with Duke. There was no getting around one simple fact: After the guest stars left, I would be working alone with John Wayne and "Wild Bill" Wellman.

I had just worked on a picture in which two eager young studs lost their cool in a fight scene, with a broken nose and three misplaced front teeth as mementos. I didn't know what to expect from Duke in a scene where Hollywood's most famous fist was to be planted in my face.

He made it look as if he had torn my head off. But, luckily, his early life as a stunt man had made him an expert at fooling the camera. When we shot our first dramatic scene together, Big John stopped in mid-scene and started to make some suggestions. Finally he said, "Hell, you got the part. You play it!"

John Ford used to order him around like a bit player and chew him out, and Duke would take it, not only because he respected the old man, but also because Ford scared the hell out of him, as unbelievable as that may seem. There are stories by the thousand about the machismo of the John Ford stock company—Duke Wayne, Victor McLaglen, Ward Bond, and company. Once, on a quail hunt, Duke and Ward Bond were shooting. I remember the scene. The two had separated, and a quail flushed. Duke shot just as Ward walked around a big rock.

"Duke, you shot me," said Ward. "Damn it, I'm shot."

Duke walked up to Ward, tore his shirt off, looked at his back.

"You're right," he said. "I wish you could see the beautiful pattern this gun throws." In a profession of overnight success, forgotten tomorrow, Duke never changes.

What he portrays on film is a man, not a cardboard cutout. His stubborn belief in God, Country, and Honor, mixed with raw violence, humor, and a little-boy shyness, makes him one of a kind. He is also first and foremost a professional.

So many times gifted stage actors come to motion pictures with a measure of contempt for film actors. Duke may never have played King Lear, but his body English was more effective than much of the king's English. His cowboy walk and coordination make his movies do just that: move!

John Wayne was a character out of time, a dinosaur in the

days of *Voyager I*. In today's clothes, he seemed to shrink, and even his famous walk looked out of place. But in Levis and a beaten-up old hat, he was like the bear that discovered a honey tree. In buckskins, he was more a mountain man than Jim Bridger or Kit Carson. Even his politics didn't fit today's left and right, but came straight out of the mouth of an Indian scout protecting the wagon train from the Apaches. He even did a blood-and-guts super-hero opus at the height of the Vietnam antiwar protests and survived. Not only did Duke survive, but he became a cult figure for the young and restless. He was the only constant in a changing world, and the most rabid revolutionary found it hard to be comtemptuous of someone as dedicated as Duke, even if he was the enemy. One thing for sure: you'd never turn this Indian scout into an Apache.

He handled his fight against cancer as he handled the other challenges in his life, with a courage and simple faith that's consistent with the heroes he played in films. Even with one lung, a heart bypass, and a stomach made from leftovers, he was more man than anyone I know.

Midway through the picture, I caught a miserable cold, which quickly developed into bronchitis. One actor who had been passed over for the role of Sullivan hung around the set, giving me daily reports on how tired he thought I looked. "No picture is worth catching pneumonia over," he said. Like Poe's Raven, this harbinger of doom and his power of negative thinking almost did me in. I started thinking that perhaps I just wouldn't be physically up to the test. But every time my doubts started getting the best of me, I said to myself, *I'm not going to succumb. I'm going to finish this picture if they have to carry me out.* I wasn't about to let a stowaway take over my Captain Sullivan without a battle.

Our final sequence took two days to shoot. All the while, the rain machines made certain we were properly soaked so that the mood would be right for Duke to limp off into the night whistling "The High and the Mighty." I managed to croak my final lines sounding like an asthmatic Andy Devine before being carted off to the hospital for ten days with two pneumonia scars on my lungs. (Ah, for the glamorous life of an actor!)

All was not high drama on the set, however, and Wellman's test for the young honeymooning couple was a case in point. In the book, two young lovers, faced with what appears to be certain death, fulfill their mission as honeymooners, getting their own reward before going to their reward. In the picture, naturally, the end result was left to the audience's imagination and played off the varying reactions of other passengers (shock, sympathy, envy, etc.).

The handsome young couple were portrayed by two actors who were tickled pink to appear in an all-star film and eager to do anything to please. Wild William muttered something like, "Just don't be self-conscious; remember you're going to die and this is your last moment together."

The two young actors took him very seriously and played the scenes beautifully. Soon they reached the point where they weren't acting any more. Instead of saying "cut" Wellman let the filming continue. I think all three thoroughly enjoyed the scene. But, given the mores of the time, the most enjoyable parts of the scene had to end up on the cutting room floor!

Since I spent a good deal of time hiding from William Wellman, I really got to know my roommate Robert Newton, who spent most of his time on the lam, too. Bobby Newton was an original. He claimed to be a descendant of Captain Blood, the only man who ever succeeded in stealing the British crown jewels from the Tower of London. Like Errol Flynn, Newton possessed a wanderlust that had led him around the world once, if not more times, from South Africa and Australia to the West Indies, indulging in the pleasures of wine, women, song, and Shakespeare, not necessarily in that order.

As a boy, he remembered rowing Guglielmo Marconi to his ship after Marconi sent the first wireless message from Cornwall to Canada.

But his zaniest adventures took place during the war. One night Bobby, his old chum Trevor Howard, and I were swapping stories of wartime London, and Bobby revealed his wildest escapade: The Royal Navy had acquired Bobby's services as a bluejacket. When his ship docked in Murmansk, he traded his ration of ship's tobacco for some uncured fur pelts. By the time the ship had reached the middle of the Arctic Ocean, his shipmates had discovered the furs. The dirty, bloodstained skins had thawed out in the heat of the crowded mess deck, giving off a foul odor which nearly asphyxiated a segment of the Royal Navy. The crew debated whether to throw Newton or the furs overboard, but eventually settled on the pelts. Newton, innocently enthusiastic, returned to shore for more fun.

No matter how wild his escapades, it was difficult for anyone to stay mad at Newton for very long. Once the police had the effrontery to arrest Bobby for drunk and disorderly behavior—in a Sunset Strip nightclub. He promptly put on a one-man show from his cell in the county jail where he spent the night, entertaining his fellow inmates and jailers alike. He paid his $15 fine in good humor and announced that "the deputies were really lovely there, but they brought me to my cell in manacles."

As an actor, he will be remembered by most as Long John Silver, the filthy, bearded, wild-eyed pirate that sent children to bed with raging nightmares. Robert was an actor of great finesse—mixed with a delicate madness, true, but still the product of the Old Vic and a wealth of classical training. He was capable of tremendous versatility. Although he made his screen debut in a silent film advertising Ovaltine, there was little doubt that he preferred liquid refreshment that was considerably stronger.

Newton was once signed to appear in a film which was to be shot abroad. After many bottles of champagne, topped off by an imperial gallon of brandy, he boarded the plane and was later surprised to find that no one from the studio was on hand to meet him at the airport. He was recognized by one of his fans, however, who took him home. He spent a lovely two months as a guest of the family. The studio never did find out what had happened to their star, because Bobby had boarded the wrong plane and flown to the wrong country. When asked for an explanation, he said, "I knew I was supposed to go to some country that began with an *A*—Austria, Australia, Africa, something like that. I was never much for geography."

When we worked together in *The High and the Mighty*, he was embroiled in his famous bouts with the demon rum, and convinced that all bad luck was behind him. Bob fell off the wagon, however, somewhere between the point of no return and my heroic efforts to land our crippled fake plane on a fake San Francisco runway. He was jollier than usual and seemed to be forever imbibing orange juice from an old thermos. "Vitamin C, you know. It's why I never catch cold," he said, rolling his eyes like Blackbeard. Bobby played the role of a Broadway producer who never showed emotion and wore his wife on his arm like an expensive coat. Happily, his part was almost finished, except for a few shots of him facing death with a courageous smile on his face. How much was raw talent and how much was the "Vitamin C" I shall never know. But he was the happiest hero I ever saw. A self-satisfied grin wreathed his face as the special-effects man blew smoke and flames at him and he prepared to meet his maker. Forest Lawn could have used him as an advertisement for the great beyond.

"Take care of your work first," he often said. "Everything else will be taken care of."

The High and the Mighty had its premiere at Grauman's Egyptian Theater, Hollywood's monument to the pharaohs. Together with its first cousin—Grauman's Chinese Theater, farther west on Hollywood Boulevard—the Egyptian Theater was a major tourist attraction in Hollywood at the time.

Sid Grauman had been one of the film colony's original theater promoters. He lived in an era when theater builders vied to outdo each other in creating structures of epic proportions. Sid Grauman was no exception. He had come to Hollywood from San Francisco, where he survived the great earthquake. He not only built movie houses but also the Temple of Art for Aimée Semple McPherson.

The Egyptian was considered his most magnificent theater. It was designed in grandiose style, approximating Hollywood's best guess at what constituted the opulence of the Middle East. One of Grauman's first innovations at the Egyptian was the tableau, a live prologue which preceded the showing of a film. Countless stars of opera, radio, and film received their first exposure to the public there, and some, like Lawrence Tibbett, went on to gain universal fame.

Then Grauman decided that the opening of films needed special promotion. So he invited a host of stars to his openings, spread bright lights around the large court leading to the entrance of the theater, and called the newspapers. Crowds of fans jammed the boulevard in front of the theater, and the Hollywood premiere was born.

Grauman, with his distinctive haircut, was seen so often around town that one local quipster asked, "What breed of sheepdog is constantly seen with Joe Schenk?" (Schenk was a powerful producer.) The answer was, "That's no sheepdog; that's Sid Grauman."

At our premiere, John Wayne and I were supposed to carry on a little banter about our epic while the producers, agents, starlets, harlots, and the rest prepared for the long march down a long red carpet to the portals of what Egypt looked like to

THE HIGH AND THE MIGHTY

an architect from Sheboygan. Nevertheless, there was a thrill in opening a picture at the theater where the likes of Valentino, Garbo, Lon Chaney, and Doug Fairbanks had once trod the same red carpets.

During the evening, I suddenly flashed back to one night when I was a boy. My brother and I had been drawn to the converging klieg lights on Hollywood Boulevard lighting up the city. We fought our way through the crowd to the very same spot I was now standing on in front of Grauman's Egyptian. The attraction for us had been Rudolph Valentino's special handmade limousine sitting forlornly on a raised velvet platform. Nothing else. Valentino had just died.

Just how quickly the glamor of stardom dies, how long an adoring audience remains loyal to its idol, was best shown by one snaggletoothed, wild-haired dummy who kept trying to push past a harassed security guard to get into the back seat. He was telling anybody who'd listen, "Valentino's supposed to be the 'Sheik,' right? Now the son of a bitch is dead. Let's see how great a sheik he was. Let me in the back seat so I can count how many rubbers are there."

Grauman's most famous creation came five years after the opening of the Egyptian. In honor of his Chinese friends in San Francisco, he planned a new theater of Oriental design. Douglas Fairbanks, Mary Pickford, and Norma Talmadge planted their footprints in the wet cement of the large courtyard outside the theater. A new tradition was born. In the ensuing months, Grauman acquired a variety of impressions in the cement: Harold Lloyd's spectacles, hoofmarks of Tom Mix's wonder horse Tony, Betty Grable's million-dollar legs, Joe E. Brown's mouth, and Monty Woolley's beard were all imprinted outside Grauman's Chinese, along with the footprints of many of the stars who went to premieres at Grauman's.

Perhaps Monty Woolley best summed up the irreverent attitude that surrounded Grauman and his promotions. Along with his beard print, Woolley left a personal message in the cement for Grauman: "To Sid," he wrote. "Wish you were here."

The High and the Mighty premiere was my favorite of any of those Marquis de Sade spectacles to which we had to subject ourselves. Bob Fellows had endeared himself to me forever by telling everyone I was absolutely wrong for the part of Sullivan. Now the premiere was over. We were all standing outside on the red carpet with the feeling of elation that only a successful movie can bring. I saw someone walking toward me.

It turned out to be none other than our worthy producer. First came the handshake and then an embrace. Beaming with avuncular pride, he looked me right in the eye and said, "Kid, you did me proud. Some said I made a mistake casting you as Sullivan, but you were always my first choice."

Now, I thought, *here's the chance you've been waiting for. Make him pay for all the suffering and humiliation. Let him know you know you weren't his choice for Sullivan but Wellman's. Tell him even his secretary didn't see you in the part.*

Naturally, I quickly clasped his outstretched hand with both of mine, and with misty eyes, assured him how grateful I would always be for his confidence in me. I didn't grow up in Hollywood for nothing.

In fairness to Bob Fellows, I have a feeling he really did think he cast me in the picture. It's a kind of memory typical to this business. That's why, when people ask me how an actor gets cast in a movie, I mumble something in Esperanto and scurry off.

I was listed by some trade papers as a dark horse in the Academy Awards race—as it turned out, a little too dark to catch the eye of the voters.

One of the most fascinating characters associated with *The High and the Mighty* never appeared on screen. He was my friend Dimitri Tiomkin, the man responsible for the film's memorable music. Tiomkin, a Russian, became a Hollywood legend, ironically as a specialist in scoring westerns. His unique accent cannot be translated on paper; it is pure Tiomkinese.

To no one's surprise, Dimi Tiomkin won the Oscar for "Best Song from a Motion Picture." But when he ascended to the podium, he shocked the normally unflappable audience with an acceptance speech that would be the talk of the town for years to come.

"I would like to thank Beethoven, Brahms, Wagner, Strauss, and Rimski-Korsakov," he said unabashedly. Of course, film composers have always "borrowed" styles and sounds from the great masters. Tiomkin insisted that he only wanted to acknowledge the serious composers who were his inspiration. The audience thought the speech was uproariously funny, but some of his fellow composers were not amused.

Nevertheless the theme from *The High and the Mighty* went on to become one of the most successful songs ever written for a motion picture.

The High and the Mighty was a smash. Ernie Gann's novel adapted itself perfectly to the screen. Some even accused him of having written the book as a classic example of how to create a best-seller and film script at the same time.

Ernest Gann was an ex-transoceanic airline pilot and the airlines regarded him as a Benedict Arnold. The book had been bad enough, but a motion picture dramatizing a wounded plane trying to limp home over the Pacific (past the point of no return) might easily bring back steamship travel.

William Wellman had lost no time in announcing that the film had been shot with the most realistic methods available. "If we're going to make them bad, we're going to make them bad with everything there is," he said.

The public relations agencies immediately started their counterattack. No such situation ever had, would, or could, happen, they said. While Mr. Gann may have been an airline pilot, it was unfair, they screamed, and downright dangerous trying to make fiction appear to be fact.

We reminded the airlines of our efforts to present the situation authentically. (Scenes had been filmed using the Civil Aeronautics Administration communications net at the Oakland Airport and the Coast Guard rescue coordinating center in San Francisco.)

The big bone of contention was that no four-motor passenger plane had ever landed with two inoperative engines. During the last weeks of filming, a Pan Am four-engine jet staggered into San Francisco's airport with two engines out on final approach; the third gave up just before touchdown.

But Ernie was first and foremost, a pilot, and he wouldn't allow the studio to publicize the San Francisco incident, which was quickly forgotten anyway. His "fictionalized" movie became the biggest grosser of the year.

The last get-together of some of the H and M alumni took place a couple of years ago when "Wild Bill" was celebrating the completion of his book, *A Short Time for Insanity*.

The guest list was limited to those who had worked in a motion picture with him. True to his character, only real friends were allowed. Doe Avedon, who played the stewardess in *The High and the Mighty* was naturally invited, but the only reason

Don Siegel, Clint Eastwood's renowned director, was allowed past the doors of Chasen's banquet room was because he happened to be Doe's husband. Half of the "beautiful people" in town would have given their eyeballs to be a part of the testimonial for "Sweet William," but they were accorded the same deference he usually reserved for producers: none!

For me, it was the best Hollywood evening I've ever spent. For once, the clichés, the forced smiles, the phony publicists' hyperbole, the desperate "look at me, love me" of every actor between jobs, and the pompous Napoleonic rumblings of the producers were missing. This was one brawl nobody could buy his way into. Here, Mae Marsh was just as important as Raquel Welch. On this night, the lady who took James Cagney's grapefruit in the kisser was still a movie star.

Richard Arlen, looking as fit as when he personally shot up most of the German military in *Wings*, told some wild tales about the making of that classic film. Buddy Rogers, Paul Fix, Barbara Stanwyck, and many others all came to pay homage to this Renaissance man who had known General Pershing, was a member of the Lafayette Escadrille, and brought truth and guts to motion picture making. William Wellman died in 1976, as did Richard Arlen. With them died an important part of our profession.

A final footnote on Bill Wellman: During the filming of "The Untouchables," someone got the bright idea of having me appear on "This is Your Life." This particular program, in spite of my liking for Ralph Edwards, had to be the most maudlin invasion of privacy ever perpetrated on an unsuspecting victim. The poor joker who has been chosen has no idea that, for a solid month, his wife has been hauling out the baby pictures, old love letters, and names of past acquaintances he has forgotten and, in many cases, hoped he would never see again. I was told by the studio that I had to do some postrecording, a boring chore that has to be done by actors when the original sound for a show has not been properly recorded.

As I drove up to the front gates of Desilu Studios, I should have known something was wrong, because the grumpy old cop at the gate was smiling. Suddenly, a character with orange hair stuck his head through the window and muttered something unintelligible. Since I was in a lousy mood, having blown a golf game at Riviera, and was facing the prospect of recording on my day off, I pushed the orange head back from where it came.

Then the studio cop jumped in front of my 300 SL Mercedes-Benz, a gift from Desi Arnaz a month before, and put his two fat hands on the delicate aluminum hood. As I began hollering at the cop to get his meathooks off, the orange-haired fellow popped his head in again and, of course, since I was yelling, I couldn't hear a damn word he said.

Finally, with a grimace and a scream to match, came, "Robert Stack, this is your life!"

"Oh balls!" I said—which was, of course, cut out of the show.

A person's importance is usually calculated on the basis of whom they can rope into appearing on the program. It turned out to be fun having my mother, my wife, and my two kids on the show. When it looked as if no big wheels were going to show up for old Bob, I heard the voice that gave me shivers for twelve weeks at Goldwyn studios. Out strode William Wellman. Never one for small talk, he walked up to me, looked at a particular area on my shirt and said, "You should have washed your vest, Eliot. You've still got some of Frank Nitti's blood on it!"

The High and the Mighty was made twenty years ago, but if any incipient sadist wants to shake up a flight crew, just whistle the first four bars of Dimitri Tiomkin's melody as you walk past the cockpit.

Intermission

with ROSEMARIE STACK

You may be wondering why, in the middle of Bob's autobiography, I am writing a chapter of my own.

The reason is simple: Although Bob is convinced that the decision to pop the question and get married was his own idea, the truth is I gave him a little help. So, in the interest of accuracy, Bob is including my version of how we met and finally married. (Just between us, it may be because, after twenty-three wonderful years together, he wants to find out himself.)

I have often been asked how in the world I convinced Hollywood's handsomest and most eligible bachelor (a description used over Bob's protest) to get married. When we met, Bob was known as the "bachelor of the world," Hollywood's least likely candidate to settle down with wife and children.

I like to think that our marriage was made in heaven, but not in the least for sentimental reasons. When Bob and I first met, astrology was very much the vogue in Hollywood. Nearly as much attention was being paid to the stars in the sky as those on the screen. More often than not, the astrologer whose predictions seemed most accurate was George Darios; he also gave psychic readings. A friend of mine wanted to consult Darios, and since she needed a ride, I came along. George Darios communicated with the stars, both heavenly and Hollywood, in Venice, California. It was a meeting I would never forget, although at the time, I didn't even take it seriously. I wasn't especially eager to hear my fortune predicted, but George insisted he had something to tell me.

"I must speak to you," he said. "You are going to meet a tall, blond, handsome man."

It wasn't the first time I had heard that prediction. But then he became more specific.

He looks like Robert Stack," he said. "No, no, it *is* Robert Stack."

It's possible, I thought to myself. I had seen him once or twice, and we were in the same profession.

"And then," continued my new astrologer friend, "you are going on a long journey, to the West Indies."

When I heard the prediction about the West Indies, I stopped paying attention. *Ridiculous*, I thought to myself. *I'm not going to the West Indies.*

Several days later, the studio phoned and informed me that I was being assigned to a new film, *The Golden Mistress*. I had to leave immediately because of an unusually tight schedule. "And," said a voice on the phone, "it's all location shooting: in Haiti."

So, off I went on the first phase of what proved to be a really incredible journey.

I had already been associated with several major studios in Hollywood. I had been under contract to MGM, Columbia, and Charles Feldman Productions. Feldman was the producer of *A Streetcar Named Desire*, incidentally, and quite accustomed to having the last word. A major exception occurred when he played cards with the legendary Hungarian film producer Sir Alexander Korda.

One night, Feldman lost at cards, and in response to a friendly wager, sent Korda a check the next day, signed in red ink.

"Here's my check," he said, "written in blood."

A few days later, Korda lost, and he returned the compliment with a check in blue ink.

"Also in blood," Korda wrote, "but note the difference in color." It was signed, "*Sir* Alexander Korda."

In the continental United States, actors and actresses are protected by the Screen Actors Guild. An actress cannot be compelled to do her own stunts, especially if they involve dangerous activities. But in Haiti there were no such rules and regulations, and I found out quickly about the "glamorous" life of an actress on location.

The entire film involved action scenes in swamps and in the ocean. The stunt woman assigned to the film didn't look like me at all and, when the producer and director insisted that I do my own stunts, I had little choice but to comply.

"Everything will be fine," the director assured me. "You'll just do swimming. And don't believe all those stories about sharks in the Caribbean," he added. The Haitians were less optimistic. One of the scenes called for me to plunge into the water using an Aqua-lung.

"Be careful," said one of the crewmen, with a very strange look on his face. "We don't know how much air is in the lung." Although the director had promised me over and over again that they would give me some lessons at the hotel in deep-sea diving, the lessons had never materialized. So there I was, going into deep water for the first time with an Aqua-lung that might not have enough air in it.

I didn't have time to worry about air. As I swam through the warm, Caribbean waters, I quickly made the acquaintance of one of the West Indies's least pleasant tourist attractions. I felt a sharp, piercing sting in my arm. Without warning, my arm went numb. I was too terrified to even look at it; all I could think of was a shark! *I've been attacked by a shark. I've lost my arm.* I finally forced myself to look in the direction of my arm, which was growing more and more numb. Panic flashed through me, but I fought to stay in control. My arm was still attached to my body, but I felt nothing.

"You've been stung by a sea urchin," a local doctor informed me. "The sharp stingers have lodged into your arm, but eventually the skin will close over the wound, and you won't have to worry about the stingers remaining there for more than a few months."

My glamorous stay in the West Indies continued. I was chased by natives and fought the rapids; I plodded through swamps and mud while the cameras recorded my ordeal. By the time our shooting was almost over, I was ready to do almost anything just to get the experience over with.

Hal Mohr, our ace photographer, gave me some advice: "Look at it this way, Rosemarie," he said. "After this picture, anything else will be a breeze."

My last scene in Haiti was a farewell that I would never forget. There was one last surprise in the script, but I was so eager to finish (and so numb from the experience) that I didn't ask questions.

John Agar, the leading man in the film, talked to the producer on my behalf. "You can't do this to her," he said. "You've got to tell her."

The director quickly explained the scene, saying something about crabs. I wasn't listening closely, and nodded my head. It was a chase scene, and I had to run around a corner and fall, face down, in an enormous mud puddle. (When I worked as a fashion model and made the cover of *Life* magazine, I thought making movies would be a different kind of experience. I didn't know how right I would be.)

I started the scene, and when I fell into the swamp, the special-effects man released 200 live crabs, throwing them directly into my face. Most of the crabs scattered, but a number of them began crawling over me. By now I was almost in a state of shock.

All the terrible things that had happened—the sea urchin, the Aqua-lung, the mad panic of never knowing what would be thrown at me next—finally took their toll. I began crying, my tears gradually growing into a form of hysteria. The cast and crew tried to calm me down, but a crab-infested swamp was hardly a soothing place. (It would be months before I could even look at a crab meat salad.)

The next day I had my final surprise. The director had some news for me. "Great shot, Rosemarie," he said. "Unfortunately, it's so repulsive we can't use it in the picture."

Finally, and gratefully, I returned to Hollywood, to the relatively calm world of agents and producers.

Shortly after my return, my agent Bill Shiffrin called. "Come down to the office," he said. "I want to talk to you."

I went over to his office, and when I arrived, a number of contract players were gathered there to compare notes. Bill was busy, and the rest of us had nothing to do but wait. I had borrowed my brother's car and promised to get it back to him at the end of the afternoon.

Although I didn't know it at the time, Bob was also one

of Bill's clients. Bob walked in and, because he was a star, the secretary immediately ushered him into Bill's private office.

I waited and waited and, thinking of my brother, I finally told the secretary I could wait no longer.

"You can't leave," she said.

A few moments later, I was invited to join Bill in his office.

"Rosemarie," he said, "say hello to Bob Stack."

There he was: Hollywood's most eligible (and unmarriageable) bachelor.

"I'm just about through for the day," Bill said. "Why don't you two join me for a drink."

So Bill, Bob, and I went downstairs to a restaurant in the same building. It was about five o'clock. After ordering our drinks, Bill received an urgent phone call and departed. So there we were, alone. In a few minutes, Bob and I were talking as if we had met before, in a previous lifetime or another world. We seemed almost to anticipate each other's conversation. He would say something; I would jump in ahead of time. By now, I had decided that he was not only handsome, but very charming, and I completely forgot about my brother's car.

It was then that I realized George Darios's predictions had come true: I had gone to the West Indies and I had met Robert Stack. To my further surprise, I learned that George was an old friend of Bob's grandmother and mother—the whole family, in fact. There was more to astrology than I had ever realized.

It was only a matter of time before Bob and I had fallen in love. But this special time for us also presented some real problems. Bob was independent; he had dated some of Hollywood's most beautiful women. He was used to leading a sporting life—a world of shooting, boat racing, and activities more suited to an explorer or an adventurer than to a family man. I could sense that Bob was ready to get married and settle down, but I could also see he needed a little help in making up his mind. So in the fall of 1955, Bob and I broke up.

I told him that I loved him, but for us to continue together, he would have to ask me a question. It was the question he had never asked any girl; at that point, he couldn't, or wouldn't, ask me. We stopped dating, and I forced myself to go out once or twice with someone else. I knew that if I saw Bob, I would melt, and the whole purpose of not seeing him would collapse. It was the hardest decision I ever made. And I had inadvertently chosen the most difficult time of the year to help Bob make up his mind: Thanksgiving and Christmas. He called me over the holidays and we exchanged Christmas gifts. I gave Bob a weather vane, and he suspected that there was a hidden meaning in this on-again, off-again device that registered which way the wind was blowing.

Some unexpected help came from an unlikely source, Louella Parsons. "Lolly" had been a lifelong friend of Bob's family, and she decided to make her contribution to the situation. She began planting items in her column about "all my dates" with Hollywood's most eligible men. No one was more surprised than I, because I wasn't dating anyone.

Bob was filming *Written on the Wind* at the time. He would come home from a hard day's work to find an envelope of clippings from a local clipping service. If he were mentioned in one of the Parsons columns, there was always an item nearby announcing that Rosemarie Bowe was out with somebody or other.

In the darkest hours of our relationship, I spoke to George Darios. He had predicted earlier that Bob and I would marry the following January.

"Your prediction can't come true this time," I told him. "We're not even speaking."

"The stars are never wrong," George said, "nor am I. You will be married next January."

On New Year's Day, Bob called me from San Diego. "Are you free?" he asked. "I'll be in town in a few days, and I want to talk to you about something."

I knew then that it had all been worth it. He loved me as much as I loved him.

"Shall I take you to dinner?" he said.

"No," I said, "I'll fix dinner for you." I wanted this special moment to be very private.

Then I had a terrible realization—I couldn't cook.

"Mother," I yelled, *"Help!* I know how to make a martini and how to toss a salad," I said, "but how do you cook a steak?"

"Five minutes on each side," she said.

I sent mother to a movie so Bob and I could be alone. Then I crossed my fingers and worried about the steaks.

The steaks turned out medium rare, exactly as Bob liked them. He proposed and I said yes. You might think that was that, but it wasn't.

Several months earlier, one of Hollywood's gaudiest spectacles had taken place: the wedding of Jayne Mansfield. It is hard for me to realize that there are many people too young to remember Jayne. At the height of her fame, she lived in an enormous pink stucco house in Beverly Hills, complete with a swimming pool containing the message, "I love you, Jayne" at the bottom of the pool.

Jayne was married in a glass church. Some spectators, angry at not being able to get in, threw rocks at the church, while an army of reporters and photographers attempted to storm the barricades to get a picture of the bride and groom.

When Bob and I began talking about our wedding, he had one condition. It could not be a Hollywood wedding like the one Jayne Mansfield had had. He wanted it to be absolutely secret, a quiet, dignified ceremony in private, just for the family, calling as little attention to ourselves as possible. I shared Bob's feelings about the private, personal nature of a wedding. But we had one problem: our agent Bill Shiffrin.

Bill was still busily working on behalf of our mutual careers, and now he informed me that I was in the running for a starring role in a major motion picture to be produced at Goldwyn studios. I had already been interviewed for the part and now I was summoned to a meeting with the film's star Anthony Quinn.

I knew that the producers were nearly ready to offer me the part. I couldn't walk down the aisle and make a film at the same time, and I knew which choice I would make without thinking twice. The producers couldn't have been more enthusiastic. They even asked me to wear the clothes I wore to the audition in the picture. I couldn't go into Saks Fifth Avenue or Magnin's for a wedding gown, because the press would find out. So my mother made my wedding dress by hand.

I was asked to read a script for Tony Quinn. I knew the only way to discourage them from offering me the part was to appear to be nervous in delivering the cold reading of the script. I had been packing and planning for the wedding; I was desperate to extricate myself from this film offer.

So I delivered the reading, and spoke the lines in a hesitant, halting manner.

"That's right," said Tony Quinn, nodding approvingly, "she's found the character's second level of nervousness—exactly what we need!"

Finally Bob and I decided to tell Bill we were getting married. He was delighted, and told Tony Quinn that I was otherwise obligated for the next few months. It was a graceful exit, no feelings hurt; they assumed I had accepted a better offer and, in a sense, I had!

I had been raised as a Lutheran and I wanted to be married in church. There was a Lutheran church in Beverly Hills, so I made an appointment with the minister. A serious, somber young man.

"What is the groom's name?" he asked.

"I can't tell you," I replied. I explained that my fiancé was famous, that he didn't want publicity, and that we were afraid someone at the church might leak word of the wedding to the press. The minister looked at me as if my fiancé were an escaped convict. I suspected that he was prepared to investigate me to find out if there would really be a wedding at all. A few days before the wedding, he called.

"As your minister, I have to counsel the bride and groom." We swore him to secrecy and invited him to my apartment to meet Bob. It was really happening. After all our trials and tribulations, Bob and I were finally going to be together. We were eager and excited.

"Are you really sure you want to get married?" the minister said. I nearly fell over. What followed was incredible. He began to go through a prepared list of questions we had to answer. The questions were supposed to predict our chances of having a successful marriage.

"Too many people rush into marriage," the minister told us. "My wife and I have very little in common except religion. Marriage is a serious business."

This wasn't the Lutheran view with which I'd grown up.

I looked at my mother, and she looked at me. After waiting so long for Bob to propose, here was a minister trying to talk him out of the wedding!

"I'm not getting married to be serious," Bob said. "I'm getting married to have fun."

"What?" said the minister, who evidently did not think of marriage in these terms.

"My work is serious business," Bob continued. "I have all

my share of frustrations and insecurities in pictures. I'm going to get married to have a good time."

"Huh?" said the minister.

"I have a great girl and I love her," said Bob enjoying himself greatly, "and that's that!"

The minister did not appear optimistic about our chances for success in our marriage but, happily, twenty-three years later, Bob has been proven right.

At last we were married, and went to Hawaii for our honeymoon. Bob and his brother Jim had a friend, an Englishman, who managed a hotel in Hawaii. To make sure the overseas operator wouldn't leak the news of our wedding to the newspapers, Jim didn't say anything about Bob's marriage. He just explained that Bob wanted the bridal suite. The manager chuckled and told him he'd take care of everything.

We went straight from the church to the airport and flew directly to Honolulu.

When we walked down the steps from the plane Bob's friend greeted us with beautiful flowered leis. And something else; he had brought along his girl friend—and the prettiest girl he could find as a date for Bob. I knew when Bob promised me a honeymoon I would never forget, he had something unusual in mind, but I didn't expect to share him with a date.

"I'm married," said my new husband, happy to display his wedding ring.

"You're kidding," said Bob's friend, who had misunderstood his instructions, obviously.

And so we had a glorious Hawaiian honeymoon. The girls, even the one who had expected a date with a most eligible bachelor, came up to our suite to congratulate us.

We settled down to our life together in California, doing all the zany, madcap things Bob is going to talk about in the upcoming pages of this book. We have two wonderful children and, to his surprise, Bob has found he likes marriage and being a father. George Darios is past ninety and still predicting. As for Bob, he is convinced that my story of how we met and married is utter nonsense, and that our marriage was entirely his own idea!

8

Deirdre

Glamor is in the eye of the beholder, but in many situations a pair of bifocals helps. In any case, a good imagination, romantic lighting, and a gallon of Chanel No. 5 or Brut can take the place of good looks. I know of one rumpled, mousy little guy who hung around the edge of Hollywood, not even accepted at Schwab's. One night, as a gag, he was carted along to a party with the Beverly Hills—Bel-Air crowd. No one paid any attention to him. Finally the hostess asked, "Who is that strange little man?" The guy who had brought him answered, "He's the enforcer for the Cleveland mob." Suddenly this little character was eyed by every good-looking doll in the room, including the hostess, and was offered five business deals. So, "It ain't what you do or the way that you do it," as the song goes, but what they *think* you do.

Norma Jean was just as pretty before her famous calendar shot, but afterwards, as Marilyn Monroe, the public's imagination had something to work on. The illusion of glamor is also very much a product of the makeup people at the studios. Danny Kaye saw one of Hollywood's reigning beauties before make-up went to work; his only comment: "She looks like a white doorknob."

Deirdre was no doorknob. (Her name wasn't really Deirdre but, as they say, her name has been changed to protect the innocent.... Maybe we'd better just say her name has been changed.)

Deirdre walked through the gate of MGM with enough vitality and plain old sex appeal to bring a leer to the face of the old studio cop—who we thought was plumb out of leers. She was from a small town in the South. Her family were sharecroppers and she was about the most beautiful thing I had ever seen. She quickly picked up on Hollywood and was, in turn, picked up by a young actor who quietly married her. She soon found out she was interested in music—well, not so much interested in music, as in musicians. As her career took off so did her tastes, which ran to bullfighters.

During this time, the lady had evidenced no interest in me and, anyway, the competition was so heavy I knew I didn't qualify—or wouldn't survive the life-style if I did. (This was, obviously, before Rosemarie took me on.)

I was so wound up in the *Death in the Afternoon* syndrome that, after *Bullfighter and the Lady*, I couldn't turn myself off. I was having dinner one evening at the Naples Restaurant, just up from Columbia studios on Gower, in Hollywood. I was demonstrating the fine points of the *veronica*, *chicuelina*, and *revolera* to a chum by waving a napkin around. I turned my head and, looking me straight in the eye from the next booth (like a bull, or, in this case, a *vaca* about to charge) was our glamor girl from the South.

"How does it feel, Bobby, to face an animal that wants to kill you?" she purred. "I've always wanted to know." She spoke in that breathy, urgent voice so familiar to millions. Until then I'd only enjoyed those sensuous tones on the silver screen.

If he digs death and the bullring, she had to be thinking, *he can't be as square as I thought*. She caressed her lovely lips with her pink tongue and continued to cast her spell.

"Why not drop by the house, so you can explain it to me? The help are on vacation, and we won't be disturbed." With this, she slowly broke eye contact and walked away as only she could. My chum gave me a lascivious grin and I hastily paid the tab and ambled out as casually as I could.

Her house was nestled on top of Mulholland Drive with a dandy view of the city. As I walked into the living room I noticed the view because the house lights were romantically dimmed, and I almost broke my neck stepping down to the sunken living room floor.

"Fix yourself a drink. I'll be right out," came from what I figured was the bedroom. I had poured gin on the rocks and was just about to add a small amount of vermouth when she appeared. Actually, she had been standing in the shadows watching me make the drink and then stepped into the moon's path. She was wearing a filmy "shorty" nightgown which slowly seemed to disappear as she moved into the backlight.

She looked like an early UFA still of Dietrich in the *Blue Angel*, only in her birthday suit. I stood there holding the vermouth bottle in midair giving fervent thanks to Duke Wayne for casting me in *Bullfighter*.

She took the glass from me and purred, "How did you know I like my martinis without vermouth?" She smiled that famous smile. "Tell me, Bobby, how does it feel?"

"Great," I said, "just great."

"I mean to face something that wants to destroy you? Is it exciting? My God, it must be!"

I thought, who should know better than you, my pet, who has wounded more male vanities and caused more potential suicides than anyone in town? But I made myself the largest martini I could and dutifully played out the game. She nestled in the big leather chair and looked at me as if I were telling her a bedtime story—which I hoped I was. When I got to the part about choosing the fighting bulls on horseback with Boetticher, she said, "But what would have happened if the horse had fallen or stuck his foot in a gopher hole?" I gave it my best David Niven roguish grin and said, "Those are the risks."

I was beginning to feel strangely lightheaded after only one martini, so I made another. Now it really became interesting. She began to tell me about a good-looking young couple she had recently met. A charming pair of kids who someone said liked to share sex. Deirdre professed a certain amazement at the idea of a foursome, but then suggested asking them over for a drink "a little later."

My beautiful nymphomaniac was slowly moving in and out of focus and my head seemed to be filled with carpet tacks. My knees suddenly began to tremble and perspiration began to stream down my face. If this was passion, I thought, something must have gone wrong with the machinery.

When my teeth began to chatter I knew I was in trouble. This was definitely not good healthy lust; it was the flu. Of all the miserable, lousy, putrid times to get it, this had to take the cake.

My potential roommate noticed my condition. She put her hand on my blistering brow and said soothingly, "Poor baby, you're sick. You'd better get to bed."

I really was sick, because I mumbled, "I'm sorry. I've got the flu and I don't want you to catch it. I'm really sorry." I staggered to my car and drove home to bed, cursing all the way. I sweated my way through three pairs of pajamas during the night before the phone rang mid-morning with a cheery Gil Stuart on the other end.

"Get your butt out of bed. We're going to the bullfights. Two tickets on the shady side—I won in a gin rummy game." I was about to beg off when I stood up and, then wonder of wonders, I felt fine. The flu had been only the twelve-hour variety.

So off we went to beautiful Tijuana, land of tequila and the trots. The smattering of Rollses, Bentleys, and Mercedeses outside the bullring was proof that a Hollywood favorite was appearing and the crowd had showed up to be recognized. The moguls would explain the gory details (usually incorrectly) to their girl friends, who would spend most of the *corrida* in the dirty bullring john being sick and unable to watch.

We were late and the *paseo* had begun, so Gil and I did our best to get to our seats quickly. I stumbled over handbags, *botas*, and bodies to get seated. When I took my seat, opened the program, and turned around to see if the plaza was filled, I found myself face to face with a ravishing brunette in a skintight gaucho outfit with a black sombrero and an expression to match. You guessed it—*Deirdre*!

Here I was at a bullfight, fit as a fiddle a few hours after being stricken with my deadly disease. Her expression was stony. She looked at me for a long beat, produced her famous smile, and drawled, "My, what an amazing recovery." She then changed seats with her escort and that is the last time we ever spoke, but it was far from my last involvement with her.

The story goes on.

Despite the public's enthusiasm and acclaim that followed

the premiere of *The High and the Mighty*, the most important (for me) screening of this film did not take place in Hollywood, but in the south of France. There, in a villa surrounded by tall trees and the quiet seclusion of the French sountryside, Darryl F. Zanuck, the undisputed ruler of Twentieth Century-Fox, watched the film. He liked what he saw.

Since the beginning of my career as an actor, I had never enjoyed the active sponsorship of a single powerful studio. My brief, ill-fated association with Liberty Productions had not produced one role, and even Liberty had been a unique combination of independent producer-directors, not a studio.

Zanuck called my agent Bill Shiffrin, and announced that he wanted to sign me to a contract. I would be under contract to Twentieth Century-Fox, apparently with the full support of its all-powerful boss. I still had a one-picture option per year with John Wayne, as the result of *The High and the Mighty*, but this didn't preclude my signing on with Fox, a sure sign that my career, at least, was about to take off like a rocket.

I arrived at the Fox lot, which is located in one of the most beautiful and streamlined sections of the city, near a series of country clubs, golf courses, and tennis courts. As I walked through the gate, I noticed a familiar face staring at me. It was Dan Dailey, whom I hadn't seen since the '40s. He quickly appointed himself a welcoming committee of one. "Hello, Bob," he said with a big smile. "Welcome to Penitentiary Fox!"

My first assignment on the Fox lot was not long in coming.

I was told to go to Sam Fuller's office. There I met a man who was short in stature and long on whiskers. He hadn't shaved for a week, and had a long Havana cigar pointed at me like a .45-caliber pistol. He thrust his lantern jaw aggressively in my face when he talked. But even the smoke screen of rich Havana leaf couldn't hide the glint in his blue eyes. He didn't know me from a hot rock but, in five minutes, he cast me as the lead in *House of Bamboo,* a high-budget, Cinemascope gangster movie set in Japan. He had the little-boy enthusiasm and controlled craziness that usually goes with big talent, as well as the courage to do all the things directors of lesser talent wouldn't touch for fear of getting in trouble with the brass. Sam is the Peck's Bad Boy of Hollywood, one of the biggest lumps of raw talent ever to invade Tinseltown. His love for all dogfaces and, in particular, the army's First Division, "the big red one," is manifest in the patch he wears on his windbreaker and the ruby cufflinks I gave him, spelling "one."

Sammy Fuller and Darryl F. Zanuck enjoyed a close, strange relationship. Darryl saw in Sammy Fuller a soul mate, a compatriot, and a fellow delinquent. No matter how far out Sammy might go, Darryl went along with him. He regarded Sammy with a sense of ironic humor that amazed the more conventional executives at Fox. One day, Sam brought a loaded 9mm Luger to the projection room. After a test of one-upmanship and several declarations of "I bet you haven't got the guts," the spectacle began. The head of one of the biggest studios in the world and his favorite director sat like teenagers while the bullets screamed and ricocheted off the cement walls. When a quiet stillness finally settled over the room, they both broke out in uncontrollable laughter.

Once, in a film called *The Steel Helmet*, Sammy did not have enough money in the budget for a tank, so he had one painted on cardboard. He shot scenes through foliage so that the greenery swayed in the breeze directly in front of the lens, making it look like a jungle scene.

In another low-budget feature, *Shock Corridor*, the script called for a scene in a long corridor in a mental hospital. Fuller built a short set and used midgets in the distance to give the impression of receding space.

I knew from the beginning that *House of Bamboo* would be no piece of cake. Japan had survived General MacArthur's presence. But we weren't sure about Sammy Fuller's.

The Japanese were obviously sensitive regarding displays of weapons. The war had ended not too long before, but Sammy behaved as if he were preparing for World War III. He prowled about the streets of Tokyo like a latter-day Wyatt Earp, with two .45s strapped to his sides. Instead of saying "roll 'em," Sammy's signal to the cameraman to start shooting was a couple of shots from his blazing .45s. Sammy was undaunted by the panic he caused; he was like a kid playing cowboys and Indians.

Sammy decided that we should use realism in the film. In one sequence, I was supposed to be unshaven. I grew the shaggiest beard I could and wandered around Osakasa, the skid row of Tokyo, as instructed. "Let the local drunks get accustomed to your face," said Sammy. I spent three days grubbing around garbage cans like a displaced wino.

Then it came time to shoot. I was supposed to run a mile through the back alleys, pursued by an assortment of extras and local talent. I was wearing a hidden microphone, and the cameras were discreetly camouflaged. The crew stood poised to catch the reactions of the locals when someone screamed, "There goes the man who stole the pearls."

Since no one had been told I was an actor, and since there was no movie camera in sight, the problem, of course, was too much authenticity. When I started running, I realized the crowd was full of skid-row characters, who might think I really had stolen some pearls. An assortment of knives and other deadly weapons were sprinkled throughout the crowd.

When we reached a blind alley, the Tokyo police were there to try to explain to the raggedy crowd that it was all just make believe. I was lucky not to get a real knife in my ribs. After three days of preparation and insane risks, the film was underexposed, and this sequence never appeared in the movie. So much for naturalism.

We were dealing with two different cultures; explaining our director defied translation. In certain sections of Japan, several generations of a family live together on specially constructed houseboats. The boats are tied together and form a "boat city." The waterline remains the same for years; the boats don't leak because they tar them. The families pursue a daily routine in relative tranquility. When we loaded the Cinemascope cameras on these boats, they settled into the water dangerously low.

The local politicians who controlled the area had been given financial inducements to permit our filming. The money was supposed to be passed on to those whose boats we used. It wasn't. No one even bothered to inform the poor people who actually lived on the boats that their sampans were about to become sinking sets for *House of Bamboo*.

This is called stealing a shot. The actor is allowed to wander around incognito until the locals accept him as one of their own. With the use of radio microphones and hidden cameras, the effect can often be very realistic. Sometimes, too realistic!

In one sequence, I had to jump from one sampan to another, duck in, go through, and come out the other side. I burst in for my grand entrance, surprising a grandfather, his grown children, and a family who hadn't been advised that their dinner would be interrupted. I continued the chase scene, running through the boat several times. The third time, the grandfather, with long whiskers and a determined look in his eye, was standing there with a butcher knife. He was ready to defend his family's honor and their home, and stood poised to plant the blade in yours truly.

"Get someone down here!" I screamed, trying to call for help. I threw my hands up in the air and began bowing.

"Ah-so, ah-so," I said, "American... friend." My monologue in the Japanese equivalent of pig Latin did nothing to assuage the poor man's panic—or mine. Finally, the assistant director came down into the boat to explain that I wasn't a marauder bent on violence. The poor grandfather put down his knife, while I insisted that these people be paid for the intrusion.

It was incredibly cold, despite the fact that our story was supposed to take place in spring. One poor fellow from special effects had to climb the trees and glue paper cherry blossoms to the top branches while it was snowing. All the while, Shirley Yamaguchi and I were playing a love scene in our make-believe spring.

We held up a train in one sequence, infuriating the Japanese unions who wanted us ousted from the country. We had a fight sequence, neatly choreographed before Sam shot it. I was to take a punch and fly backward through a shoji door made of rice paper. Suddenly, in the middle of the fight, Sammy emptied a barrel of *pachinko* balls on the floor before my entrance. These ball bearings, used in the famous Japanese pinball game, made it impossible for me to stand up. My legs went in every direction and choreography went straight into the Pacific. There was just enough actor in me to slide across the room and wind up near Bob Ryan's feet (Bob played the mobster in our film). As soon as the take was over, Sammy started running. He kept that enigmatic smile on his face, but stayed just far enough away so that he'd have a good head start if I tried to stuff him in the pachinko barrel.

Sammy's penchant for saying "surprise" to actors was not exclusively his. John Ford was a master of such techniques. The night before Victor McLaglen was supposed to shoot his big scene in *The Informer*, Ford told him that shooting had been postponed and he wouldn't have to work the next day. McLaglen went out on the town and got appropriately blasted only to be awakened by Ford at six the next morning with the news that the picture would in fact be shot that morning. He poured coffee down his throat and prepared for action. When they arrived on the set, Ford called McLaglen every epithet you can think of.

"You stupid Irish bástard," he said. "What the hell did I ever see in you?"

McLaglen was so furious that tears streamed down his face. You could see the muscles bulging through his clothing.

Under his breath, Ford muttered, "Roll 'em." While the cameras rolled, McLaglen turned in the best performance of his life.

Time hasn't changed Sammy Fuller a bit. He shot a picture called *Dead Pigeon on Beethoven Street,* completely financed by a German studio with a full crew and cast working in English. He got permission to shoot a locomotive suspended from the ceiling in the Krupp ironworks. He even got permission to shoot in the house where Beethoven was born. The German authorities originally had denied permission, but they changed their minds when Sammy discovered that he had slept under the piano in the house several years before, as a GI. He remembered the incident and the government was so astonished that they agreed to permit his cameras inside the building which is regarded by most Germans as a shrine.

As usual, no one seems to be able to say no to Samuel Fuller. He's an original, in Hollywood or anywhere else.

Nothing could have provided a greater contrast to the hijinks of *House of Bamboo* than my next Fox adventure.

Good Morning Miss Dove was one of those pictures that they don't seem to make any more. It was adapted by Eleanor Griffin from Frances Gray Patton's novel. The film told the touching story of a schoolteacher, a wealthy, lighthearted girl at the turn of the century, who gave up a chance for romance and excitement to devote herself to others. As time passed, she became a spinster geography teacher who influenced the lives of generations of students. I played a doctor who helped her recover from an illness. Miss Dove was played by Jennifer Jones.

Henry Koster, who had presided over my osculation scene with Deanna in *First Love,* was our director. Jennifer was shy. Very shy. In one scene, as the doctor, I was supposed to give her the knee-reflex test. She kept looking at me, saying, "Do you have to do that?" (In other words, did I have to put my hand on her knee?) I laughed and finally said, "Jennifer, I'm the doctor, you're the patient, and it's in the script." She was the only really shy actress I've ever worked with.

Little did I know that around the corner a surprise was in store, one I would remember for the rest of my life.

One day my agent called. He was bursting with enthusiasm. "I've got something great over here," he said.

"All right," I said. "Send the script right over."

"It isn't a script," he said. "It's a girl."

"In that case," I said, "I'll come over to see you."

I didn't lose any time. When I walked through the door of his office, I found myself facing the most beautiful girl I had ever seen. She was wearing a simple dress, had a magnificent tan, and possessed the most beautiful body I had ever seen... the most beautiful eyes and hair... in short, a girl I had to meet. It was, of course, Rosemarie.

"Who's that good-looking guy she's with?" I asked Bill.

"That's not a guy," explained my agent, with the logic known only to agents, "that's an actor."

He arranged the introduction and we all went downstairs to a place called the Harlequin for a drink. It didn't take long for either of us to find ourselves deeply involved in a serious romance.

The last thing I contemplated, however, was marriage. My parents had been divorced, my brother was divorced, and most of my friends had experienced an unhappy marriage at one time or another. I explained to Rosemarie that I really had no choice. My whole life had been structured for bachelorhood. All my racing boats were one-seaters. I lived on the assumption that he who travels fastest travels alone. I knew that if I killed anyone while racing, I would be the only casualty. I had simply never expected to fall so deeply in love with anyone.

As proof that there are no set patterns in life, after we were married, I spent a good deal of my time taking photographs of my daughter on a bearskin rug, changing diapers, and engaging in other kinds of domestic activities. In what was perhaps the ultimate shock to a lifelong bachelor, I discovered that I liked family life.

But that's how the story *ended*. I had no idea what ending to expect when Rosemarie and I began seeing each other. I just knew that we were seeing each other more and more regularly, and that we both had less and less desire to see anyone else.

And then there was the episode of Bella Darvi....

Bella Darvi was a petite, green-eyed fashion model and

onetime Polish refugee. She had endured the horrors of wartime Europe and embarked upon a new life when my friend Alex D'Arcy introduced her to Darryl Zanuck.

Zanuck decided to make Bella his protégée. (In fact, her professional name "Darvi" had been coined by Zanuck as a combination of two first names, his own [Dar] and that of his wife Virginia [Vi].)

One day I received a telephone call from a man named Red, who worked in the Fox publicity office. He told me that Zanuck wanted me to escort Bella to a premiere. I knew that the Fox grapevine regarded Bella as Zanuck's girl friend, but I thought that if he wanted me to act as her escort, I would.

The evening was a minor disaster. On the way to the theater, I sensed that we were being followed by another car. If we turned right or left, our uninvited tail followed us. I tried to do my best impression of Humphrey Bogart and nonchalantly ignored the unwanted company, but I knew we were in for trouble. I just didn't suspect what kind.

On the way into the theater, as Bella and I walked down the aisle to our seats, we ran directly into Rosemarie, who naturally assumed that I was dating someone else. Tears followed, and I knew that even if I told Rosemarie the truth, it would sound like a very tall tale.

The other tail, our uninvited tail, was very much with us on the way back to Bella's apartment. I dropped her off and went home, glad to see the evening end.

The next morning, I received a telephone call. Darryl Zanuck wanted to see me. His office was half the length of a football field. He stood behind the desk, brandishing a sawed-off polo mallet, looking out the window.

"Sit down, Bob," he said. "I want to talk to you, man to man."

So far, so good, I thought to myself. *He's going to tell me I'm in line for Bill Holden and Gregory Peck parts.*

"I know you're a young, virile guy," he began. "I just want a straight answer."

I could feel the blood rush to my face, and a vein in my temples began throbbing ominously.

"I have no official hold on Bella," he said. "She's free to do what she wants."

Good Lord, I thought. *The date was her idea to make him jealous*.

"I had you followed," he continued. "I know you went back

to her apartment and spent twenty-seven minutes there."

How could one lousy drink have taken twenty-seven minutes?

"Now, Bob," he said, moving in for the kill, "man to man, I want to know if anything happened."

I explained to Darryl that I thought I had only been following his instructions.

"What instructions?" he thundered. "What do you mean?"

I managed to convince Darryl that no actor would be insane enough to flaunt a relationship with the protégée of the most important man in films and then play ducks and drakes with her while the same important man held his career in his hands.

He seemed to finally accept my explanation. But, as I looked back, I saw him take one last swipe with his polo mallet and decapitate a geranium.

Eventually, Bella broke off her relationship with Zanuck. Her career ended sadly, as she became a compulsive gambler who usually bet $1,000 a throw in Monte Carlo. She died in Monaco, still a young woman, after gambling away nearly 1.5 million dollars in the casino.

As for the helpful, red-haired publicist who had engineered my evening with Bella, he was never seen on the Fox lot again.

Two weeks later, Darryl left Fox to become an independent producer, and Buddy Adler took over his job. The surest road to disaster in Hollywood is to know, or be brash enough to remember, the humblest origins of any of our great leaders. I had known Buddy Adler when he ran a small movie house on Santa Monica Boulevard. In addition, I had been hand-picked by his predecessor for a contract at Fox. In short, I was as welcome in the new regime as root rot.

One of the scripts I was soon offered was called *No Down Payment*. It was a story about a group of suburban couples who moved into a housing project and watched their lives fall apart. The character the studio wanted me to portray was a loudmouthed bigot with a violent temper, a man capable of committing rape, and a racist to boot. At first I couldn't figure out why I was suddenly being groomed as a replacement for Bela Lugosi.

If I've learned anything in pictures, I've learned there is no proscenium arch. The public usually believes you are whatever you appear to be on the screen. You don't take a curtain call when it's over.

For this reason I turned down *No Down Payment* and my good friend Cameron Mitchell was talked into it. The review in *Variety* said, "Without a doubt, the most repulsive character of the year was played by Cameron Mitchell in *No Down Payment*."

Soon after that I was offered a "garbage film," a script so terrible you simply have to turn it down. When I did, I found myself back on suspension. All this isn't meant to make me into an Oliver Twist character, but to illustrate that acting is only a small part of being a successful actor. Fox didn't really want me, but they didn't want to let me go, either. To get me out of Penitentiary Fox, my agent Bill Shiffrin came up with an idea. He bought two shares of Twentieth stock and confronted Spyros Skouros, the president, at the stockholders' meeting.

"Why are you crucifying Bob Stack?" Bill demanded. "What's he ever done to you?" It was the best performance Skouros had seen all year.

On the way out, Spyros put his arm around Shiffrin's shoulder and said, in his best Zorba accent, "Why you do this to me? Why you make trouble when I do nothing bad?" They walked arm in arm down the main studio street. If anyone had seen the president of Fox with his arm around my agent, we would have owned the joint. The street is always crowded at lunchtime with executives exchanging starlets' numbers and conducting similarly important studio business. Just my luck, this particular day it was deserted from one end to the other.

Our daring effort had run into a stone wall. Next, Bill sneakily called John Wayne and asked him to exercise his option on me for a single picture—a clause that would enable me to work legally at another studio. My old pal Duke agreed, and instead of worrying about my next job, I started learning my lines for *Written on the Wind*. The role proved to be a fantastic challenge, and the executives at Fox soon saw their suspended actor playing the best role of his life in a film at another studio.

Filming *Written on the Wind* proved to be one of those rare experiences when everything came together all at once. Our director Douglas Sirk was wonderfully talented and, for some reason, showed constant faith in me. When we first began talking about the role, I had asked all the wrong questions.

"I can't figure out why you want me for this role," I began.

"Because," said Sirk, "you are a good actor."

"But I've never done anything like this before."

"I know," said Sirk, shrugging his shoulders, "but you are still a good actor."

But Sirk was also demanding. There was no way to get by with "good enough" when he wanted a scene to be "good." He was a perfectionist. He worked my tail off. Rock Hudson, Lauren Bacall, and Dorothy Malone made up the rest of the cast. The two central figures were brother and sister, social misfits and heirs to a Texas oil fortune. My character was a tormented man, a dypsomaniac, haunted by fears of impotency. Rock played the major role. Lauren Bacall was my wife, whom I'd stolen away from Rock, and Dorothy played my sister, a wanton woman who was so frustrated over her failure to interest Rock that she seduced every man in sight.

The film called for me to express emotions I had never felt or even thought about before. It was the kind of part an actor dreams of getting before the fears set in, when he wonders if he'll cut it or make a fool of himself. Douglas Sirk had been the director who had guided Rock through his first big film *Magnificent Obsession*. Even though Rock was now a major star, Doug could still maintain absolute control over the film.

Written on the Wind was like a parachute jump. Every day, I prayed my chute would open. When it came time to prepare for my delirium-tremors scene, I literally had nothing but my imagination on which to depend. I didn't want to go to a drunk tank as Susan Hayward did for *I'll Cry Tomorrow*. I wanted this to be my character, not a copy of an anonymous unfortunate. Finally, my old friend George Shdanoff came up with the answer. George once ran a theater with Michael Chekhov, and had numbered among his students Elia Kazan, Yul Brynner, Gary Cooper, Patricia Neal, and Jack Palance. He gave me the key in one brilliantly visual sentence.

"You're in a coffin," he said, "the lid is being forced down on you. You are trying to push your way out."

Happily, it did the job. Doug Sirk came from the rushes beaming and gave me the best compliment I've ever received. "The rushes look great," he said. "Everybody in the projection room agreed: You make a wonderful maniac!"

Lauren Bacall was half convinced that I was slightly off my rocker and it was only after an hour of cajoling that I convinced her I wasn't really going to decapitate her during the miscarriage scene.

One of Louella Parson's legmen was on the sound stage the day I shot my big scene with Bacall. When I let out a scream and proceeded to beat the hell out of Betty Bacall, I saw him slink out the door.

The next day, word came to my agent that Stack was a first-class ham, chewing up the scenery, and an embarrassment to watch. But Doug Sirk seemed satisfied, and that was all that mattered.

Dorothy and I had most of the intense and dramatic scenes. Rock, a gentleman as always, and one of the nicest people in our business, let all our juiciest histrionics remain on film, not on the cutting room floor. Since I was a loan-out actor and Universal was his home base, he could have used his influence to have the heart cut out of my part. But he let the script run exactly as written. I can't tell how many others in this survival profession would have done things differently.

I have often been asked since then how many slugs of Old Crow it took to be drunk enough to play the part. Now I have heard that Marlon Brando got bagged for *The Ugly American*, and it's more than a rumor that the cast of *Easy Rider* had to be tied down so they wouldn't float away. But a drunken or spaced-out actor is usually about as exciting as the bum next to you at any bar.

To the consternation of the Fox executives, who in those days wanted desperately to keep contract actors in their place, I was nominated for the Academy Award. Suddenly, their whole suspension procedure was out the window. Instead of rendering me unemployable and out of funds, they were forced to sit by and watch me win an Oscar nomination at another studio.

The prevailing view then at Twentieth Century-Fox was that actors were children and the parent (the studio) had to keep the upper hand. Marilyn Monroe was denied a dressing room on the set, because Lou Schreiber, a pocket-sized executive with a peculiar sense of priorities, didn't want her to develop a big head. Later, when Marilyn married Arthur Miller, she told the studio what it could do with its dressing rooms and everything else on the lot. Darryl sent Schreiber to New York, hat in hand, with instructions to bring Marilyn back or face the consequences. Although Schreiber terrified everyone else, he himself had no desire for a session with Zanuck and his sawed-off polo mallet. He had to get down on his knees and beg before Norma Jean would return to the lot.

I was naturally pretty happy about my nomination and excited by the results of the *Variety* poll, which were soon announced. The *Variety* poll is regarded as an important test in the industry, because the same people vote in the trade-paper poll as in the actual Oscar selection. Dorothy Malone was also nominated for an Oscar, and when Dorothy and I both won the *Variety* poll, things were really looking up!

Winning the *Variety* poll made me take my chances seriously for the first time. No one is ever told directly how to vote, but mention can be made of the fact that an Oscar brings in added millions to a studio. Since a large studio must be financially healthy to furnish jobs, it takes an employer only a few minutes to realize where his own best interests lie, relative to the question of which studio wins the most Oscars.

Jack Lemmon once said that the Oscar race is a popularity contest. It is also an auto-da-fé, with jealousy, love, and hatred in every ballot. The Academy of Motion Picture Arts and Sciences is made up of members proposed by their peers. In some cases, studios proposed members, paid their initiation dues, and controlled blocks of votes. Since an Oscar can virtually guarantee extra millions at the box offices, the major studios don't take the competition lightly.

After my nomination, I was invited to Buddy Adler's office at Fox for a meeting. I realized that since I was an Oscar nominee, the studio wanted to patch things up. But I never imagined what a surprise was in store for me. I went to Buddy Adler's Twentieth Century-Fox office and sat watching his manicured nails delicately riffle the pages of a script whose title was casually covered by his gold cigarette case.

"You've never had a major studio behind you before, Bob, but I want you to know we're behind you one hundred percent." If my smile looked a little jaundiced it was because I remembered the advice to a young sailor on a long sea voyage: If you've got to bend over, make sure no one's behind you.

Buddy went on. "Your chances of winning the Academy Award look good, and we think this should be the perfect follow-up."

He slowly picked up the gold case, took out a cigarette, and pushed the script toward me. It was upside down, but every actor worth his salt learns to read upside down, that way he can keep up with what scripts are making the rounds in various offices.

First I read the author's name, one of the most honored of the macho literary giants. The title was one of his best efforts, a post—World War I story of a lost generation.

Buddy looked at me. "And do you know who's playing the female lead opposite you?"

I knew I wasn't expected to answer, so I waited. Finally, it came.

"Deirdre!"

Oh, my God, I thought to myself. *Of all the love goddesses in Hollywood, it would have to be that one.* What could I say? I imagined the conversation going something like this:

"Well, Buddy, she might not want me in the picture!"

"Why not?"

"Because, one night some years ago, we had a date, and when we came back to her house, she got into a transparent negligee, and the bedroom door had been open."

"So?"

"Well, I broke out in a cold sweat."

"Yeah, anybody would. Then what?"

"I drove home."

"You *what*?!"

That explanation wouldn't work, even though it *was* the truth. I shut up, keeping my male reputation intact, thanked him profusely, and left.

The lady was living in Spain at the time, between bullfighters. The first subtle heralding of doom came in the form of a telegram: "Not Stack in the lead, no way!! Deirdre"

Her sister, who was a doll, wrote her saying what a dandy actor I was, and reminded her that, after all, I was up for the Academy Award. The studio even sent a publicist to Madrid to sell my virtues. They thought it was my lack of stature as a star that was putting her off. They never did know it was my lack of stature as a stud. In Hollywood, the former is usually preferable to the latter.

The wrap-up came in the next telegram: "Mention anybody's name but Stack! Final!"

By then, the studio had a firm contract commitment with me for the lead. Yet even I had to admit Deirdre was born to play the jaded, decadent playgirl of the lost generation.

The legal eagles finally figured a sneaky way out, but not without complications and some heavy expenses. The studio simply bought out the producer and director and replaced them with new people. Now the project could be regarded as a legally different one from the one which had been promised me by Buddy Adler.

Instead of being seen as the injured party, the studio could only remember that I had been a problem for them and had cost them a bundle. I was now a loser as far as they were concerned. Ty Power, my good friend and a gentleman of taste and talent, took over the part.

Our profession is built on double and triple ironies, however, and the picture turned out to be a flop. The film did give my old chum Errol Flynn the part he was born for, that of a drunken soldier of fortune.

Unfortunately, during this hassle, the studio lost its enthusiasm for my potential Academy Award. At this time, Twentieth Century-Fox controlled the largest block of votes in the Academy. The first inkling that all might not be well occurred when Bill Shiffrin went to see one of the top publicists at Fox.

"Are you pleased that Stack is up for the Oscar?" Bill asked.

With expressionless eyes veiled behind his thick glasses, the publicist answered softly, "He's not going to win."

"Come on," Bill insisted, "he's just won the *Variety* poll and it's never been wrong."

Again, even more softly, came the reply: "He's *not* going to win."

The newspaper polls kept coming in; I won them all. Still, I was jumpy on the night of the Awards. I got there early and had to drive around the block until someone besides the TV technicians arrived. Tony Quinn had been nominated in my category, but he was not considered a favorite. As I walked into the auditorium, Tony was being interviewed. He assured the fans that being nominated was the real honor. Mickey Rooney, my brilliant, crazy friend, grabbed me and said, "It's between you and me, Bob; the rest are nowhere."

Tony Perkins, Mickey, Don Murray, Tony Quinn, and I all had aisle seats. We had been instructed to avoid thanking everyone in the phone book if we won. Each of us had the same gray, waxen expression that accompanies pure panic covered by a tight-lipped smile. I clasped Rosemarie's hand and whispered that the cameras would be on all of us.

"No matter what happens," I said. "We mustn't change expressions."

The male supporting award would be announced early in the program, so at least it would soon be over.

Now it began. The nominees were announced. Mickey turned around and gave me a wink.

"The winner is," said the voice on stage, followed by a ghastly pause, "Tony Quinn."

There was a sharp intake of breath from the audience.

"That silly character was only on film for five minutes with a rubber nose," said Mickey. "We've been robbed."

I looked over at my lady. Her expression hadn't changed, except for two big tears which were slowly running down her cheeks into the smile lines on her face.

Tony is a good actor, but a few facts can't be argued. Tony had a movie coming up soon at Fox while my picture had been made at Universal. In addition, I was on suspension at a studio with the largest block of Academy votes. Their publicist had knowingly predicted that I would never win. It was also true that Tony, who is a good friend, had turned in a superb performance the previous year in *La Strada*, and many actors win the Oscar for a performance given the previous year. Bill Holden's *Sunset Boulevard* Oscar had been given to him for *Stalag 17*. Jimmy Stewart should have won the Oscar for *Mr. Smith Goes to Washington*, but his award for that tour de force came later, when he won an Oscar for the *The Philadelphia Story*.

I ran into Jimmy at a party later that night.

"Don't worry, Bob," he said. "You'll win next year."

I said, "Yeah, Jimmy, but what if I don't get another part like that one next year?"

The topper of the evening came when the Academy's highest accolade, the Irving Thalberg Award, was given to Buddy Adler. Mickey Rooney jumped out of his seat and said, "That does it! Come on, Bob, let's get the hell out of here!" he bellowed loud enough for all to hear. Then he strode up the aisle past the studio bosses, producers, and agents and out of the theater, leaving me wishing I had had the guts to follow him.

The next morning, I got a wire from Alex Kerr, my old

friend who'd been on the all-American skeet team with me many years before. It said simply, "This one was yours."

I'm not bitter about the Academy Award, just a whole lot wiser. On Academy night, I still root for my favorites like any other fan. Only Rosemarie looking at me out of the corner of her eye seems to notice a certain gray, waxen expression covered by a tight-lipped smile, reminiscent of that night many years ago.

My years at Fox were not particularly happy ones, to put it mildly. But that was years ago, and Fox has changed. A classy gent called Dennis Stanfill is president of Twentieth today. Dennis was a Rhodes scholar, but in spite of that, he's responsible, with Alan Ladd, Jr., for putting together the most successful movie in Hollywood's history, *Star Wars*. He also bypassed Twentieth's past problems with actors by casting R2D2 and C3PO, a couple of tin robots, in the leads. Who knows, there may even be a Twenty-first Century-Fox someday.

My own period under contract to Fox in the fifties finally came to an end. But, to this day, when someone tells me he's one hundred percent behind me, I make sure, like my legendary nemesis Al Capone, that I keep my back to the wall.

9

Join the Movies and See the World!

Join the movies and see the world! A motion picture filmed on foreign location can be all things to all people. To a starry-eyed beginner, it's the best of both worlds: a chance to work in his or her chosen profession, plus a free trip. But there are also characters, like one I knew at Twentieth Century-Fox, who are kept under contract because of their girl-collecting talents on behalf of the execs and visiting firemen. He got paid in an interesting way. First, he'd be given a list of foreign location films. He'd take his choice; then just the right part would be written into the script for him—not too small, but not big enough to keep him from enjoying his prepaid hustler's vacation. I think he still holds one world's record.

Fourteen minutes from the time the plane touched down in Tokyo, he managed, with some help getting through customs and an experienced driver with a limousine, to get the junior exec in his charge installed in a geisha house, where the young man was given a crash course in East-West horizontal relations. His wife—who was left home while her husband learned the business—still can't get over her spouse's unflagging interest in things Oriental.

"Can you believe it?" she says, "Kimonos... that's all he ever wants me to wear."

The truth is, when a film crew goes on location, no one—not the producer, the director, or, least of all, yours truly—has the slightest idea what will happen next.

For example, my warmest memory of location shooting took place in a less-than-exotic location: sunny San Diego, California.

In 1957 we were shooting *Tarnished Angels,* a reteaming of Rock Hudson, Dorothy Malone, and me. My head may have been devoted to the script, but my heart was really back home where Rosemarie was about to make me a papa for the first time.

We were in the middle of a tense scene in which I gave Dorothy Malone away to a dirty old man (played with glee by Bob Middleton). Suddenly, the sound men began hollering. Out of nowhere an old plane was diving straight for the cameras; behind it, trailed a tatty old banner proclaiming in letters four feet tall: It's A Girl!

Rock Hudson had arranged with the hospital to send word immediately when the baby was born. He had then hired a stunt pilot and gave him instructions to tow the appropriate message behind the plane. It's a moment I've never forgotten. Anybody who tells me that Rock Hudson isn't a first-class gent had better put up his dukes. We named our daughter Elizabeth after my mother; if all location experiences were like that one, it would be a happy world, indeed.

I thought my wild and woolly experiences in Japan during *House of Bamboo* had prepared me for anything, but I learned that the only thing you can expect in pictures is the unexpected. The idea of filming aboard a luxury liner sounds as if the cast and crew are exposed to weeks of uninterrupted luxury. Well, not exactly. I found out why when I participated in my first "disaster" film.

The definitive catastrophe motion picture would be a home movie shot by a passenger on the *Titanic*. Short of that, this breed of film has been a bonanza for special-effects men and held audiences spellbound since the days of D.W. Griffith and C.B. DeMille. For the price of a ticket, you can shiver deliciously in your seat while Steve McQueen and Paul Newman brave the perils of fire, flood, and whatever other disasters

Irwin Allen figures will make him a fortune. Irwin is, of course, the creator of *The Poseidon Adventure*, *The Towering Inferno*, and *Swarm*,

Long before Irwin got the idea to turn an ocean liner upside down, a character named Andy Stone thought of using the real thing. No special effects for Andy; he actually planned to destroy a liner and photograph the process. Thus began a film called *The Last Voyage*, which was shot on location and, for yours truly, very nearly lived up to its title.

Andy's most incredible experience involved his taking on the Defense Department. He was making an outer space film, and in the course of his research, he met the famed Dr. William H. Pickering of Caltech, who told him that rivalry between the various military services was delaying the American space program. (This was in 1957, when we were competing against the Soviets to see which nation would launch the first Earth satellite.)

Andy came up with a plan which called for MGM to provide 5 million dollars to launch an American satellite. The studio agreed, but Andy was never able to reach President Eisenhower. If he had, we would have won the space race before it started, and our satellite, not Sputnik I, would have been first to circle the globe.

The Last Voyage was the precursor of all the great disaster films; it was, in many ways, a motion picture ahead of its time.

The hallmark of the film was to be realism. Instead of merely working on a set, Andy decided to use a real boat. So he started searching for a luxury liner. The motion picture was to portray the sinking of the ship, focusing on the efforts of a husband to save his wife, who was pinned in the wreckage of their cabin, and his daughter, trapped on an inaccessible ledge.

Andy combed the shipyards of Europe, trying to find the chief prop. He said it was like searching for an iceberg and gave up in discouragement. Obviously, he received little encouragement from the shipping lines, for "Do you have a spare luxury liner I can sink?" was hardly the way to win popularity and influence with any of the big shipping companies.

Andy heard a number of rumors that the *Ile de France*, a noble ocean liner dating back to the 1920s, might be heading for salvage and available for sale. He called the French Line.

"Salvaging the *Ile de France*?" said a startled executive. "Absurd, Monsieur."

Yet within sixty days, however, Andy had the ship.

Rosemarie and I arrived in Japan. We met the rest of the cast of *The Last Voyage*, all old friends—Dorothy Malone, who played my wife, Edmond O'Brien, and George Sanders.

The true story of *The Last Voyage* has remained a mystery for many years, even to many of us with access to the bits and pieces of the puzzle. Only in recent months has Andy Stone revealed to me the complete details of what took place behind the scenes in Osaka—a harrowing tale.

Our problems started from the first day of shooting.

Although Andy was nominally in control of the ship, the real owner was the Japanese salvage company. This company had only rented the ship to the Stones because they couldn't take the *Ile de France* into dry dock until they finished salvaging a freighter which had sunk in Osaka harbor.

Andy told us that we were going to take part in the actual flooding of an ocean liner. No one realized, however, that the Japanese salvage company had no intention of letting Andy go through with his plans. If Andy were permitted to flood the engine room, for instance, none of the valuable ship's properties could be salvaged.

Our Japanese friends had concocted a clever scheme. They would rent the liner to the Stones at enormous fees and prevent them, with stalling tactics, from doing anything to the ship. Eventually, they would reclaim the liner and take it to dry dock for salvage—leaving Andy, the cast, and crew, and MGM's 1.5-million-dollar investment sitting right in the middle of Osaka harbor!

I quickly became aware that something strange was going on, as our shooting schedule was inexplicably plagued by delays.

"Why aren't we shooting?" I asked one day.

"The Japanese salvage company won't let us use the liner today," said Andy. "They said it's too windy to take the ship out." He pointed to the smokestacks. The smoke was sailing straight up into a windless, cloudless sky.

Andy began receiving a variety of threats, some anonymous, others directly from the Japanese shipping firm which owned our liner. All these messages made one thing clear: The company had no intention whatsoever of living up to its contractual obligations.

Andy decided that the only way he could force the company to stop intimidating us was to refuse to pay the bills.

What none of us knew was that, while we were busy memorizing our lines and concentrating on the difficult action of the film, Andy had encountered another crisis. The Japanese interpreter who handled communications with the shipping company came to him with an incredible story. He said that his eight-year-old daughter had been attacked on the way to school and raped. Along with the assault had come a message revealing that anyone who defied the shipping company would be injured or killed.

Andy began eating his meals in his hotel room, turning off all the lights. He suspected that organized criminals might try any form of violence in order to retaliate against members of our company. He received a threat that Japanese gangsters would blow up the boat that brought us out to the *Ile de France* every day unless we capitulated and started paying the bills.

Andy is a fighter, a throwback to the old-style directors who started the film industry. He was not about to be intimidated by anyone. So he decided to try to sink the ship "visually," creating an optical *impression* that the ship was going down.

One member of the group seemed oblivious to it all. Although I was nominally the star of the ship, George Sanders did not waste time with protocol. He arrived on board the *Ile de France* in his captain's uniform and installed himself at the captain's table where the crew brought him his choice of food and wine for the rest of the picture.

On the instructions of "Captain Sanders," two square portholes were cut in the side of his cabin. If something went wrong, the rest of us might be trapped on board, but our brave "captain" would have a means of exiting to safety.

At last we came to the key scene, the flooding of the ship. Andy had been having terrible problems with the insurance man. His initial meeting with Andy had been a distaster. He asked for a bribe; Andy said no; and the relationship deteriorated from that point on. The insurance man cooperated in every way with the Japanese shipping firm, frustrating our every attempt to flood the ship. Andy came up with an ingenious scheme. The contract said we couldn't shoot unless the insurance man was present. Andy somehow got hold of a beautiful Japanese girl and persuaded her to seduce the agent and take him away for the weekend.

"Everybody's happy," said Andy. "He's having fun and we're making a picture."

The minute the insurance man and his lady friend were out of town, Andy began protesting his absence. He threatened to sue the company who then instructed Andy to proceed without their representative. Andy started cranking up the cameras. The special-effects men decided that the only way to sink the ship visually was to put the cameras inside and photograph the sea rushing in. Using fireboats, which shoot streams of water several hundred feet high, they stretched giant hoists up the sides of the ship through the portholes, and sealed them off. Sandbags were placed all around the arc lights. There were knifeblade switches on the arcs, and the slightest contact with water could electrocute someone nearby.

The water came through with such ferocity that we literally were thrown head over heels. Electricity combined with salt water to produce a small electrical storm on board. Great waves poured through the ship.

Eddie O'Brien, according to scripted instructions, fought his way through the waves and stumbled over the sandbags to the main dining room. He had to battle his way through thousands of gallons of water and arc lights spitting sparks like Dr. Frankenstein's infernal machine.

Eddie turned to Andy in a rage. "You son of a bitch!" he bellowed, "You compulsive masochist! You have a death wish! You can kill yourself—but you're not going to kill me!" Eddie continued in his stentorian tones for a few minutes and then stormed off the ship. It is understandable that he found the experience unusually terrifying. So much water had come into the superstructure that the ship began to list. Eddie couldn't see that well, and the ship really appeared to be going down.

Eddie's agent, also in a rage, called Andy.

"Mr. O'Brien will not come aboard ship unless it passes his inspection. You're going to capsize the boat!"

When Eddie arrived the next day, he inspected the angle of the ship in the water and agreed to go on working. "I have a new scene for you," said Andy, smilingly presenting him with an addition to the script. The scene was shot with no difficulties. As we left the *Ile de France* that night, Eddie was handed an airplane ticket. "This is your ticket back to the mainland," said Andy. "The new scene you shot today . . . well, I wrote you out of the picture!"

Happily, Eddie and Andy eventually overcame their difficulties and today the two are on good terms.

The use of the real ship made *The Last Voyage* exceptionally hazardous. When we ran up and down ladders, instead of finding neatly designed stairs built for the action of the film, we found ourselves on ladders with forty-five years of grease and slime on them.

In one sequence, Dorothy Malone was supposed to be trapped under the superstructure of the ship, while the water rose around her. This was shot with a set built into the swimming pool. We first made sure the Japanese crewman in charge of flooding knew our signals.

He smiled, nodded, and said *"hai, hai"* (yes, yes). When Andy told him to stop, he kept on smiling, did nothing, and damn near drowned Dorothy.

Great chunks of glass flew freely through the air on deck as dynamite explosions rocked the boat with regularity.

Among the most poignant scenes in the film were those involving the relationship between the father I played and his small daughter. I knew going into production that these scary scenes involving the child would be especially difficult. Tammy Marihugh played my daughter. When we first met, I suggested we play a little game. I would always call her by the name of her character in the film. I asked her to call me daddy instead of Mr. Stack.

It is important for people outside the film industry to realize the difference between an actor who is simply giving a performance and an actor who is expressing emotions because he is being photographed in a realistic situation. A man who is actually being dropped into a cauldron of boiling water may be inspired by his terror to execute a more dramatic performance than an actor being tossed into imaginary flames. But the whole purpose of acting is to act, not to simply photograph emotions which have been induced by the director's chicanery.

Our most difficult scene involved my climbing with Tammy over a seventy-three-foot drop. Rosemarie enjoyed coming to the set, but on the morning we were to shoot the scene, I suggested she go shopping. (She tends to have a strong sense of anticipation.)

"You're going to do something crazy again," she said.

"Not at all," I said, neglecting to mention the eleven-story drop. "I just thought you'd like to go shopping."

Before we began shooting, a board was set across the enormous hole in the deck. Tammy and I were each provided with a piano wire around our waists. We were assured that it was attached to a cable and that, in case anyone slipped, the cable would see to it that we didn't fall eleven stories.

Hal Mohr, our cinematographer, turned to Tammy's father, who stood there with a big grin. "If anything happens to this little girl," Hal said, "I'm going to beat your brains out with this wrench."

The board did not look like a firm base, as it lay stretched across the giant, gaping hole. Tammy climbed out on the board. She was absolutely terrified and, I might add, in good company. When she reached the middle of the board, special effects rotated the board slightly, to make it appear ready to collapse.

Tammy started to cry. She turned back to me and said, "Daddy, daddy, help me." It was a more realistic plea than any mere performance could have been. I was terrified myself, but I came to the rescue as the script demanded. Hal Mohr put his wrench away, and Tammy's father could breathe a sigh of relief.

There were no easy scenes in *The Last Voyage*.

We had surmounted every type of difficulty—threats of violence, blackmail, and extortion. We felt we had finally finished facing unpleasant surprises. But the worst surprise was still to come. Around 4 A.M. one day, one of Andy's assistants called and said that the Japanese company had ordered our film crew and cast locked off the ship. Andy enlisted the aid of our chief underwater-demolition expert Commander Fain, a war hero whose life story had been filmed by Warner Brothers.

The Stones and our cameraman arrived at the side of the ocean liner. On board were Japanese crewmen, reinforced by armed thugs with a variety of weapons including knives and saws. They were prepared to kill the Stones to prevent them from gaining access to their camera equipment. There was a rope hanging down the gangplank. Andy seized the rope and, like a born buccaneer, began climbing up the side of the ship. Suddenly it was no longer a movie, but a case of piracy on the high seas. The Stones finally reached the main deck. An armed man charged at Andy, and his assistant threw himself in front of the director.

"You've got to kill me first!" he screamed.

A Japanese steward approached the Stones carrying an enormous sword. He was prepared to decapitate them if they took a step toward their equipment. Virginia Stone greeted this marauder with a strong kick in the groin. A photographer from *Life* magazine in the boat at the side of the *Ile de France*, yelled "Do it again! Kick him—but this time while I'm in focus!"

Somehow, the Stones managed to retrieve their equipment.

As their launch proceeded down the canal back toward the hotel, it was followed by a police boat. Reporters were swarming around the dock. To our surprise, customs cleared us instantly; we had expected an inquisition.

"Of course they cleared us," said Andy. "Commander Fain arranged for a US warship to follow us. We told them that if anything happened to us, the marines and the navy would blow the *Ile de France* out of the water."

I thought I had seen enough of ships to last a lifetime, but my shipboard adventures were only beginning. I couldn't resist the chance to play the title role in a historical epic, *John Paul Jones*, a film shot entirely on location.

Doing the life of a major historical figure is a little like having your first love affair. The experience may be terribly meaningful for you, but your audience is usually less than satisfied. All those complicated costumes, wigs, and makeup are as comfortable as a hair shirt, and does the audience dig it? No way. They're waiting for slave girls, slave boys, concubines, and queens to appear in the briefest costumes decency allows.

As a small boy, I saw the C.B. DeMille epic *Sign of the Cross*, starring Fredric March, Claudette Colbert, and Elissa Landi. Fredric March was given the choice of living a lascivious, debauched life with the queen, played by brunette Claudette Colbert, or a dubious future based on purity and dedication with blond Elissa Landi. Claudette was dressed in revealing cuplike arrangements and very little else, which meant she was a wanton woman. Elissa Landi wore a kind of long, white nightshirt which showed she was pure. The scene in which Claudette takes her nude bath in asses' milk is still crystal clear in my mind. I can see that opaque liquid caressing her lovely body, her beauteous bosoms appearing and disappearing as she moved. Maybe I was just a horny little kid, but I remember thinking that Freddy March blew it. I would never have walked off into the lion's den with the blond in the nightshirt. I would have gone for a milky swim with the lascivious brunette queen in her birthday suit. And that's how C.B. DeMille made his millions on costume pictures and biblical epics. Give them enough "t and a" to keep everyone's libido operating, mixed with a little something for the sadomasochists when all the luscious, undulating, bad ladies are burned, drowned, crushed, or chewed up in righteous retribution. You can't even fault the moral. The good folks always survive— in a boring fashion, maybe, but they do survive.

My involvement with *John Paul Jones* was again masterminded by whoever controls the law of irony. Back in 1959 a bunch of us were coming back from a western location in Red Rock Canyon, the classic spot for westerns ever since Tom Mix, and someone brought up the subject of sadistic directors. We kicked it around for a while, and one name kept leading the list. I made the most noise and even told a story to make my point. It was when Barbara Stanwyck was filming *California* with Ray Milland. Barbara refused to work until the director in question apologized to an actor he had misused and humiliated, and she made the director do it in front of the entire crew.

Barbara is one of the special ladies of our profession. She and Carole Lombard were the best this business ever produced. They both were examples of a super blend of guts, talent, and humor. After a harrowing day on a miserable location, Carole was the one who came up with the classic, "Who do you have to screw to get off this picture?"

(Van Heflin, a young, ambitious New York actor, was cast with Barbara in a western and figured he would use all his stage tricks to take advantage of this break. He practiced for hours rolling a silver dollar from one finger to another as a piece of business. During rehearsal, Barbara asked, "Are you going to do that in the take?"

"No," said Van, "I'm just practicing a trick."

But when the camera was rolling, Van began playing with the silver dollar during Barbara's lines. About halfway through the scene, the crew began to laugh. Van turned around and saw Barbara slowly lifting up her dress. "What are you doing?" asked Van.

Barbara beamed innocently. "I'm going to show them a trick a hell of a lot more interesting than yours.")

Ten days after my brave speech about directors and human rights, I got a call from my agent. He told me to go to a house in Beverly Hills, as someone wanted to have a look at me.

"This guy wants to see if you're too tall," explained my agent. "So wear moccasins and slouch and sit down every chance you get."

"What's it for?"

"The lead in *John Paul Jones*."

The man who met me at the door had brilliant blue eyes, a ruddy face, and crew-cut, sandy hair.

"Come in, come in," he said. "I'm John Farrow."

It can't be, I thought; it's too much. But here it was: John Farrow, of course, had been Barbara Stanwyck's director in *California*.

I closed my eyes. I could see one of the lesser gods looking down, his laurel wreath set on the back of his head, and, with a Mona Lisa smile, saying, "You asked for a big movie? You've got it! Just so it comes out even, you've got John Farrow for six months. Let's see how you handle your human rights."

John Paul Jones was a major historical figure and he had a fascinating life. His travels and adventures led him to many parts of the world. Not only were his naval exploits unprecedented in the history of the country, but his experiences in Europe were equally astonishing.

He was one of the sexiest, most colorful characters in American history, with decadent partners like Catherine the Great of Russia, whose orgies and bizarre tastes had made even blasé European royalty shiver deliciously. Certainly, John Farrow had a reputation as a swinger; since he was writing and directing the opus, it was bound to be provocative.

Strangely enough, however, he had also written a book about Catholicism, and the Church had made him a Papal prince. Which side of him would win out on the script of *John Paul Jones*, the prurient or the pious? In spite of Farrow's personal peccadillos, the kama sutra I expected turned out to be more like Mother Goose, and John Paul Jones became, like Elmer Gantry or Reverend Davidson in *Rain*, the opposite of what he was cracked up to be.

This proved that the best screenwriters are not on the side of the angels. In spite of the taming of *JPJ*, it was an exciting project with a long schedule, foreign locations, and millions to spend. We had a good cast: Charles Coburn as Benjamin Franklin, Marisa Pavan (Pier Angeli's sister), Jean Pierre Aumont, David Farrar, Peter Cushing (as my noble adversary who inspired me to say "I've not yet begun to fight"), and Bette Davis in a guest appearance as Catherine the Great.

Rosemarie was about to have our son Charlie, so she stayed at home. I left for Europe, and Rosemarie joined me as soon as she could bring the new baby.

Farrow engaged his cousin Captain Alan Villiers as nautical expert. Villiers, the man responsible for the sailing of *Mayflower II*, a scale model of the original ship, was world-renowned for his expertise in boats.

We shot much of the film on location: at the King James Palace outside London; in Versailles; in Williamsburg, Virginia; and Denia, Spain. Denia is an almost forgotten little town nestled in a miniature harbor on the Mediterranean coast, halfway between Alicante and Valencia. There were a handful of toy-making factories in town and a well-established export industry specializing in apricots.

The action of the film was supposed to take place in nineteenth-century Scotland, not twentieth-century Spain. We were prepared to convert Denia into a Scottish village. The stone fort used in the naval battles was authentic. Although it had been built by the Moors, it projected a definite Norman feeling.

Villiers remembered having seen some ancient hulks of sailing ships lying on a beach in Sicily when he served there during the war. He went back to Sicily, found two of the hulks, towed them to Rome, restored them, and launched his ships. The cost came to $300,000 before the vessels were ready to sail dramatically into the harbor of Denia. One ship was a perfect replica of the *Bonhomme Richard*, and the other duplicated the *Serapis*. Even the uniforms were authentic. The researchers working on the film discovered the actual tailoring house which had manufactured the uniforms worn by Jones and his men. The company was still in existence and, like most British craftsmen, the tailors were able to go through the records and discover what their ancestors had done hundreds of years ago.

Unfortunately, the uniforms were made of a heavy, thick material. They were interesting to look at and would have been fine in Scotland, but were miserable to wear in Spain during the height of summer. I felt less like a great American naval figure than a candidate for the main course at one of Colonel Sanders's friendly neighborhood stands. Denia was as close as I ever expect to get to Hades. The people were friendly, but the weather was impossible. In addition to our thick jackets and trousers, we had to wear powered wigs. Whenever people comment about Chuck Heston and his well-earned salaries in an assortment of biblical epics, I remind them that a man who puts on a suit of armor under the Spanish sun is definitely earning his pay.

Unfortunately, one of the battle sequences was shot very near the coastline, in an area that served as one of the main outlets for the local sewage system. As the "sailors" were blown overboard by the exploding cannon, they had to tumble into the water—holding their noses. No one could have paid me to take a swim in those waters. But the stunt men, unintimidated by man, beast, or odor, held their noses and plunged in with gusto.

Filming *John Paul Jones* gave me an opportunity to work with Charles Coburn, who played the mischievous octogenarian Ben Franklin. Coburn was a veteran of sixty-five years in show business. He loved good cigars and was proud of his collection of monocles. The monocle, which he wore because he needed a lens for only one eye, became his trademark.

"They only cause one problem," he said once. "They drop in the soup all the time."

Coburn simply refused to age. He learned to drive a sulky at the age of seventy, took up Latin, and waged a one-man campaign to staff the drama departments of colleges with professional actors.

If working with Charles Coburn and Bette Davis was one of the nicer aspects of *JPJ*, the same could not be said for doing business with our producer, an old-fashioned promoter named Sam Bronston. Sam had discovered that many large corporations had enormous assets in Spain which were frozen unless they were reinvested locally. Pierre Du Pont, under Sam's influence, agreed to put up five million dollars in frozen funds to produce our movie. Sam's financial manipulations rivaled those of an international diplomat. He raised huge sums of money as if by magic. His wheeler-dealer ways with cash extended to the cast and crew. One day he showed up on the set with an enormous carpetbag full of exotic currencies—pfennigs, pesetas, francs, lira, and a variety of others I had never seen before, announcing that the currency represented my week's salary.

"I don't know what this stuff is," I said. "It could be Confederate money. Give me something I can spend in the good old US of A."

Bronston was never at a loss for words. In the course of shooting, he managed to run up an enormous tab at the local bars. Instead of cash, he closed out his accounts with the Spanish bartenders by inviting them to the set to watch the filming. But, in spite of it all, I liked old Sam—he did give me the part!

One of Sam's biggest coups was obtaining permission from the Spanish government to shoot scenes in the royal palace in Madrid; we enjoyed a breathtaking banquet in the enormous state dining room. The throne room in the royal palace served as the film's setting for the court of Catherine the Great. By draping a silk banner bearing the double-headed eagle of Imperial Russia behind the throne, the room—with deep carpets, mirrors, chandeliers, and red tapestried walls—was completely transformed. Our splendid Catherine the Great, Bette Davis, was a real doll, even passing out cigars when word came that Rosemarie had given birth to a son.

Location protocol is fairly well recognized, and there are few exceptions. First star billing gets the preferred chateau, villa, apartment, hotel, etc., and the rest get theirs in order of importance.

I was the star, at least contractually, so I was to be given, according to the producers, a luxurious villa with gleaming marble steps and pillars, on the beach at Benidorm.

Rosemarie was the first to notice a small spot in the ceiling over our bed, which seemed to change in shape and size from day to day like a cancerous growth.

"Don't worry, honey," I said. "It's just a spot."

"Maybe so, but it's right over our bed and it makes me nervous."

"Just don't think about it; maybe it'll go away." It got to be a routine. Every night when I'd get home, we'd check the spot and note its progress.

"Look at it now," said my bride. "It covers half the ceiling. I'm going to sleep downstairs."

"Wait a minute," I said. "What do the local Spanish ladies say?"

"That it's a stain and just needs painting."

"I promise it'll be checked out tomorrow. Let's get some sleep."

Next morning at breakfast, we heard a horrendous crash. All the plaster on the ceiling, along with one hundred gallons of water, cascaded onto the bed where our bodies had lain ten minutes before.

No one seemed particularly surprised. All the houses had water storage tanks on their roofs, but then they didn't all have storage tanks that leaked. Finally, the rumor got back to us that the German builder blew all his loot on the marble exterior so he could rent it to the Americans.

The view was magnificent; the sea was a remarkable azure blue, and our replica of the *Bonhomme Richard* proudly rode at anchor. Only the smell was terrible. I could never discover where the elusive stink originated. One day, while baby-sitting for our eighteen-month-old Elizabeth, Rosemarie noticed an old rubber hose running out to the garden. Of course, anyone who'd build a leaky cistern over the bed would have to find an equally clever way to handle human waste. It's a miracle no one in our fancy marble villa contracted typhoid. But these were only details. Spain, under any condition, is worth the trip. The country and its people are ageless, with a character not even the tourists can ruin.

Denia, on the opposite side of a mountain range, was our main location. Each day we'd have to drive an hour and a half each way on hairpin mountain roads. The means of transport again conformed contractually to my unique star status. I was given the honor of having the only Lincoln on the Costa Brava.

No one mentioned that it was twenty years old. The color was grasshopper green and, unfortunately, so was the driver. Every time I'd leave in the morning in what Rosemarie called the "green hornet," she'd get a lost look on her pretty face.

"Be careful," she'd say, as if I had any control over my destiny. The Denia drive was as challenging as any I've known. What made it so unique was that normal concepts of road and auto safety were absolutely reversed. My enthusiastic driver had read somewhere that, in the event of a front-wheel wobble, the best remedy is to increase speed and drive through it, a procedure that was always attempted at the most twisted part of the road with a 2,000-foot drop-off into the canyon below.

As the steering wheel would begin chattering, the driver would look at me with a big grin and say, "Don't worry, me fix." Then he'd jam his foot on the gas and we'd go lurching around the curves like a drunken roller coaster. Sure enough, when we got to a straight stretch, the wobble had stopped. I used to think he scared the wobble out. One day Bruce Cabot, who was impressed by my private limousine, asked if he could join me. Bruce, who's never been known to steer away from the good life, was appreciative.

"Your own private car and driver," he said. "Beats hell out of that two-hour ride in the bus." When we got to the twisty part of the road, Bruce shot upright in his seat. "Hey, look at the steering wheel," he said. "The car's got a front-wheel wobble."

"Yeah, I know," I said. "He's got a way of fixing it."

"How?"

"Just watch," I said.

Our driver, who was aptly named Jesús, gave Bruce his customary grin, stomped on the gas, and we were off.

"Jesús," said Bruce.

"Si, señor," said Jesús.

We lurched around the turns, going faster and faster. "Jesus Christ," said Bruce. (This time, Jesús knew he wasn't being addressed.) "What's he doing? Trying to kill us? Slow down, damn it, slow down!"

But Jesús, with his patient smile, said, "Don't worry, me fix," and kept right on going. Finally, Bruce picked up the big leather script cover given to him by Errol Flynn and started beating our driver over the head.

"You damn maniac," he said. "Stop the car and let me out of here! Stop the car or I'll beat your brains out!"

Jesús jammed on the brakes. We slid sideways and came to a halt pointing in the wrong direction. He turned slowly and said, "You should not do that, señor. It can be dangerous stopping like that."

Bruce got out, waited for the bus, and never again mentioned how lucky he thought I was to have a private car and driver.

You might think the collapsing ceiling cured me of a desire to make films abroad. But every picture is different, and the fact that the roof may fall in during one film doesn't mean that the next one won't be a real gem. In 1967, I began a multilingual, multinational production that nearly blew up the Berlin Wall.

Doing a motion picture in two languages is an experience not many actors are fortunate, or unfortunate enough, to be able to have. To do one in three takes one beyond the pale. In this film I had the dubious pleasure of participating in a derring-do, hidden-treasure stinker called *The Corrupt Ones*, an apt title, no doubt referring to the desperate desire for financial gain of any actor willing to take on such a project. I also did it because I thought the director, James Hill, saw something in the script invisible to me. Hill's *Born Free* had been a classic of sorts and, with my usual desperate search for an element of class or talent, I hung my hat on him. He was obviously more at home with lions.

This was my first involvement with a multinational production—which merely means the production is financed by a promoter who has gotten his money from four or five different countries. Each investor usually insists that a star from his own country be added to the cast. It starts getting interesting when you meet the rest of the cast and realize most of them don't speak English.

Not only don't they speak English, but nobody speaks the same language. A scene becomes rather like a debate at the United Nations without the benefit of a translator. The first day, I worked with a wonderful Italian character actress, who had no knowledge of English. She had memorized the English dialogue but based her pronunciation on Italian phonetics and syllabication. Her accents were all on the wrong syllables.

I couldn't understand a damn word. The director saw I was lost, so he worked out signals and simply waved to me each time I was supposed to start talking. There was more to come. The third character—a big, fat German actor, one of Berlin's top comedy stars—made his entrance. He slapped me on the back and, with the authority only thirty years of stage work can bring, boomed, "Sixty-four, thirty-five, fifty-three, seventy-two?"

The "seventy-two" had taken on the intonation of a question, so, like the Mad Hatter at an "unbirthday party," I read my next line. My walking cash register picked up his cue and we finished the scene. This is called "doing it by the numbers."

The numbers game may be a sneaky ploy, but only actors of remarkable talent can get away with it. I'll make you a bet Laurence Olivier couldn't play a "seventy-two" with as much authority as my German friend. The trick, of course, is to apply as much facial expression to this gibberish as one would to a scene written by Willie Shakespeare. After the shooting is completed, other actors dub the English dialogue; only lip readers know the difference. Stanislavski's book, *The Actor Prepares*, didn't devote a chapter to this phenomenon, because no actor is prepared for the first time he plays a scene "by the numbers," not even a Russian.

There's an old Hollywood saying: The tougher a movie is to make, the lousier it turns out. This production was no exception.

Arthur Brauner was the German producer. He made his fortune by arriving in postwar Berlin with a bag of money and buying a studio for next to nothing. The studio was something of a curiosity.

Rising ominously from the midst of the sound stages was a tall, skinny tower that seemed to serve no purpose. I was midway into the movie before a wandering cab driver explained its use. No one in the production company seemed to want to discuss it.

Our large, ugly tower, it turned out, was used by Hitler to manufacture poison gas. Small wonder our producer got such a bargain; there were no other bidders. Between the gas tower and the Berlin Wall, the atmosphere on the set was not best described as "a lot of laughs."

I was warned that I had better bring my own stunt man,

since there was a rumor in Hollywood the Germans didn't use makeup for the blood effects. So my old chum and stunt double on "The Untouchables," Bill Catching, was included. The day he arrived, I wasn't working, so he was put in charge of explosives which, of course, he knew nothing about. On the first test run, he wondered why his helper was using such a long fuse. After it went off, blowing out three of the cafeteria windows and scaring the socks off everyone else, Bill finally asked, "What in the hell kind of powder was that?"

"Not just powder," said his grinning helper, "but to make it better, I added my own secret, a little nitroglycerin."

If an actor is called upon to die in a movie, the idea is to make it appear believable without actually finishing him off. He may be needed for retakes. The farther away you get from Hollywood, the nearer you get to fiction's becoming fact. Maybe the Europeans have been through too many real wars to take any wounds acquired in make-believe seriously. Bill Catching, my stuntman and double, found himself responsible for laying out the bomb effects for a sequence in which we were all escaping from Chinese Communists (I forgot to mention that part of *The Corrupt Ones* was shot in Hong Kong). Naturally, the escape from the Chinese Communists was shot in Berlin, in a park adjoining the Berlin Wall. No one thought it a good idea to mention that Bill and his assistant, "the mad bomber," were going to set off explosions of blasting power and nitro a few hundred yards away from the guard dogs and tank traps of East Berlin.

Elke Sommer and I made our escape from the German actors (made up to look like Chinese) as Bill set off the first explosion. There was a great roar; a ball of fire rose thirty feet in the air, and the leaves were blown off the surrounding trees. At first there was absolute silence. Then the guard dogs began their frenzied patrols. The rings that keep them chained to their individual cables hissed as they lunged 100 yards one way and then back, all the while making that eerie sound only the Doberman killer can produce.

By the time the second explosion was detonated, I could see the flash of binoculars from a tower a quarter of a mile away. Before Bill could set off the third, an East German helicopter swooped down, took a look, and disappeared back over the wall. When the third explosion was touched off, we heard an answering roar from the other side. But this was no special effect. It was heavy artillery. Jimmy Hill's six months with the lions of *Born Free* must have inured him, because he kept right on filming; every time Bill touched off his make-believe mayhem on the west side, it was answered like an echo from the east.

This went on for a few more minutes, until two carloads of red-faced West German police arrived and ordered us the hell out of there. Later, over a bottle of schnapps, we tried to reconstruct what had happened. We must have totally blown the minds of East Germany's highly professional surveillance teams. First, a massive, unidentified explosion near the wall had been verified by their reconnaissance helicopter. The pilot had reported probable war games involving a troop of Chinese Communists. Nobody could have understood what it meant, but it was obviously some sort of provocation. The provocation part they thoroughly understood, because the East German chopper pilots used to love to harass the Allied—and, in particular, the American—forces. (I played golf one day on the US Army golf course which adjoins the Berlin Wall. The jokers from the other side would suddenly pop up over the Wall and, scooting along about twenty feet off the ground, knock everybody flat.)

In any case, since they couldn't figure out what in hell was going on, they must have decided to use the old monkey-see, monkey-do gambit. You make a noise and I'll make a bigger one.

After the incident of the explosions near the Berlin Wall, Bill was no longer kept on as a special-effects man. But his next job as stunt coordinator was no piece of cake. Bill has always tried to lay out his stunts so the actor can be photographed in close-up and show how courageous or stupid he is. In the more dangerous master shots, Bill does the stunt himself. In one scene, the hero (me) was caught by the dirty guys and dragged behind a speedboat at night, his hands tied behind his back, like a soggy James Bond. Bill, who makes all the tough ones look easy, helped me into a wet suit, because it was mid-December. Unfortunately, Bill's boat driver got into his car and left (it was 2 A.M., and the driver had a strong union).

I was stuck with a dud who'd been drinking since early afternoon; he slammed into the end of the boat dock on the way out. I jumped into the icy water, grabbed the rope to make it look as if my hands were tied, and we were off. I'll say we were off! He jammed the throttle wide open and, as we flew past the cameras, I looked like a racing hull in full plane, my shirt and pants flapping along behind me.

After a conference and a replacement wardrobe, we tried it again, only more slowly. It was suggested that the close-ups of me holding the rope were not good enough; we were asked to use a knot that would make it appear I was really tied up.

"You can always let go if you get into trouble," the director announced.

This time, as we came by, there was nothing to photograph. The boat was going so damn slow, and the angle of the rope was such, that I was dragged to the bottom like a human dredge.

Bill finally hauled me up—my eyes full of mud and muck in my hair—looking like a ratty Ophelia. I was beginning to lose my enthusiasm. Around 4:30 A.M. we finally got the shot, but not before I'd inhaled half the lake. When the sequence appeared on the screen, it lasted about ten seconds, and you couldn't tell who (or what) was being towed behind the boat.

As they say, the tougher the movie is to make...

My leading lady, Elke Sommer, had to be the most luscious blond of the year; she turned the town on its ear. As we met, her first seductive line was, "I bet I can beat you running." So she set up a footrace and I had to knock my brains out trying to beat her before we got down to discussing script. Maybe we should have kept running. She was amazing, never complained, did her own dangerous stunts like a Teutonic Pearl White. Nancy Kwan was another lovely addition to our smorgasbord; Christian Marquand representing the French contingent.

Christian was something else—a Gallic charmer who was equally successful with both sexes. He was a great friend of Marlon Brando, who is said to have named his son after him. One day his visitor on the set would be a beautiful blond, the next it might be another blond almost as beautiful, but a male. Christian was equally attentive to both, and made sure they were seated comfortably, invariably in my chair. Once he asked me if I'd read Terry Southern's *Candy*. I assured him I had read the history of this young lady who found fulfillment through incest, an orgy with a masochistic hunchback, and masturbation with a coat hanger. He then told me he was going to produce it as a movie. The cast would star Marlon Brando, Richard Burton, James Coburn, and, just possibly, me.

"Would I like to play the lascivious doctor?" I thought Christian had as much chance to produce a picture with Brando, Burton, and Coburn, as Linda Lovelace had to be voted Miss Teenage America. So I wished him well, waved good-bye to Mr. Ulrich's wall and Mr. Brauner's tower, and flew back to a blander kind of insanity.

The proof that I have no idea what this business is about came on my return. When I read my first *Daily Variety*, it announced that Christian Marquand had signed Brando, Burton, and Coburn to do *Candy*, with Terry Southern writing the screeplay in a multimillion-dollar production.

Anyday now, I can see the headline in *Daily Variety*, "Linda Lovelace voted Miss Teenage America."

Of course, every trip outside the USA hasn't been quite so traumatic. Rosemarie and I have made some wonderful friends and encountered some incredibly talented filmmakers in all parts of the world. The affection of fans who have seen you "speaking" their language in a nondubbed version of a film is particularly gratifying.

In 1968, for example, I went to Paris to begin working on *Le Soleil des Voyous* (*The Day of the Delinquents*), with Jean Gabin—the French Spencer Tracy, who first achieved stardom in Jean Renoir's unforgettable classic *Grande Illusion*. Gabin and I had a wonderful relationship. He was not especially fond of Hollywood or American films. His own experience in Hollywood had been a disaster. He was living with Marlene Dietrich at the time and, when he arrived in Hollywood, the studio immediately marcelled his hair (shades of my old widow's peak!). Gabin, who was tough as nails, decided he looked like a fruitcake and went back to France, convinced that Hollywood destroys French actors.

Gabin was a fascinating man to work with. I spent most of my time learning my lines, since the entire picture was shot in French slang. The studio provided me with a coach, a Russian lady who knew all the appropriate lingo. I lived at the Georges V in Paris, missing Rosemarie who had to stay home with the kids. I spent Christmas alone and swore I'd never leave home again.

So, the next time you hear that your favorite actor is shooting abroad, he may be relaxing under the stars in Acapulco or sunning himself on the French Riviera. Or he may be in a bombing raid on the Berlin Wall. Only the producer knows for sure, and he won't admit anything—at least until after the contracts are signed.

10

"The Untouchables"

Or, How I Caught Capone, Won the Emmy, and Acquired a Lifetime Machine Gun

The television industry is full of ironies. "The Untouchables" was not originally supposed to be a television series. When the show went on the air, it wasn't supposed to be a success. I wasn't supposed to be playing Eliot Ness either. No one expected Al Capone to get off scot-free, of course, but otherwise, "The Untouchables" was one surprise after another.

Shortly after I finished *John Paul Jones,* the 5-million-dollar epic was dubbed *John Paul Gonzales* by a wiseacre aware of the absurdity of making a film in Spain about America's greatest naval hero. The last thing I ever expected to do next was a prohibition-era TV show. I told my agent Bill Shiffrin that it was old hat, downbeat, a sure loser. I also said that I'd do the damn thing just to prove my point.

It all started when Oscar Fraley wrote the original book. Desi Arnaz decided to produce the most expensive show ever made for television. It was to be a two-part film about the struggle between Eliot Ness and Al Capone. The part of Ness was originally offered to Van Heflin; when he decided he wasn't quite robust enough for it, they turned to Van Johnson. He said yes, but his wife objected, and they came to me. I knew exactly what the right answer was: I said no, just like the others. My agent, however, insisted that I change my mind, and after a violent argument, I finally agreed. But I was less than enthusiastic. I went to costuming with smoke coming out of my ears. I found a tailor greeting me with the 1930 suits already cut for Van Johnson. With a broad Roumanian accent he greeted me: "Messtaire Zzzhonson! Your clothes are ready."

Trying not to wonder if the rest of the production would go the same way, I said, "T think you've got the wrong guy. I got the part—my name is Stack."

The director for the two-part story of the forming of "The Untouchables" was Phil Karlson. Quinn Martin produced both episodes for Desilu.

Phil Karlson is an example of a guy who loses himself in his work. He can deal in violence and brutality on the screen, and some of his work was regarded as the precursor of Sam Peckinpah's. But he's a quiet, gentle man who wears a ratty-looking red sweater, which he thinks brings him luck. He may still have it, unless the moths have finally devoured it. His personal, Joe Milquetoast manner contrasted sharply with the controlled mayhem of his product. Phil was ideally suited to "The Untouchables."

Everyone thought the show would be a one-shot affair. Once we caught Capone, there wasn't supposed to be anywhere else to go. No one realized at the time that we were formulating a branch of theater wherein the character actor (a different one each week) became the star.

Tom Moore of ABC was the first to envision a series based on the two-parter. At that time, Bill Orr, my old chum and an executive of Warner Brothers, was trying to sell a show called "Public Enemy" using all the great stock footage from the Edward G. Robinson—James Cagney era. Orr was told to forget it. "No one is interested in downbeat stories about gangsters during prohibition," said the executives. That same week, "The Untouchables" hit the air and broke the Nielsens wide open with a 36.1 rating.

A series can sound like a good idea and prove otherwise. When you commit yourself to the same concept every week, it's a little like getting married. You may start out on cloud nine, but the wrong partners can turn things upside down. It's bad enough in a single film. In a series you find yourself thinking of long-term associations. A producer can out-interfere the most militant mother-in-law, and it may seem like a lifetime commitment.

The thought of doing a TV series scared me to death. Desi Arnaz was the real reason I took the jump. I told him, "Desi, if you promise me as an actor, not as an executive, to do a good show, I'll believe you."

He said, "Baby, we're gonna make the best damn television show on the air." He never let me down.

Desi was the ideal producer, and the captain of what proved to be a super team. When we started, I said to myself, *Don't count your residuals before they're hatched*. But I knew that we would have a quality show, regardless of how the public reacted. Fortunately, they liked it as much as we did.

Ness and his men were the only constant factors; Nitti, Maddog Coll, and others were instantly recognizable, and that was one of the big reasons for the show's success. We began going right through the underworld, and every week we featured someone who was internationally known, publicized in all the papers of the era.

The fun started with the first two-part film, and it never ended. Neville Brand created the part of Al Capone and Bruce Gordon was Frank Nitti. Brand had been a war hero behind enemy lines with the OSS. He was schooled in violence, and perfect for Capone. They only thing he liked better than danger was booze. Because Brand was supposed to speak in an Italian dialect, the studio got him a dialogue coach. Brand drove him down to his place at the beach for the "lessons" where the dialogue coach began to realize that Brand's talents were not confined to acting. Instead of the coach's teaching Brand an Italian accent, Brand taught the dialect specialist how to drink. He nearly managed to destroy the poor fellow and got him loaded every night.

The dialogue coach crashed their car straight into the studio's gate. Nevertheless, when Brand showed up for work, he was dynamite in his role, even though his Italian accent left something to be desired. The first time he had to threaten those dedicated federal agents, he said, "That'sa wat'sa gonna happena to Meester Nessa." That's the closest he ever came. It was enough to make a good mafioso cry in his lasagna. But the audience didn't seem to care, so maybe Brand's method of preparing a part was right after all.

My concept of Ness was actually a composite of three of

the bravest men I ever met. Audie Murphy was one—taciturn, almost shy, and a one-man army! Buck Mazza was my roomie in the navy, and as a dive-bomber pilot became the most decorated flyer in the fleet. Since he never wore his wings or decorations, I didn't know he was a flyer. One drunken night, I patiently explained to him how to fly a dive bomber. To his credit, he never said a word.

The third was a stunt man named Carey Loftin. It was Carey who had saved my life after my motorcycle crackup in the Mojave. All three had one thing in common: They were the best in their fields and they never boasted!

In our story conferences, we discussed humanizing Ness. We had an opportunity to make some plans with our initial two-part program. (Each episode lasted for forty-seven minutes, not counting commercials.) This is a very small frame of reference for revealing a man's personality.

For some time, actors had experimented with a variety of mannerisms, bits, and props as a means of building a particular character. Bat Masterson, for instance, was identified with the cane he carried. Chester, the deputy on "Gunsmoke," had his limp. Edd Byrnes, Kookie on "77 Sunset Strip," always appeared combing his hair. I decided not to use any accents, physical handicaps, or props in building Ness's character. I felt that an air of mystery should surround Ness. He was unpredictable. He never exploded in the face of disappointments; he concealed his inner fire and frustration, but he could blow up when least expected to do so.

With so many character actors playing gangsters, I felt a natural temptation to try to match their flamboyance in my characterization of Ness. I always considered myself more of a character actor than straight lead, and refusing the temptation to be flashy was not easy, particularly after having received an Academy Award nomination for the flakiest character of the year in *Written on the Wind*.

But I decided that my character should be a counterpoint to all the gaudy pin-striped suits, bias-cut dresses, sexy broads, loud jazz, prostitutes, and machine guns. Ness would be played *against* the flamboyance of the villains. The villains could create the unreal atmosphere of the underworld. I decided to lead the audience along as a protagonist. The strange presence and silent looks provided a richness. That's where the power lay in this character.

Bruce Gordon turned in a fantastic performance as Frank Nitti. With Capone in prison, he became the regular villain once we started making regular series episodes. He was absolutely magic. Bruce managed that oneness with a part that rarely happens. He made Nitti unforgettable, a combination of chilling evil, ironic humor, and sex. In fact, he was a real crook; he stole most of our scenes.

Bruce is a tremendously versatile actor, at home in all kinds of parts, including Shakespeare; but after "The Untouchables," he *was* Frank Nitti wherever he went. He was so identified with the role that if he played Macbeth, people would expect him to end the play by sending the strongarm boys after the witches with machine guns. It's a prime example of how an actor can be so good in a particular role that it hinders rather than helps his career. We killed Bruce off about three times, but always resurrected him. By now I realized that the show couldn't afford to lose Ness's greatest antagonist. Luckily we didn't shoot our stuff in sequence; we could always jump back and revive Nitti whenever we needed him.

Technically, the show was difficult, even dangerous. We had five or six cameras at times, and we almost killed one cameraman. In one of the show's classic episodes, a truck had to go through steel doors with enough power and speed to knock the doors sky-high and go zapping into a 5,000-gallon tank of beer. (Actually, they used soapsuds or detergent, but it looked like the real thing.)

Our stunt man said he didn't know if he could get through the door and hit the tank hard enough. There were two cameras outside and three inside, one low and one up high, and one zooming in for special shots. We could only do the scene once. When the stuntman drove through the door, he hit the vat, which exploded, cutting the bands that wrapped around the vat. The bands whipped around the truck and the windshield; one wrapped around him, and he wound up with a pair of broken ribs. That wasn't all. One massive brewery door flew off and ricocheted under one of the cameras. The cameraman was led away in shock. Two feet higher, and he would have been crushed.

At first, we used real glass instead of breakaway glass. Once I was supposed to use an axe to break down a door. The door came back and hit me. The axe flew right past my nose and stuck into the wall. It could have cut my whole head off.

But we dealt with problems like this all the time. The show was young, and we didn't think about danger until later. Our stunt men were among my greatest friends; they were the most important contributors to that kind of show. Carey Loftin was one of the classic examples of a fine stunt man; Bill Catching was the best double I ever had. We had a whole crew of stunt men for the falls.

The stunt men really make these shows work. Without them, an action show has no style, no dash. The old cars were painted to look as if they were new, but you never knew if the brakes would work. Our crew had to handle these cars, period trucks, and even explosives.

The special effects man was A.D. Flowers. He's won more awards than any actor or director in the business. A.D. was responsible for the special effects on such television shows as "Combat" and in films like *Tora, Tora, Tora,* and *The Poseidon Adventure* (which added another Oscar to his shelf). We were blessed to have him for four years. He made the show function simply because we were the first television show to use cause and effect. We used squibs and explosives, and showed the effects actually happening. The television audience could see the glasses and mirrors blowing up after seeing a guy with a machine gun. None of the other shows ever did that because it was too expensive and time-consuming. Our special-effects crew would take a hairline wire and put an explosive inside each glass. The explosions would be controlled by a master keyboard. I always insisted that just shooting blanks in a scene was meaningless, like watching a kid with a cap gun going *bang, bang.* But if you hear the *bang,* and see the result, it's a completely different situation. If you can blow a water pitcher into 1,000 pieces, the audience instantly accepts the terrible potential of a Thompson submachine gun.

The director took a back seat on the stunts involving my close shots with explosives, glass, fire, etc. A.D. and I would work out the timing. After a while, it became automatic, as if it were a dance routine. If an actor doesn't have coordination with the special-effects man, he can literally lose his head.

A case in point was a Ma Barker show. One of the boys on that episode was new, and he didn't understand enough, or was too nervous, to get his timing right. He got involved in the scene and waited too long. Somebody was supposed to machine-gun a room, and an antique grandfather's alarm clock was to explode. It drove about three or four inches of splinter into his behind, which really must have hurt. It was a miracle that more of us weren't seriously hurt.

I remember one poor bastard who practiced by himself all morning for the big moment: driving the getaway car. The hoods ran out and hopped in the car, while he gunned the motor and put it in gear—reverse, of course. He managed to scatter an already jumpy camera crew, knock down the assistant director, and run over the director's foot. Not everyone was ready for "The Untouchables" or carried enough insurance. Of necessity, our directors were always on their toes.

All actors have a classic answer to the question, "Can you ride a horse, swim, drive a car, etc.?" Yes. Then they rush for a crash course. In the case of 1930s cars, it was usually an experiment in terror. To the uninitiated, the stick shift was as easy to understand as Arabic. Since no one expected us to stay on the air more than a year, the cars were all rented. I have a fond memory of racing toward the camera in my 1930 Buick, hitting the brakes, losing them, and going straight through the sound stage wall.

From the beginning, our show had a strong team spirit. In Hollywood, actors often become typecast. But actors don't like to be pigeonholed, and never want to feel that the only roles for which they are suited are determined by their physical appearance. On "The Untouchables," the characters who assisted Eliot Ness in pursuing the bootleggers were portrayed by actors who were cast according to a Hollywood tradition: Everybody played something he wasn't.

Paul Picerni, with an Italian family background, played Hobson, a typical midwestern American. The Italian character of Enrico Rossi was played by Nick Georgiade, of Greek descent. Youngfellow, an Indian, was portrayed by Abel Fernandez, whose background was Mexican. Abel was a gentle giant, a former California heavyweight champion. He wouldn't deliberately hurt a fly, but his powerful right hand once smashed an opponent's jaw in six pieces.

Paul, Nick, and Abel were not only Ness's right-hand men on camera, but my good personal friends through those wild and wacky times. Testimonials can be square enough to line the pages of a geometry book. But putting together a television show is like coordinating a football team. The star may be a good quarterback, but the blockers and tacklers make things work!

Our program provided an opportunity for character actors to feel like leading men on film. A character man could be a star on Broadway, but very seldom in the context of a character role on television. That's why we had such a happy company. I kept telling them that the better they were, the better I would be, and the better the show would be.

Telly Savalas had a delightfully despicable quality, perfect for "The Untouchables." The ladies soon started tuning in to watch Telly and Bruce Gordon. This was long before double-breasted vests, lollipops, and crooning turned him into the bald Burt Reynolds of television.

Joe Wiseman's performance as the homosexual convict in an episode called "Detective Story" must have set back the gay lib movement twenty years! For pure unadulterated evil, he was the master. He could raise the hackles of the most hardened TV viewer by merely slithering into a room and slowly turning toward the camera. He was better than a car full of tommy guns or a body hanging on a mast hook.

However, like most New York actors, he was unaccustomed to Hollywood props and special effects. In one scene, he was to take an axe and destroy a brewery. With his usual fire and abandon he tore the whole set apart and, in a final burst, started on the real pipes and valves. Unfortunately they were not rigged to break. The axe ricocheted off the metal, and cut through his Achilles tendon. I never felt so sorry for anyone in my life. We had a part written for him as a cripple a few weeks later. "The Antidote" was one of our half-dozen top shows, and Joe's best performance in the series... but it's still a lousy way to get a part.

We also shared some lighter moments with Joe Wiseman. Because my blue eyes photograph gray in black and white, our cinematographer Charles Straumer arranged for two pink eyelights. These lights make blue eyes appear black and more visible on the screen. Wiseman, whose dark eyes don't need the pink lighting, insisted that he receive equal treatment. So Charlie, with a great flourish, set up a whole bank of pink eyelights. Joe succeeded in looking like a Toulouse-Lautrec study in pink; but his eyes still photographed brown!

Many of the New York actors who appeared as guest stars

had stage backgrounds and were devotees of the "method," the acting technique identified with the Actors Studio.

Simply put, method actors try literally to become the characters they portray. Sometimes they use animals or objects as images to help them along. I recall my own memories of my brief encounter with method acting. As a young student, I slithered around the stage saying to myself, "I'm a snake, I'm a snake." I don't know if it improved my acting, but rolling around on the floor certainly loused up a good pair of pants.

Method actors are devotees of realism. They think an actor should be only minimally removed from actually living the part he plays. Although the "method" has produced some of the country's finest actors and actresses, it can be carried to extremes. Many method actors have deserved their tremendous public acclaim. But you never know what to expect next. Our worthy director, Paul Wendkos, once was driven to beating on the walls when he tried to convince Cloris Leachman not to play a character with a limp and a Balkan accent since the character was only from Brooklyn! Cloris was a darling to work with, but she can get carried away with her enthusiasm for authenticity.

Since a television show is shot on different days, it is important that actors match their shots. If an actor picks something up in his right hand on Monday night, he must be careful to use the same hand when shooting resumes Tuesday morning. Rip Torn, a New York stage star, in high good humor, refused to match any shots. He was convinced that by changing things from scene to scene, he achieved more spontaneity. One time he would appear with his hat on, then off, tie askew, then straight, eating left-handed in one take and right-handed in the next. There is a special padded room for film editors who have tried to piece together his scenes.

In a series as weird as "The Untouchables," few things came as a surprise. But Peter Falk did! Having worked with such free spirits as Rip and Cloris, I thought I was prepared for anything. But when Stu Rosenberg, our director, brought Peter out from New York for the part of a small-time hood, I had no idea what to expect.

Peter believes in analyzing the smallest piece of action in a scene. Since method actors are concerned with motivation, they don't want to just make entrances and exits. They always want to know why a piece of action is necessary.

If a New York stage actor demands to know why he can't whisper his way through a part the night his play opens on Broadway, his director must have an answer. ("The audience can't hear you!" is usually a good reason.)

In our first scene together, Peter announced his plan of action. He picked up a bottle standing on the table. "Before you say your line," he suggested, "I'll take the top off the bottle; then I'll put it on. Then I'll take it off again; then maybe I'll say something about it."

I knew that the script said nothing about bottles, although I thought our script girl would need one, trying to keep track of Peter's dialogue.

"I don't care what you do," I said, laughing. "Just wave a handkerchief when you're through and I'll start talking!"

So Peter improvised. In one scene, he was interviewed by Mafia dons. He took that scene, overlapped dialogue, sat down, banged on a table, invented his own speech, and waved his arms like a traffic cop. By the time he made his exit, slamming the door as he went, a star was born!

Peter was probably ahead of his time. He was to have the perfect vehicle as the wily, bumbling Lieutenant Columbo, and in his rumpled coat he does just as much creative improvising as ever. I enjoyed working with him, even though any relation between what was in the script and what was on film was strictly coincidental with Peter. He made just as good a gangster as he now makes a Columbo.

Another mainstay of the show was Keenan Wynn, an old friend. I've known him all my life. There's an easy way to describe Keenan: He's mad. Mad, but fantastically talented! His personality is a compound of his family tradition and his own natural instincts as a roustabout. He was the original motorcyclist in Hollywood, long before Steve McQueen. (He used to ride with McQueen until he decided to slow down.) The man on the motorcycle has always been identified with a mystique of wildness, which extends to Keenan's entire lifestyle. Keenan has always been a terrific racer, and was ideal for "The Untouchables." (In the opening two-part production, he played a close friend of Ness; he was ultimately machine-gunned by some of the Capone-Nitti enforcers.)

Jack Warden, another of our standbys, has since gone on to greater glory as the dirty old man in *Shampoo*. I always felt he had that potential, but we couldn't afford Julie Christie to prove it. It's good to see a friend find his proper niche in this great business of ours.

Pat Neal had too much class for our show, but did it anyway, and in the doing, proved that talent is boss. A super lady! She's a cherished friend who, as far as I'm concerned, can do no wrong.

My first encounter with Pat was in an acting group. She played Blanche in *A Streetcar Named Desire*. I had worked with such actresses of talent as Bette Davis, Barbara Stanwyck, Carole Lombard, and Elizabeth Taylor, but wasn't prepared for the presence and sheer power of this one. She took my character—Stanley Kowalski, who is supposed to be dominant—swept him into the wings, and turned the scene into a virtual soliloquy.

I used to regret not having more scenes with the heavies. Ness was never invited to those meetings Frank Nitti always had in the back room. Sometimes, in fact, the actors playing the roles of the good guys never even met those playing the bad guys off screen. A guest star might appear and, by the time I arrived on the lot, he could have disappeared just as quickly. Flashing his evil smile, Frank Nitti would order the execution of some helpless victim who, when successfully machine-gunned, would hurry back to Broadway and the relative safety of downtown Manhattan traffic jams.

A classic example of never meeting one of the guest stars was my experience with a promising actor who played a small part on "The Untouchables." He played the part of a young narcotics addict and quickly became a corpse. Candy Bergen later called me and said she had enjoyed watching me co-star with Bob Redford. I couldn't remember ever doing a picture with Redford; then I realized that he had been on "The Untouchables," and we had never met.

Like Redford, Lee Marvin, Carroll O'Connor, and Jimmy Caan were eager to appear on "The Untouchables." Many a major star used the cold slab on the set of our Chicago morgue as a launching pad.

For all the good times and laughter, there are moments of poignancy in any theatrical experience. "The Untouchables" was no exception. Every actor looks forward to working with the colleagues and stars he has admired throughout his career. I had long admired Thomas Mitchell, who came to us as a guest star near the very end of his career. A distinguished trouper, he was modest and retiring. But it soon became clear that he was no longer able to remember his lines with ease. When he offered an apology for forgetting a line, I said, "Mr. Mitchell, we're just honored to have you here. Everything will be all right."

So much attention is focused upon the glamor of stardom and the glow of spotlights, that people forget the cold reality that pervades our industry. An eminent doctor or lawyer can retire from his practice and enjoy the respect of his younger colleagues. But an actor can only expect honors in proportion to his last week's reviews. Europeans may give a standing ovation to a revered singer whose voice has faded, out of affectionate regard for the talent that existed. The American film industry is far more pragmatic.

The actor, like the proverbial clown behind the mask, must face his moments of truth alone. Like old soldiers, they don't die, but often fade away. I will long remember Thomas Mitchell as a gentleman and artist who thought of the present, accepting yesterday's honors with a quiet modesty that can provide an example for us all.

There is no doubt which scene in "The Untouchables" stands out in my mind as the most potentially evil—as well as the most risky in terms of audience acceptance: *bacio di morte*, the kiss of death, that classic Sicilian gesture when the Capo kisses a Mafia soldier on the mouth before sending him out as executioner! Although the scene was fine in script form, we were uncertain about how it would work on camera. First of all, two men had never been photographed before kissing on TV. Secondly, if the scene got a laugh, the whole Capone mystique would be out the window. Neville Brand played Capone, and Frank De Kova, the killer, and you couldn't buy two deadlier kissers; so far, so good. The next step was to get these two macho monsters to osculate for the camera. They're both professionals and they knew that the scene, if done right, could be the most effective and talked about sequence in the picture. But now, they were both suddenly hesitant, and only great persuasion from Phil Carlson got things moving. When the camera started rolling, the scene began to take on a life of its own.

The set was deadly quiet. When Neville locked eyes with Frank De Kova, tipped back his hat, and slowly kissed him on the mouth, the overtones of menace and death were so strong that after a cut we all stood around in eerie silence. Later I found out that just before the take, some jokester in the crew had told Neville that, even though De Kova looked rough, he was really a fag. Then, of course, he told Frank the same thing about Neville. Naturally, it wasn't true. Part of the deadly atmosphere came from their suspicion of one another.

One of our best episodes was "The Rusty Heller Story." When it came time to cast the lead, the producers drew up a list of actresses as possible stars. The last name on the list was Elizabeth Montgomery. I had known Liz's father Bob Montgomery; I went shooting with him, and took him to dad's duck lodge when I was a kid. I'd only known Elizabeth as a young socialite. When the girls at her finishing school talked about making a debut, I'm sure they weren't thinking about the kind Liz made in her first appearance on "The Untouchables," in the role of a tough young southern hooker. I'd learned from parts I'd lost that you must be objective in your judgment: The fact that I knew this girl and her background was no reason to disqualify her from consideration for the part. The producers didn't always ask my opinion about casting, but in this instance, I'm glad they did.

Anyway, she took the part and ran away with it; she got an Emmy nomination and, I think, should have won it. Dame Judith Anderson won the award for Medea, which was shot in Scotland on location over a thirty-day period. Liz turned in a smashing performance in six days. It was the only time that Ness became emotionally involved. The episode had a touching and gentle poignancy to it.

We were also fortunate in having top directors. Wally Grauman and Stu Rosenberg were two of the best. Wally was a man of small stature, handsome, and an ex-fighter pilot in the air force. He loved the ladies, and the ladies loved him. He was terribly aggressive with a terrific pride and a fully developed ego. He couldn't stand having anything come out with his name on it that wasn't first-class.

Wally did his homework, but there was nothing academic about the way he solved our problems. We once had a Mardi Gras sequence in which Wally promised us a whole carnival on our small sound stage. First, he helped himself to a collection of masks and costumes and props from another set on the Desilu lot. (We never learned if the producers of that other show knew that they were making a contribution to "The Untouchables.") Then he instructed the extras to march through and around the stage, constantly changing masks and costumes off camera. Soon he had twenty extras looking like two hundred. Plays like this gave us the reputation of being the best-produced show on television.

Stu Rosenberg was wacky, but brilliant. One day he asked me if I liked the "roll 'em" expression used at the beginning of every shot.

"Not particularly," I said.

"Then let's use 'swordfish'!" said Stu. If visitors to the set were surprised by the "swordfish" opening, it's easy to guess what they thought when Stu closed the shots with an imitation of Porky Pig—"Th-th-th-that's all, folks!"

We used some theater actors who were accustomed to indulging themselves in long pauses between words. (There were enough silences to make the sound stage as quiet as a librarian's haven.) Stu let the actors have their fun, but he cut out all the pauses during editing, taking advantage of the low cost of black and white film. (The network never commented about this particular mischief of Stu's, but Eastman Kodak was delighted!)

Our working conditions were incredible. Normally, I would get up around six-thirty to start shooting around eight. Friday was always a late day or night. Near the end of the series, I wound up doing two shows at once and doing retakes on another. As for the sponsors, they saw us in an uncomplicated light. They simply assumed we were nuts and stayed away.

When a network plans a season, a few shows tend to be special favorites of the top executives. It's rather like an auto company launching new lines of cars: There's room for everything from a sleek Rolls-Royce to a compact economy model. In our opening season, ABC did not think of us as a Rolls-Royce; we were more in the little red wagon category.

That year the network had decided to reach out for class, spending heavy exploitation money on James Michener's "Adventures in Paradise." Our show came in the back door, until we went on the air. Since we were like the ugly duckling that turned into a golden-egg-laying goose, and since our home base was out in the sticks, at Desilu's Culver City lot, we were left pretty much to ourselves.

I wasn't sure whether it was the "swordfish" gambit, Stu Rosenberg's Porky Pig imitation, or the constant gunfire and explosions that drove our script girl into hysterics. But somehow word got around that "The Untouchables" was a fairly weird show.

Every once in a while, just to remind the network we were around, I'd give Ness a little rope. At the end of a hard day's work, we would shoot some second versions of scenes the public would never see. One of the accepted clichés would be Ness testing the booze and spitting it out. One day, we shot a sequence in which he tasted it, loved it, and got smashed. Another time, Ness was wounded and in the hospital. We shot a second version in which Eliot jumped out of bed, tore off the nurse's uniform, and chased her around the room. Strangely enough, the front office, which saw these sequences, never acknowledged our creativity.

We worked very hard. Rosemarie used to bring an old checkered tablecloth to the studio, and we'd have a candlelit dinner after a day's shooting. When we were first married, I had described the romantic type of life I thought we would have together. The candlelight seemed right in place, but I never anticipated such a setting: an old back alley, surrounded by machine guns and garbage cans.

Eventually we became involved in several controversies over violence and the use of Italian names on the program. The question of censorship soon became the central aspect of many of our discussions. We had three or four producers each producing his own program, seldom touching base with each other. As a result, we found ourselves being judged on the basis of individual taste (or lack of it) as displayed by a particular producer in a specific episode. I remember one episode in which a fellow in a hospital scene pulled out a tube that was used to transfuse a patient; great globs of blood ran down the fellow's fingers as he went down the fire escape. In another episode, the story line dealt with hoods who were smuggling prostitutes into the country. Instead of releasing them, when Ness showed up, the gang decided to machine-gun them off camera.

One of our experiments in realism produced a surprising result. We had a special vest that was guaranteed to elicit emotion from the most plastic performer. Even our jaded crew used to gather around and watch some poor devil inadvertently give a great performance.

The vest was lined with steel. Squibs—small explosives

connected to hairlike wires—were laid in across the steel, with cloth set over the squibs. Squibs were then laid in a line across a wall, and the hoodlum stood in the middle of a gap in the line. When all was ready, A.D. Flowers would start the explosives across the wall, across the actor, and on to the other side. When this was later cut in with a close-up of a machine gun, the effect was startling.

We found it best not to explain too thoroughly to the actor. When that vest began exploding, many an actor really thought he had been shot, but the actor in him made him finish the scene and later accept the applause that always went with it. Anyway, we were never sued—at least, not for that!

We always did our best to be accurate. Walter Winchell did the narration leading into the beginning of each episode. At one time, the network was thinking of using someone with a pretty voice. Desi kept saying, "Oh, no, you've got to have Winchell. Winchell is the period." Much of the tone and style of "The Untouchables" was derived from our newsreel quality. We had actual shots of the assassination of Mayor Anton Cermak, when he was killed instead of Franklin Delano Roosevelt. We cut out the sequences of newsreel film and matched the newsreel footage. We couldn't improve the quality of the newsreel footage, so we worked to give our own film a grainy quality. I looked ten years older than I was because of this newsreel style. That's one of the reasons why some people think I'm ninety-five years old today.

Strange as it may seem, some of Chicago's more notorious hoods loved the show. They didn't see themselves as villains on the screen. They were curiously interested in the show's accuracy. Anyone who thinks only schoolteachers and librarians spot inaccuracies in the films they see is underestimating your basic, everyday gangster.

"That killing didn't happen the way you said it did," they would declare. "There's a big difference between knocking somebody off in a barber chair and rubbing him out in a back alley." Naturally, mobsters didn't write such protest letters to *TV Guide*. But in their own circles, they watched "The Untouchables" to make sure that the wrong man wasn't given credit for something he didn't do. Even our thoroughly competent research staff couldn't match the hoods for accuracy in determining precisely who dumped whom into the Chicago river.

The subject of organized crime was regarded as a highly sensitive topic in those days. One of my favorite scripts was Ben Maddow's brilliant work, "The Noise of Death." J. Carrol Naish played the old don in this episode about *omerta*, the Mafia's law of silence. *The Godfather* has more recently explored many of the complex relationships in the underworld. But in the late fifties, it wasn't a popular subject. The FBI denied that the Mafia even existed. This was before the Appalachian meeting and so, despite the high quality of the episode, "The Noise of Death" was never rerun.

Mobsters who didn't like the show regarded its actors as belonging to the same category as chorus girls or ball players— as hired hands. They turned their wrath upon the sponsors and Desi Arnaz, the top executive of Desilu. Desi received an anonymous phone call threatening to "blow his brains out" if the program wasn't withdrawn. One of our sponsors, Liggett & Myers Tobacco Co., also had its problems. They discovered that their cigarettes were left on docks all over the country. The head of the Longshoremen's union in New York was one of the Anastasia brothers, also numbered among our archcritics. Rumor had it that Liggett & Myers would continue to have shipping problems until they dropped "The Untouchables." But we were so hot by then that other sponsors jumped in and we kept right on going. (We had the highest rating of any show in Chicago, where most of the hoods had their headquarters.) Not all the hoods' reactions were to be taken seriously. Inside the most terrifying mobster there often lurks a remnant of the little boy he used to be. (Admittedly, he may have been a rotten kid whose idea of "the numbers" at age ten had nothing to do with arithmetic.) But a rough exterior may conceal the spirit of a person who longs to be away from the complex adult world of crime and punishment and desires a nostalgic return to his youth as the neighborhood bully.

Peekaboo is not the game usually associated with a real-life "godfather," but Rosemarie and I encountered a classic example of one such man who never grew up. Some time after the premiere of "The Untouchables," we were invited up to Cal-Neva for the opening of a famous nightclub singer's act. She was rumored to be the girl friend of a powerful underworld figure. Although Sam Giancanna has been called "public enemy number one," he was murdered last year, so it is no longer necessary to preserve his anonymity.

After the girl's performance, we went backstage to say hello. In the course of our visit, Rosemarie and I had the strange sensation that we were being watched. (We both realized that we were under the scrutiny of a mysterious eyeball peering at us through a crack in the door.) A few days after we left Cal-Neva, it was revealed that a notorious syndicate boss had been on the premises.

Some months later, the singer happened to drop by our home. Rosemarie couldn't keep from mentioning that we knew about her boyfriend's proclivities as a Peeping Tom. (We never did figure out what he had expected to prove by eavesdropping on our conversation.) Our singer friend quickly enlightened us.

"He would turn purple if he knew you hadn't been fooled," she said. "He went right back to Chicago and told all his friends he had really put one over on Eliot Ness!"

Here was a man who was tough enough to strike fear into the hearts of most of the country's mobsters. But he couldn't resist behaving as if he were five years old, to impress his buddies in Chicago.

There's a strange affinity between the hoodlums and show business. Many of the earlier leaders of our profession came from spots like Hell's Kitchen, and stepped into a brand-new medium that was regarded as about as respectable as the numbers racket. The heads of our major studios found it was convenient to deal with gangsters in Hollywood.

Why do hoods want to get involved in motion pictures? Pretty much for the same reason everyone else does. They want to be part of the most glamorous arena in the world.

How about being in the position of hiring or firing a Raquel Welch, Julie Christie, or Farrah Fawcett-Majors? Being able to brag to a relative in Sheboygan that you had to turn down Robert Redford because you just didn't see him in the part is great for the ego. If you get lucky, you can get a fat return on that laundered loot you brought in from Mexico.

Actors also have an odd fascination with the underworld. For some it's just an extension of the way they've always lived. Some of our most macho sex symbols came from the roughest parts of our asphalt jungles or from the coal mines of Pennsylvania. The camera picks up what Stanislavski called "the second level," the "gut" or "driving" level.

So much of that titillating undercurrent of violence that can also be translated as sex is not so much a performance as the real thing covered by a performance. And then there are those who get their kicks associating with, or fantasizing about, gunsels. One of our most successful performers has been quoted in a national magazine as saying that if he hadn't made it in show business, he would have been a gangster. He was a close friend of last year's "public enemy number one" before his friend was sent packing to the great crap shoot in the sky. This phenomenon isn't limited to the USA. Alain Delon became France's leading male sex symbol by playing gangster roles, and numbers some of France's real mobsters among his biggest fans.

Delon met some of the leaders of the French underworld before becoming a star, but he considered them friends long after a public acknowledgment might have proven embarrassing.

"They are like me," he told an interviewer. "They give their trust only once."

Delon's shady friends nearly proved his undoing. A young Yugoslav who worked as his secretary (and was romantically involved with Delon's separated wife) was found murdered near a Versailles garbage dump. The young man was suspected of planning orgies for French VIPs and later blackmailing them. He left a letter suggesting that the police contact Delon in the event of his violent death.

If the unsolved murder did nothing for Delon's popularity with the police, it did nothing to damage his movie career. His name appeared on a list of France's ten most admired men, and the public was sympathetic when he accused the French police of treating him unfairly.

As for gangsters themselves, on either side of the Atlantic, they love to associate with film people, and are usually frustrated hams themselves. Aside from old-line Mafia Capos who disappear behind the family, the others are front and center hamballs who love the spotlight.

"The Untouchables" managed to get in more trouble in a shorter time than any show on TV. One of our biggest problems was the charge of an ethnic bias in our scripts. Many of the villains, from Capone and Nitti to the least important, small-time thugs, had Italian names. (No one seemed to notice that one of Ness's closest lieutenants, Enrico Rossi, was also Italian.)

No one ever suggested even remotely that Italian people as

a whole had a leaning toward violent crime. But the controversy began. Despite my being brought up in Italy, I found myself having to defend our approach.

I had grown up with a great love for many things of Italian origin. My childhood had been spent in Europe, and my first copybooks were in Italian. I wrote in Italian before I wrote in English. Italian opera was a part of my family background, since my own relatives had "Italianized" their names when they sang in Europe.

It's difficult to imagine an issue which could unite such diverse people as Frank Sinatra, Cardinal Spellman, and J. Edgar Hoover. But our show succeeded where others failed. All three men hated "The Untouchables." Together with Senator John Pastore, the powerful chairman of the Senate Communications Subcommittee, Frank Sinatra and Cardinal Spellman objected to the large number of Italian gangsters on the program. J. Edgar Hoover didn't think that the show was accurate in its depiction of the T-men. Senator Thomas Dodd opened a hearing by the Senate Subcommittee on Juvenile Delinquency. (Tom Moore of ABC had to appear three times as a witness.) If two government investigations weren't enough, Newton Minow, chairman of the Federal Communications Commission, decided to hold hearings of his own, devoted to the subject of violence.

But we were dealing with a specific period of history in which a number of actual hoodlums had Italian names. The controversy which engaged the support of Frank Sinatra and Cardinal Spellman began when a New York politician was running for reelection in the Bronx. His sister was on one of the boards of an Italo-American society. I felt he wanted to hitch his wagon (or bandwagon) to an explosive, political issue. He made some charges and capitalized on the notoriety available. He also got reelected.

Eventually, we did stop using Italian names, switching to an unrecognizable nationality which would baffle a roomful of genealogists and send a Berlitz instructor scrambling for his dictionary. We were criticized for telling the truth about real gangsters, and supported by some for turning our attention to people and events that never existed!

We featured a group of Italian gangsters because the particular mobsters the real Ness pursued happened to be Italian. It was entirely innocent. Our research was very thorough.

Members of the producers' staff would check the telephone book of a specific city in a given time span. If we were doing a story set in Chicago in 1935, we would be certain that no person with a name we were using lived in Chicago at that time except, of course, our lead gangster.

None of us could ever forget an incident that happened one night after the studio's office was closed. The telephone kept ringing and finally one of the members of our crew picked up the receiver. No one else was in the office, and he came back to the set, not knowing whether to laugh or run. He had spoken with a lady with a marked Italian accent. He said, "You won't believe what just happened."

The lady asked him, "Is this 'The Untouches'?"

"Yes, ma'am," he said. "This is 'The Untouchables' office."

She said, "Why do you always show Italiana people as bada people?"

"Look, madam," he said, "I just picked up the phone. I don't even work here."

The lady was relentless.

"Italiana people are gooda people, peace-loving people like Marconi, Christopher Columbus, Enrico Caruso."

He said, "Lady, I don't even work here."

She snapped, "You shut up anda listen to me! Italian people make America a wonderful country. You keep showing us as bad people."

"Lady!" he said.

"You shut up and listen to me," she continued. "If you don't stop showing Italian people as bad people, and start showing us as good, peace-loving people, some night, someone is going to throw a bomb and blow up your damn studio."

Danny Thomas took that story and developed it into a twenty-minute act. He had a smashing success with it, but he never paid me a nickel.

Al Capone's son tried to file suit against Desilu for a million dollars. He had known Desi Arnaz very well. In fact, they had grown up together, and Desi had had to resolve an emotional crisis of his own when he decided to produce the show. Capone's son called him and said, "Please don't do this. Everything about Dad has been buried now." But Desi said that if he didn't do it, someone else would. Anyone can reprint the editorials about Capone—they belong to the public domain—

calling him every dirty name in the book, and his relatives would have a hard time effectively objecting. There is a strange acceptance of this fact by criminals and gangsters. They usually love publicity. Invasion of privacy is less important to them because, more often than not, they love to see themselves on the screen.

By the time the series went into its final year of production, we couldn't use Italian names—or any others that could be identified with a specific nationality or minority group. We wound up using Chinese names and, of course, Ness never got close to Chinatown except, perhaps, to eat dinner.

We didn't introduce any black characters at all. We were already in terrible trouble with the Italians, and nobody knew whether black actors would want to be included, or how a black audience might react. Anyway, blacks had nothing to do with organized crime during that era.

An actor, particularly a TV-series actor, has to face many special problems. On one hand, his success is immediate and international, and he finds himself beloved by millions; on the other hand, his feeble, weekly efforts are judged by critics as though he were attempting Hamlet. I suppose "The Untouchables" was the most loved and most despised TV series ever made. John Crosby called it an abomination, the worst show on the air. Ed Friendly, a producer of documentaries, aired his unfriendliness in the trade papers, complaining that garbage such as ours was in the top ten while his classy efforts were in the basement. So it went, until one day—July 8, 1962, to be exact—a respected novelist, a center of continuing controversy herself and the author of *The Fountainhead* and *Atlas Shrugged*, came to our rescue. Ayn Rand's article, "The New Enemies of The Untouchables," appeared in the *Los Angeles Times*. She explained, with a novelist's skill, what Eliot Ness and his friends were all about, and maintained they were not as bad as some people suggested.

She said, "When a culture is dominated by an irrational philosophy, a major symptom of its decadence is the inversion of all values. This can always be seen clearly in the field of art, the best barometer of a culture. In today's flood of criticism and abuse unleashed against the television industry, it is the best program that has been singled out for the most persistent denunciations. That program is 'The Untouchables.'"

Miss Rand disposed of our chief critics with the same finesse that the real Eliot Ness used to rid Chicago of a whole gang of bootleggers.

Leonard Goldenson told my business manager that our show built ABC. Until then, the American Broadcasting Company had always failed to make a showing in the Emmy Awards. ABC was the "other" network, but our show received six nominations and four Emmys the first year. I take much more pride in what we were able to do as a team than in anything I did individually. The program was the precursor of a type of quality rarely achieved on television in those days. Its crudity and violence might amuse or infuriate viewers today; but, for its time, it was a remarkable show.

Eventually, the show went into international syndication. Not long after, Bruce Gordon and I were walking on the Champs Elysées and virtually created a traffic jam. Bruce and I were innocent but, to the Parisians, Eliot Ness and Frank Nitti were walking together, side by side. I didn't completely realize the impact of the show until I got away from the studio and saw the reactions of people around the world.

They used to call us the fanatics, and we took great pride in killing ourselves with work. It was really a special form of insanity, seventeen- and eighteen-hour work days. But in television, if you work on a show that produces a special magic, it has a whole life of its own. Personal ambition goes out the window, and you find yourself taking pride in the show you're doing. It is far less a matter of work than the chemistry and empathy and the almost paternal feeling of responsibility toward thirty-five people. (As a result of our schedule, the California legislature passed a law limiting television overtime!)

David Janssen once said, "A TV series is like making love to a gorilla. It's not when you want to stop, it's when she lets you."

There's no doubt in my mind that one of the lowest points in my life came when my health forced me to stop work on the series. The loss of something familiar, something taken for granted, wreaks great havoc. When I hemorrhaged a vocal cord on "The Untouchables," I found what life can be like without communication.

After a while, I began to crawl into myself and let the world go by. I tried to imagine life without making a sound. I even fantasized trying to act by scribbling on a blackboard and holding it up to the audience. I became depressed and developed, if not a death wish, a "no-involvement in life" wish. After three months, I went to the Scripps Clinic in La Jolla, and they gave me a clean bill of health. Like the hotel doctor in Paris who diagnosed my Hong King flu as homesickness and kept asking the chambermaid for her opinion, the doctors at Scripps couldn't understand why my voice wouldn't come back. I still sounded like Andy Devine. I was sent to a "specialist." My first hint that this gent was not of the pulse-taking, knee-jerking school of medicine came when, out of the blue, I was thrown, "Did you get along with your father?"

Oh, oh, I thought, here comes your first horizontal fifty-dollars-an-hour encounter—at least the first with a guy in a white coat. I've never been a fan of Hollywood psychiatry, peopled by actors who fill the day with sexual hang-ups revisited at a dollar a minute.

Since I was stuck, I played out the charade.

"I never really knew my father."

"Really?"

"He died when I was very young."

"I see," he said, and slowly moved forward in his chair. "Would you like to lie down? You'll be more comfortable?" he offered.

"Before I do, doctor," I said, "can I ask you a question?"

"Of course," he said with a professional smile.

"It must take years of hard work and dedication to be a specialist in your field." Now he looked a little surprised.

"Yes, it does. Why do you ask?"

"Well, I know the work you do is very important; you can bring solace to the emotionally destroyed and deprived, even those damaged in combat." He was looking at me curiously.

"Yes, that's my job."

"Then why did you choose a place like Beverly Hills to practice?"

He sat back in his chair and slowly let out a breath. His eyes never lost their searching look, but his mouth wore an ironic half smile.

"I don't think you need my services, Mr. Stack," he said. "Whatever is wrong with you is not in my department." He stopped me at the door. "Incidentally, Mr. Stack," he said, "I *live* in Beverly Hills!"

"Touché, doc," I said, and left.

The most traumatic event connected with "The Untouchables" happened off camera one windy day.

In the north country, they're called williwaws. They go by the name of *mistral* in France, and Santana in Southern California, but no matter what you call them, they are winds that spell trouble. Santa Ana (or Santana, if you prefer the popular version) occurs when the winds force their way through gaps in the mountains; friction heats the air, and the result is a hot blast that puts everyone's teeth on edge. It's also a bank holiday for arsonists, who creep oot of their rat holes to take advantage of a condition that's an answer to a pyromaniac's dream. Some Santa Ana nights, the brush fires rage from the Hollywood hills to Malibu and light up the sky like the Fourth of July in January.

On one particular hot, windy day, we were shooting exteriors for "The Untouchables" at Desilu, in Culver City, an adjunct to the main studio in Hollywood. This ancient studio dates back to the days of Thomas Ince. It was bought by David O. Selznick for *Gone with the Wind*. During the burning-of-Atlanta sequence, Clark Gable led Vivien Leigh to safety through a conflagration that destroyed all the standing sets. It was finally bought by Desi Arnaz for its forty-acre back lot, where Eliot Ness and his friends ran wild over a replica of Chicago, vintage 1929.

We had just finished a shoot-out with the baddies, and the Thompson .45s were still red hot, when someone noticed a pillar of smoke to the north.

"It must be a brush fire in Beverly Hills," someone said.

Victor Paul, one of our stunt men, took a long look. "Brush fire my butt," he said. "Those are houses burning and that's not Beverly Hills, it's Bel-Air." He took a quick look at my face and started to move. With their accustomed precision, four of my doughty gang commandeered a 1930 Buick, and we were off, followed by the hysterical shrieks of the assistant director who lived in the San Fernando Valley, and whose only concern was the next shot. When we got to the Bel-Air Gate, it was a madhouse. Fire engines were lost in dead-end streets with names no one could pronounce. Water pressure had gone down to zero because everyone was watering his roof. Burt Lancaster and Joe E. Brown had houses that were listed as burned. The gates were closed to all traffic, but the shock of seeing Eliot Ness with his Untouchables screeching up in a vintage Buick so confused the cop at the gate, he waved us in. The fire took everyone by surprise, and as Zsa Zsa Gabor, that famous Hungarian collector of jewels and husbands, said, "There can't be a fire in Bel-Air—not with the taxes we pay!" But there was, and it was a dandy. We got on the roof and tried to keep it watered, while palm trees exploded in colorful bursts up and down the block.

Mother, who was smarter than the rest, had installed a sprinkling system on her roof "just in case." We had all kidded her.

"What are you planning to do?" we said. "Grow a victory garden?" But now no one was laughing. When she had to evacuate her house, she calmly turned on the rainbirds and let them do the work. Her house was the only one on the block that didn't suffer fire damage.

Mother was accustomed to being prepared. In the thirties, she also was the only one in the family who had put away a little cash in a box in the basement "just in case." When Roosevelt closed the banks, she ended up feeding family and friends who were caught short. It took me a while, but I finally began to pay close attention to mother's "just in case."

Rosemarie and I had just finished building our dream house. We had sold off the old Colleen Moore home, subdivided the remaining property, and talked George MacLean, a gifted free spirit of an architect, into stuffing a house between the circa 1929 pool and tennis court. The result turned up on the cover of *Architectural Digest,* and many thought it was MacLean's best effort. The last of the furniture had arrived only the week before, and now I was on the roof, hoping to save eighteen months' worth of plans and dreams (paid for by my countless encounters with Chicago's denizens) from becoming smouldering charcoal. I was desperately trying to make the hose produce more than a dribble, when I noticed a Rolls-Royce drive up with two of the strangest characters I had ever seen. They were dressed in ancient seamen's costumes, complete with pigtails. The familiar voice gave him away.

It was Gil Stuart, three sheets to the wind, with an equally anesthetized companion.

"Quit mucking about on the roof and let us in. We're going to help you break your lease."

I let the two mad characters in, and immediately they went

to work moving all the furniture down to the garage. Then they each inhaled a large beaker of Cutty Sark and stumbled back into the Rolls.

"Thanks," I yelled after them.

"All right, old sod, we've got to go and help some of the other poor buggers."

"That's damn nice of you."

"Just trying to make up for our sinful ways. Keep your pecker up." And off they roared. A few minutes later, the wind changed miraculously; the fire hurdled over Beverly Glen Boulevard, just before reaching our house. It took me a week before I got Gil's story. He was working at MGM on *Mutiny on the Bounty* when he and his companion decided in the middle of a take to sally forth on their errand of mercy. It wasn't until I saw *Mutiny on the Bounty* that I realized who Gil's mystery companion was. Appearing over titles with Marlon Brando and Trevor Howard was a very heroic-looking Richard Harris, in the same outfit he wore as my furniture mover. But he was never as heroic in the movie as he was on a certain hot and windy day in Bel-Air.

Midway through filming of "The Untouchables," *Look* magazine decided to put me on the cover with an accompanying story. Earl Theisen, a top documentary photographer, was given the assignment.

"You understand our editorial policy, Bob," he said. "Nothing is faked; everything has to be for real."

"That's okay," I said.

"All right, let's join the narco squad on a raid!"

So off we went, downtown to the Los Angeles Bureau of Narcotics. The angle was fairly obvious: stick the phony Ness in a real-life situation and see what happens. The only problem was that the other participants in this play didn't have a script and might not take direction. I felt a little as I had when I entered the bullring for the first time and realized my opponent didn't know it was only a movie. Theisen had several chums on the narco squad, and they made us welcome. First we took a tour of Main Street where the winos were into their second quart of dago red. The hookers, with their clown faces and ancient eyes, spotted our unmarked car a block away.

"How?" I asked.

"Well, I guess it's the way cops sit in a car. Not like a regular John."

"Hey, what about hitting Annie Mo?" said one of the cops.
"Who's Annie Mo?" I said.
"That's our nickname for a 300-pound lady who has a house with lots of beds and all the customers to fill them."
"A cathouse?"
"No, not a cathouse. I guess you could call it a 'horse house'—a place to mainline heroin and then sleep it off."

By now we were somewhere near the Los Angeles River in East Los Angeles.

"How's your night vision?" one of the narcos asked our driver.
"What's night vision got to do with it?" I asked.
"Well, Annie is about as sharp as they come. She's got her house on top of a hill with a 360-degree view of everything below her. There's a bumpy, one-way dirt road to the house, and she's up there with ten-power binoculars that can spot headlights a mile away. Our only chance to catch her holding drugs is to barrel up there with no lights and burst in."
"Okay, here we go. Hang on."

The lights were off, and we were flying up a rutted trail to nowhere. I couldn't see a damn thing. Suddenly our driver Bill hit the brakes, and we went into a familiar slide. The car door flew open, and we all stormed out. Someone hollered, "Police, open up!"

Nothing happened. Then they broke the door down. So far, it was the same script I'd been doing for six months. The door flew open, and the narco squad stood there with drawn guns.

"Nobody move!"

It took a split second for our eyes to adjust to the light, and, even then, I couldn't believe it. There, sitting on the floor like a Mexican version of the Waltons, were five little kids, each chewing on a big piece of watermelon. The smallest one looked up at the Bureau of Narcotics' finest and never stopped chewing. Only when he spotted me did he put down the watermelon and break into a big grin. He turned to his 300-pound mother, who was equally unruffled, and then looked at me as if it were Christmas Eve and I were Santa Claus. "Hey, ma," he said, "it's Eliot Ness!"

Then he offered me a piece of his watermelon.

I had one hell of a time looking steely-eyed for the rest of the bust. The back room wasn't so funny. There the customers had just partaken of Annie's hospitality and were in varying states of semi-consciousness. The heroin addict, after a fix, is not the same person as the maniac who can kill when his supply is cut off. He's vulnerable and usually just wants to be left alone. I felt the despair of these poor souls who were fantasizing a better life in Annie Mo's back room before going back to the dreary reality of being aliens in the City of the Angels, a city that had belonged to their people not too many years before.

One handsome twenty-year-old came up to me and gently asked, "Why did you do this, Mr. Ness? You've always been my favorite. I'd never do that to you."

This is no apology for the drug addict. It's just easier for me to understand those with no hope looking for a substitute life in a hypodermic needle than the joy boys and girls who have too much of everything and "drug-out" for kicks.

At Annie Mo's, everybody rushed around in different directions. Some empty heroin capsules were found in the garden but, after ransacking the house, we found nothing else.

"Where's the heroin that goes into these capsules?"

"You know, Sergeant, from many times before, there's no heroin here."

"Then what are the empty capsules for, Annie?"

The narc knew we had nothing, so the two were talking like old friends.

"Aspirin, Sergeant. I fill them with aspirin for my headaches. I get a headache every time you guys break down my door."

"And what about all your guests in the back room with holes in their arms?"

"Friends, Sergeant, friends who have no place to stay. You might call it charity."

In a tragic way, I guess you might.

After my evening with the narcs, *Look* magazine put my face on the cover! Rosemarie had already been on the cover of *Life*. But perhaps the most exciting moment occurred on a Burbank sound stage as Rosemarie and I waited for the announcement of the 1960 Emmy Awards.

When the 1960 nominations were announced, I learned I had been nominated for an Emmy for the role of Eliot Ness, a role that was intended for someone else in a series which wasn't supposed to go beyond the second episode. But show biz has always been full of surprises.

I approached the Emmy with a jaundiced eye. I felt that I had been robbed of the Oscar for *Written on the Wind*. The only memory of that debacle was the nomination adorning my wall at home, black-bordered and already peeling at the edges like a tatty death notice.

The next day Van Johnson, the original choice for Ness, sent me a telegram: "Dear Bob. It couldn't happen to a nicer guy. What've you turned down lately?"

I also brought a little of the movie actor's attitude to commercial television. In those days, film actors said, "The money is good, but it's still just TV." I didn't think seriously about winning the Emmy. But Rosemarie and I made our way into the studio in NBC's main building in Burbank.

A bank of spotlights illuminated the golden ladies. As one cynic said, "The Emmy looks like a refugee from an Easter pageant playing basketball!" When we sat down, I caught my first glimpse of the statuettes.

"Hey, they're kind of pretty, aren't they?" I said.

This particular Emmy presentation would honor Bob Newhart's maiden performance on television, and a host of famous guests were present to hand out the awards.

Even today, I have a collage of memories: Fred Astaire on the crawl, looking me in the eye with a big grin, saying, "And the winner is..." No tears for Rosemarie this time—but a big kiss, that endless walk to the podium, the mumbled acceptance speech, and, for the first time in my life, an ovation, even from the press box. Who said TV is something dumb? It was a moment I'll never forget. By the time the evening had ended, not only had I won my first award for a part I never wanted to accept, but the show that wasn't supposed to work was the success of the year!

A television series can be an incredible, wonderful, terrible, exciting, exhausting, and unique experience. In the case of "The Untouchables," it proved to be everything it could be for me: a chance to be part of a team that worked together to produce a television series of quality. I wouldn't change a thing if I could do it all over again...except, of course, that acceptance speech. The very next day, I thought of the perfect acknowledgment in response to the Emmy:

"I'd like to thank those people most responsible for this

show's success: Frank Nitti, Machine-Gun McGurn, Greasy Thumb Guzik, Maddog Coll, and especially the man without whom "The Untouchables" could never have happened: Al Capone!

11

Beware the Smiling Lion!

Africa! I'd dreamed about it all my life. As a boy I sat spellbound while Harry Carey's *Trader Horn* and Frank Buck's *Bring Them Back Alive* took me with them on their wild adventures. Later, I graduated to Hemingway and Ruark who further whetted my appetite for the Dark Continent. I felt about Africa like someone in love who is afraid to make the wrong move and spoil it all. A safari had been proposed to me many times, but I felt I wanted to share my first experience with somebody special, and I turned down all the invitations.

My "somebody special," Joe Foss, was a war hero and the ex-governor of South Dakota. He had the physique and raw-boned features of a working cowboy too long in the sun. Joe organized a pheasant hunt in South Dakota every year during the hunting season, and that's where I first met him. He was sitting in the middle of a South Dakota cornfield, guzzling a beer, and cleaning a pheasant. Without looking up, he said, "Why don't we go to Africa?"

I figured that he was just shooting the breeze, so I said, "Sure, why not?"

"Okay," he said, "you'd better get your shots."

A week later, he called me.

"Did you get your shots?" he demanded.

"What shots?"

"Get moving," he continued. "Roone Arledge of ABC wants to do a show called 'The American Sportsman.' We get our trip to Africa!"

Each safari begins for the traveler with the mandatory shots for typhus, typhoid, etc., and ends up with tetanus in case you are bitten, disemboweled, scratched, or stomped upon by whatever wild resident may reverse the procedure and hunt you.

The only mention made of snakes was a throwaway at the end of a brochure in the doctor's office.

"Snakes such as the cobra, black mamba, and Gaboon viper are not usually encountered on safari." The tag caught my eye and stayed with me for at least three weeks.

"But it might be a good idea to remember all these are deadly, poisonous." As it later turned out, both the cobra and the Gaboon viper were highly visible; only the black mamba, which reaches a length of ten feet and propels itself through the tall African grass fast enough to catch a horse at full gallop, lived up to the brochure... thank God!

Before leaving for Africa, we stopped in New York to assemble and try out equipment. A Winchester .458 is the biggest production rifle made and since there are no rhinos, Cape buffalo, or elephants on the North American continent, there is little reason for an American hunter to shoot these monsters. We went to a range, and I was handed a gun not unlike the .50-caliber machine gun I used when I taught aerial gunnery in the Pacific. When I pulled the trigger I thought my collarbone was broken.

The man on the target said, "You're in the bull at six o'clock. Do you want to shoot a group?"

"A group, my behind," I said. "I hope I never have to shoot this thing again."

The premise of ABC's show was to take two well-known shooters and let the audience experience with them their first safari in Africa. General Joe Foss had won the Congressional Medal of Honor for shooting down a mess of Japanese Zeros and was equally good with a rifle, so I had my work cut out for me.

We flew to Nairobi, where we were introduced to a professional hunter who would be our teacher, companion, and buffer against disaster in the weeks ahead. For this job, Joe Foss had chosen Bill Ryan, a small wiry Irishman with a sense of humor and an arm held together by metal rods. He was born with the sense of humor; the arm was the result of an idiot client who froze under pressure like Hemingway's Francis Meocomber and shot Bill instead of a charging rhino. The .458 almost tore his arm off, and it was pieced together like a jigsaw puzzle. As Bill later told us, "My first mistake was getting in front of this particular chap; the rhino started trotting, then broke into a run, but they often do this and turn away at the last moment. Suddenly I heard shooting behind me and fell to the ground. 'You bloody fool, you've shot me,' I shouted at my client, who was standing behind a tree, four .458 shell cases on the ground around him. 'I didn't shoot, I swear,' he said. 'I never fired one shot.' His eyes were glazed and he was in shock. No one could convince him that he'd fired his gun, let alone shot me."

Tony Archer, another hunter, looked like a young Van Johnson, and was a dedicated naturalist and conservationist. He had also killed his first elephant, a rogue that was laying waste to the surrounding farms, at age thirteen. He was a tough taskmaster.

"My job is to get you close to the animals," he announced tersely. "Yours is to do your part well."

I spent many hours with this strange, quiet young man, and like to think I became his friend. He was another of Africa's contradictions, a professional hunter dedicated to the preservation of his country's wildlife.

The life-death cycle is what Africa is about. The animal you will harvest has been cleared by the game commission to keep a balance in the herd. Some animals like the cheetah, are off limits as endangered species, and protected. The money a hunter pays for his license will more than help keep the balance.

Poachers who destroy everything for their profits in fur, hides, and ivory are the ones who behave irresponsibly. For example, poachers set wire snares half a mile long and drive wildebeests into them. The animals are left to strangle to death, and all the poachers take are the tails. These are sold in curio shops as fly whisks. Elephants are shot with poisoned arrows and tracked until they die. This may take days, and many escape to a lingering death. (Ironically, the elephant is also killing himself and changing the whole topography of Africa. His diet of hundreds of pounds of leaves and greenery a day has turned what used to be forest into great plains. They're literally eating themselves out of their country.)

Our first stop in Nairobi was at Ahmed Brothers for our hunting outfits. This is a gigantic store full of exotic smells and pictures of their famous customers—various maharajahs, including some of the greatest African hunters of all, bearded characters of the past—all looking terribly at ease and very glamorous. I had nearly chosen an outfit, which looked like the one Stewart Granger wore in *King Solomon's Mines*, when Tony Archer led me to the opposite end of the store.

"Get cracking, Bob," he said. "No more playing tourist. It's time to get you outfitted." Here they hauled out bolts of fungus-green cloth and disillusionment began to set in. In green shirt, pants, and jacket, I looked like a large grasshopper. I did manage to wangle a wonderful, big Borsalino hat, but when I was about to add a leopard-skin band, Tony put his foot down.

"I'd be afraid to be in the same camp with you wearing that bloody leopard band," he grumbled. "You look like a fruitcake."

That took care of the glamor.

We arrived in Africa on the heels of a problem so terrifying that most people tried not to discuss it at all. The words *Mau Mau* and *Uhuru* were seldom used, but you could feel it in the air. Somehow one of our pistols got lost in shipment, and endless hours were spent with local police before it was located and we were allowed to leave for the Kenya highlands and our new base. I began to realize that below Nairobi's big-city façade was the smell of revolution and change. I even came to learn that Tony Archer, my gentle naturalist friend, had done his share of "nightwork." When the Mau Mau began their siege of terror, killing and burning out whole families, the men best qualified fought back the only way they knew. No questions were asked if a young man left a party early. Soon the fancy duds were exchanged for dark hunting clothes and burned cork. The professional hunter was doing "nightwork." The real tragedy is that both sides dearly loved their Africa; I have never seen more warmth, respect, and pride between the professional hunter and his black crew than I saw on this safari.

We flew by twin-engine Cessna to our base camp, 150 miles

west of Nairobi near Narok. From the air, our green tents melted into the rolling hills.

Early in the morning, we were awakened by a smiling face, a voice that said, *"Jambo, bwana"* and served tea the way only the British can make it. Breakfast, at least until the eggs ran out, was anything from omelettes and French toast, to pancakes. (You quickly learn the necessity of collecting camp meat when gazelle steaks and wood pigeons give way to that tired old standby, tinned beef.)

Bob Ruark best describes the mix of emotions Africa causes in his *Horn of the Hunter*. There is the simple affirmation that being alive is very special. Then there is a sensation that no words can describe, the oneness, the feeling of having been there before, maybe a karma or two ago. The garbage of civilization gets washed off first, but it only takes one solitary walk at sunrise or dusk to experience the heightening of all your senses to a degree that almost hurts. Your senses become crosswired and you feel yourself absorbing the sounds and colors. You are in harmony with the shapes around you, the vivid atmosphere. That's what Africa is about, and if you don't experience it, you don't see it.

When we were packing to leave Los Angeles, my beautiful Norwegian wife kept stuffing a heavy goose down coat in my case.

"I'm not going to Norway," I said. "I'm going to Africa."
"I know that," she said. "It's a 'just in case.'"
"Just in case what?"
"Just in case it's not like in the movies."

Now you know why my marriage has lasted twenty-three years. I don't know where in Africa Frank Buck, Tracy, or Bogey shot their films, but I know, sure as hell, it wasn't in the Kenya highlands. The first night, a pail of water outside our tent froze solid. The following morning, I could have sold the down jacket for $1,000 to my companion who'd seen the same movies. The greatest test of bravery was not facing an angry elephant, Cape buffalo, or lion, but getting out of bed at night and making the 100-yard trek to the two-holer. As soon as the fire began dying down, the fun began. We zipped ourselves into our tents to keep out the snakes. The first night a hyena prowled around my tent for an hour like an insane jogger. If those ghastly sounds he made were laughter, then a vampire is a mocking bird. He was quickly joined by a big male lion letting go with a roar in stereophonic sound so loud that it seemed as if it were inside the tent. The feeling of confidence you get from that one-fourth inch of canvas between you and the great outdoors is as great as you would have facing Machine-Gun McGurn with a water pistol. Those damn lions in *Bwana Devil,* who ate up half of Africa in 3-D, began taking over my dreams. I nearly felt a burst bladder might be better than taking my last walk. Eventually, I realized every other greenhorn has gone through the same thing, and KerDowney claims it has never lost a client. So, flashlight in hand, I carefully unzipped the tent and stepped outside, remembering to zip it back up to keep out the "nonexistent snakes." That 100 yards of stumbling over branches (each looking like cobras), holding my breath along with my bladder so nothing unfriendly would hear me, is about as brave as I'll ever get. Why didn't I just open the tent and let fly? I'll tell you why: It just isn't done. The protocol on safari doesn't allow it. When you are in the bush, miles away from anywhere, and you must follow nature's call, even the toilet paper is buried. Then no one will ever know you were in Africa. The main reason for burying it is an esoteric one: Stumbling on any reminder of civilization out there in the wilds of Africa destroys the intimate relationship between man and environment. Even the beer cans are first burned in the fire and later buried so that hyenas, who fancy the varnish, won't dig them up. Every effort is made to let you feel no one has preceded you.

Upon arrival in camp, Bill Ryan gave us a lecture.

"Don't ever go anywhere without your gun. The country looks innocent, but there's always potential danger." I thought the country looked amazingly like Arch Oboler's Paramount Ranch, but I was careful to follow Bill's advice.

Joe Foss was the first to prove that even the best-laid plans go astray in a hurry on safari.

"I'm going to take a walk to the top of the hill and back," Joe announced. "I'm going to get me some exercise."

"Don't forget your gun," I said.

"Oh, hell," breezed Joe, "there's nothing this close to camp."

A few minutes later, Bill Ryan walked by.

"Where's Foss?"

"He took a walk up that hill," I told him.

"Good Lord, and this is only the first day."

"What's wrong?"

"That hill has the highest concentration of black cobras in Kenya."

"I thought you never saw a snake on safari."

"Only if you go looking for them."

It was quite a sight to see little Bill Ryan chewing out General Joe Foss like a private in boot camp. But Joe had his own ideas, even including a prebreakfast, mile-long jog in his shorts with red ants printed on them.

A big black-maned lion, my nocturnal companion, had established residence near the river a mile from camp. We could hear him announcing his territorial imperative with a great roar. One morning I fully expected him to finish with a burp, leaving us with one less man for breakfast.

Luckily, Joe and I knew how to handle a gun, but neither Bill nor Tony knew we knew. So we went out to "sight the guns" to find out if the guns shoot where they are aimed. (They could go off in transit.) But for the professional hunter and his tracker to evaluate their chances of survival, this procedure is essential.

Since the hunter normally walks in front of his amateur client, who is waving around a .458 a couple of feet from his back, his curiosity is understandable. I'd rather trade jobs with Evel Knievel than with Tony or Bill. I guess we passed, because they were all smiles after our practice shots; now we were set to start.

"The American Sportsman" was to be the first program of its kind with sound on film. If the network had known the problems the decision would cause, the producers might have changed their minds. Every word, sigh, or groan was to be recorded to give the audience a sense of being there with us. This is done with a temperamental device called a radio microphone, which even picks up heartbeats. All other African shows had been filmed MOS (as pronounced by an early German sound engineer, "*mit* out sound"). Sound effects and narration were added later on at the studio. Our dictum, however, had been handed down by ABC: "No matter what happens, not one foot of film will be shot without sound." There were other rules, much more bizarre, laid down by some executives whose expertise on things African was based on a visit to a zoo. All film was to be shot in full sunlight, not shade. I could see us dancing around, trying to work a charging Cape buffalo into the proper light. But the smiling lion was the maddest of the lot.

"It is imperative that nothing be done to a lion when it appears to smile like a cat," the network told us. "It is imperative that the lion look ferocious and, if possible, in the act of charging before being fired upon."

Our professional hunters were quick to point out that a lion was just as liable to bite your head off while smiling as while scowling, and that nothing in their contract dealt with an animal's facial expression. They were suddenly playing their game by a different set of rules. Two of our newest arrivals, David Ommaney and Theo Pottgeiter, were particularly jumpy. David had just been released from the hospital and was recovering from leopard bites. Theo had shot the leopard while it was sitting on David's chest chewing on him.

The night before I was to go after a Cape buffalo, we all gathered around the roaring fire, drinks in hand, and the conversation began. Much like the toreros I met while filming *The Bullfighter and the Lady*, the professional hunters gave me a working over.

"Would you say, David, that the leopard is the most dangerous animal in Africa? After all, you were almost done in by one."

"Yes, Theo, because a leopard is so quick. It's on you, its teeth in your neck, and can disembowel you with its hind legs in a matter of seconds."

Terry Mathews, our camp manager, then joined in the act. "Sorry to disagree with you, fellows, but in my opinion nothing is as dangerous as a lion in heavy cover. He'll backtrack and stalk you. By the way, a fellow from San Francisco—you may know him—had his head taken off by a lion in Bechuanaland last week; it made a nasty mess."

Now it was my loyal hunter's turn. Tony said, "Well, I hate to disagree, but I think the elephant is the most dangerous animal in Africa, because he has so many different ways of killing you. He can not only step on you or stick a tusk through you, but he can slowly kneel on you or uncoil his trunk like those party favors you blow on New Year's Eve and split your head like a pumpkin."

Bill Ryan, who'd been puffing thoughtfully on a pipe, slowly got up, knocked out its contents with his crooked arm, and finished the conversation.

"As you know, fellows, I'm senior to all of you, and I know which one scares hell out of me: the Cape buffalo. He's born angry, and when he charges, he comes straight at you at twenty-five or thirty miles an hour; you can not turn him. You either kill him or he gets you. He's got good eyesight, a good sense of smell, good hearing, and he's incredibly agile. When a buffalo gets a man down, he pounds him. He never leaves his prey as other animals do; he just cuts him to ribbons with his hoofs. He's the hardest of all African animals to kill."

There was a pause. Then in unison, each one of these miserable bastards lifted his glass.

"Good luck tomorrow, Bob."

When the sun rose the next morning (I was halfway hoping it wouldn't), there was a wind and the temperature was only a couple of points above freezing. Our job was to stalk a Cape buffalo in bright sunlight. This already goes against normal procedure, since the buffalo usually hangs out in the shady forest during the day, only moving out just before dusk. The addition of a cameraman, his assistant, a sound man, and the director, to the professional hunter, tracker, and me, made us as inconspicuous as Coxey's Army. As we weaved our way over the African landscape like a drunken conga line, I kept thinking that our only chance for success was to find a retarded buffalo. And by God, we did; he was an old fellow taking a nap in the noonday sun. We crept up closer and closer, until I could make out every crack and chip in those ancient horns. I thought if we got any closer, we could attack him from the rear. Tony had a crazy grin on his face. He whispered, "They said they wanted us to get up close."

The buffalo has a constant friend that serves as his charm; he's called the tick bird. He rides around as a passenger and gets to eat all the ticks he wants in return for signaling impending danger. The delinquent bird finally saw us, let out a squeak, and began flapping its wings. Now everything happened at once.

"Watch it, be quick. He might charge," said Tony.

"Hold it, damn it, hold it," the sound man suddenly yelled. "The sound is out."

The buffalo, a deadly black bull close enough to hit with a rock, lurched to his feet. He took one amazed look, spun, and was gone into the brush. We all just stood there for a minute. Finally the sound man said, "I see, somebody knocked a connection loose. The sound's okay now." The only sound he got was a string of cuss words no network would pass.

So ended my first day of big-game hunting. Back at camp, Bill Ryan read Tony the riot act.

"Good Lord, man," he thundered, "you know better than that. You were almost on top of that buff."

Tony wore his Van Johnson smile. "Just following orders, Bill. You must get as close as possible to the animal so the audience can experience the thrill of being there."

"Balls," said the senior professional hunter.

The next day, Tony killed an eland for camp meat. A few seconds after the shot, a group of figures materialized on the horizon. They looked like the angular stick men in ancient cave drawings. As they approached, I could see the familiar red ochre dye, the capes, and ever-present spears of the Masai *moran* (warrior).

The Masai are the African tribe least bastardized by Western man's progress, and there are some travelers who have become so fascinated, they have stayed and made a life study of these amazing people. Sophisticated women have fallen helplessly in love with these lofty warriors. It's as if outsiders try to find strength from the Masai's unique culture. There is a story about a Masai chief's son who was sent to England for a formal education. He graduated from Eton, and returned home in top hat and morning coat speaking the king's English. The next day he was back in red ochre, with a cape and spear, as if he'd never left.

The Masai live by a Spartan ethic of survival. In the circumcision ceremony, the "doctor" does the job with the most primitive of instruments. The young man is allowed to stand in a freezing river before the ceremony to deaden a little of the pain, but he must not change expression throughout the ceremony. To prove himself self-sufficient, a young warrior is turned loose miles from his manyatta—an igloolike house made of straw and cow dung—and is made to live off the land for a week with only his spear as provider.

Before the British outlawed it, a traditional lion hunt followed this test. Top honors went to whoever could grab the lion's tail. This took care of the overpopulation problem. Small wonder a Masai walks with that look of superiority.

By the time our two Masai reached us, Tony had skinned the eland and was beginning to butcher it. Without looking up, he cut a slab of meat from around the heart and liver and gave it to them.

Now I understand their sudden appearance. These impressive giants are protein-starved. Since they would never think of killing their own status symbol, cattle, they subsist on a combination of the animal's milk and blood, and scrounge for other meat wherever they can. Tony's gift led to an invitation to their manyatta, where we were greeted warmly and invited inside. Accepting the combination of urine and cow dung as building materials took a little adjustment on my part, but a smile worked wonders and soon we were all chums—urine, cow dung, flies, and all.

That night I was awakened by a racket in the mess tent. It sounded as if someone was playing "The Anvil Chorus" with the pots and pans, accompanied by cuss words in Swahili. I stumbled out and saw our cook using the refrigerator for target practice. Wrapped around the old-fashioned refrigerator motor was black hose at least seven feet long.

"What is that?" I asked Bill Ryan.

"What's it look like?"

"A black hose."

"Then that's what it is."

"Why is the cook throwing pots at it?"

"Pay no attention to him; he's drunk."

The next morning, a Polaroid picture made the rounds of the breakfast table. It was of David Ommaney, the camp wag, seated Hindu-style, his eyes crossed, his cheeks puffed, blowing on a stick as if it were a flute. The object of his serenade was a deadly seven-foot black cobra, its head held up by a string tied to a low hanging branch.

If you didn't look closely, it looked as if David were a first-class snake charmer. But he was actually a first-class liar.

"A trick I learned in India, working for the Maharajah of Cooch Behar," he announced. "You know, music soothes the savage beast and all that. Don't want you to worry, Bob. It never fails."

Strangely enough, from then on I didn't worry. I finally had something concrete to hang my hat on. These hunters were just like the boat racers, motorcycle nuts, stunt men, and bullfighters I grew up with. Here was something I understood. The accents may have been different, but they had one thing in common: They were out of their skulls.

A funny thing happens when you get behind the viewfinder of a camera. You feel removed from reality. You feel as if you are in charge of the situation, godlike, and writing a script. A friend of mine was photographic officer aboard an aircraft carrier in the Pacific at the time when the suicidal kamikaze pilots were raising havoc with our fleet. During an attack, he got behind his camera, framed the diving Japanese Zero perfectly in the finder, and followed him through our barrage of five-inch cannons, through the 40mm's, through the 20mm's .... By now the plane was so close that all that was left was the .50-caliber machine guns which serve defenders as a desperate last resort. About 150 yards above the flight deck, the pilot was hit and the Zero screamed into the ocean a few feet off the port beam in a ball of fire. My friend never took his eye off the finder and got it all.

"Son of a bitch, what a shot. I got it all." He looked around and saw he was talking to himself. Everyone else had jumped over into the nets surrounding the flight deck.

Then he ran up to the bridge. "Captain, Captain, I've got the greatest kamikaze shot you ever saw." There was no one in sight. Slowly, the four-striper uncoiled himself from under a table.

"You stood out there alone during this entire dive with just a movie camera?"

"Yes, sir."

"That took guts."

It was only then my friend realized what he'd done. He mumbled something about just doing his job, went to his quarters, and threw up. He told me later he always felt that as long as he was looking through his viewfinder, nothing could touch him. This probably explains the high mortality rate among combat photographers.

The same kind of dedication almost lost us Jimmy Crabe, the younger of our cameramen, when he ran into an elephant.

"There he is, Joe. He's a big one," whispered Bill Ryan. "Looks like he's got good ivory, too." Jimmy crawled on his stomach between Bill and Joe and the elephant. The telltale bobbing of the head-and-ear flapping that precedes the charge never bothered Jim. He was on his stomach, camera to his eye, as if he were filming a picnic. Suddenly the elephant came around a tree and headed straight toward Crabe.

"Good Lord," said Joe Foss. "He's big, but he's only got one tusk."

Bill said, "He may be short one tusk, but if you don't take him you're going to be short one cameraman."

Joe made a perfect brain shot and, like my friend's kamikaze flyer, the one-tusker came a few feet from mashing him into strawberry jam.

The one-tusker was greeted back in camp with customary respect. Joe took some ribbing.

"Know of a good dentist, Joe? Maybe he can make you one very big false tooth."

It was decided we should change scenery and head up to the NFD (Northern Frontier District). This lonely, godforsaken area looks very much like the valleys of the moon—not a shrub or vestige of greenery anywhere. It was near the Olduvai Gorge where Leaky found the remnants of the oldest *homo sapiens* and shook up every anthropologist in the world. Butting up against Ethiopia is Lake Rudolph, home of thousands of crocodiles and the Nile perch. The Nile perch, unique to Lake Rudolph, is the granddaddy of the goldfish, and can weigh up to 200 pounds. The natives of the area have a peculiar abnormality caused by their diet of fish only. Their shins and thigh bones bend forward, which gives them the appearance of moving when they're standing still.

Before leaving for the NFD, I noticed some murmured conversation and worried looks.

"I'm not so sure we should go that far north."

"Ah, hell, there are too many of us and too many guns."

"The guns are what worry me. You know the Shiftas as well as I do."

Finally I got into it. "What are Shiftas?"

Bill Ryan explained: "The Shiftas are Somali bandits. Sometimes they cross over the border looking for weapons. But don't worry, there are too many of us."

There was only one small hotel and one boat on the gigantic lake. The proprietor and his young wife were the only Caucasians for a hundred miles around. But it's thrilling for a fisherman to know he's the only one dropping line where the fishing is fabulous and the fish unique to the area. It's as close to heaven as he's going to get.

The next day, we all made bets on who'd catch the biggest

Nile perch. Bill Ryan came along reluctantly and turned green in fifteen minutes, but he brought in the first fish. I was next and hauled in a ninety-pounder. Joe, who'd been bragging about his prowess, had not a bite until we were almost finished, then latched onto a monster. Joe's "Nile perch" finally surfaced. The face was definitely unlike a perch's. It had bulging eyes and long whiskers like Fu Manchu. General Joe had caught the world's biggest catfish. This, coupled with his one-tusk elephant, gave us enough material with which to work him over the rest of the trip.

At that time, Lynn Temple-Borham was senior game warden of all Kenya and perfectly cast for the part. Six-feet-four, ramrod straight, with a mane of white hair and a Teddy Roosevelt mustache, he was not to be taken lightly. He was the law of the bush, the scourge of the poacher, and protector of the Masai. After Uhuru, he returned to England, only to be called back by the black government to resume his job. The aloof Masai thought enough of him to offer him 500 acres of their land and some of their precious cattle if he'd stay. All in all, he was quite a guy.

He was wearing the familiar green uniform and carrying an old, beautifully carved .470 double-barreled Rigby rifle, held African-style over his shoulder, muzzles forward. He had a chore for us.

"Gentlemen, the job has to be done! Whether I kill the lion at night with a spotlight to blind him, or you shoot him as sportsmen on your license, is up to you. He's killed too many Masai cattle; next he'll be on to the children and women."

So began my lion hunt, with a corny B-grade script and a game warden from central casting. The only difference was that this wasn't Paramount Ranch and Arch Oboler wasn't there to yell "cut."

The first thing I noticed the next day was an addition to our crew. He walked directly in front of me, carrying a bag painted white with a blood-red cross on it. I was told that the first-aid bag is absolutely necessary with lions. Their claws and teeth are highly septic and even if you survive a mauling, the infection can still kill you. There's a mystique about a lion. The other animals may be equally dangerous, but the African male lion really *looks* the part. He is more intimidating than the Cape buffalo, elephant, or leopard.

Happily for us, we had no problem with the "smiling lion"

bit. Our lion was a real heavy, a cattle rustler, a potential threat to men, women, and children.

We spent five days tracking our quarry; we were always a half a day behind. Our time was running out and we were down to our last day. Our first break came from an old Masai we found leaning against a thorn tree; he was stoned on honey beer. The Masai culture is far superior to ours. While the young are busy living their lives, only the old are allowed the luxury of alcohol to heighten the past and dim the present.

The old man explained in the international language of the drunk that a big black-maned lion lived only a short way from here. A very big, very old lion with a couple of teeth missing. I asked Tony how the Masai could know a couple of teeth were missing.

"Damned if I know," he said, "but it's his country and there's a lot we don't understand."

It was up to Tony now. We followed the old warrior's directions. Two hours later we found the old man was right. The lion was big, black-maned, and lunching on a Masai steer he'd just killed. We stalked him bent over at the waist; my nose was resting on the red cross bag in front of me, my aching back making me wish I'd kept up my Jack LaLanne exercise class. Tony and I crept behind a bush and waited for Jim Crabe and his camera. The sound man was in a tree a quarter of a mile away. I could hear the lion roaring and chomping from the other side of the bush, and I could feel my adrenal glands emptying like a leaky hot-water bottle.

Tony said, "We'll step away from the bush and you take him."

"How close is he?" I asked.

"Why?"

"How much time will I have if he charges?"

"We'll have to play it by ear."

Just as we began our move, Jim Crabe said, "Hold it, the damn sound is out again." He pointed to our bearded sound engineer frantically waving a handkerchief, the signal to hold everything.

I've done some pretty hairy things in my day, but waiting behind that bush for ten minutes while Leo growled and chewed his way through a steer only a few yards away, tops them all.

By the time the radio sound equipment was working, I was so emotionally exhausted I could hardly get off my knees. This time, we stepped away from the bush. The lion looked up, growled, and I shot him dead. I must admit, I never checked to see if he was smiling.

The old man must have told his chums because, in a few minutes, we were surrounded by Masai. Lynn Temple-Borham pointed me out to the new arrivals as the bwana who had killed their cattle killer, and I could have run for mayor of Nyrok. There was much backslapping, jumping around, and spear shaking. Then the old man slowly walked over to the dead lion, opened its mouth, and pointed with a stubby finger. You didn't have to understand Swahili to see he was pointing to two missing teeth. He gave me a big grin. I gave him one back, just as big. I walked over to him and held out my hand. He held out his. We shook hands and that was just about the best day of my life.

We left for home the next day, but not before Tony Archer discovered a Gaboon viper coiled a few feet away from where we sat. He picked it up by the tail as if it were a garter snake, and casually pointed out its bizarre yellow, orange, and black paint job. He then released it.

"Aren't they supposed to be deadly?"

"Oh, yes," he said.

"Why didn't you kill it?"

"No point. They've got more right to be here than we have."

Just before we left, we got some really shocking news. Bill Ryan had been right to be uneasy about venturing into the NFD. Only a day or so before, the proprietor of the little hotel at Lake Rudolph and a Catholic priest had taken a jeep to pick up supplies. They were ambushed by Somali bandits who took their guns and killed them. Then they skinned them and left them for the vultures and hyenas. Everytime I show my 16mm movies of Lake Rudolph, almost everyone remarks how utterly peaceful and serene the lake appears to be. And I remember that incident.

Bill Ryan said it best. "Whatever you think Africa is, it usually isn't."

I left Nairobi feeling seven feet tall. It only took two days in Tinseltown to bring me back down to four-feet-eleven.

After a couple of weeks, Nyrok, the Serengeti, and Lake Rudolph began fading away until a phone call brought them back into sharp perspective. Johnny Brandeis, one of my proxy fathers during my growing-up period, had been badly mauled by a lion not far from where our base camp had been. I went to see him when he got back.

"How'd it happen, Johnny?" I asked.

"Just got careless," he said, "but I've got no complaints. It was a great safari."

He died a short time later.

12

Welcome to Grauman's Chinese—East!

"How'd you like to go to Vietnam?"

The question took me by surprise.

"What in hell for?" I said. "I've already been in one war, two wars ago."

"To visit the troops."

"And do what, tap-dance and sing?"

"No, this would be to visit the hospitals. Just you and your escort officer, no jokes."

"Okay," I said, "why not?"

And so, this simple conversation began my visit to wartime Vietnam. Henry Fonda suggested that I take a ten-second Polaroid camera with me, while Bob Mitchum tried to prepare me for what I would find.

"Whatever you see, don't react," he said. "Don't change expression."

"Hell, I know that," I said.

"I know you know that, but it is not going to be easy. You're not going to talk about Vietnam at cocktail parties, like every dummy who's been no further away than Tarzana. In fact, you'll find you won't talk about it at all, except maybe to some other silly bastard who's been there."

On my arrival in Saigon, I met my escort officer. Hal Hoyt was a major in the Green Berets, of medium build, blond, hair in a crew cut, and sporting a brand-new Distinguished Service Medal. His main claim to fame was for developing the floating cities of the Mekong Delta, built on fifty-gallon steel drums that rose and fell with the tide. He also, incidentally, commanded the most raggedy-looking troops in the US Army—a combination of US Army, South Vietnamese, Chinese mercenaries (better known as bandits), and North Vietnamese.

The North Vietnamese were not listed on the roll call as North Vietnamese, but everyone knew they were there. I think that Hal's biggest disappointment had to do with Fred, the company barber. He was so good that the guys from miles around would make the trip to see him. One afternoon, he complained that he was sick, and he left early. That night, the North Vietnamese mounted an attack, blaring trumpets and all. They were finally beaten back, but not without leaving a few hanging on the barbed wire. The next morning, there were many sad faces when Fred the barber was discovered hanging on the wire in full North Vietnamese uniform.

Hal's only comment was, "Damn it, we'll never find another barber as good as Fred."

Hal was due three weeks' leave after his tour of combat, and some fast-talking public relations man convinced him it was his duty to use it squiring me around. He was invaluable, particularly at those devastating moments with the badly wounded. To him, it was business as usual, and he kept me from falling apart. We found the ten-second Polaroid camera worked miracles. Usually the patients would see us come in with a camera and figure some bum had wandered in looking for publicity. But after the patient realized the ten-second picture was his to send home, we owned the joint. Even those with tubes and hoses in them wanted their pictures taken.

The conversations went something like this.

"Hi, want to get your picture taken? You can send it home. Tell them Donald Duck dropped by." I have no idea if we did any good, but what the hell, we tried!

Soon after arriving, I met a soldier I'll never forget.

We were taken to a big base hospital outside of Saigon where we were met by a colonel who was chief medical officer, and taken to the main ward. On the way in, I noticed a glass-enclosed room out of the corner of my eye. It was brightly lit, with what appeared to be a giant silk worm's cocoon resting on a table. There were four nurses and a doctor hovering over it. When we'd finished in the wards, the colonel told me there was a young helicopter pilot who'd like to say hello. His chopper had been shot down while he was evacuating the wounded. He rode it down and it exploded around him.

The doctor led me toward the little glass room.

I thought, *Oh, my God, I'm not ready for this. It's only my first day.*

Through my mind flashed Irwin Shaw's description of "the Burn," the German tank commander in *The Young Lions*, completely encased in bandages, who taps out a message asking the character named Christian to kill him.

Then I thought, *Damn it, you're here! You're supposed to be a plus, not a minus.* The nurses were carrying on a lively conversation around the boy in bandages.

"Want to say hello to Robert Stack, Lieutenant?"

The mummy had no mouth. There was a straw-sized hole where the mouth should have been, and just a small hole for each nostril. Only the eyes were not covered. He'd been wearing goggles when he crashed. The eyes were pale blue, crystal clear, and looking at me.

"How's it going, Lieutenant?" I said.

"Okay," said the eyes.

"Not bad having four beautiful nurses?"

I thought, *What a stupid thing to say*. But he understood.

"It's okay," said the eyes.

One of the nurses said, "He's leaving us tomorrow, graduating to the burn center in Honolulu."

I said, "That's the best hospital of its kind in the world, isn't it?"

"Yes," agreed the nurse.

There was a pause.

Now his look had an urgency, as if he wanted to make sure I understood. I locked eyes with him and listened. I mentally shut off all the sound around me and listened to him.

"Thanks for coming, Mr. Stack. I appreciate it." he seemed to say.

"Glad to know you, Lieutenant," I said, "Good luck."

The eyes held me; there was more to say. "Don't worry, Mr. Stack, don't worry. I'm going to be all right. No matter what happens, I'm going to be all right." I leaned closer. I looked deeply into the blue eyes, through the blue and into something as eternal as birth and death.

I didn't have to speak. "I know," I told him silently.

"Good, I'm glad." Then his right eye closed and opened. A nurse thought he had something in it and brought cotton and a solution, but I knew better. He had winked.

Our itinerary, set up by the USO, quickly went by the boards. Hal's comment when he read it was, "Nothing's happening in these places. Let's get out with the grunts [dogfaces, infantrymen]." Hal had so many combat ribbons, we didn't need special orders. The field commanders treated him like a long-lost son. I soon realized I was along for the ride.

I want to establish now that there is nothing as worthless as an actor in the middle of a war, getting in the way of the professionals. So there will be no tales of derring-do from me. I wound up in places I had no right to be, because I was too dumb to know any better and my escort officer was too dumb to be scared.

We also did our job. Hal and I covered many wards and saw many patients, including those in intensive care and recovery. We wound up in places like Dong Ha, the outhouse of creation, where the wind never stops. The chopper dumped us off and refueled with the rotors turning in case of attack. A young Catholic chaplain in battle dress was trying to conduct services for the dead in an open field. The dirt was in his eyes, the purple cloth blowing over his face. His pooped audience of a dozen or so filthy infantrymen hung on his every word as they never did in church. The rifles and helmets of the three killed were framed in the foreground.

My only other memory of Dong Ha is of a somewhat lighter nature. I found myself seated, enjoying nature's call in a six-holer, three on each side, with a general directly opposite me. I wish I could say we conversed, but we sat opposite each other a foot apart, and he never once looked up from his *Stars and Stripes*. However, I can still say I did business with a general.

We said good-bye to the marine commandant at Dong Ha, and flew back to Saigon. A week later, he was killed in a chopper flying exactly the same route at the same altitude.

Back in Saigon, there was a brand-new topic to kick around the bars—the Dragon Lady. This lady of the night more than lived up to her reputation in Steve Canyon's comic strip. She rode to combat on the back of a motor scooter, directing her driver to find a solitary, preferably drunk, American officer. She would then scoot up, ask for a light, calmly blow her victim away with a 9mm automatic, and scoot off.

After five or six stories of her successes, the military didn't drink less, they just didn't walk the streets alone as much.

Finally, one ingenious fly-boy figured out a solution to the problem of the Dragon Lady. The real problem in fighting back was that military personnel were not allowed to carry firearms unless on guard or police duty. One night, he made sure to be the last one out of the club. Then he leaned against a lightpole, all alone, an overcoat over his arm. The Vespa with the beautiful North Vietnamese putted up to him. She smiled, held the cigarette prettily, the other hand in her pocket.

"Could I have a light, Captain?" she said.

His foot shot out and knocked over the scooter; he whipped a .45 out from under his overcoat and blew a large hole in the Dragon Lady and her driver. He then folded the overcoat over the gun and slowly walked back to his quarters.

Hal kept getting more restless. After all, our junket was taking the place of his thirty-day leave.

"If I can get a chopper, do you want to take a trip up north?" he said.

"How far north? To Hanoi?"

"No, just to the DMZ [Demilitarized Zone]. I've spent the whole damn war down south in the delta," Hal went on. "It might be interesting for a change." He was right; the trip was very interesting.

Our helicopter pilot was a second lieutenant, really impressed with Major Hoyt and his ribbons, and anxious to please.

"Where do you want to go, Major?"

"How about Contien?" That was a familiar name. Then I remembered: Contien was the base that had changed hands back and forth so many times no one could keep track. It adjoined the "zone" all by itself in the middle of nowhere. This week, it belonged to us. We flew for about an hour, and then the pilot said, "Are you *sure* about Contien, Major?"

"Yeah, why not?" said Hal. "Can't you get in?"

"I can get in, all right," said the pilot.

"Then what?"

"They're under fire. I can shut off the power and windmill it in [drop it straight down], but there won't be anyone around to greet you. They're all underground."

Finally I came alive. "We're going to windmill it into Contien, while they're under fire, and everyone is underground but us? I may be nuts, but I've got a way to go to catch up with you."

Hal never changed expression. "Okay, let's try Khe Sanh."

From the sky, Khe Sanh looks like a big soup bowl surrounded by parsley. The bowl is the base and landing strip, the parsley the forest that completely encircles it. At the time we were there, the forest was harboring an unknown number of North Vietnamese regulars. As the chopper settled to earth, we felt as if we were landing on a target to be fired upon from any direction at the whim of an unseen enemy. After an hour at Khe Sanh, I had a stiff neck from looking over my shoulder. The first person to greet us was a black master sergeant with a big grin and three Purple Hearts.

"I'll be damned," he said, "you're the first civilian outside of engineers we've seen in six months. What the hell are *you* doing here, Mr. Stack?"

I threw my escort officer a look.

"I'll be a son of a bitch if I know, Sergeant."

He walked us toward the underground sick bay. "Not many patients here, Mr. Stack. The evacuation choppers take them straight to the field hospital."

"Three Purple Hearts, eh, Sergeant. How long you been here?"

"With the time I spent in hospitals, about seven months."

"Seven months?" I said.

"Yeah, things can heat up pretty good around here. We sure appreciate your coming up here. No USO folks ever made it this far north before." *And never again,* I thought.

Absolutely nothing happened at Khe Sanh. It was a beautiful day, the sun shone, the birds twittered; but, as we took off, I grabbed a helmet off the rack and sat on it.

If I was going to get a Purple Heart, it wasn't going to be there!

Hal Hoyt's tour of the Orient continued. We flew over the ancient walled city of Hue, an architectural marvel. The TET offensive a few weeks later ruined a good part of it. The North

Vietnamese took most of the city's intellectuals, "liberated" them into open ditches, and covered them alive. Hal noted the Vietnamese adage: You can get too smart for your own good.

It was a miserable, rainy day. Everything was mud and my escort officer was beginning to drive me nuts. No matter how lousy things were, he was cheerful as a chipmunk.

"Know where we are?"

"Yeah," I said, "right in the middle of nowhere, under Niagara Falls! Hell, no, I don't know where we are! I *never* know where we are."

I looked at the terrain below.

"This resembles Dien Bien Phu," Hal said.

"Where Ho Chi Minh pushed the French out of Indochina?"

"You got it," said Hal. "See that valley? They came through a valley just like that when they made their attack."

I looked around and again was struck by the deceptive peace of the place. Another look at the giant 155mm mobile artillery and the rest of the modern hardware was a reminder that battles are fought over and over in the same places. Only the faces and the equipment change.

The colonel was surprised but tickled to see us, and gave us his private chopper. "I may need it back in a hurry," he said, "but why don't you take Mr. Stack up to the observation post; it's kind of lonely up there. The men would be happy to have a little company."

The observation post was on top of the biggest hill in the area, and could only be reached by chopper. (At least that was the fervent hope of the lieutenant in charge.) Any visitors who came by foot would be North Vietnamese. This was a particularly sensitive spot, as it was the only place that commanded a view of the entire valley. The enemy were shy about being spotted and kept lobbing artillery and rockets, flattening the top like a bulldozer. This was the place I had been asked to visit, to bring good cheer to the men.

"Only stay a few minutes," said the colonel. "We don't want to bring too much attention to them. They have enough problems."

The chopper stayed low until it got to the base of the hill, and then zoomed up like an elevator, slid sideways, and landed hard. I stepped out of the chopper into knee-deep mud, tripped, and fell flat on my face as I turned to Hal to congratulate him on this new adventure. The chopper revved up, side-slipped off the mountain, and was lost in the rain. I stood there like the "indomitable mud man."

"Any idea how we're supposed to get down?" I said. "Or do you plan spending the week here?"

Before my fearless leader could answer, a very young second lieutenant appeared from between two sandbags. Wiping the rain off his glasses, he held out his hand and said, "Welcome, Mr. Ness." He read my harried expression and said, "We don't leave choppers up here, they make too good a target."

Then with a hollow laugh, he said, "Speaking of targets, we'd better go below."

I followed the teenaged lieutenant down some steps into a bunker. There I met four other soggy soldiers, manning observation equipment. I autographed a couple of moldy T-shirts and a canteen. The lieutenant played it straight and announced, "I guess this is as good an observation post as there is." He was as proud of his ratty underground digs as Conrad Hilton of his entire chain.

"See out there, Mr. Ness?" he said.

I took a look through the slot in the bunker; even in the rain, the entire valley floor stretched out like a giant bowling alley. I could see why the Viet Cong were so interested in subletting the lieutenant's bunker.

"And see out there on the hill?" he said. The top hundred yards were absolutely bare. Below was an ugly jungle of blasted trees interlaced with shocks of jagged metal and barbed wire.

"That took a lot of work," he said proudly, "but it's going to be worth it. It'll do the job." He made it sound as if it were the gardens of Versailles.

He paused, then looked back down the valley. As he turned, the mask of command slipped and he looked at me with the youngest, loneliest look I'd seen in this war. "Don't you think so, Mr. Ness?"

How in hell did I know if the VC could overrun this lieutenant's observation post? They'd done it once before, to the French.

"Well, I'll tell you, Lieutenant," I said, "if I were the VC, I sure as hell wouldn't try to go through that mess."

He grinned as if he'd just made Eagle Scout.

"You been out here long, Lieutenant?" I said.

"No, sir," he said, "this is my first command."

"No kidding?"

"Yes, it's not exactly the way I imagined. Nothing is, I guess. But it's a very important job; we're the eyes of the whole battalion. That's the way me and the men look at it." Son of a bitch, he meant it. I could feel the throb of the incoming helicopter. We shook hands.

"Good luck, Lieutenant."

"Drop by any time you're around, Mr. Ness."

"Sure," I said. The lieutenant and his crew were waving enthusiastically as we lurched off and dropped down the mountain. The farther away we got, the more puny and helpless the observation post appeared, until the bald spot disappeared in the mist. I wasn't sure who had boosted whose spirits, as I kept thinking, *Was I ever that young?* If I never was, I suddenly wished I had been.

Fearless Hal knew someone in Pleiku, so away we went. On my arrival, much was made of the fact that I was given the VIP tent. It was like every tent in the military, with one marked exception: It had an adjoining bomb shelter. I asked, like a dummy, who woke whom up in case of a rocket attack.

"All you do is jump in when the first rocket hits," came the reply.

"What about a direct hit?"

The big fat sergeant laughed.

"You Hollywood guys got a good sense of humor," he said. "In that case you don't have to worry about the bomb shelter."

The wards were all the same. The wounded were living out their suspension in time, as if whatever happened would go away if nobody moved. I had to keep telling myself we were doing some good. Some would turn their faces to the wall. Then we'd walk by and go to the next bed.

"Want to get your picutre taken?" It didn't change.

In a hospital recovery room—I forgot where—I finally fell apart. There was no way not to see him. The net of crossed webbing used in multiple-wound cases was strung five feet off the floor. The young soldier lay there like an El Greco painting, his skin painfully white in his nakedness, his arms forming the crucifix. The webbing made him appear to be the helpless victim of a giant spider.

I thought: *How long have I been out here? It's time to go home.*

A thin weary doctor with hairy arms interrupted my fantasies. "This boy is something special. He must have read about Sergeant York, because he tried taking on the North Viet army on his own. He did it surprisingly well, too. He'll be coming out of it any minute now."

As we approached, I could see he was about nineteen, with a baby face like another one-man army named Audie Murphy, from another more honored war. He was deathly still. Slowly, the eyelids began to flicker.

"Incidentally, he's being put up for the Congressional Medal of Honor. Why don't you say something to him, Mr. Stack? I know he'd appreciate it."

His eyes flicked open.

He had no idea where he was. I leaned over, next to his ear and tried.

I honest to God tried, but finally none of it worked—no more "how's it going, you're going to be just fine." I wished I had the gift of Hank Fonda, who brought peace and hope to all the kids he touched. I started with, "Everybody at home is very proud of you." Then I couldn't say any more. I knew I was lying through my teeth. The boy never moved. He kept staring at the ceiling, lost in his own world. Then I blurted, "I want you to know I'm very proud of you."

Those damn tears I promised would never come began pouring down my face. Hal put his arm on my shoulder and we walked out. "You know something, pardner," he said, "I think we're due for a vacation."

Until now, the closest I had got to getting my feet in cement was when Eliot Ness began doing a job on the Mafia. But all that changed when Hal decided that we should take a little vacation from the hospitals. He chose, not surprisingly, a location directly adjoining the DMZ. Any farther north, and we would have been holding hands with Ho Chi Minh. My grandmother had an expression for a place that was way off the beaten path: "That's where God lost his boots." That was Cua Viet.

"This spot is different," said Hal. "It's on the ocean, with a big sandy beach and a steady breeze to cool you off."

If Hal Hoyt handled the chamber of commerce for the River Styx, he would fill it with angels. Our first view of Cua Viet did not quite match Hal's description. The day was grimly overcast, the ocean whipped into a gray green froth, and the beach looked like the Sahara covered with beetles. As we began letting down, these became amtracks and other amphibious machinery. I also noticed that each 50-caliber waist gun was actively manned. We had an LSA (Landing Signal Officer) to bring us down on a metal carpet so the chopper wouldn't disappear in sand up to its rotors. If ever a place had an atmosphere of otherworldliness, of something seen through the eyes of Ray Bradbury, this was it. Even the Polaroid snaps I shot convey a feeling of impending doom. The palm trees were bent double in the "prevailing breeze," and everybody on duty wore goggles to keep from sandblasting their eyeballs. I could certainly see this spot was different.

The interesting part of going into advance areas is that your presence comes as a complete surprise to the people stuck there. Cua Viet had long ago been forgotten by everyone but the North Vietnamese. The DMZ had become an area to infiltrate at night for a possible surprise attack instead of a no-man's land for both sides. Some enthusiastic Seabees had built an outdoor theater to show movies, forgetting this was not Hollywood and Vine. The premiere screening was a smash, literally. The troops finally got to see a movie, but the VC now had a nifty target on which they could zero in with their newly arrived 180mm Russian rockets with warheads as big as watermelons. As soon as the projector started whirring, a VC rocket team managed to sneak into no-man's land and set up shop. This took them about an hour. Then the rockets came. The last half of the movie ran while the audience was underground. This got to be a routine, and the biggest complaint was that they never got to see how the movies ended. I spent most of my time in Cua Viet narrating the second half of a dozen motion pictures to an avid audience.

"See, damn it, I told you. The big-titted broad did it."

"You thought it was the fat guy with the cigar."

The general even choppered in to see what we were doing there. He kept looking at me, if not suspiciously, then with ill-concealed curiosity. "This certainly is an unexpected pleasure, Mr. Stack. What can we do for you? How about some lunch?" He stopped. "No, wait a minute. Our cook shack took a direct hit."

We walked over to a beat-up shack made of ammunition boxes, sporting a sign on the wall that read Limberdick Lounge.

No one offered to explain, so I guess it was self-explanatory. The cook came out with a tray of hard-boiled eggs. "It looks like 'The Untouchables' down there. We've got canned tomatoes all over the place. This is going to have to be it." Of all the dismal places I visited, this one on the DMZ, adjoining the Ho Chi Minh trail, had the loosest, most casual atmosphere. I decided that the men had to act that way, because they knew what was going to happen. It was just a matter of when. But now I could feel a kind of excitement in the air.

A sergeant with ribbons from two wars came up to me. "Mr. Stack, we don't get many visitors. Make that *any*. Well, we'd like to commemorate your visit, so we worked out a little ceremony in your honor." He led me to a spot under a blasted palm tree. There they formed a circle around a block of wet cement that had scratched on the top, Grauman's Chinese East. I took my cue and with proper ceremony, planted my boot in the wet cement and got set to inscribe the message.

TO THE GUYS AT CUA VIET, THANKS FOR THE HOSPITALITY.
GOOD LUCK.   Robert Stack

As I began to walk away, the sergeant said, "Would you mind adding something, Mr. Stack?"

"Of course not. What?"

It was something that was on everyone's mind. Now the last line read: Good luck with the 180mm's.

After Cua Viet, I'd had it with Hal Hoyt's magic tour, and went to the source. The USO said, "We have no idea where you've been, but everybody seems to be happy, so I'm not going to ask any questions."

"We figure you're due a few days off," I was told. Before Hal Hoyt could open his yap and send us to Hanoi, I said, "How about the fleet?" I was in the navy almost four years, but I'd never been on a destroyer, and I said I'd like to see a new slant-deck carrier like the *Forrestal*.

I looked over at Hal triumphantly and, for the first time, I saw a flash of insecurity, a small break in his cheerful chipmunk grin.

"We're going to spend three days on boats?" he said.

"The word is *ships*." Then I slapped him on the back. "You're in the navy now, Major."

It's interesting how many politicians, TV commentators, columnists, and cocktail-party pundits had the answers on Vietnam. Actually, Jane Fonda is one of the few who got there, but she was so far north she was looking at a different war. Even the combat correspondents I met saw a lot of it through political convictions. Somehow you see it differently through the eyes of the wounded. You spend three weeks with a few thousand men in varying conditions of disability or disfigurement, and you don't have time for the guilt and masochism of the moralist, the whining self-justification of the deserter, or the pompous, cold self-righteousness of the military. Vietnam was a dirty war, and so was the rape of Rome.

It was not right or wrong, it just was. The worst part is not that we should never have been there, or even that we lost, but that most just don't give a damn. The same poor bastards that I saw would have been heroes in any other war. Many, on their return to the States, had to lie about being in Vietnam to get a job.

Shortly after I returned to the States, I learned that Cua Viet had been overrun by the North Vietnamese. Many of the men who welcomed me, with courage and good humor even though they knew their own days were more than likely numbered, were casualties.

I often wonder what happened to my cement footprint. I don't think the North Vietnam commander that overran Cua Viet took care of it. Chances are he never heard of Grauman's Chinese.

13

A Tube for All Seasons

Somewhere in the dark, mossy recesses of my subconscious lurks a bizarre character, who, like Dorian Gray's sequestered portrait, I've imprisoned and tried to forget. But sometimes, after a late snack of chili and tequila, or one too many glasses of dago red, he invades my dreams like an unwanted weed. This apparition first leaps into close-up like a TV commercial, flailing the air with a sword and shouting some gibberish in French. *"Coeur et courage,"* he yells. "Heart and courage." This makes no more sense in English than it does in French.

This character is wearing an outfit of powder blue stretch pants, silk flowing shirt, hip-high boots, a red sash around his waist, and matching bandana on his head. He looks like a refugee from a gypsy tearoom. I snap upright in bed, the sweat running off my brow.

"I paid you off like Faust, you miserable phantom," I say. "Get lost." But now it's too late, and the reels are turning. The show has started and I can't stop it.

Back in the 1950s, I got the best reviews of my life in that good movie with the terrible title, *The Bullfighter and the Lady*.

Even *Time* magazine singled me out as a young actor with great potential. Much of the potential went out the window on my next film, *My Outlaw Brother*, a piece of Limburger that put a temporary damper on the careers of Robert Preston, Mickey Rooney, and me—and finished off Eliot Nugent, the well-known Broadway director.

I played two characters: the good, innocent ranchero and, at night, the evil despoiler of virgins and innocent folks. My makeup as the evil despoiler of virgins was a cross between a rubber Halloween mask and Jo Jo, the dog-faced boy, fur-covered and hunchbacked (thanks to the stuffing from a car seat). No matter how much I tried to be scary, I'm afraid I wasn't too impressive. I remember that the scenes with Bob Preston took forever. He'd start out on target, but then I could see the telltale stomach contractions. Soon he was in hysterics. The only one I scared was my horse, who bucked me off during my most evil scene, when I was setting fire to the mayor's house. Happily, I fell on my back and the car seat stuffing took the worst of it. I wish I could have used the car seat stuffing on the reviewers.

During the inevitable inactivity that follows a turkey, my press agent, a lovely ex-actress named Helen Ferguson, came up with a radical idea. I know that up till now I've always said "The Untouchables" was my first TV-series effort, but I'm afraid that's wishful thinking. It's time I let you in on a secret not even my closest friends know. Helen walked up to me tentatively and said, "We've always agreed that activity breeds activity, right, Bob?" I could see she was holding something behind her back.

"Yeah, right," I said. "What have you got behind your back?"

"Now I don't want you to get mad," she said, "it's just an idea."

"What?"

"This."

She presented me with a very skinny-looking script, with IDEA FOR TV SERIES printed across the top.

"You want me to do one of those things?" I asked, outraged. "A cheesy half-hour show each week? Only unemployed actors do that kind of garbage." There was a lengthy pause, during which no one spoke.

"Okay," I said, "it can't hurt me to look at it."

The blood-red title superimposed over crossed swords came leaping off the page at me: "The Phantom Pirate."

The active imagination that wins Academy Awards also sinks studios, and the actor's best friend, which can also be his worst enemy, began chugging away. All the Rafael Sabatini books I'd cherished since childhood began forming a montage—Scaramouche, Captain Blood.... In a flash, I could see myself sliding down the sail of a pirate ship like Doug Fairbanks, and making shish kebabs of the enemy with the ease of Errol Flynn.

"Not a bad idea, Helen," I said. "Not a bad idea." Little did I know.

I met my producer in a studio on Santa Monica Boulevard. The "studio" was the size of a two-car garage. He looked like a used-car salesman about to sell me an Edsel.

"You see, Bob," he explained, "there's not really much difference between making motion pictures and series TV. What we do now is make a pilot or sample film to show potential buyers." Finally I woke up.

"You mean we might not even get on the air?"

"Of course, there's always that chance," he said, "but with you as our star, and this great story, we're a cinch."

My new leader had a nervous twitch, and fingernails chewed off to the first knuckle–a stark contrast to his air of complete confidence. My agent, with the smile of a white slaver who'd just sold a warm body, nodded in agreement.

As I was leaving, I was casually reminded the Phantom Pirate was a great swordsman.

"Do you know how to use a sword?" said the producer.

"No."

"Don't worry, you'll pick it up in no time."

I soon found that learning the art of fencing in a couple of weeks is as easy as playing a Rachmaninoff concerto the first time you see a piano. It's like no other sport in the world, and uses muscles you've never even been introduced to.

Al Cavens is the son of the great Belgian Olympic champion and head of the Belgian Fencing Academy who taught Douglas Fairbanks his fabulous style. This took months of arduous training and even Fairbanks, who was Hollywood's best athlete, found it no piece of cake. Poor Al had two weeks to make old "stumble foot" Stack look like Fairbanks's hero.

The tennis court was the scene of my daily torture.

"Advance, retreat, lunge, recover, lunge," Al kept yelling, until I was barely more than a mass of charley horses. I cursed every Sabatini book I'd ever read. I learned that the joyous flamboyance of Fairbanks and Flynn in their sword fights was as cheerfully choreographed as a complex dance routine.

"Come on, Bob, think," he would say. "Cheek, head, okay, now the parry, parry, cart, counter, parry, lunge—hold it!" Each move has to be right to match the opponent's move. If you try to improvise you can pull the foil into your eye just the way Flynn did once after too little rehearsal and too many vodkas. Remember when the camera rolls, you won't be wearing a protective mask.

I must say here that TV series of the 1950s were like the old silent two-reelers—frantic and fast. One of the biggest successes, "Wild Bill Hickok," with Guy Madison as the lead and Andy Devine as his sidekick Jingles, was as simple as a comic strip and as popular with the kids as bubble gum. Jack Webb's "Dragnet" had the perfect formula and he made a fortune. Except for a few exteriors of police cars, the main plot always featured an interrogation. He stuck the actors against a wall avoiding the problem of building sets, and used cue cards to save time never moving the camera. Even so, his "just want the facts, ma'am" made "Dragnet" a classic. The name of the game was quick and cheap; take the money and run. Into this formularized routine I thought I would jump as the Phantom Pirate, bringing a little class to the boob tube.

I'd read just enough books on theatrical costuming to think I could make the Phantom Pirate not just a run-of-the-mill pirate, but something different. To say I achieved my goal would be an understatement. The idea, I said, was to keep the costume tight around the hips, with a loose flowing shirt to symbolize freedom and devil-may-care abandon, like Olivier's Hamlet, and a sash around the waist, a trademark of all reputable pirates. The bandana was Helen's idea of a romantic touch. The wardrobe test was made, and in the projection room, I had the first inkling of what was to come. After the lights came up, Helen said, "I think you look simply wonderful, so romantic," As we filed out, I overheard the assistant cameraman whisper to his boss, "They ought to call it 'The Phantom Faggot.'"

We shot the titles at Santa Monica Beach, and I got my first introduction to TV-series economics. I was to appear hanging from the rigging of a ship with my most adventurous grin as the credits unrolled. My first question seemed a logical one.

"Where's the ship?"

"What ship?" came the reply.

"What do you mean, what ship?" I said. "The one whose rigging I'm supposed to climb to shoot the titles."

"Oh, you mean the truck," came the reply. "It's over there."

Parked not far from where we stood was a beaten-up truck with a platform from which sprouted a mast, a small piece of sail, and a couple of ropes for the rigging.

"Just hang onto the rope and look out to the sea. Nobody'll know the difference."

I was told that, in deference to my stature in motion pictures and the glamorous subject matter, great care would be taken in the future to assure authenticity. "We're going to use real boats and shoot on distant location." Well, they weren't *quite* real pirate ships; they were whatever they could find that would float with phony ship rigging glued to the side. Of course, the cameramen would be careful not to photograph from low camera angles, showing our glamorous pirate ship as the lowly barge or scow it was. "Nobody'll know the difference" was the standard reply.

Our "distant location" was Catalina Island, a few miles off the California coast, and the meeting place of all the fishing boats from Long Beach to Santa Barbara. We got up at 4 A.M., got into our scow with the fringe on top, and chugged toward our destination. The barge with the camera and lights had left two hours earlier. We were almost there when we ran into a fog bank.

It was four hours, with everyone hollering and doing foghorn imitations, before we found the camera boat. The fog was too thick for even our hyperactive producer. But did he give up? Not for a second! This was TV.

"Get ready for the great sword fight," he announced. "We're going to Griffith Park."

There are very few places in today's Southern California that look like the Sherwood Forest described so vividly in the script. Our chosen location was made famous many years ago by Sam Goldwyn: When he was approached about filming on distant location, he said, "A rock is a rock; a tree is a tree. Shoot it in Griffith Park."

Griffith Park is on the way to Pasadena, and has the obligatory trees and rocks that have served the movie industry for fifty years. It also has bridle paths, lots of dogs, and the calling cards horses and dogs leave behind. Walking through the park is more like negotiating a mined field. The "great sword fight" featured a troup of stunt men, most of whom were at home on motorcycles and horses. They were visibly uncomfortable as pirates with rapiers and sabers. Those with beards were the baddies, and the rest were the clean-shaven good guys. Al Cavens was by far the best with a sword, so he kept switching hats and beards like a quick-change artist. He would leap at me from behind the rocks and trees, yelling *Aha!*" As soon as he had his back to the camera, he would talk me through a routine and cover my mistakes with broad moves and much waving of the arms.

"All right, advance, advance, lunge, good. Now here I come. Cart. No, watch it, that's counter of cart. Okay, okay, don't stop. Keep smiling. I'm going for your head, right cheek... left cheek. Good. Now lunge, *aaahhh*... that's good. You've killed me. Okay, Cut!"

The Phantom Pirate was not only a master swordsman, but also a master of disguises. You'd think I would have learned my lesson after *My Outlaw Brother*, but there isn't an actor in the world who doesn't relish the misery of gluey spirit gum and the itchings of hair-lace mustaches and whiskers. But the worst of all is a process known as "laying on a beard." This qualifies as an extension course taught by the Marquis de Sade. The entire face, up to the eyes, is coated with spirit gum, which is allowed to dry until sticky. Then the end of a "rope" of hair is laid on the tortured skin and cut down to the desired length. The entire mess feels as though you've been tarred and feathered. The actor can now experience the rosy glow of masochism that goes with "suffering for his art." There's an important rule of thumb: the heavier the disguise, the heavier the talent required to make it work. Many actors, and especially beginners tend to confuse self-indulgence with performance and think that a beard gives them dramatic license. It takes a Paul Muni or Laurence Olivier to handle heavy characters. But they were not available, so I jumped enthusiastically into spirit gum—beard, mustache, and all.

No one seeing "The Phantom Pirate" had any idea who the weird characters were. I groveled, slouched, and stomped through the scenes like a refugee from *Dracula* or *Franken-*

stein. The audience, I knew, would spend half its time trying to figure out who I was.

We also had our problems with the law.

"Where's Bud?" someone would ask.

"In jail."

"He can't be in jail. He's already been established as the good guy with the big hat. He's the only stunt man we've got who can handle the roof fall."

Bud had been a tumbler, and was a specialist in falls from the roof. The insanity continued.

"Why's he in jail?"

"His wife put him there."

"What'd he do to her?"

"Nothing. He just didn't pay the alimony, and she called the sheriff."

"Well, you call the sheriff and tell him he's holding up the production."

Sure enough, an hour later, poor Bud arrived with an embarrassed-looking sheriff in tow.

"Don't let him escape, sheriff," someone would say. "He's a dangerous man."

"Hey, Bud, if you'd done more stunts at home and less in Studio City motels, you'd be a free man."

When Bud's workday was over, he took off his big hat and skinny mustache. The sheriff stuffed him into a black-and-white and hauled him off to the pokey. This became a daily routine; the sheriff was the best audience we ever had.

Somewhere along the line, the producer suggested that we needed a rallying cry. "You know," he said, "something original like Remember the Alamo, Damn the Torpedoes, Full Speed Ahead, or Praise the Lord and Pass the Ammunition." Al Cavens, who spoke a kind of pidgin French, suggested *"coeur et courage."* This, he said, gave a European dash to the project. One of our loyal troops piped up, "We're all supposed to yell whatever he just said?"

"Yeah."

"What the hell does it mean?"

"Heart and courage."

"What's that supposed to mean?"

"It doesn't have to mean anything; it's just a trademark."

"If we don't know what it means, how's the audience supposed to know?"

The troops were told to forget the audience and shout the line, setting the art of piracy on the high seas back a few hundred years. We never came close to sounding like Frenchmen. The rallying cry sounded more like an advertisement for an East Indian restaurant. It came out "curried courage," or, as one wag put it, "a well-known pirate delicacy, old curried dog."

By now the Phantom Pirate has lived up to his name, vanishing without a trace. An actor should really be protected from himself! The difficulty of swordplay, the arduous stunts and fast tempo of filming convinced even my best friends—those sophisticates of show business, the stunt men—that we had a smash. Actually, my phantom friend was only behind the times. This poor, stretch-panted, silk-shirted buccaneer would be too straight in the company of today's Bionic Man, Wonderwoman, and Spiderman, with his magic web and insect mask.

But even the disappearance of the Phantom Pirate had the customary complications. When our effort was finally put together and shown to potential buyers conditioned to westerns and cop shows, it was greeted with an eerie silence. One critic summed up all the general feeling.

"All the guys wear wigs and big faggy hats, while Stack jumps around in bright blue long johns. What the hell kind of audience would tune that in?"

When the producer realized his "lavish pilot film" hadn't sold, he subtly hinted that the name of Robert Stack would assure the sale of the Phantom Pirate pilot to local TV. Only by giving him back my salary did I get a written guarantee that "The Phantom Pirate" would remain a phantom and never see the light of day. The Phantom only appears at night, and only to me.

The pace of TV often came as a rude shock. I appeared on "Playhouse 90," "The Theater Guild," "Celanese Theater"—all the quality live TV shows—to demonstrate that I wasn't just a "movie actor." Since live television in those days was run by theater people, it was more like doing a stage play. Many film actors wouldn't touch live TV. "Good God," they said, "what do you do if you blow your lines?" The typical live show would be rehearsed for two weeks or more. Then would come the madhouse of the multiple cameras and technical rehearsals. There was never enough time for a costume change.

Following a hurried countdown, the electrifying words "on the air, live" boomed forth. Survival was the key ward. This was before the security of video tape; whatever happened damn well happened on camera.

Live TV had moments of high drama—the golden years of Rod Serling, Paddy Chayefsky, James Costigan, and Reginald Rose. But there were other moments, equally unforgettable, that could only happen in an era when we thought we could do anything, and almost succeeded.

I have an image of Maurice Evans, that distinguished Shakespearean actor, being carried out dead on his shield: Thinking he was off camera, he opened his eyes, only to see the lens still on him, and the red camera lights glowing.

With a muffled "oh, my God," he snapped his eyes shut and proved that, on live television, you can die twice on the same night.

Sometimes doing it well wasn't as important as just getting through it. John Frankenheimer, the *enfant terrible* of live television, who has since graduated to such classics as *The Manchurian Candidate, French Connection II,* and *Black Sunday,* had the job of putting together the first "Playhouse 90" combining film *and* live actors on stage. The intercutting had to be absolutely perfect for the show to work. The subject was Manolete, with Jack Palance as the tragic torero. Rehearsals were like a fire drill with everyone going to the wrong lifeboats. Dress rehearsal was a shambles and the show was never finished. On the air, it came together but, surprisingly, it was not a good show. Jack Palance looked like a fugitive from *Carmen*, and the complicated techniques were only confusing, not dramatic. But John was all smiles.

"Not one of your best, John," said a critic, sourly.

"Who cares about being best," said John, philosophically. "It was the first time we got through the damn thing all the way."

In "Panic Button," an updated version of Dostoevski's *Crime and Punishment,* I played Raskolnikoff to Lee J. Cobb's inspector. Once we were on the air, there was no protection, no chance to be saved in the cutting room, none of the retakes that rescue an actor in a motion picture. When you are up against a giant like Lee J. Cobb, the odds are strong that he'll chew you up and spit you out in little pieces. I had seen Cobb do *Death of a Salesman*. I still think his was the best performance I've ever seen on stage. I was his fan—suspicious, but still a fan.

My old and dear friend Rod Serling had done the teleplay, and Frank Shaffner (of later *Patton* fame) was the director. Vera Miles played my wife, and Leif Erickson and Marian Seldes completed the cast.

During rehearsals, Vera spent most of the time knitting. Shaffner spent most of the time admiring her bosoms, and I spent my time trying to figure out what in the hell Cobb was saying.

In our TV drama, Cobb mumbled so incoherently, he could have been reading his lines in Swahili. I had to look at his lips to know when he'd finished. Luckily I remember the words of wisdom given me by a Group Theater graduate: "Hang loose during rehearsals, but hang on to your hat when the curtain goes up. Expect the unexpected."

My only confrontation with Mr. Cobb (who turned out to be a gentleman in every respect), came when he said, "Mr. Stack, it appears to me your character might be—"

Before he could finish, I leaped in with, "Mr. Cobb, Dostoevski wrote us each a highly complex character. In the short rehearsal time left, we'll each be lucky to do justice to them." After a long Macready pause, one eyebrow slowly lifted, he looked me straight in the eye for the first time. Next came an appraising squint, with the beginning of a smile. "Of course, Mr. Stack, of course."

I took a deep breath, and Mr. Cobb went back to his mumbling.

It happened in dress rehearsal. After two weeks of rehearsals, I'd gotten used to Lee Cobb as an eighty-year-old hunchback with a speech affliction. As we started dress rehearsals, his first words hit me like a slap in the face. "I want the truth" was a knife to the vitals, and it built from there. It was the most amazing metamorphosis I have ever seen. He was the classic symbol of authority—shoulders back, eyes piercing, even the droopy cigar was having an erection.

Nothing I'd ever learned equipped me to handle this. He played me like a harmonica. But the master had taken pity on me. He gave me the shock treatment at dress rehearsal so I could adjust to it on the air. There were no tricks this time, just pure unadulterated talent and, my God, how that man could listen. He made everything I said seem important. In the courtroom scene, he led me into the best TV performance I'd ever given.

Later we had a couple of drinks, and he told me he'd just recovered from a heart attack. He also told me a story about Frank Sinatra with a promise not to repeat it.

Lee Cobb had been doing a movie for the King brothers when he had his heart attack. The King brothers tried holding up the picture, but it looked as if Lee would be in the hospital for too long a time. Frank walked into Lee's hospital room.

"You don't know me, Mr. Cobb," he said. "My name is Frank Sinatra. Your hospital expenses are taken care of for as long as you have to stay here. I don't want you to worry about anything. I talked to the King brothers, and they're going to hold the picture until you're ready."

For once, Cobb was speechless.

"Why?" he asked Francis Albert.

"Because you're America's greatest actor, and it's my privilege."

Lee pushed the drink away. "He made me promise not to tell anyone, but you've known him a long time, and you know something else. There's no one else in this world that would (or could) do something like that for me. Not my closest friends, not even my family. He was a perfect stranger. I'd better never hear anybody rap this man while I'm around."

Lee Cobb is no longer around. He was the victim of a second heart attack. Frank Sinatra was right; he was America's greatest actor, and it was a privilege to be on the same stage with him.

At the final countdown, I could feel the octopus in my stomach and the shortness of breath that heralds a live ninety-minute show. When the count got to five, Lee walked by, gave me a slap on the back, and a crooked grin. The octopus swam away and my breath returned. The final 4-3-2-1 came. The floor manager pointed his finger, looking like Uncle Sam in a World War I poster. We were off.

After the initial shock that television gave the major studios, desperate measures were applied to meet the enemy. Motion pictures over the years had become a way of life—from the kids and the Saturday-afternoon serials to the once-a-week habitué who traded his workaday world for a buck's worth of enchantment. But the means with which to destroy this upstart drowned in a sea of confusion, and each Napoleon in his own studio had a different idea. Fox was the dumbest of the lot.

I was told I had been assigned to "Fox's answer to TV." The studio was going to take its biggest hits and remake them with multiple cameras for the small screen. (This was a highly complex technique only veterans of live TV's "Playhouse 90" knew anything about.) The remake was to be of *Laura*. I was going to play Dana Andrews's overly romantic detective; George Sanders was to usurp Clifton Webb's role; and a beautiful English actress named Dana Wynter, not Gene Tierney, was Laura.

The director, who had not asked for the idiotic assignment, got so tangled up in the cameras and the seven-day schedule, it took us fourteen days to finish it. Upon completion of our effort, someone upstairs suddenly realized what they had just done was make a cheesy copy of their own classic. So why not just release the original *Laura* on television?

I think our answer to TV ended up as a few thousand guitar picks. Many years later I found myself doing an even worse version of the poor defenseless film, for just as idiotic a reason.

David Susskind called me with "a great piece of natural casting. It will be the talk of the business," he said. "We'll get ratings never seen before, when we do *Laura* with Jackie Kennedy's sister Lee Radziwill as the ghostly enchantress!"

"Has she ever acted before?" I said.

"It doesn't matter," said David. "Michael Cacoyanis, the director of *Zorba the Greek*, and Truman Capote say she's a natural." I should have remembered that *natural* and *amateur* are usually interchangeable.

"Okay," I said, "I'll call you back, David."

I checked around town and found that five actors I knew couldn't wait to embrace Princess Radziwill and the worldwide publicity, as well as a free trip to London. So, like a Sunset Strip hooker, I naturally said Yes.

In the lobby of our London hotel, I ran into my old chum George Sanders.

"Welcome to London, old man," he said. "I hear you're doing *Laura* again."

"What are you doing here?" I asked him.

"You'll be pleased to know that we are once again united,"

drawled George. "My Waldo Lydekker and your detective didn't do enough damage to the original film. We're going to try again, but this time we have the advantage of a leading lady with no acting experience at all, so I think we'll succeed."

John Rich, our director, was chubby, myopic, and a highly talented man who might best be described as "oversexed." Our rehearsal hall overlooked King's Road, where mini-skirted dollies paraded their goodies. On windy days, I could see that John's mind may have been on Laura's Park Avenue apartment, but his libido was definitely on King's Road.

Our leading lady had frosted brown hair, the unmistakable Bouvier eyes set wide apart, and a slightly pointed chin. She was always dressed to the nines. This was Princess Lee Radziwill, or, as she had chosen to act under her maiden name, Lee Bouvier.

After the first reading, it was obvious that we had our work cut out. Besides George, my old partner in crime, the rest of the cast included Arlene Francis and Farley Granger, both experienced pros. For a first reading, the cast and director sit around a table and get to know each other and familiarize themselves with the story. No one expects a performance this early in the game, but when it came Lee's turn, she sounded as if she were reading "the gray cat jumped over the spotted dog."

The next step in putting a show together is to "get it on its feet." The cast begins to move, as the director works out crosses and camera angles. The scripts are still in hand, but now communication begins and parts of scenes start coming alive. I discovered, to my amazement, that Lee Radziwill had no idea how to move. On her first stage cross, she walked like a mechanical doll, a dead giveaway of an amateur.

There's an old theater story about a director who went out on the street looking for the perfect prostitute. He found her but, as soon as she found herself in front of a camera, she began doing an imitation of Queen Victoria. No amount of direction could make her be herself. Being yourself is acting natural in unnatural situations, and it often takes years of practice.

It wasn't Lee's fault. Cacoyanis and Capote had convinced her that because she had so much natural charm at cocktail parties, she would be perfect for Laura.

"You *are* Laura," they told her. "You'll just be playing

yourself." Capote was supposed to write the final screenplay, but perhaps he knew something the rest of us didn't. He took off unexpectedly for the Bahamas and we heard nothing more from him.

Lee never acknowledged any insecurity, no matter how terrible the rehearsals. Finally, even David began to panic as the shooting drew closer and the production still resembled a junior-high-school effort.

We were told that a press conference had been scheduled; Lee's debut could be covered by all the wire services. My life flashed in front of my eyes. This fiasco was not only going to be aired on prime-time TV, but every paper in the world would cover JFK's sister-in-law in her television debut—her debut and my demise.

The press hovered around the princess, and finally one journalist wandered over to me. He was an old man with half-moon glasses, from the *London Times*.

"And what do you do, young man," he said kindly. "Are you a technician?"

Instead of blurting out, "I'm playing the lead in this turkey," I nodded my head sagely and buried my beak in the nearest martini. Six months earlier I had received the *Télé Sept Jours* award and the trophy from *Cinémonde* as France's most renowned TV star. But the British censors had kept "The Untouchables" off English airwaves, and I wasn't about to change my luck now.

Lee was very social and couldn't get her priorities in order. Acting was all right as long as it didn't interfere with her important social engagements. Into the final week of rehearsals, she still didn't know her lines and was late for rehearsal. The brass suddenly decided that she should be replaced.

With a professional actress, the dismissal could have been easily, though brutally, accomplished. But Lee was the sister-in-law of the President of the United States, and to casually dismiss her would have been the deadly icing on the cake for this ill-fated and dubious project.

John Rich was instructed to be so professionally tough on her that she would withdraw. Ostensibly, she would quit rather than be fired. The cast refused to go along with this scheme, feeling that no matter how inadequate a performer she was, we could not allow her to be mistreated this way. We decided to use the last week as a crash course in acting for our poor, put-upon Laura.

The show was unlike anything I'd ever seen before. *Newsweek, Time,* and other assorted national magazines watched from a glass-enclosed booth where champagne, smoked salmon, and caviar were presented like offerings to the pagan gods for mercy.

We managed to get through it, more or less. When we got to the scene in which the detective gives Laura the third degree, David had some advice for me.

"Scare the hell out of her!" he whispered. "On her close-up, nothing's happening!"

I don't think Godzilla at his worst could have broken down Princess Radziwill's cafe-society cool, but I did manage to induce a faint expression of surprise when I suddenly threw a chair across the room and began poinding on the table and bellowing at her. After twenty-two takes, we were running out of chairs, my hand hurt, and I'd lost my voice entirely. But Susskind did get the rudimentary beginnings of a scene.

Farley Granger was cast in the Vincent Price role of Laura's bungling fiancé. During our love scene, however, Lee murmured in my ear, and in the forgotten microphone for all the press to hear, "You kiss better than Farley Granger." This little gem was printed verbatim in the next issue of *Newsweek*.

We all got to like Lee Radziwill and, having spent these many weeks trying to help, protect, and instruct her, we felt almost responsible for her. It's only ironic that when asked by one of the *Newsweek* reporters if she was grateful to the rest of the cast for all their help, she said, "No, they just did their job, no more!"

The Universal I knew is no more. It is now owned by Music Corporation of America, a mammoth organization that used to be a theatrical agency. In fact, they were my agents, twice; in the sixties, the agency became so huge that Attorney General Robert Kennedy forced them to choose between either running their studio or running their agency, not both. They chose the studio, which is by far the most solvent theatrical operation in the world.

Universal tours for visitors to Hollywood are an innovation and a clever way of killing the pig and recording the squeal.

They not only succeed in publicizing their product, but entertain at the same time. The tours also bring a lot of money into the studio bank accounts. Once a well-known actor got tired of all the fans being hauled past his dressing room to catch a glimpse of him. He blocked the street with his car. Within minutes, word came down from the black tower ordering him to either move his car to allow the tours to proceed as planned, or depart from the lot. The car was moved.

Another character actor, known for his war record and extracurricular boozing, decided to greet a tour trainload by unzipping his pants and giving his autograph in a highly unconventional manner. Word came from the tower that this actor could seek further employment at some other studio. He has not worked at Universal since.

The top Universal executives are mostly ex-MCA agents. This is about like a patient finding that his psychiatrist has become his boss. An agent is an actor's confidant, his crying towel; he knows his client's every weakness. Universal knows how to handle actors.

My old friend Jennings Lang, a Universal vice-president, flew to London to talk me into signing a picture-TV deal. (Notice that the motion picture part is always put first in the offer.) Universal had signed Tony Franciosa and Gene Barry for a three-star TV concept and needed a third body to complete the act. He began optimistically.

"You're probably not going to believe this, Bob," he said.

"You're probably right, Jennings," I said, "but go ahead anyway."

"I know you're a motion picture actor," he continued. "So to prove our good intentions, we'll guarantee you one major picture a year along with the classiest, most expensive television show on the air. It's called "Name of the Game."

Then he moved in for the kill. "Furthermore, you'll have as your leading lady in the first picture... BibiAndersson."

The name of Bibi Andersson did it. Here was a chance to work with Ingmar Bergman's protégée, the superb actress of *My Sister, My Love* and *Personna*.

Then the script arrived, and the picture in which I had been promised first-star billing had an unlikely title, *Story of a Woman*. We shot on location; Cortina d'Ampezzo, Stockholm, and Rome with Rosemarie and the kids made a nice trip.

Unfortunately, despite good reviews, the movie came in over budget and didn't make a nickel.

Thus was forged my future (and highly convoluted association) with MCA-Universal.

The idea of putting together twenty-four ninety-minute shows a year, using three actors who'd had their own successful TV series, was a courageous one, to say the least.

Sid Sheinberg was a tall, shy, rumpled-looking fellow who had just graduated from Universal's legal department to become boss of all TV. He has since gone on to greater glory as leader of the *Jaws* project, and has for the first time made Universal a power in theatrical films.

The first photo session was an indication of what was to come. It was a rat race, with Tony Franciosa, Gene Barry, and me jockeying for preferred positions. Left is good because your name is listed first. Being closest to camera is good because you look bigger. Being highest is good, as it makes you look important. And it's good to have your better photographic side showing. Claudette Colbert used to have sets rebuilt to accommodate her never having to show the "wrong" side.

What makes a photo session really suspenseful is that after the fooling around, all someone has to do is flip the negative, and everyone is reversed. This is especially tricky with *TV Guide*, a small weekly that has the largest circulation in the world, and knows it. If a performer displeases them, he gets the "label treatment." If he appears on the cover, the label with the name and address of the subscriber will be cleverly placed to cover his face like a giant Band-Aid. The treatment was given to Tony Franciosa when he failed to appear for a photo session the year before. Tony used more moves than a belly dancer, but still appeared headless to all of *TV Guide*'s subscribers.

This same magazine must have a live-in witch who can read the future; they always seem to know if a show will be canceled—even before the network knows it. To celebrate such an event, *TV Guide* often does a cover in living color, accompanied by a flattering story about the poor wretch about to be axed. For a borderline-rated show, a *TV Guide* cover can be as cheerful as a eulogy. Nor is this most-read of all TV publications above stirring up the pot to see what comes to the top.

A good way to do this is to assign a critic to review a show he detests. For example, when Roone Arledge (the boss man of sports and TV news at ABC), Joe Foss, and I did the first "American Sportsman" on safari in Africa, none of us expected it to be reviewed; no hunting show had been up to then. But *TV Guide* assigned Cleveland Amory, that preservationist of everything from the vampire bat to the malaria mosquito, to critique our African journey. He was particularly suited for the job since he had recently blasted Kirk Douglas, yours truly, and other "criminal" sporting types in a book he was trying to peddle. I can't really blame Cleveland; he was just "doin' what comes naturally." But, in the final analysis, television reviewers are as useless as tits on a bull. A good review has as little effect on the success of a show (the success quotient is the Nielsen rating) as a bad one has on its failure. "The American Sportsman" has enjoyed a decade of success and is still going strong.

Getting back to the "Name of the Game," the idea was an original one: three actors in three separate shows held together under the umbrella of *People* magazine. We each had our own production, but we were supposed to appear occasionally in each other's show for the sake of continuity. This went by the boards after Tony's first appearance as guest star with Gene Barry. Gene was overjoyed to play the Hearst-like boss of *People* with Tony and me as reporters. Tony and I were just as happy to let him have it. In the first guest scene, Tony was supposed to come into Barry's sumptuous office, look suitably impressed, and expectantly and respectfully take a seat. Instead, Tony made a breezy entrance, took a casual look around, loosened his tie, blew away some imaginary dust, carefully wiped the spotless chair, and then stretched out on the conference table. He had just reduced Barry's Hearst-like character to newsboy without a single line of dialogue.

Tony hadn't done a series in a while, and soon he began to worry about all the dialogue. One day I bumped into him over coffee.

"How are you doing with all the lines?" he asked.

"Okay, I guess," I said.

"Sure a lot of dialogue to learn."

"Sure is."

Tony paused and gave his nicest lost-little-boy look.

"I'm going to use a prompter."

"Idiot cards?"

"No, a teleprompter."

"Do you know how to use those things? I hear it takes practice."

"I'll make it work," said Tony.

The decision made, he walked off, his old jaunty self again.

Tony's first teleprompter trauma involved a wonderful old character actress who was imported from Europe for the show. The first time Tony began to read his words off the electric box instead of looking at her, the old lady just stood in shock. She'd never seen TV's substitute for memory before. The second time they ran through it, she started moving all over the set, and finally stood in front of the teleprompter, trying to catch Tony's eye. Finally, she broke the rehearsal wide open.

"Why you look at stupid black box, and not at me?" she said. "In all my life, I never work with actor who not look at me. You come here, young man." She went over to Tony, pulled him to her, and set him like a child on her lap.

"You got to look in my eyes and we do good scene together. Forget stupid black box. Just look in my eyes." Together they finally did the most moving scene in Tony's series. But TV pressure being what it is, Tony didn't give up the stupid black box. He just stopped importing old character actresses from Europe.

My film with Bibi Andersson had not been a smashing financial success. With a film factory like Universal, generally if you bomb out commercially on your first shot, that's the last chance you'll get. But since "Name of the Game" was doing well on television, Universal had to face the hated picture deal each year. The second year produced a legal battle when the studio tried canceling. The Universal brass offered Geneviève Bujold, the Academy Award nominee for *Anne of a Thousand Days* (opposite Richard Burton), a minor supporting role in my film. Geneviève naturally refused. This seemed to surprise no one in the Universal tower. In fact, a foul rumor went around that the whole procedure had been planned to provide an excuse to abandon the picture—not an unusual studio maneuver. (Once an actor is already committed to a television series, an excuse, no matter how flimsy, can be found to scuttle his film commitments.)

I threatened to sue, and got as far as getting a court date before I was paid off, in small amounts over a year's time.

But the Bujold episode was only a sneak preview of what was to come the third year: Richard Burton, the Great Diamond, Henry Hathaway, and a mysterious fellow called Harry Tattleman.

By the third year, the federal government had banned cigarette advertising on television. The network and the studio were suddenly both afraid that no other sponsor would cover "the most expensive show on TV." So "Name of the Game" was dropped. Actually it could have gone on for another three years, if anyone had had the guts to stay with it.

When a studio uses movies to entice an actor to do television, its interest in the movies disappears in a hurry if the television commitments don't work out. I had an idea of what to expect next.

The studio was forced by contract to submit three properties with million-dollar budgets to me. If I turned them all down, they were off the hook. I had to read the first two with a vomit cup, and the third was a piece of cheese, almost as bad, called *Raid on Rommel*. The producer's name on the script was Harry Tattleman. The fact that I had never heard of Harry Tattleman confirmed my ignorance of a particularly clever ploy used by Universal to salvage something from an expensive but unsuccessful film.

In a walk-up office, far from the madding crowd, a Harry Tattleman can carefully choose and edit visuals, special effects, hundreds of extras, foreign locations, and expensive sets—all of these films simply reels of leftover, loser films. They are glued together by a skilled editor; he can then add any necessary new footage photographed on a mini-schedule and using a less expensive cast. A script is developed to use all the impressive old footage (only the backs of the original actors' heads are allowed to show), while close-ups of the new "stars" are inserted into an entirely new plot.

The studio may gross enough to make up the deficit incurred by the original film, since the contract players who "star" in these epics have little choice of material.

Raid on Rommel was just such a project, based on the movie *Tobruk,* starring Rock Hudson and George Peppard. Pieces from that earlier movie were rearranged like the pieces of a jigsaw puzzle. Of course, a new "script" had been concocted and I was offered the job of replacing Hudson and Peppard in the close-ups.

Since this was the studio's third submission, I had a dandy choice: I either took it or blew a lot of money. I took it.

I called the studio and said, "I'll do it."

"Do what?" came the reply.

"Raid on Rommel!"

"Are you kidding?"

I wasn't kidding, but I decided to make the studio work for it.

I demanded a private projection room to run all the film of Rommel's desert saga, documentaries of tank warfare, any German films available ("to get the feel of the period") and then scheduled my first production meeting.

Harry Tattleman is a very nice gentleman and I hope by now he's recovered.

I began with, "You understand, Mr. Tattleman, this must be a million-dollar picture. Even though there is a three-week schedule, it will be the most expensive three-week picture ever made. Sixty percent of the film is already shot and I'll have a CPA determine its value. The rest of the million will have to be spent on cast and production. James Mason and Laurence Olivier would be good, I think."

"Mr. Stack," he said, "these pictures don't cost anywhere near one million. I've never had a star like you in one of these pictures. And Mason and Olivier—it's unheard of!"

I continued to play the game.

"Then this will be a new experience for both of us," I said.

My agent called me a few days later. "Guess who your co-star is in *Raid on Rommel*?" he said.

"Mickey Mouse?"

"No," he said. "Richard Burton."

"Look, I'm in no mood for fun and games."

"Honest to God, he said he'd do it."

"Has he lost his mind?"

"Beats me, but it makes for an interesting discussion. You're guaranteed first billing in the contract."

In Puerto Vallarta, Richard Burton was being bombarded by scripts by all the studios. In the middle of all of them was *Raid on Rommel*. No one had bothered to tell him that the opus had already been cast.

Richard, as the story goes, needed money to cover the insurance on the diamond he had presented to Elizabeth Taylor, an event which had been dutifully covered in detail by the world press. He chose *Raid on Rommel* because it could be made on a cheap budget in Mexico and he would have a big piece of the action, with no taxes.

When Burton accepted, he insisted that Henry Hathaway, a veteran film director, be a part of the deal. Of course, Universal didn't tell Hathaway, either, that his picture already had a leading man. Like Scarlett O'Hara, they decided to worry about that problem later.

Henry Hathaway, one of Hollywood's legendary directors, was an old friend. Film critic Arthur Knight once called Henry the least appreciated director in town. His credits ranged from the first American color outdoor film, *Trials of Lonesome Pine*, to such classics as *Lives of a Bengal Lancer*, *Peter Ibbetson* (with Gary Cooper), and *The House on 92nd Street*. Now, at an age when lesser men might be thinking about retiring, Henry had just finished his greatest triumph, directing my old pal Duke Wayne in *True Grit*.

I had never worked with Henry before, but I knew his reputation as a director of the "spare the rod" school in dealing with actors. In short, he was a great chum away from the set, but when it came to making pictures, there was no question as to who was in charge.

There are very few moments when an actor can face the powers that control his destiny and not be squashed in the process. My moment came outside the Universal commissary one sunny Tuesday afternoon at one-thirty. Out strode Henry Hathaway, a symbol of all the authoritarian directors of Hollywood, cigar clenched in teeth, jaw thrust forward, clouds of expensive Havana leaf forming an effective smoke screen to keep away peasants and unemployed actors.

His gimlet blue eyes noticed me. He paused, made his decision to stride over to me, and announced: "The studio tells me they're trying to find a part for you in my picture. Sorry, kid, there's nothing there you could do. Burton's got the only part."

A slow flush began at my toes and worked its way to my face; the flush of power. "Henry, I've been thinking it over," I said. "I'm just not sure you're the right director for my picture."

"What the hell are you talking about?" growled Hathaway. "Your picture? You're not even in it. It's Burton's picture."

"Henry, you better call the legal department. They'll explain it all to you."

"I'm not calling any damn legal department."

"Well, I'd just hate to see you make your plans and then have to change them. I'm playing the lead in *Raid on Rommel*, not Richard Burton."

He almost bit the cigar in half. With one last piercing look in my direction, he was off.

The next day, I dyed my hair blond. Actually it came out nearer to orange, since the young man who took care of the dye showed up bagged and dropped part of the stuff on the bathroom floor. But at least it proved to one and all that I was serious. For three months, every time I went skeet shooting or played golf, some bastard would whistle or greet me with "hey, Red, throw me a kiss." The closest the studio ever got to the truth was to ask Richard if he'd mind my co-starring with him.

Richard, the gent that he is, said, "Of course not." By now I felt a little guilty and, with as straight a face as I could muster, I told Henry that I would agree to let Richard Burton play my part if I were paid off (in full) to assuage my humiliation over losing such a golden opportunity.

The studio quietly agreed.

Raid on Rommel was badly reviewed and a box-office failure. To this day, I still can't believe that two such heavyweights wanted to do something I tried so hard to avoid.

I still wonder what Harry Tattleman said when they told him, "Stack's decided not to do *Raid on Rommel*. Richard Burton is going to do it."

I first saw Richard Burton as Prince Hal at Stratford-upon-Avon. Humphrey Bogart, Lauren Bacall, Radie Harris, a New York syndicated columnist, and I decided to take a trip to Stratford. Bogart, the big star, was given a Rolls-Royce, though no one told him it was a 1929 model. I tagged along in my nondescript Ford. By the time Bogie arrived, after covering miles of cobblestone roads on the 1929 hard-pressure tires, he disappeared into a local pub; only Betty's expert persuasion could get him into the theater.

Young Burton was the most electric actor I'd ever seen. Even Bogie said, "The kid is good." Betty and Radie's only comment was "my God, he's sexy." I've never seen a performer handle the classics with such joy and gusto. His particular Welsh madness, the glorious voice, and that go-to-hell look in the eye were devastating. Later we went back to an ancient English manse he shared with the equally mad Hugh Griffith (the Falstaff to his Hal). As we entered, we heard the baying of hounds. Corgis from everywhere leaping over the furniture as if they were running in the Grand National Steeplechase. The baronial living room had a massive fireplace, but hiding furtively in its center was a tiny electric heater, the only source of warmth for the entire house. Richard had now donned a raggedy green turtleneck sweater, the same one I saw him wear a week later at a formal party.

He was Laurence Olivier's protégé, and could have been the greatest actor in the world. Many have said that Richard should have allowed his potential to develop, as Olivier had. But I'll make you a wager that if Richard were given the choice today between Shakespeare and Liz Taylor, or between the green turtleneck and the good life, he wouldn't change a thing.

To keep the record straight, I have no vendetta with Universal studios. Doris and Jules Stein are close friends. I've known Lew and Edie Wasserman since I first started in the business, and two nicer people would be hard to find. UI would have been a super place to work if my first picture had been a box-office smash. But MCA was never geared to wait for a return on its investment. I've still got a soft spot in my heart for Universal, because of my kiss with Deanna and my Academy Award nomination for *Written on the Wind*. Most of all, I am grateful to UI for a personal favor: When Rosemarie was almost killed in a terrible automobile accident during the days of "Name of the Game," they turned over an entire studio trunk telephone line to me so I could get her the best possible medical attention. Now if they could just find Harry Tattleman a decent script!

People outside our racket make the mistake of thinking the television business is rational. Well, it isn't. There's a great big puppet master in the sky who pulls the strings. Sometimes he gets the strings all tangled but, after all, he's only human. Well, no, as a matter of fact, he's not human, so I guess he just likes working with tangled strings. This, of course, explains the success of "Charlie's Angels," a police drama about three beautiful detectives. They look like fashion models, have perfect hairdos, sexy clothes, and are undercover (in more ways than one). They take orders from a boss they never see, but he tells them what to do through a loudspeaker. I was once finishing a movie for television called *Murder on Flight 502*. It was a bad copy of *The High and the Mighty*, but it gave Rosemarie, our daughter Elizabeth, and me a chance to work together in the same film. My leading lady was a gorgeous blond model with a good tennis game, but not much experience as an actress. However, she had one quality that really impressed me: a sense of humor about herself. When "Angels" set the TV tubes on fire, she was asked the reason for their phenomenal success. Most performers usually take advantage of this question and make pompous noises about how great the executives, producers, writers, crew, and fellow actors are. Farrah Fawcett-Majors replied, "We became number one when we all decided to take off our bras." She has since made enough money—thanks to her famous photo, Farrah dolls, and a three-million-dollar contract with Fabergé—to buy her own studio.

Did you like the movie *M*A*S*H*, and think the series based on it is the best show on television? Surely this was not an accident, right? Wrong!

I was at Martin Ransohoff's house last year, when an executive told me *M*A*S*H* was born because of a lousy transoceanic phone connection. He said one of the Twentieth Century-Fox brass in London gave the go-ahead for the film thinking his representative in Hollywood was talking about another film under discussion. When he returned, the conversation went something like this:

"Who gave the okay for this turkey?"

"You did, sir."

"Are you nuts, a comedy about medics in Korea, covered in blood? And for a leading man, we've got Barbra Streisand's ex-husband; no one's ever heard of him!"

Actually, many Academy Award winning performances have resulted from the same type of situation. I can't forget *It Happened One Night*. Clark Gable had been misbehaving at Metro, his home studio; to put him in his place, the studio lent him to Columbia for "a little 'nothing' picture" with an unknown director named Frank Capra. The studio figured he'd turn it down and go on suspension. But Clark needed the money, and history was made. The movie was a smash, and Clark became such a sex symbol that when he decided not to wear an undershirt, he did the same thing for the poor manufacturer of undershirts that Farrah Fawcett-Majors did for the makers of bras. The hitchhiking scene with Claudette Colbert is still used as an example of what motion picutre comedy is all about. The "unknown" Frank Capra became one of Hollywood's legendary directors.

Such accidents continually happen. An old friend and many times guest star on "The Untouchables" decided to try his hand at carrying his own show. Before it hit the air, he had so little confidence in the project, he apologized for it in every interview he gave. Its initial reception was negative: "racist, an exercise in bigotry, an unhealthy step backwards." The public, however, fell in love with Archie Bunker and his family, and Carroll O'Connor became the country's most beloved bigot.

Styles in TV series are as changeable as they are for women's clothes. A while back, westerns were "in." Then came doctors and lawyers, followed by cops and private eyes. They then dissolved into the funny cop, and finally, today, TV is dominated by "t and a" (tits and ass).

The reason for all this is not only a change in taste. After all, Adam dug what Eve was all about. But the influence of pressure groups on the networks can't be underestimated. A famous jingle of the sixties, Make Love, Not War, has suddenly become the answer for networks besieged by those protesting violence on the tube. Other various protective groups are now hung up by the antiviolence crusade, since they can't logically be against everything and, after all, sex is certainly not as noisy as violence.

This has given the networks a hook that appeals to dirty old men of all ages. So in one TV series, "James at Fifteen," young James gets involved with a luscious, nubile Scandinavian lass of sixteen, has an affair, worries about having made her pregnant, and later thinks he has contracted gonorrhea, pointing up the moral that sex is only dirty or censorable after sixteen. The producer proclaimed, perhaps rightly so, that he was merely "telling it like it is." But the fallout from this particular segment of the show was an eye-opener. No guy I ever talked to gave a hoot about James and his problems; all they wanted to know was the name of the sixteen-year-old Swedish dish. Each one of these studs was over eighteen, but the young girl was so luscious and, more to the point, so available, that each one of these average American viewers was a vicarious statutory rapist. For the impressionable "sickie" viewer, this type of show could be a strong catalyst for the violence of rape, and end by being more harmful than the violence of general mayhem in the action shows.

As short-shorts become shorter, braless bosoms larger, and the girls younger and dingier, TV has literally become the *boob* tube; men all over the country are canceling their *Playboy* subscriptions. Don't get me wrong, I'm not a moralist. I'm just mad we couldn't have put more pizazz into "The Untouchables." I can remember when a cleavage had to be covered by fabric or a cloth flower sewn to the top of the dress. Hookers on our show were as sexy as Whistler's mother. I'm not complaining; I just wish the party had started earlier.

For a guy who's continually being called Sam Straight, I've managed to play young empty-headed comedians, a weird, bearded hunchback, a fruity-looking pirate, America's top naval hero, a schizoid airline pilot, a drunken psychotic wife-beater, and finally, the scourge of the Mafia. But leave it to Quinn Martin—my old partner in crime, the producer of "The Untouchables"—to come up with something no one had ever thought of before. He sent me a script for a TV movie called "Most Wanted." There were five characters: an electronics expert; a hippie street cop; a black major; a middle-aged, retired police captain; and a lady police psychiatrist, who was the lead. The cryptic note attached by my agent to the script said, "Quinn wants you for the lead."

Okay, I thought. *Quinn made a show about prohibition when everyone else turned down the idea. Maybe he has another, even more daring project, something like an Untouchable who went to Sweden and came back as policewoman Angie Dickinson.*

The psychiatrist in this particular show was supposed to investigate a group of nuns who had been raped, and, using her feminine wiles, find the culprit and bring him to justice. To show you how important any one actor (or even a particular sex) is to a TV show, "Most Wanted" became a vehicle for me as a TV series without a sex change. All the psychiatrist's lines were simply given to the police captain.

Our opening program was scheduled for the same night as another equally bizarre effort which preceded us on the air. "Charlie's Angels" featured cops who wore bikinis and false eyelashes, and both shows had the very same high rating.

Many years ago, in old Hollywood, a bewhiskered, sandaled, raggedy character called Peter the Hermit would occasionally come down from the hills. No one knew whether he was a great teacher or a little "teched" in the head, but he told me something I've never forgotten. It's helped me through some times that defy explanation.

"Remember son," he said, "everything is nothing and nothing is everything."

The everything part started like gangbusters. ABC, the network that won its first Emmy through our "Untouchables," now ranked first among the three major networks. We were set for Thursday night, in a perfect ten-o'clock time slot, following Karl Malden in the very successful series, "The Streets of San Francisco." Every executive told us what a smash we'd be; at the party for the ABC affiliate stations, I got a rousing ovation.

Without warning, the pit boss in the sky switched the dice. Fred Silverman, then golden boy of ABC, broke the rules and changed the master schedule to confound the other networks. The net result was that we were moved to ten o'clock on Saturday night, a time slot often referred to as "the graveyard shift." For ten straight years Carol Burnett had destroyed all opposition.

"We realize it's a tough time slot, fellows," we were told. "But we think your show is strong enough to do what no ABC show has ever done. It's really an honor. We're going to give you the chance to knock off Carol Burnett...and this we'll promise you. If you win, you'll be heroes to everyone at the network."

I got hold of Quinn.

"I don't want to be a hero. Let Karl Malden have the honor," I said. "If 'Streets of San Francisco' doesn't make it, he's always got American Express Travelers Checks to protect him."

CBS had comedy locked up on Saturday night with "All in the Family," "The Mary Tyler Moore Show," "The Bob Newhart Show," and "The Carol Burnett Show." After ten years, Carol's audience of loyal fans never let her show drop below thirty in the Nielsen ratings. Only something like *Star Wars* could turn Burnett's loyal family into Benedict Arnolds. ABC had tried everything and failed dismally. Now NBC was planning to program a library of motion pictures on Saturdays. They dubbed this mixture of "a few biggies and a lot of leftovers" The Saturday Night Movie. We knew that no *single* TV show could break that CBS rating, but we didn't know what effect the NBC *movies* would have on Carol Burnett's ratings or on ours.

Today, TV series no longer have the break-in time of the past. Some shows have needed half a season and lots of changes before they soared to the top of the ratings. Today, unfortunately, a network executive runs so scared that success must be instant. If a show doesn't "grab heavy numbers" right away, the executive responsible for the show may suddenly decide to "go into independent production." This is equivalent to an actor's "developing a property." Both terms mean the same thing—unemployment!

The opening show of "Most Wanted" ran right into John Wayne (the NBC movie) as its competition. Next came Clint Eastwood, and then Burt Reynolds. We knew there had to be a *Beach Blanket Bingo* or *Teenage Werewolf* in the NBC movie library coming up soon—if we could just hold out. The next week, NBC served up their first bad movie and a funny thing happened. Carol Burnett kept her usual thirty Nielsen rating, but we stole enough viewers from NBC's movie to give ABC their first Saturday night victory. That's the way it happened. When the NBC movie was strong, Carol won with her army. When it wasn't, we won.

So, here's Peter the Hermit's script so far. We started with "nothing": the offer of a story with a female lead which became "everything" of a pilot film that had a great rating and was placed on ABC's preferred Thursday slot, back to the "nothing" of being moved to Saturday night's graveyard shift opposite the tremendously talented Carol Burnett, back to the "everything" of stealing the movie audience and giving ABC its first Saturday night fever. And so it went, from success to disaster.

We were preempted so many times no one knew when the show was on. (An audience expecting "Most Wanted" might find itslef watching a Miss Teenage America contest, specials on abortion and wife-beating, and political plugs by candidates.) Still, at the end of the season, we somehow had worked our way up into the top ten. When we got to number seven, we gave a big party to celebrate the good news. The next day, we were canceled!

Some time later, a rumor working its way around the studio reached my ears. At a board meeting our producer got into an argument with the head of the network. To make a point, in anger, he threw an ashtray down on the desk. Unfortunately, it took one bounce and hit the network president in the chest.

The next day, not only "Most Wanted," but "The Streets of San Francisco" and all the producer's pilots were canceled. Two weeks later, the network head left ABC for NBC.

No matter how hard I tried to live by Peter the Hermit's formula, I had to ask the obvious. *I know none of it's supposed to make sense,* I thought, *but I've been told for twenty years nothing matters but the numbers. No show in the number seven spot has ever been canceled.* I flashed to an echo of the past. "No one who's won the *Variety* poll has ever lost the Academy Award.... And the winner is... Tony Quinn."

But then I felt a glow of well-being. *What the hell?* I thought. *Knowing would take all the fun out of it. Because after all, everything was all right, and nothing mattered. Or was it the other way around? In any case, I'll let Peter worry about it.*

A couple of months ago I received a bottle of champagne and a card which read, "'Most Wanted' is the number one television show in France and Mexico. Congratulations!"

So the game goes on.

When I was approached a short time ago to host a TV special dealing with crime in America, it seemed a natural, given my association with fictional crime. The idea was to interview three real underworld characters. The questions were only to be disclosed on the air and, to protect the guilty, two of the three were to wear ski masks.

As it turned out, my growing-up years at Tahoe had hardly prepared me for this experience. The three gentlemen to be interviewed were: Joey, a garrulous, self-proclaimed hit-man; Tony, who had turned informer when the syndicate threatened his wife; and an old Hollywood underworld character called Mickey Cohen. I began to realize that I was dealing with the real thing when Tony made his entrance flanked by two uniformed guards with guns. A lot of the procedure dealing with these "most wanted" types was set up without our knowledge.

The first incident occurred when the poor makeup man came through the back door carrying his makeup kit. He was slammed against the wall by the armed guards; his makeup kit went flying.

"What's in the box, buddy?" they demanded.

"Makeup," came the startled reply. His eyes were fixed on the .38 pressed against his navel.

Suddenly, from the land of make-believe, we were hauled into an arena where none of us belonged. The producer had forgotten to tell us that there was a $500,000 contract on Tony, and that none of the crew was supposed to use that door.

Rosemarie's parting words as I left the house were, "Remember, you're not dealing with actors. Don't do anything crazy."

I assured her not to worry. "They're wearing masks," I said. "No sweat."

"I know," she said, "but are you wearing one?"

If ever I saw death, I saw it in Tony's eyes. He had resigned himself to the inevitable. The guards' precaution of moving him to a different hotel every day didn't help. As he slipped the ski mask over his face, the effect became really weird. His mouth moved, but the eyes never changed; they looked like two gravestones.

Now we began the interview.

"Were you a member of the mob?"

He nodded affirmatively.

"Have you ever killed a man?"

He answered yes.

I should have had enough brains never to ask the next question. "Would you tell us the name of your last victim, and describe the circumstances under which you killed him?"

Out of that ski mask peered the eyes of an attack dog about to go for the jugular. In a deadly whisper, he said, "You know better than to ask that!"

I looked up at the director in the control booth for his support, but he was the same shade of gray I was. I remembered Rosemarie's parting words and wondered what in hell I was doing there.

I deleted the other inflammatory questions, and we were happily through with Tony.

Joey was a horse (or a hood) of another color. You couldn't shut him up. He kept offering information of which I wanted absolutely no part. When he was asked if he thought the underworld had made an attempt on the life of Fidel Castro, he took the ball and ran. A simple yes would have been fine, but he went on to describe the would-be assassin as a great swimmer who was dropped off the shore of Cuba with a scoped rifle in a waterproof bag. He even gave us the killer's name and identified the mob that supplied him.

Out of the corner of my eye I could see the director giving the cut sign to shut him up. I thought I would get away from the prepared script and ask my own questions to cool things down.

"Joey," I said, "I can't understand why Sam Giancanna, Chicago's contribution to the underworld, was killed with a .22-caliber pistol. Hit-men have always used .38s and .45s in the past. Why shoot him six times in the mouth with a .22?"

"Seven times," Joey said.

The pause must have lasted ten seconds.

I didn't want to mention the fact that all the newspapers said he had been shot six times—or find out how he knew about the seventh shot. I just wanted to go home.

Mickey Cohen, our third guest, was a shadow of his former self. He'd been beaten terribly in prison. His speech was slurred and his walk was a tentative shuffle. At one time, this little character had attracted the attention of studio executives. A newswoman named Florabelle Muir had sponsored him, and the dollies had hung around in droves. He and Ben "Bugsie" Siegel were fixtures in Hollywood. Like Jimmy Cagney and Edward G. Robinson, they were regarded more as characters than as actual hoods. But make no mistake, they were the real thing.

Bugsie went to that great crap table in the sky when he forgot to furnish the Vegas mob with a lump of money from a shipment of drugs. He told them the shipment had been hijacked. True to their code of not wasting anyone in the Vegas city limits, they waited until he reached Beverly Hills before they blew him away.

Mickey almost got his opportunity to be listed in the mob's who's who (who *was* who) one early morning on Sunset Strip. He was walking out of a strip joint when, from across the street, a hit man jumped up from behind a billboard and let go with a sawed-off shotgun. Mickey's bodyguard was hit, but Mickey moved so quickly that he was flat on the pavement before the gun went off.

Now, however, Mickey made a pathetic figure. His garbled verbal ramblings didn't make much sense. Toward the end of the show, I asked him why he had become involved with the rackets.

"Well, you got a profession, ain't you?" he said. "I'm just earning a living like any other citizen. There's always gonna be guys like me. Somebody's got to do this job."

So much for the future of law and order.

Epilogue

Several months before my mother passed away, I discovered an old photograph of Rudolph Valentino's wedding party. There, as clear as could be, was mother, a member of the wedding. When I asked her about the photo, and why she had never told me about the Valentino wedding, she said simply that I had never asked her. Past glories and triumphs provided a treasure trove of rich memories for her, but she believed in leaving them where they belonged—in the past.

Perhaps it runs in the family but I, too, have always believed in living today for tomorrow. I do not keep scrapbooks or spend time dwelling on yesterday. Hollywood has changed radically since I began in pictures; the ingenuous innocence of Deanna's era has given way to an audience that can only smile indulgently when reminded of the teapot tempest surrounding our first kiss. The wild, macho days of Tracy and Gable had a spirit all their own. I was fortunate, young as I was, to be a part of the incredible fun and good times.

Happily, and much to my surprise, mother did keep scrapbooks. In an old tin strongbox—along with her autographed pictures of Thomas Edison and Wallace Reid, and her lifesaving certificate—were dozens of photographs of a life I was too busy living to frame and remember.

But now the memories came flooding back. The frightened, tearful boy crying in French and Italian at Ellis Island gave way to a young athlete stumbling into the wonderfully wacky picture business. And almost overnight, it seems, Deanna's *First Love* became the intense, wild-eyed madman of *Written on the Wind*.

In some ways, my life was like a movie, full of twists and turns. What an impressive cast of characters I worked with along the way: mother, with the style and grace of a bygone era; dad, roaring through life as if he wanted to outrun it; Gil Stuart, charging around Hollywood like a British Don Quixote, armed with the best intentions and the worst of luck; Carole Lombard teaching me what glamor meant; and Gable, with a little help from his best scotch, telling me what the responsibilities of an actor really were.

And there were so many others: Harry Fleischmann showing me how to be a man by example; Al Jepson living life at 1,000 miles per hour; Luis and Felix Briones, ready to die on camera rather than turn in a bad performance; and that nameless soldier in Vietnam with a boy's years and a man's courage. Duke Wayne cast a heroic shadow as a model for me and so many others.

But it is time to move on. Have things really changed that much since that day when I wandered onto Joe Pasternak's set at Universal?

While spending a few uncharacteristic moments thinking about yesterday, the phone rang. My good duck-hunting buddy John Milius was about to produce a thirty-million-dollar film called *1941*. Steven Spielberg, director of *Jaws* and *Close Encounters of the Third Kind* hadn't found anyone he thought was right for the role of General Joe Stilwell. Every actor in Hollywood was ready to give his eyeteeth for the role, but Spielberg turned thumbs down on so many that John accused him of wanting to dig up the original.

"Hey, Bob," John said, "thanks for a great duck shoot."

"Glad you enjoyed it, John," I said.

"How'd you like to play Vinegar Joe?"

"Who?"

"General Joseph Stilwell."

Holy Toledo! I thought, *a quantum jump into a thirty-mil-*

lion-dollar motion picutre, a chance to work with the wunderkind of Hollywood, a part light years away from Eliot Ness.

After I unglued my tongue from my palate, I said, "I'd like that very much, John. But I'm curious. Why me?"

"Well," said Milius, "when we were up at the duck lodge, you ordered us around like a general commanding his troops! And since you wear goggles when you shoot, we started thinking about General Stilwell and his glasses!"

For a moment, only a moment, I was back on that sound stage in the era of the real General Stilwell. For no reason, Joe Pasternak had popped that most improbable of all questions all over again. "How would you like to be in pictures?"

Of course, I thought to myself, *but there won't be a widow's peak this time.*

"One thing, though," Milius went on. "We're going to have to rearrange your hair. In fact, we're going to cut it off."

"It's okay, John," I said. "For Gerneral Stilwell, I'll cut my throat."

I wish my friend Peter the Hermit were still around. He'd just nod his head and give me his strange enchanted grin. With memories of Jack Pierce and the widow's peak dancing in my head, I called my barber. As they say in France, *"Plus ça change, plus c'est la même chose."*

So here I go again, wondering where it all will lead. In pictures you may end up as Rocky—or just punchy. I'm more than grateful for the good times. I've had a ball.

And what about that question my friends were asking me on the first page of my story? Who am I? Probably someone who enjoys finding out every day, trying to guess what's around the bend, and absolutely convinced that whatever it is, every day should be an adventure. Of course, I may end up as I did in the *tienta,* facing a charging pair of horns and asking myself, "How did I ever get into this?" But then I'll smile because I know that not knowing is one of the special joys of living.

Index

Academy Awards, 45–46
Academy of Motion Picture Arts and Sciences, 84, 224
Adair, Jack, 32
Adler, Buddy, 220, 224–27
Agar, John, 203
Allen, Irwin, 231
Amory, Cleveland, 330
Andersson, Bibi, 328, 331
Archer, Tony, 285–86, 289–93, 297–98
Arledge, Roone, 284, 330
Arlen, Richard, 198
Armillita (bull-fighter), 165–67
Arnaz, Desi, 252–54, 267–68, 272, 276
Astoya (mystic), 38–39
Avedon, Doe, 188–89, 197–98

"Baby Leroy" (Ronald Leroy Winnebrenner), 80–81
Bacall, Lauren, 222–23, 335
Badlands of Dakota, 77–79
Bankhead, Tallulah, 150–51
Barry, Gene, 328–30

Barrymore, Diana, 76–77, 111–12
Barrymore, John, 138, 144
Beatty, Warren, 26, 75
Behymer, Lynden Ellsworth, 12
Belasco, 149, 151, 152–53
Belcher, Marge, 35
Benchley, Robert, 85–87
Benny, Jack, 62, 105–07
Boetticher, Budd, 165–68, 174–76, 182–83
Bogart, Humphrey, 144, 219, 335
Bond, Ward, 96, 190
Bonelli, Richard (a/k/a Richard Bonn) (uncle), 31, 38–40
"Bones" (Cal-Neva Lodge boss), 28–30
Bottome, Phyllis, 95
Bowe, Rosemarie. *See* Stack, Rosemarie Bowe
Brand, Neville, 254, 263–64
Brandeis, Johnny, 298–99
Brando, Marlon, 249–50
Brauner, Arthur, 246, 250
Briones, Felix, 169, 175–77, 347

349

Briones, Luis, 168–70, 175–81, 183–84, 347
Britton, Barbara, 157
Bronston, Sam, 242
Bujold, Geneviève, 331
Bullfighter and the Lady, The, 4, 164–84, 210, 211, 290, 313
Burnett, Carol, 340–41
Burton, Richard, 250, 331–36
Bwana Devil, 155–60, 288

Cabot, Bruce, 244–45
Cacoyannis, Michael, 324–26
Cal–Neva Lodge (nightclub), 27–30
Capone, Al (in "The Untouchables"), 6, 18, 252–56, 263, 272–73, 282
Capote, Truman, 324–26
Capra, Frank, 129–30, 337–38
Carrillo, Leo, 18, 23
Catching, Bill, 247–49, 257
Cavens, Al, 315–16, 318
Champion, Gower, 35
Chennault, General Clair, 124
Chevalier, Maurice, 80–81
Chung, Ma, 124–25
Clayton, Billy, 44–48
Clift, Montgomery, 104
Cobb, Lee J., 321–23
Coburn, Bob, 98
Coburn, Charles, 240–41
Coburn, James, 250
Cohen, Mickey, 342–45
Colbert, Claudette, 237–38, 338
Cole, Nat King, 27
Confessions of a Nazi Spy, 95
Cooper, Merion, 113
Corrupt Ones, The, 245–49
Courtship of Miles Standish, The, 84
Coverman, Ida May, 27
Crabe, Jimmy, 294–95, 297
Crawford, Broderick, 77–79
Crockett, Dick, 160–61
Crosby, Bing, 130
Cukor, George, 109–11

Cummings, Bob, 186
Curtis, Tony, 79

Dailey, Dan, 95–96, 213
Darios, George, 200–01, 204–05, 208
Darvi, Bella, 218–20
Date with Judy, A, 142–43
Davis, Bette, 137, 240–42
Davis, Sammy, 27
Davis, Sammy, Jr., 144
Day of the Delinquents, The (*Le Soleil des Voyous*), 250
Dean, James, 162
DeCarlo, Yvonne, 79
Defiant Ones, The, 79
DeHaven, Gloria, 139
deHavilland, Olivia, 137
Deirde (pseudonym), 210–11, 225–26
DeKova, Frank, 263–64
Delon, Alain, 270
DeMott, Lt. Thomas, Jr., 127–28
Dempsey, Jack, 19
deSegurola, Andrés, 68–69
deToth, André ("Bondi"), 158–59
Devine, Andy, 52, 57, 78
Dietrich, Marlene, 250
Disney, Walt, 35, 83
Dumont, Jack, 33
Dunaway, Faye, 26, 69
Durbin, Deanna, 1, 6, 13, 68–71, 74–77, 89, 217, 346, 347

Eagle Squadron, 111–113
Easton, Jon, 91–92
Edwards, Nate, 169–70
El Capitan College of Theater, 37

Fairbanks, Douglas, 315–16
Falk, Peter, 260–61
Farrow, John, 239–40
Fawcett-Majors, Farrah, 337–38
Feldari, Eric, 103
Feldman, Charles, 201
Fellows, Bob, 186, 195–96
Ferguson, Helen, 314–15, 316

INDEX

Fernandez, Abel, 258
Fields, W. C., 80–82
Fighter Squadron, 143
First Love, 70–71, 74–77, 217, 347
Fitzgerald, F. Scott, 87, 100
Fleischmann, Harry, 42–48, 50–53, 347
Fleming, Victor, 57
Flowers, A. D., 257–58, 267
Flynn, Errol, 134–41, 226
Flynn, Norma, 139
Fonda, Henry, 300, 309
Fonda, Jane, 311
Ford, John, 188, 190, 216–17
Forever Amber, 176
Fortuna, Diego, 176
Foss, Joe, 283–85, 289, 294–95, 330
Foy, Bryney, 158
Fraley, Oscar, 252
Franciosa, Tony, 328–31
Frank, Anne, 89–90
Frankenheimer, John, 321
Franklin, Sydney, 165, 183–84
Frankovich, Mike, 107–09
Frazier, Brenda, 62
Fuller, Sam, 213–17

Gable, Clark, 50–51, 57, 70, 72, 96–104, 120, 144, 337, 346–47
Gann, Ernest K., 185, 197
Garbo, Greta, 105, 109–11
Garden of Allah, 81, 86–88
Garland, Judy, 2, 25, 26–27
Garnett, Tay, 123
Garroway, Will, 31
Garson, Greer, 137
Geisler, Jerry, 135
Georgiade, Nick, 258
Gilbert, Billy, 83
Girl of the Golden West, 149–51
Golden Mistress, The, 201–03
Goldenson, Leonard, 274
Goldwyn, Sam, 317

Good Morning Miss Dove, 217
Gordon, Bruce, 254–56, 259, 274
Grable, Betty, 85–86
Granger, Farley, 325–27
Grant, Jimmy, 175
Granville, Bonita, 96
Grauman, Sid, 194–95
Grauman, Wally, 264
Grauman's Chinese Theater, 194–95
Grauman's Egyptian Theater, 194–95
Griffin, Eleanor, 217
Gunzberg, Dr. (3-D inventor), 155–56, 159

Hale, Alan, Jr., 160
Hammerstein, Oscar, II, 161, 163
Hansen, Betty, 135
Hardin, Ty, 146
Hargrave, Homer, 133
Harlow, Jean, 104
Harris, Radie, 335
Hart, Lorenz, 161
Hathaway, Henry, 334–35
Havoc, June, 149–53
Hayworth, Rita, 35
Hecht, Ben, 105
Heflin, Van, 238–39, 252
Hemingway, Ernest, 164–65
Herbert, Hugh, 83
High and the Mighty, The, 185–99, 213
Hill, James, 245–46
Hilton, Barron, 102
Hommes, Ray, 101–03
Hope, Bob, 130
Hopper, Hedda, 26, 69, 137
House of Bamboo, 213–17, 230
House of Wax, 158–59
Howard, Trevor, 192
Hoyt, Hal, 301–05, 309–11
Hudson, Rock, 145, 222–23, 230
Hughes, Howard, 50, 52–53
Hutton, Barbara, 9

Ile de France, 231–37
Invisible Man, 72
Iron Glove, The, 160

James, Harry, 85
Jepson, Al, 53–64, 347
John Paul Jones, 237–44, 252
Johnson, Van, 57, 252–53, 281
Jones, Jennifer, 217–18
Journey's End, 91–94

Karloff, Boris, 67, 72
Karlson, Phil, 253
Katzman, Sam, 160–61
Kelly, Frank, 47
Kennedy, George, 65
Kennedy, John F., 88–89
Kennedy, Robert F., 327
Kerr, Alex, 43, 48
Korda, Sir Alexander, 201
Koster, Henry, 71, 74, 217

Ladd, Alan, Jr., 228
Laemmle, Carl, 66–67
Laemmle, Carl, Jr., 67
Lake Tahoe, 26–32
LaMarr, Barbara, 103–04
Landi, Elissa, 237–38
Lang, Jennings, 328
Langner, Lawrence, 149, 150
Last Voyage, The, 231–36
Laura, 324–27
Leachman, Cloris, 260
Le Soleil des Voyous (*The Day of The Delinquents*), 250
Liberty Productions, 129–30, 213
Lindbergh, Charles, 19–20
Little Bit of Heaven, A, 83–84, 114
Loftin, Carey, 57–59, 64, 257
Lombard, Carole, 26, 57, 96–98, 102–03, 104–06, 238, 347
Lubitsch, Ernst, 105–07
Lugosi, Bela, 67, 72
Lund, John, 151

McCormick, John, 131–33
McEvoy, Freddie, 134
McLaglen, Andy, 164, 167
McLaglen, Victor, 3, 25, 216–17
McLarnin, Jimmy, 22
MacLean, George, 277
MacRae, Gordon, 162–63
Maddow, Ben, 268
Malone, Dorothy, 222–24, 230–32, 235
March, Fredric, 237–38
Marcum, Max, 45
Marihugh, Tammy, 235–36
Marquand, Christian, 249–50
Marshall, Armina, 149
Martin, Quinn, 253, 339
Marx, Harpo, 143
Mathews, Terry, 290
Mayer, Edwin Justus, 106
Mayer, Louis B., 27, 68
M'Divani, Alexis, 8–9
M'Divani, David, 8–9
M'Divani, Russa, 8–9
M'Divani, Serge, 8–9
Men of Texas, 78–79
Miles, Vera, 322
Milius, John, 347–48
Miller, Arthur, 223
Minchie (college friend), 37
Miranda, Carmen, 142–43
Misfits, The, 104
Mitchell, Cameron, 221
Mitchell, Thomas, 262–63
Mitchum, Robert, 300
Mix, Tom, 144
Mohr, Hal, 236
Monroe, Katherine, 13
Monroe, Marilyn, 103–04, 209, 223–24
Monroe, Rear Admiral William R., 13
Montgomery, Elizabeth, 264
Moore, Colleen, 130–34
Moore, Tom, 253, 271
Morgan, Frank, 50–51, 95
Mortal Storm, The, 77, 95, 107
"Most Wanted," 339–42

INDEX

Mozzetti, Joe, 53–57
Muñoz, Señor, 174–75, 183
Murder on Flight 502, 337
My Outlaw Brother, 314, 318

Nash, J. Carrol, 268
Nazimova, Alla, 86–87
Neal, Patricia, 262
Negri, Pola, 9, 105
Ness, Eliot (in "The Untouchables"), 2, 6, 18, 61, 252, 254–55, 258, 262, 266, 273–74, 280
Newton, Robert, 189, 192–94
Nice Girl, 77, 85
Nitti, Frank (in "The Untouchables"), 6, 254–56, 262, 274, 282
No Down Payment, 220–21
Nugent, Eliot, 314

Oboler, Arch, 155–60
O'Brien, Edmond, 232–35
Oklahoma!, 161–63
Olivier, Lawrence, 106, 336
Ommaney, David, 290, 293
Orr, William T., 96, 145–46, 253
Ouspenskaya, Maria, 96

Padilla, Ruben, 169–70
Paine, Norman Reilly, 112
Palance, Jack, 321
Parrish, Helen, 70
Parsons, Louella, 26, 50, 69, 107–08, 133, 140–41, 205
Pasadena Playhouse, 35–36
Pasternak, Joe, 69–70, 348
Paul, Victor, 276
Perez, Silverio, 173
Perry, Mamie (grandmother), 11–13
Perry, William (great-grandfather), 12–13
Phantom Pirate, The, 314–20
Picerni, Paul, 258
Pierce, Jack, 71–75, 110
Poitier, Sidney, 79

Pottgeiter, Theo, 290
Powell, Dick, 57
Powell, William, 96–97, 104
Power, Tyrone, 226
Preminger, Otto, 114–16
Preston, Robert, 314
Price, Vincent, 158
Pride and Prejudice, 37
Prince, Arthur, 34–35

Quinn, Anthony, 206–07, 226–27

Radziwill, Princess Lee, 324–27
Raft, George, 144
Raid on Rommel, 332–35
Rand, Ayn, 273
Rank, Arthur, 113–14
Raphaelson, Samson, 105
Ray, Charles, 84
Reagan, Ronald, 51
Redford, Robert, 262
Reid, Wallace, 15–16
Reynolds, Quentin, 112–13
Rich, John, 325, 326
Rigg, Lyn, 161
Ritz brothers, 80–82
Rodgers, Richard, 161
Rogers, Ginger, 52
Rogers, Will, 18, 24
Roland, Gilbert, 168, 175
Rooney, Mickey, 27, 226–27, 314
Rose, David, 27
Rosenberg, Stu, 260, 264–66
Ruffo, Tito, 40
Ruman, Sig, 106
Rutherford, Ann, 79
Ryan, Bill, 285, 288–96, 298
Ryan, Bob, 216

Sabu, 107–08
St. Johns, Adela Rogers, 15, 133
Salome Where She Danced, 79
Sanders, George, 232–33, 324–25
Satterle, Peggy, 135
Savalas, Telly, 259
Saville, Victor, 95

Scheuer, Philip K., 142
Schreiber, Elsa, 162
Schreiber, Lou, 223–24
Schumann-Heink, Ernestine, 68
Scott, Ralph Cook, 49
Screen Actors Guild, 16, 202
Sennett, Mack, 18, 24–25
Shaw, Artie, 27
Shdanoff, George, 222
Sheinberg, Sid, 329
Shiffrin, Bill, 186–88, 203–04, 206–07, 213, 221, 226
Siegel, Don, 198
Silverman, Fred, 340
Sinatra, Frank, 27, 271, 323
Sirk, Doug, 2, 221–22
Skouras, Spyros, 221
Skinner, Tom, 91
Smith, C. Aubrey, 114
Sommer, Elke, 247, 249
Sorrel, Helena, 92–93
Southern, Terry, 249
Spielberg, Steven, 347
Stack, Charles (son), 240
Stack, Elizabeth (daughter), 13–14, 230, 337
Stack, Elizabeth Modini Wood (mother), 6–8, 9–11, 13–18, 24–25, 29–34, 38, 64, 277
Stack, James Langford (father), 6, 16–21, 23–24
Stack, James L., Jr. (brother), 6, 22–26, 29–30, 32–36, 59, 61, 86, 92, 101
Stack, Rosemarie Bowe (wife), 200–08, 218–19, 227–28, 230, 232, 235–36, 240, 242–44, 250, 266, 268–69, 277, 280–81, 287, 336, 343
Stanfield, Dennis, 228
Stanwyck, Barbara, 238–39
Sterling, Bob, 146–48
Stevens, Craig, 146–48
Stevens, George, 129–30
Stewart, Jimmy, 96, 129–30, 227
Stone, Andy, 231–37
Story of a Woman, 328

Straumer, Charles, 259
Stuart, Gilchrist, 92, 93–94, 113–19, 212, 277–78, 347
Sullavan, Margaret, 95
Susskind, David, 324–27

Tarnished Angels, 230
Tattleman, Harry, 332–33, 336
Taylor, Elizabeth, 142, 333, 336
Taylor, Robert, 51–52, 72–74
Temple-Borham, Lynn, 296–98
That's Entertainment, 102
Theisen, Earl, 278
Thiess, Ursula, 160
3-D motion pictures (*House of Bamboo, House of Wax*), 154–59
Tiomkin, Dimitri, 196, 199
To Be or Not to Be, 96, 103, 105–07
Tobin, Eugene "Red," 112
Todd, Mike, Jr., 159
Torn, Rip, 260
Tracy, Spencer, 70, 148
Tunney, Gene, 19
Turner, Lana, 76, 85
Turner, Roscoe, 26

"Untouchables, The," 2, 6, 43, 61, 65, 111, 121, 153, 198, 247, 252–82, 311, 314, 326, 338–40

Valentine, Joe, 70
Villiers, Captain Alan, 240
von Zell, Harry, 93–94
Vye, Murvyn, 149–54
Walsh, Raoul, 143–45
Wanger, Walter, 111–13
Warden, Jack, 261–62
Warner, Jack, 2, 138, 143, 158–59
Wayne, John, 4–5, 144, 164–68, 175, 185–88, 190–91, 194, 211, 213, 221, 334, 347
"Weird Frank," 30–32

INDEX

Wellman, "Wild Bill," 186–92, 196–99
Wendkos, Paul, 260
Westport County Playhouse, 149–52
Williams, Guinn ("Big Boy"), 3–4
Williams, Kay, 103
Wills, Jerry, 26
Willson, Henry, 145
Winchell, Walter, 267
Winfield, Ed, 55
Winnebrenner, Ronald Leroy, 80–81
Wiseman, Joe, 259
Wood, Charley (a/k/a Carlo Modini) (grandfather), 11–13, 16, 41
Wood, Elizabeth Modini. *See* Stack, Elizabeth Modini Wood
Wood, Flissie (aunt), 14–15
Wood, Mona (aunt), 15, 31, 34, 39
Wood, Perry (uncle), 10, 41, 123
Wooley, Monty, 195
Wright, Cobina, Jr. ("Little Cobina"), 61–62
Wrightsman, Irene, 134–36
Written on the Wind, 2, 100–01, 208, 221–22, 255, 281, 336, 347
Wyler, William, 67, 129–30
Wynn, Keenan, 57, 261

Yamaguchi, Shirley, 216
Young, Robert, 95

Zanuck, Darryl F., 213–14, 219–20, 223–24
Zhdanov, George, 162
Zimmerman, Baroness von, 11
Zimmerman, Fred, 163

MS READ-a-thon— a simple way to start youngsters reading

Boys and girls between 6 and 14 can join the MS READ-a-thon and help find a cure for Multiple Sclerosis by reading books. And they get two rewards — the enjoyment of reading, and the great feeling that comes from helping others.

Parents and educators: For complete information call your local MS chapter. Or mail the coupon below.

Kids can help, too!

Mail to:
National Multiple Sclerosis Society
205 East 42nd Street
New York, N.Y. 10017

I would like more information about the MS READ-a-thon and how it can work in my area.

MS Mystery Sleuth

Name _____
(please print)
Address _____
City _____ State _____ Zip _____
Organization _____

78F

Glittering lives of famous people!
Bestsellers from Berkley

____HITCH: THE LIFE AND TIMES OF
    ALFRED HITCHCOCK   04436-X—$2.75
John Russell Taylor

____LADD: A HOLLYWOOD
    TRAGEDY   04531-5—$2.75
Beverly Linet

____LIVING IT UP   04352-5—$2.25
George Burns

____MERMAN:
    AN AUTOBIOGRAPHY   04261-8—$2.50
Ethel Merman with George Eells

____MOMMIE DEAREST   04444-0—$2.75
Christina Crawford

____MOTHER GODDAM   04691-5—$2.75
Whitney Stine with Bette Davis

____MY WICKED, WICKED WAYS   04686-9—$2.75
Errol Flynn

____NO BED OF ROSES   05028-9—$2.75
Joan Fontaine

____SELF-PORTRAIT   04485-8—$2.75
Gene Tierney, with Mickey Herskowitz

____MISS TALLULAH BANKHEAD   04574-9—$2.75
Lee Israel

____DINAH!   04675-3—$2.50
Bruce Cassiday

____BRANDO FOR BREAKFAST   04698-2—$2.75
Anna Kashfi Brando and E.P. Stein

____THE THIRD TIME AROUND   04732-6—$2.75
George Burns

Berkley Book Mailing Service
P.O. Box 690
Rockville Centre, NY 11570

Please send me the above titles. I am enclosing $_____
(Please add 75¢ per copy to cover postage and handling). Send check or money order—no cash or C.O.D.'s. Allow six weeks for delivery.

NAME_____

ADDRESS_____

CITY_____STATE/ZIP_____ 6F